Pb-I-344

MIGRANT LABOUR IN EUROPE 1600-1900
The Drift to the North Sea

Jan Lucassen

Translated by Donald A. Bloch

CROOM HELM
London • Sydney • Wolfeboro, New Hampshire

© Jan Lucassen 1987 English Edition
Croom Helm Ltd, Provident House, Burrell Row,
Beckenham, Kent BR3 1AT

Croom Helm Australia, 44 Waterloo Road,
North Ryde 2113, New South Wales

British Library Cataloguing in Publication Data

Lucassen, Jan
   Migrant labour in Europe 1600-1900.
   1. Migrant labour — Europe — History
   I. Title
   331.12′7′094   HD5856.E85

ISBN 0-7099-4117-X

Croom Helm US, 27 South Main Street,
Wolfeboro, New Hampshire 03894-2069

Library of Congress Cataloging-in-Publication Data

Lucassen, Jan.
   Migrant labour in Europe, 1700-1900.

   Includes index.
   1. Migrant labor — Benelux countries — History — 19th
century. 2. Migrant labor — Germany — History — 19th
century. 3. Migrant labor — Europe — History.
4. Migrant agricultural laborers — Europe — History.
I. Title.
HD5856.B47L83   1986   331.5′44′094   86-16832
ISBN 0-7099-4117-X

TO MY PARENTS

Typeset in 10pt Times Roman by Leaper & Gard Ltd, Bristol, England
Printed and bound in Great Britain

CONTENTS

List of Tables

List of Figures

Foreword and Acknowledgements

1. Introduction   1
   The Subject   1
   The Concept of Migrant Labour: a Working Definition   1
   The North Sea System: the Choice of Research Setting and Period   5
   Sources   7

Part One: A Description and Analysis of the North Sea System: the Northern Region of the French Empire c. 1811   19

Introduction   21

2. Migrant Labour at Macro-level: Geographic Patterns in 1811   23
   Geographic Patterns in General   23
   Characteristics of 'Pull Areas'   27
   Characteristics of 'Push Areas' and 'Neutral Areas'   29
   Conclusions Concerning Patterns of Migratory Labour at Macro-level   39
3. Migrants Under Way   42
4. Migrant Labour at Meso-level: the Work   52
   Work in Agriculture and Forestry   52
   Excavation, Dredging and Cutting Peat   63
   Industrial Jobs   76
   Work in the Transport Sector   86
   Work in the Trade and Services Sector   88
   Summary and Conclusions   92

5. Migrant Labour at the Micro-level:
   the Migrant Worker and his Household 95
      Introduction 95
      The Income Structure of a Migrant
      Worker's Household 95
      Changes in the Work Cycle 97
Conclusion 100

Part Two: The North Sea System in Wider Perspective: Migratory Labour in Western Europe *c.* 1800 103

Introduction 105

6. Other West-European Migratory Labour
   Systems *c.* 1800 107
      The Existence of 'Pull' and 'Push' Areas 107
      The Major Migratory Labour Systems 107
      Work and Work Cycle in Major
      Systems of Migratory Labour 113
      The Relationship Between 'Pull' and
      'Push' Areas 119
      The Drawing Power of Large Cities 122
7. The Absence of Migratory Labour Systems
   in Central and Eastern Europe 125
      The Situation *c.* 1800 125
      Consequences of the Abolition of Serfdom 126
Conclusion 128

Part Three: The Rise and Fall of Systems of Migratory Labour 129

Introduction 131

8. The Rise of Systems of Migratory Labour:
   a Case Study of the Emergence of the North
   Sea System 133
      Conditions for the Rise of Migrant Labour
      from Westphalia to the Province of Holland,
      the Heart of the North Sea Coast 133

	The Actual Development of Labour Migration from Westphalia to Holland	145
	The Development of Non-seasonal Labour Migration to the North Sea Coast	155
	Development of Labour Migration to the Extreme Ends of the North Sea Coast	158
	The Emergence of Other Systems of Migrant Labour	164
	Migratory Labour and Economic Fluctuations, 1600-1800	169
9.	The Demise of the North Sea System and Changes in other European Systems of Migratory Labour	172
	A Statistical Description of the Waning of Migratory Labour in the North Sea System	173
	Developments in the Labour Market in the 'Pull Area' of the North Sea System as a Possible Explanation for Declining Migratory Labour	178
	Development of the Labour Market in 'Push Areas' of the North Sea System	184
	Conclusion: the Disappearance of the North Sea System	194
	Developments in Other Systems of Migratory Labour 1800-1900	194
	Summary	203
	Migratory Labour and Economic Trends: the Kondratieff, 1800-1900	204
	Changes in Systems of Migratory Labour: Summary and Conclusion	206

Summary and Final Remarks   207
Appendix 1   217
Appendix 2   230
Appendix 3   268
Notes   279
Bibliography of Primary and Secondary Sources   312
Index of Place Names   328

LIST OF TABLES

2.1	Number of Linen Looms per 1,000 Inhabitants, First Half of the Nineteenth Century, Flanders, Westphalia, Twente	31
2.2	Some Characteristics of the West and East of Tecklenburg, Early Nineteenth Century	33
2.3	Linen Production and Migrant Labour in Several Kreise of the Regierungsbezirk Minden c. 1840	34
2.4	Distribution of Belgian Farms According to Size-category in 1846	36
8.1	Population Developments in the Province of Holland 1514-1795 (in 1,000s)	134
8.2	Land Reclamation and Dike Construction on the North-Holland Mainland 1600-1800 (in km^2)	137
8.3	Ground-work and Peat-dredging in Holland South of the IJ. 1600-1800 (in km^2)	139
8.4	Population Development in Four 'Push Areas' of the North Sea System 1600-1800	143
8.5	Hauptfeuerstätten and Nebenfeuerstätten in Osnabrück 1663-1801	144
8.6	Development of the Number of Migrant Workers in Several Locations and Regions of the North Sea System 1806-11	148
8.7	Voyages from Hasselt and Fees Paid by Skippers from Hasselt to their Guild per Voyage, May to December 1728 and March to April 1729	150
8.8	Labour Migration from Amt Syke 1718-1808	154
8.9	Anual Hiring of VOC Personnel from Maritime Provinces Compared to the Annual Increase of Provincial Manpower Supply on the Non-agrarian Labour Market in Holland and Friesland c. 1650-1795	158
9.1	Foreign Migrant Workers in Germany c. 1910 by Country of Origin	189
A1.1	Migratory Labour in the North of the French Empire in 1811	225
A2.1	Number of Migratory Workers from Galicia to	

	Castile and the East of Léon 1767-c. 1900	232
A2.2	Migratory Labour in Italy c. 1810, in Absolute Numbers and Related to Numbers of Inhabitants	258
A3.1	Migratory Labour from Regierungsbezirk Minden 1811-61	270
A3.2	Migratory Labour from Regierungsbezirk Münster 1811-61	272
A3.3	Migratory Labour from the Environment of Steinfurt 1811 and 1828	273
A3.4	Migratory Labour from Landdrostei Aurich 1811-c. 1900	273
A3.5	Migratory Labour from Landdrostei Osnabrück 1811-c. 1900	274
A3.6	Migratory Labour from Landdrostei Hannover 1811-c. 1900	275
A3.7	Migratory Labour from Landdrostei Stade 1811-c. 1900	276
A3.8	Migratory Labour from Oldenburg 1811-1900	276
A3.9	Migratory Labour from Lippe-Detmold 1811-1923	277
A3.10	Migratory Labour from the Electorate of Hesse 1865-84	278

LIST OF FIGURES

1.1	Political Status of Territories Within the Study Area in 1811	9
1.2	Départemental Divisions in the Study Area in 1811	10
2.1	'Pull Areas' in 1811 Which Attracted a Minimum of 500 Migrant Workers	24
2.2	'Push Areas' in 1811 From Which a Minimum of 500 Migrants Departed to Seek Work Elsewhere	25
2.3	'Push Areas' of Migrant Labourers and Areas of Linen Manufacture, First Half of the Nineteenth Century in Westphalia	32
3.1	Most Important Routes Followed to the North Sea Coast by Migrant Labourers	43
5.1	Examples of the Work Cycle of Westphalian 'Heuerlinge' in the Eighteenth and Nineteenth Centuries	98
6.1	Currents of Migratory Labour in Europe at the Beginning of the Nineteenth Century	108
6.2	Leading 'Pull Areas' in Europe at the Beginning of the Nineteenth Century	109
6.3	The Most Important 'Pull Areas' in Europe at the Beginning of the Nineteenth Century and their Distance from Each Other	111
6.4	Work Cycle: Irish Migrant Worker's Household in the Nineteenth Century	114
8.1	The Work Cycles of Labourers and Small Farmers from Certain Rural Areas in North-Holland, Before and After c. 1650-80	135
8.2	Work Cycles in Rural South-Holland, Before and After c. 1650-80	142
8.3	Proportion of Rural Population in the Arrondissements of Zuyderzee and Bouches de la Meuse Made Up by Migrant Workers 1811 (in per cent)	147
8.4	Transport of Migrant Workers from Hasselt to Holland, Estimated as a Function of the Hasselt	

	Skippers Making Regular Journeys to Amsterdam 1617-1812	152
8.5	Political Division of Several 'Pull' and 'Push Areas' within the North Sea System from the Seventeenth to the Nineteenth Centuries	154
8.6	Reconstruction of Recruitment of VOC Personnel, Dutch vs. Foreigners, by Decades during the Period 1630-1795	157
8.7	Development of Turf Production and Population in the Ostfriesland Bogs 1748-1900	160
9.1	Development of Migratory Labour from a Number of German 'Push Areas' in the North Sea System during the Nineteenth Century	176
9.2	Comparative Development of Migratory Labour from German 'Push Areas' to the North Sea Coast during the Nineteenth Century	177
9.3	Changes in the Work Cycle of Various Workers Active in Domestic Industry and of Migrant Labourers — Changes Brought About by the Mechanization of the Textile Industry in the Nineteenth Century	187
9.4	Number of Three Leading Categories of Migrant Workers Originating from Lippe-Detmold 1811-1923	192
A1.1	'Pull' of Workers in 1811 per Département in Absolute Numbers	226
A1.2	'Pull' of Workers in 1811 per Département, Related to Number of Inhabitants	227
A1.3	'Push' of Workers in 1811 per Département in Absolute Numbers	228
A1.4	'Push' of Workers in 1811 per Département, Related to Number of Inhabitants	229
A2.1	Political Geography of Italy in 1810	236
A2.2	Migratory Labour in Central and Northern Italy at the Beginning of the Nineteenth Century	259
A2.3	'Pull' and 'Push Areas' in Great Britain and Ireland c. 1800-10	267
A3.1	The Netherlands and a Number of German 'Push Areas' 1815-66	269

Plates

1: An Official Completed Questionnaire Form, 6 December 1811
2: Prins Hendrikkade in Amsterdam *c.* 1870
3: Ostfriesland *Mieren* (Ants) Mowing Grass Early in the Twentieth Century
4: Workers Turning the Hay, Friesland, Early Twentieth Century
5: Grain Reapers, Probably in de Liemers *c.* 1930
6: Madder-diggers in Zeeland 1830
7: Oak-strippers in Drenthe *c.* 1940
8: Turf-diggers in a High Peat Bog in Drenthe, Nieuw-Amsterdam *c.* 1910-20
9: Workers Digging Low Peat in the Bogs of South Holland and Utrecht *c.* 1850
10: Female and Male Bleachers, the Haarlem Dunes *c.* 1615
11: Aerial View of a Timber-raft on the Rhine 1782
12: Itinerant Tinker at Work in Front of a House Somewhere in the Province of Holland, First Half of the Nineteenth Century
13: A Slovakian Vendor of Medicinal Herbs in Front of the Inn 'De rustende jager' (The resting huntsman), First Half of the Nineteenth Century
14: Mowers' Market in Hungary 1943
15: Sale of Statuettes from Lucca in a Dutch City 1846
16: *Hannekemaaier* (Migrant German Mower), of the End of the Eighteenth Century
17: The 'Kamper Steiger' (Kampen Jetty) in Amsterdam, Seen from the Nieuwe Brug *c.* 1765
18: Savoyards in Rotterdam, Second Half of the Eighteenth Century
19: *Hannekemaaiers* Under Way, Friesland 1896
20: Polish 'Beet-Girls' in the Fields of Søby Søgård on Funen Island, Denmark, in the Spring of 1913

FOREWORD AND ACKNOWLEDGMENTS

Birds of passage have inspired many observers of migrant labour. In Spain people spoke of the *golondrina*, the passage of swallows, in Sweden of *Sommarfågel*, summer birds. In the Dutch province of Friesland some migratory labourers were compared to *Sneeuwganzen*, snow geese, and in Germany some to *Wanderfögel*. Such metaphors convey the notion that migratory labour was something unavoidable, fulfillment of natural law, inevitable, mechanical. Yet, however appealing such figures of speech may be, they are not adequate to depict the complexity of the phenomenon of migratory labour in its historical perspective, certainly not when our over-riding interest in the past is in helping us to clarify contemporary forms of labour migration.

This English version of *Naar de Kusten van de Noordzee* differs in certain respects from the original Dutch text of 1984. It has been pared down somewhat, especially Appendix 1. On the other hand certain passages in the original have been revised and further elaborated, benefiting from the use of additional source materials since first publication. Such new material concerns, for the most part, areas outside the North Sea System, Spain, for example, as well as Italy, Scandinavia and Russia.

The many whose help was essential for the realization of this book have been thanked in the Dutch edition. Here I would like to single out, once again, T. van Tijn and R. Penninx for their continuing help. For this English edition I have incurred new debts of gratitude: to Leo Lucassen for the maps, graphs and figures which appear here; to Peter Boorsma for information with regard to migratory labour in Spain; to Don Bloch for his resourceful translation; to Richard Stoneman, senior editor, for his enthusiastic encouragement; and, above all, to Lieske Vorst, whose support never flagged. Translation of the text was possible, it remains to be acknowledged, through the generosity of the Dutch governmental organization ZWO (De Nederlandse Organisatie voor Zuiverwetenschappelijk Onderzoek).

Jan Lucassen
Gouda

1 INTRODUCTION

The Subject

Migrant labour and foreign workers — for many the first associations which these phenomena summon up today involve the arrival of, largely, men from less developed Mediterranean countries in western Europe as a consequence of strong economic growth after World War II. We are far less inclined to think back on earlier migrant labourers in the Netherlands, the *hannekemaaiers*, for example, the *poepen* or the *mieren*, colloquial names for Germans who drifted to the lowlands to find work during peak labour seasons. Indeed, whatever image of such workers people may have, likely as not it is a blurred, inaccurate one. Not only the general public, but historians too have paid little serious attention in the past to these labour migrants and the journeys they made.

This, I believe, has been an unfortunate lapse. In the following pages I hope to demonstrate the importance of migrant labour to the labour market on the North Sea coast and in a significant number of other locations in western Europe. Indeed, the importance of such workers who left home to find work elsewhere extends beyond the labour market; their lives shed light on the social and economic history of their times as well.

To begin with, this study concerns migrant labour early in the nineteenth century in the Netherlands and adjoining areas of Germany and Belgium. The phenomenon is also viewed, however, in a broader, European perspective. Finally, the time period under consideration is extended, enabling the migrant labour situation at the turn of the nineteenth century to be placed within the historical development of migrant labour from 1600 to 1900.

The Concept of Migrant Labour: a Working Definition[1]

Man both produces and consumes; and as a rule he undertakes these activities not individually but within a larger social context. We can consider the household as the most significant unit of consumption in society. Although households may be made up in every imaginable way; in western Europe, since approximately 1500, the nuclear family, parents with their children, has dominated.[2] Such families are, generally speaking, tied to one specific location, the family's dwelling.

For a family to be able to consume, one or more of its members must have an income. The income should be at least sufficient to sustain its source — for most people this source will be their own forces of production or to put it even more simply, their own muscles and brains. In studying a labour market, i.e. the relation of work to be done in a given location to the availability of workers capable of doing it, we may raise the question of how, from where, households acquire their incomes (or where indeed the households are based to which those workers employed in a given place belong). For any given moment in time the following possibilities need to be considered: (a) people work at the same place in which they live — this obtains for farmers, craftsmen and self-employed professionals, as well as for workers in domestic industry; (b) people work away from the place where others in their household live. Under these circumstances, distance and necessary travel time may vary, so that the following distinction is of cardinal importance:

• every day the worker travels from home to place of work and back again; if the journey takes the worker outside his own municipality, he is said to be a commuter;
• the distance from home to place of work is such that the worker returns home only once a week, month, or year; here we speak of migratory labour.

Through time, however, a person or household may also change its place of residence, either 'moving' (within the same municipality), relocating (within the same country), or emigrating (beyond national boundaries). In conjunction with any such move it is possible for a person or household to undergo a transition from one form of work (e.g. migratory labour) to another (e.g. commuting, or work at home). Such a transition, however, is not invariably the case. Here at the outset I want to state very clearly that migratory labour as analysed in these pages does not entail any permanent change of residence.

Various factors can determine when a migrant worker leaves and returns to the household to which he belongs, and how long he stays away. His work may be confined to a specific period. It is possible his employment lasts only as long as it takes to finish a particular project, such as the digging of a canal or dredging of a harbour. It is also possible his job depends upon the season of the year: many activities, especially in agriculture, can only, or preferably be carried out at a special time, or within a short, fixed period. In Holland, for example, grass is at its highest in June, when seed formation has not yet taken place. This, then, is the month for mowing, or else the hay yield will be less or of an inferior quality.[3] Certain tasks could *not* be performed at certain seasons, and therefore the rest of the year had to be utilised for their execution. A prominent example here are brick-works, idle in northern countries during the winter because rain and frost make it difficult to model bricks, and next to impossible to dry them for firing. Brick-works operated accordingly from March until October.[4] Given the seasonal nature of much work undertaken by migrants, for the remainder of the year they were obliged to hunt for alternative employment, frequently close to, or at home.

If instead of considering the demands of the work which a migrant worker did away from home, we look at the various possibilities open to him to find employment elsewhere, then once again we encounter the seasons as a determining factor. There were chores, for example, which required his assistance at peak times on his (small) farm at home. Only when his manpower was not needed *per se*, would he be free to travel out to find work. A well-known example of such a cycle of indispensable/dispensable labour involves mountain dwellers who during the six months of winter could do no work at home and therefore descended to the plains to find employment for this half of the year, especially in large cities.[5] To be sure, the attunement of these two varieties of seasonally dependent work — jobs abroad and jobs at home — will emerge as a central idea in the pages to come.

There were other migrant workers, however, whose work was not tied to any particular season. Such labourers usually made one trip home each year, often to share Christmas, Easter or some special fair with their families. Here we are dealing with the following groups:

• itinerant workers who attempt to master a particular craft or skill, such as the German *Wanderburschen*, the English Travelling Brothers and the French *Compagnons*[6].

- mercenary soldiers[7]
- seamen on intercontinental voyages[8]
- domestic servants[9].

This list is, however, by no means exhaustive; it simply mentions a few numerically important groups. In general, migrant workers who did such work do not appear in the discussion which ensues; they do not figure sufficiently in the sources which I consulted for me to be able to say anything useful about them.

Packmen, or *marskramers* (hawkers, vendors, pedlars) and wandering performers who earned their living by entertaining the public (minstrels, carnival folk, circus artists and actors)[10] — such figures, until the end of the nineteenth century, usually had a fixed abode where, frequently, they remained throughout the winter. Their activities were of such a nature that clients needed them but once, or a few times during the year. Packmen in particular will figure prominently in this survey of migrant labour.

Among those who held jobs that were not tied to any given season we find the first — and the most — migrant workers who exchanged their come-and-go existence for migration proper, i.e. for permanent resettlement. Not only the nature or duration of the particular jobs involved but also the age of those who practised such occupations, may have promoted this transition, for these workers were usually young and unmarried. Either they were already entirely self-sufficient, financially-speaking as well, or they remitted a share of their earnings to their parents in expectation of future marriage and the setting up of an independent household. As the work which migrant workers performed during the nineteenth century that was either on a project basis or seasonally determined declined, the likelihood increased that for economic reasons migrant workers would decide to leave home for good and set up their households elsewhere.

In the text of this study I have concentrated primarily on large groups of workers who left clearly demarcated areas, which I call 'push areas', to perform seasonal tasks in other areas just as sharply defined, which I refer to as 'pull areas'. The composite of such independent and sharply outlined 'push' and 'pull' areas I have designated a 'system'.

Migratory labour as described above has until now been the subject of comparatively limited research. What has been written is largely descriptive in nature. Few theories explaining the phenomenon have thus far been advanced,[11] and this has made it impossible for me to begin my study of the history of migrant labour in a particular location by applying an already existing theoretical framework. Instead, as I proceed with the description and analysis of migrant labour on the North Sea coast, step by step I will attempt to formulate meaningful hypotheses which may prove more widely applicable, helping us to understand where, when and why we may expect to see foreign workers in large numbers appear, and where, when and why such figures may also be expected to disappear from the scene.

In my presentation I emphasise two underlying assumptions derived from analyses of contemporary labour migration in western Europe.[12] In the first place we may postulate that the migrant worker anticipates advantages accruing from his travels; by leaving home he hopes to earn more in the same time than he could by simply staying at home. This point of departure means that we should inquire into the economic structure of 'push areas', examine the kinds of work performed by migrant workers, assess their wages, and consider the time(s) of the year when they leave home.

At the same time, and as importantly, I suppose that those who employed migrant workers did so because they believed it to be beneficial to their interests. This point of departure invokes the question why, if a supply of local manpower was available, migrant workers were preferred to local workers.

The pair of assumptions I have chosen to adopt as premises, that both workers and employers behave rationally in their choice of actions, motivated in large part by potential profits, mean that I have chosen to approach the subject of migratory labour from an economic point of view. The disadvantage of doing so is that social and psychological aspects of migrant workers' lives, and therefore the full, human complexity of their decision-making processes, are all too likely to receive inadequate illumination.

The North Sea System: the Choice of Research Setting and Period

The migrant labour system central to this study, the 'North Sea System', consisted on the one hand of a 'pull area' formed by what I will hereafter refer to as the North Sea coast — the strip of coastal land from Calais in France to the German Butjadingen — and on the other hand of 'push areas' comprising a hinterland stretching for hundreds of kilometres to the east, and to some extent, to the south.[13]

In the seventeenth century the heart of the 'pull area', the Seven United Provinces, the most important of which was Holland, were far more developed economically than all their neighbours. It was at this time that a migrant labour system emerged there.[14] Study of the possible connection between migrant labour and economic development is therefore, obviously, indicated. Yet the remarkable fact that the migrant labour system persisted even after the economic star of Holland was already on the wane, arouses curiosity. My choice of what period to concentrate on in studying the North Sea System was largely determined by the availability of an extraordinarily rich historical source, responses to a questionnaire administered in the French Empire c. 1811. The data then accumulated offer a unique opportunity to appreciate the dimensions of migratory labour throughout a large part of western Europe. During the years covered by the questionnaire (roughly 1810-13), the various regions of the North Sea System belonged for the most part to a single state. Prior and subsequent to this period they were divided up among at least three governmental entities as far as 'pull areas' were concerned, and among no less than some tens of units with different sovereignty as far as 'push areas' were concerned, a situation which virtually eliminates the availability of any set of uniform historical sources.

The condition of the labour market which we encounter around 1811, however, is the consequence of previous developments. It cannot be understood on the basis of any analysis confined merely to the 'French era'. For this reason we must move backwards in time to trace the beginning of the North Sea System — and forward in time to follow its demise. We can place the emergence of the system during the second half of the sixteenth century. Our analysis of the system's gradual growth will consequently involve us primarily with events during the seventeenth and eighteenth centuries. By the nineteenth century the system was in decline, and it would disappear before the turn of the present century.

In the course of examining the North Sea System I will also refer to migrant workers elsewhere in Europe and to the rise and fall of other migrant-labour systems. Attention is devoted to such systems in England, France, Spain and Italy primarily to test the

Introduction 7

validity and general applicability of concepts derived from observations within the North Sea System. First and foremost, however, available sources compel us to concentrate on a thorough analysis of the North Sea System at the start of the nineteenth century.

Sources

General

A migrant labour system entailed advantages for both 'push' and 'pull' areas. Most governments in both parts of the system realised this in time. With the exception of a few trade and financial regulations, as a rule governments tried not to impose any judicial obstacles to the free movement of workers.[15]

This meant that there was also no extensive system of registration which the authorities might influence or control. As a consequence, source material concerning migrant labour is extraordinarily scarce. The great exception is the government of the French Empire. Obliged by the insatiable appetite of its war machine for cannon fodder, the Empire made manpower recruitment for the army a matter of higher priority than the maintenance, despite its profitability, of migrant labour. The First French Republic and the First French Empire engaged in steadily more extensive military operations. Although at first there was a sufficiency of volunteers, in 1793 all Frenchmen became obliged in principle to fulfil military duty, and the ranks of the army were filled by levies. In 1798 the draft (*conscription*) was introduced, imposing compulsory military service on all French males between the ages of 20 and 25. Subsequently, manpower needs were established annually and induction into the armed forces determined by lottery. As more and more *conscrits* received the call to join up, the number who failed to appear increased, to the considerable chagrin of the responsible prefects. One reason for the poor rate of compliance had to do with the seasonal nature of migrant labour: at the moment many *conscrits* received their induction notice at home they were simply not present, but rather at work somewhere possibly hundreds of kilometres away. This is probably why the Minister of the Interior drafted a questionnaire in 1808 concerning *migration temporaire*.[16] As new territories were incorporated within the Empire, newly appointed prefects were promptly confronted with an avalanche of forms with questions, forms which had been filled in throughout the rest of the Empire during the preceding years. Thus, Count De Montalivet, Minister of the Interior, insisted on 13 November 1811 that his prefects in Holland — the kingdom annexed just the year before — complete the questionnaire submitted to them concerning *migration temporaire*. The questionnaire had already been administered in the southern parts of the Netherlands which were previously absorbed into the Empire, and in Belgium; it remained to be administered in German territories about to be added to French dominion in 1811. Responses to the questionnaire submitted between 1808 and 1813 have been preserved in Paris. For the most part responses relevant to the North Sea System cover the years 1810-12. For the sake of convenience, following De Montalivet's usage when he issued his request to the 'Dutch' *départements*, we will, however, speak simply of 'The Questionnaire of 1811'. It should be mentioned at once that the French regime never managed to process these data which it collected, no less publish any commentary on the phenomenon which prompted the questionnaire. What is unique about the questionnaire is that it represents the only source of information throughout the history of the North Sea System which pertains to practically the entire area involved. Only a small part of the eastern half of the area fell outside the domain of the Empire: of interest to us were the Grand Duchies of Berg and Hesse, the Principality of Waldeck, the Kingdom of Westphalia and the Principalities of Schaumburg-Lippe and Lippe-Detmold, all territories to the west of, roughly speaking, the Hamburg-Kassel line (see Figure 1.1).

For some decades already in this last-mentioned area registration had been in effect for subjects departing to work elsewhere. Such registration is also available for the years around 1810, so that the Principality of Lippe-Detmold, although it was able to maintain its independence, can be included in this study on equal footing with the French départements.[17] As far as the remaining areas of interest to us outside the French Empire are concerned, it is particularly regrettable that the Kingdom of Westphalia kept no administrative records about the movements of its migrant workers; in this respect the other places mentioned are of secondary importance. We are not totally without information, however, since each French département had to report not only where local residents were going to work but also from where

Figure 1.1: Political Status of Territories Within the Study Area in 1811

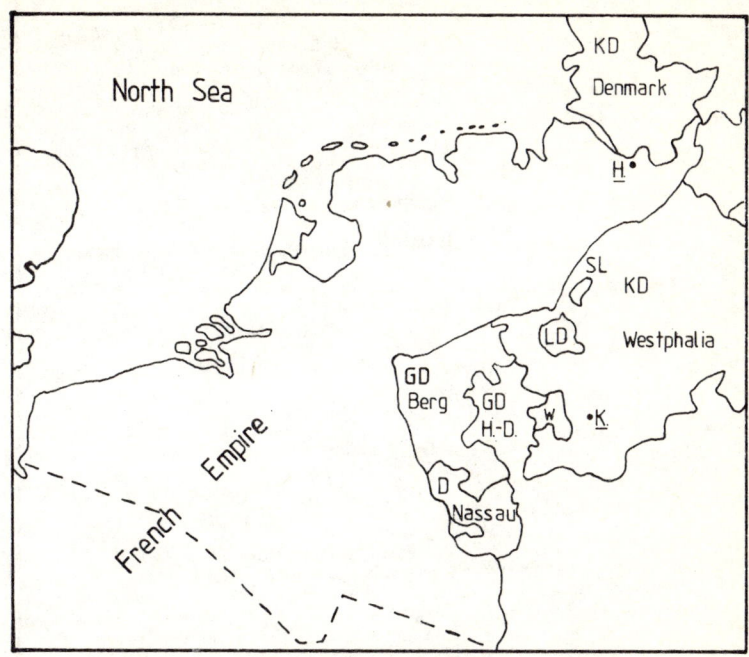

SL	Schaumburg-Lippe	K	Kassel	KD	Kingdom
LD	Lippe-Detmold	H	Hamburg	GD	Grand duchy
W	Waldeck	H-D	Hesse-Darmstadt	D	Duchy

――― approximate southern borders of départements, included in research concerning the North Sea System

arriving migrant workers were coming. In this way an appreciable amount of data about 'border zones' have passed down to us.[18]

In an effort to understand the dynamics of the North Sea System, I have processed the answers to the Questionnaire of 1811 from the northernmost 31 French départements, together with statistical data from the Princedom of Lippe. As far as possible I have made use of the answers provided by the lowest administrative echelons: what the *maires* (mayors) had to tell the sub-prefects, and what these in turn had to say to the prefects.

Responses to the Questionnaire of 1811 from the following départements have been studied (see Figure 1.2):

Figure 1.2: Départemental Divisions in the Study Area in 1811

B. e ...... Bouches de
oc. Occidental
or. Oriental
sup. Supérieur

Inf. Inférieur
Z.Z. Zuyderzee
S. et M. Sambre et Meuse
Mo. Moselle

— — — — — Hannover-Kassel line

• in northwest Germany: Bouches de l'Elbe, Bouches du Weser, Ems Oriental, Ems Supérieur, Lippe (plus migrant worker registration from the Principality of Lippe-Detmold);
• principally in what is today The Netherlands: Ems Occidental, Frise, Bouches de l'Issel, Issel Supérieur, Zuyderzee, Bouches de la Meuse, Bouches de l'Escaut, Bouches du Rhin, Meuse Inférieure;
• principally in what is today Belgium: Lys, Escaut, Deux Nèthes, Dyle, Jemappes, Sambre et Meuse, Ourthe;
• principally in what is today Luxemburg: Forêts;

- principally in what is today the German Rhine valley: Roër, Rhin et Moselle, Sarre, Mont Tonnerre;
- principally in what is today northern France: Pas de Calais, Nord, Ardennes, Meuse, Moselle.

For other migrant-labour systems at the beginning of the nineteenth century — systems which provide material for the drawing of comparisons with the North Sea System in Part II of this book — I have used information from the French questionnaire in part (data relevant to Swiss and Italian départements), and in part diverse literary sources (including publications about Denmark, England and Spain, and Chatelain's standard work on France).[19]

In drawing up accounts of historical developments in, for the most part, Dutch and German territory, I have relied on widely scattered archival sources and literature. The same extreme variety characterises my sources for the descriptions of places, journeys and kinds of employment which take up most of Part I. Specific references are cited throughout in the notes to each chapter.

Qualitative sources and literature about the North Sea System deal in large part with the Netherlands and Westphalia, while migratory labour in Belgium is, in particular, much less well documented.

Responses to the Questionnaire of 1811

The exact form of the questions which the French Minister of the Interior posed to his prefects can be read in a letter which survives in Paris written in 1811 and addressed to the Prefect of the Département of Meuse Inférieure in Maastricht:

> Je désirois pour completter des recherches fort avancées, obtenir de vous des renseignemens sur les ouvriers et journaliers originaires de votre Département qui peuvent être dans l'usage d'en sortir périodiquement, à certaines époques de l'année, pour aller se livrer dans d'autres parties de l'Empire, ou dans les pays étrangers, à divers travaux. Je vous prie dans le cas ou ces sortes d'émigrations auroient lieu dans la contrée que vous administrez, de m'indiquer le nombre, au moins approximatif, des personnes qui s'y livrent, les cantons dont elles sortent, les époques ordinaires de leur départ et de leur retour, les pays où elles se rendent, les professions qu'elles y exercent, et enfin autant que possible le montant des sommes q'on estime qu'elles

peuvent rapporter dans leurs foyers pour prix de leurs journées. Supposé que des individus étrangers à la portion de l'Empire que vous administrez, soient de leur côté dans l'habitude de s'y rendre, pour y être employés aux travaux de l'agriculture ou des arts mécaniques, je vous engage à me procurer à leur égard des informations analogues à celles dont je viens de vous entretenir. Je compte, pour avoir ces éclaircissements aussi promptement qu'il sera possible, sur votre zèle et votre attention.[20]

Freely translated, what Paris wanted to know from Maastricht, just as from all other prefects, was the following:

I would gladly receive information about the day labourers from your département whose custom it is to leave the département for some length of time during the year in order to take up employment of various kinds in other parts of the empire, or beyond. Concerning these individuals, I would like to know: their number, in any event an estimation; the canton from which they depart; the time of the year when they usually go away and come back; their destination; the occupation which they exercise elsewhere; the earnings which they are able to bring back with them when they return home. Should such individuals come from other places to work in your département, then I would like to receive the same information about them. For as quick and thorough a response as possible, I am relying on your diligence and perspicacity.

Not only did the minister in this way pose the first question of this study; we are also now able to reap the profit of the industry and powers of observation which the prefects to whom the minister directed his demands, demonstrated at that time. In order to be able to send off their responses 'as quickly as possible', most prefects had to expend considerable effort: the information asked was not generally available for collation from standard administrative paperwork.[21] Those prefects who were ready with their reply within several weeks, did, as we shall see, a superficial job, or else administered a département where migrant labour was insignificant. Alas, for the purposes of this study, their superficiality was a grievous fault. In more than a few instances, however, a second appeal followed from Paris for more complete information.

Roughly speaking we can reconstruct four principal approaches to fulfilling the Minister of the Interior's request for information:

- the prefect decided to draft an answer on the basis of some general notes which he and his helping officials had on hand. This approach usually resulted in a rapid, or brief response. Most cursory of all was Sambre et Meuse, where the prefect merely advised the minister to consult the supplement on immigration and emigration which was part of the *grande Mémoire* of c. 1805. In this category of response also fall the départements of Lys, Escaut, Bouches de l'Elbe and Rhin et Moselle. We certainly should include Bouches de l'Escaut as well: the prefect submitted his reply on the same day the request arrived from Paris. This reply was therefore so vague that Paris asked for more information. This time two days passed while a somewhat more elaborate set of answers was prepared. Whether or not the capital rested content with this second meagre effort, it is no longer possible to know.
- The prefect decided to formulate his reply based on administrative records in his custody. This is probably what took place in the département of the Dyle, and certainly what happened, although in each instance with some variation in method, in Ems Oriental, Ourthe and Frise. The prefect in Ems Oriental extracted the data he needed from the archives of the *Kriegs- und Domänenkammer*. This former Prussian, centrally organised institution did indeed have at its disposal an extremely extensive set of records concerning the economic life of Ostfriesland. Ourthe chose to analyse its registration of passports for the preceding years (1808-10) and to use various averages thus calculated to represent the flow of migrant workers out of the département. Frise, finally, had available the results of a survey undertaken a year earlier by the *Landdrost* (governor) of Friesland concerning the appearance of foreign workers in the licensing registers of 1809.[22] The prefect simply presented the results as if they were equivalent to the total volume of migrant labour in 1811.
- The prefect decided to consult experts. Meuse Inférieure is a good example of this approach. Here five persons dispersed throughout the entire département were asked for advice — individuals who at that moment did not belong to any one administrative body. The only thing they had in common was that at one time or another they all had been members of the *conseil général* of the département. We can regard them as members of the départemental elite, deriving their position in part from large land

holdings. Along with other submissions, Ems Supérieur received — it is not certain whether this was in response to a specific request — an elaborate report from a former *Amtmann* (magistrate).

* The most frequently followed approach involved the consultation of sub-prefects, and at times of other officials in office as well, such as officers of the *gendarmerie impériale*, the mayor of Amsterdam (in Zuyderzee), or a director of police. In most instances the sub-prefects in turn consulted the heads (*maires*) of municipalities. This usually generated extensive information. Exceptions were the maires of the arrondissement Almelo (Bouches de l'Issel) whose responses were so unsatisfactory that the sub-prefect resorted instead to his own administration, which contained data about *veiligheidskaarten* (security passes — passports for travel within the Empire) that had been issued. This scrupulous but time-consuming method of collecting information from sub-prefects and maires was practised in Jemappes, Forêts, Roër, Lippe, Ems Supérieur, Bouches du Weser, Ems Occidental, Bouches de l'Issel, Bouches du Rhin, Issel Supérieur, Bouches de la Meuse and Zuyderzee. Many reminders had to be sent in these départements. That more than human neglect was responsible for the delay in forwarding answers can be discovered in a letter from the sub-prefect of the arrondissement Quakenbrück (Ems Supérieur). On 26 December 1811, he wrote: 'I trust the Prefect will excuse the tardiness with which this information has arrived but my correspondence with the *maires* was disrupted in diverse instances by floods so that I was unable to receive their responses more promptly'.

Maires were as unable as their superiors to produce the necessary information off the top of their heads. A few examples from Bouches de la Meuse help to clarify various ways of arriving at answers. In a number of places, Zoetermeer for example, licensing registers were used in which the names of workers appear who were taxed because they came from outside the bounds of the former kingdom of Holland. In Rijswijk (South-Holland) — just as in West Zaandam in Zuyderzee — employers were asked for information about whom they hired; in Ter Aar prefects elicited 'renseignements de gens experts' (information from experts). To be sure, the questionnaire was administered most professionally in this département: special forms for the purpose were even printed (see Plate 1).

In Smilde (Ems Occidental) the maire used the records in his administrative files concerning security passes that had been issued.

At times a maire had to contend with recalcitrant subordinates. The maire of Barkhausen (Ems Supérieur) wrote:

> After I had urged the inhabitants of my municipality twice to answer the questions put to them, whereby I added the threat the second time that whoever kept silent about his travels wouldn't be able to acquire a passport any more, the occasional exception turned up.

Open sabotage against the questionnaire, however, was rare. If in Zuyderzee a short time after the sub-prefect came to collect information, the imperial gendarmerie appeared to repeat the unanswered questions, we can detect a certain degree of public cantankerousness. At the end of December 1811 two imperial gendarmes rode through the arrondissement 'to reconnoiter concerning foreigners'.[23] In Diemen and Diemerdam this was apparently considered to be totally unnecessary, and people acted as if they failed to understand what the issue was. To questions about 'unknown foreigners', the answer was given

> to say how many of such there are, we need to be instructed exactly who is meant and how long such must have lived in the municipality, or how familiar they must have become no longer to be considered foreigners.

And in Watergraafsmeer, where, as in Diemen, a month earlier an extremely well-expressed and complete answer to the request for information about migrant workers had been submitted, when four follow-up questions were asked by the same imperial gendarmes, the local response was not untinged with grumpiness:

> 1. If what is meant by strange workers are the foreigners here, then in this municipality there are very many of these people in permanent employment ... if precise details about each year are required, this would cost at least three days to be able to collect.
> 2. This would also seem true in that case.
> 3. This is entirely unsure: the most stay on.
> 4. This one should look into at once and inquire from the 'bosses' etc.

Processing of Questionnaire Responses

In order to be able to present a total picture of migrant labour within the North Sea System, it is necessary to make the different kinds of answers submitted by the prefects and their subordinates somehow comparable. Then for the whole system it becomes possible to establish an estimate of the total number of workers seeking employment away from home, and to arrive at sub-totals per occupation. While attempting such quantification, I became repeatedly involved in weighing and interpreting responses made to the questions raised.[24]

My guiding principle in interpreting questionnaires answers was to try to avoid both over- and under-estimates. Over-estimates were in theory possible because one worker may have worked in any given year in two places and thus have been counted twice. This might be true, for example, for workers who worked in the spring in a bog or on a dike, and then during the subsequent June went out to mow grass. Because prefects refer explicitly to this phenomenon and also because I compared data from 'push' and 'pull' areas with each other, I believe that on the whole I have avoided this duplication trap. Where relevant, I have discussed the possibility of a worker's being counted more than once in Appendix I.

On the other hand, under-estimates had to be avoided every bit as carefully. These were possible because in a number of instances the kind of work a group left or arrived to perform was reported, without the number of persons in the group being specified. If it seemed reasonable to imagine that large numbers of workers were involved — i.e. some hundreds — I have tried to make an estimate on the basis of other sources. In other instances I have chosen not to attach any number to the journey in question, and have written PM (*pro memoria*) in the appropriate place. A second reason why certain kinds of labour may be under-estimated is the criterion for migration applied in the questionnaire: prefects were to report journeys across departmental boundaries. Migratory labour within the département was thus by definition excluded from questionnaire responses. Fortunately for us, however, various prefects nevertheless mentioned such internal shifts of labour. I have also taken this data into consideration whenever possible, yet in a number of instances estimates of the extent of intradépartemental migration of labour will fall short of reality because we lack more complete statistics.[25]

Looking over the processed replies submitted by the prefects in the area of the North Sea System, I am of the opinion that the Questionnaire of 1811 provides a reasonably reliable picture of contemporary migrant labour. Its accuracy appears to hold up even for the Italian part of the Empire.[26]

Finally, I must point out that during the final years of the First French Empire migratory labour was at a low ebb, both in the north and in the south of the Empire.[27] Seamen from merchant fleets were conspicuously absent from the north, forbidden to ship out in connection with Napolean's boycott of English goods (The Continental Blockade of 1806).[28] Public works such as land reclamation and the building of dikes in Holland and Zeeland stood largely still during these years.[29] For these reasons, and because of the ongoing war that drained so much manpower from the civil sector, probably far fewer migrant workers were on the road than during the preceding, or ensuing years.

PART ONE:

A Description and Analysis of the North Sea System:
the Northern Region of the French Empire *c.* 1811

INTRODUCTION

Line of Inquiry and Principal Source of Information, the Questionnaire of 1811

The question which initially concerns us in the first part of this study can be stated simply: What were the economic conditions responsible for the emergence of migratory labour along the North Sea coast in 1811? This question can be broken down into two parts: What motivated migratory labourers to look for work on a temporary basis away from home, and what induced employers to hire migratory workers? These questions can be answered at three levels.

At the macro-level, the geographical pattern of migrants' places of origin and destinations can provide a first insight into the forces at work. Indeed, wherever a clear pattern of 'pull' and 'push' areas become visible, this at once helps pinpoint potential migrants and potential employers. The Questionnaire of 1811, the principal source for material cited in the first part of this study, posed specific questions about travel from and to every département in the French Empire, requiring specific notation of the areas from which workers departed and to which they journeyed to find work. Completed questionnaires therefore offer the possibility of mapping geographically various currents in the migratory labour movement.

At the meso-level, making use of the geographical patterns sketched at macro-level, 'pull' areas can be more closely analysed. Here, the essential question concerns the kinds of labour performed by migrant workers in a given area. The motives of employers will arise for consideration while we address this question. As points of departure here, we can resort to those entries in the Questionnaire of 1811 which pertain to kind of labour, date of departure and date of arrival. These data, however, require supplementation. Consequently, I will also make use of material from as early as several decades prior to the Questionnaire of 1811 and from as late as several decades thereafter.

With the geographic pattern of labour migration as our basis once again, we can derive a clearer picture of the migrant workers themselves. What work did they perform away from home (*meso-*

level)? How did such work relate to labour at home? What portion of total household income did migrant labour account for? These questions help in composing a description of labour migration at the micro-level. Here the Questionnaire of 1811 is of but slight assistance, other sources must provide the required information.

Chapter 3 depicts the migrant worker's journey and his daily life, and describes various kinds of jobs that migrant workers performed away from home. The worker's route from 'push' to 'pull' areas is reconstructed primarily on a basis of descriptive sources. The Questionnaire of 1811 did not concern itself with workers' movements between the time of their departure from home and arrival at work site.

2 MIGRANT LABOUR AT MACRO-LEVEL: GEOGRAPHIC PATTERNS IN 1811

Geographic Patterns in General

An analysis of answers to the Questionnaire of 1811 yields a more or less well-defined geographic pattern of 'pull' and 'push' areas. If we look at the absolute totals of migrants per département who left to seek work or who arrived to find employment, then it appears that 'pull areas' were especially concentrated in the west, 'push areas' in the east. This pattern is confirmed when we compare number of transients to residential population per département.[1] Sharper patterns emerge when we examine the situation per arrondissement or even per canton within various départements. Then we can see that 'pull areas' and 'push areas' were sharply circumscribed, with hardly any overlapping (see Figures 2.1 and 2.2).

All but two 'pull areas' were situated along the North Sea coast. Moving from south to north we can differentiate: the coastal regions of Pas de Calais and Nord and thereafter, with the pattern broken by Lys as a non 'pull area',[2] the coast starting at Escaut extending as far north as Ems Oriental. Separated by Jeverland there followed Butjadingen and the estuary of the Weser in the département of the same name. There is room for discussion about whether or not the southern and northern enclaves, Pas de Calais/Nord and Bouches du Weser were an integral part of the heart of the area. The answer to this question depends materially on whether migrant workers came to seek jobs in the intermediate areas, Lys and Jeverland. Until these questions can be satisfactorily answered, I will consider the entire coast from Calais to Bremen as a single 'pull area': The North Sea coast.

There are two depártements which attracted migrant workers but were not situated on the North Sea coast: Mont Tonnerre and Roër. In Mont Tonnerre the banks of the Rhine near Mainz and Speier drew a number of workers. Yet because in comparison to the North Sea coast this isolated 'pull area' gave work to a mere few, I have left it out of further consideration in this study.

Migrant labour to the second exception, the département of Roër, was incidental. There, and in nearby Meuse Inférieure, the

24 *Migrant Labour at Macro-level*

Figure 2.1: 'Pull Areas' in 1811 Which Attracted a Minimum of 500 Migrant Workers[3]

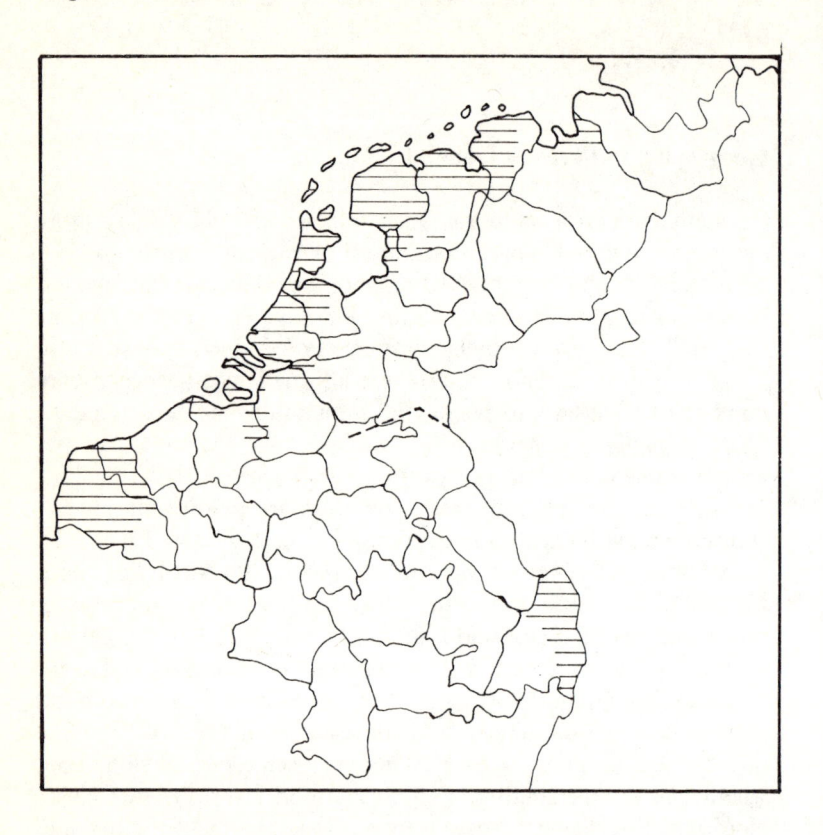

― ― ― ― ― Grand Canal du Nord

▤ 'Pull areas'

Grand Canal du Nord was being excavated at that time, a waterway to link the Schelde, Maas and Rhine. The digging drew thousands of labourers, most of them from the département of Ourthe. After the French Empire incorporated the Kingdom of Holland, however, work on the canal was discontinued and Roër ceased to be a 'pull area'.

The 'push areas' present a clear and yet less uniform picture than the 'pull areas'. Various adjoining 'push areas' are indicated

Figure 2.2: 'Push Areas' in 1811 From Which a Minimum of 500 Migrants Departed to Seek Work Elsewhere[4]

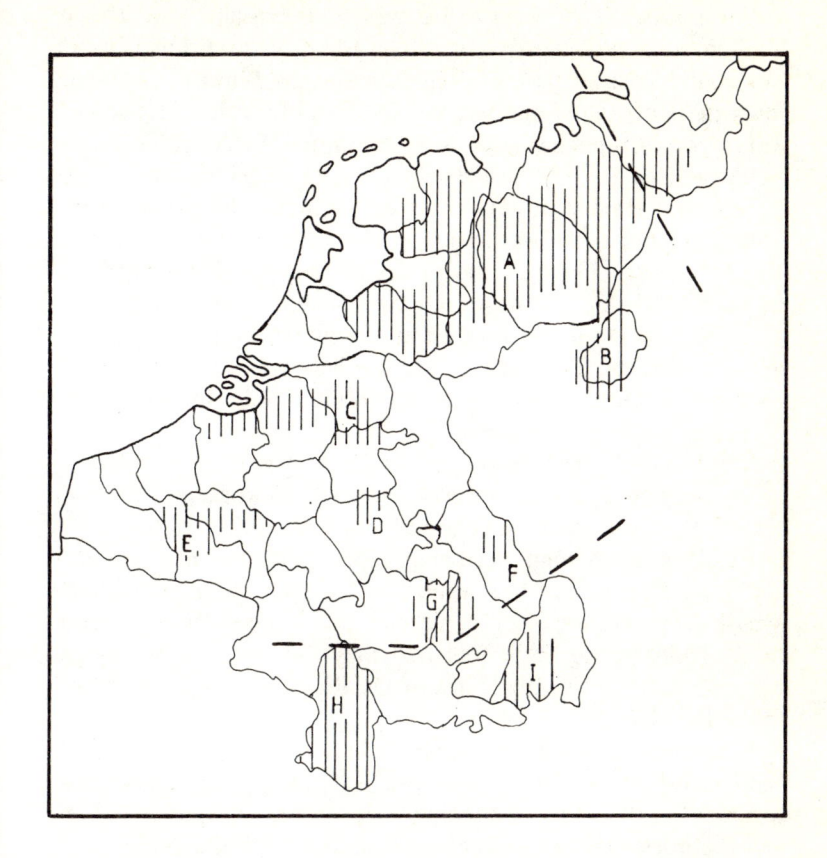

— — — 'Water Sheds'

▓▓▓ 'Push areas'

by letters in Figure 2.2. The area marked A supplied by far the most workers. It stretched from The Veluwe, Twente and the Drenthe-Frisian bogland in the west as far as the line Münster-Osnabrück-Minden-Lüneburg in the east.

The boundary which coincides with the departmental border between Bouches de l'Elbe and Bouches du Weser I would like to designate a labour 'water shed'. To the west of this 'water shed' workers headed for the North Sea coast, to its east they made for Denmark and Mecklenburg instead.

'Push area' B of Figure 2.2 was a 'peninsula' joined near Minden with 'push area' A, and consisting of the Principality of Lippe and a large part of Regierungsbezirk Minden, including small parts of Regierungsbezirke Hesse and Münster. Hereafter I will refer to this peninsula as 'Minden/Lippe/Wiedenbrück'.

'Push area' C lay further south. The département of the Bouches du Rhin with adjacent areas of Meuse Inférieure in the southeast, and, in the west, parts of Deux Nèthes and Escaut (the east of Zeeland-Flanders except for the region of Axel and the region due south of it) comprised the nucleus of 'push area' C.

'Push area' D was the smallest of all, and yet a distinct source of migrant workers. This area, to the northeast of Liège, lay for the most part in Ourthe, but also extended into Meuse Inférieure (the north bank of the Jeker).

'Push area E' was made up of the adjacent 'push areas' of Jemappes and Nord. A specific category of workers, raftsmen, came from 'push areas' F, G and part of I.

Finally, there remain 'push area' H and part of I: these are situated on the far side of the 'water shed'. Almost all migrants from Meuse (area H) went south, deeper into France. Workers from Mont Tonnerre, to the extent that they did not shift within the same département to the banks of the Rhine, probably journeyed to the Bas Rhin farther south.

In summary, the following 'push areas' appear to have been significant for the North Sea coast: the vast region due east, together with the adjoining 'peninsula' Minden/Lippe/Wiedenbrück; the area south of the heart of the 'pull areas' together with the separate 'island' Jemappes/Nord; the extremely small Liège 'island'; and lastly, the area that was the home of raftsmen in the mountain chain of Eifel, Hunsrück and Pfalz.

Within the 'push areas' data enable us to differentiate two evident 'water sheds': one between the départements Bouche de l'Elbe and Bouches du Weser in the northeast; the second which passes through the Ardennes and the Eifel in the south. (Hainaut was a transitional area: prior to 1811 workers travelled seasonally to the North Sea coast; later they headed south.)

In the east there was no 'water shed': research has failed to turn up any account of migratory labour towards the east; or, at any rate east of the line Hamburg-Kassel. Data concerning 'water sheds' and all absence of labour movement towards the eastern edge of the 'push area' encourage the provisional conclusion that the greatest distance workers journeyed in 1811 to find employment along the North Sea coast would have been roughly 250 to 300 km.[5]

Now that 'pull area' and 'push area' have been delineated geographically, three queries deserve at least a provisional answer. The first question concerns the reasons why the 'pull area' displays its particular configurations. The second raises the same issue with regard to 'push areas'. The third question involves how we should appraise the situation in 'neutral areas' where no labour migration worth mentioning, out or in, took place.

Characteristics of 'Pull Areas'

One can attempt to answer questions about the specific form of the 'pull area' by looking for shared economic characteristics within the region, but also by identifying differences with 'push areas'. Considering the fact that the two kinds of areas in general border on each other, we can expect explanations for such a well-defined border to shed light on their intrinsic differences.

First and foremost, the 'pull area' of the North Sea coast was homogeneous in that it was a region suited geographically for transport and traffic. Never more than 50 km wide, from north to south the coastal strip boasted countless sea harbours. River harbours abounded as well in the deltas.

Perhaps even more important than its accessibility by sea, or by large or small rivers, was the internal communication and travel network that existed here. Up and down the coast during the sixteenth, but especially during the first half of the seventeenth century, an extensive network of canals for ships came into being, which meant that nothing could be easier than reaching one point within the area from any other.[6] Jan de Vries, who has studied this canal shipping system using horse-drawn barges, believes it helps to explain the flourishing of the Republic of the Seven United Provinces. De Zeeuw, moreover, has demonstrated that the system of waterways also served for the distribution of peat.[7]

We can, moreover, cite additional characteristics in common for this area. The difference between the North Sea coast and the rest of the Netherlands emerged with particular clarity from the first major demographic study of the Netherlands which covered an appreciable time span: the collective work of the Wageningen School in 1965.[8] The demographic development of coast and interior differed in virtually every respect. This surely had to do with the distinct economic specialisations of the respective areas. The coast was characterised by capital-intensive agriculture (especially cultivation of industrial crops, market gardening, dairy farming and cattle breeding[9]), by industry, trade and shipping. The remaining regions were on the one hand much more oriented to extensive agriculture, and on the other hand to domestic industry; here trade and transport played but a subordinate role. Consequently, the coastal strip was far more urbanised.[10] And finally, it is remarkable how wages along the coast, whether in the Netherlands, Germany or Belgium, were far higher than they were further inland, a fact which De Meere in turn relates to differences in the cost of living between the two areas.[11]

At this point, having established that the North Sea coastal strip exhibited similar infrastructural, economic and demographic characteristics all along its length, let us look more closely at the dividing lines between 'pull', 'push' and 'neutral areas'. Soil typology appears to be a fact of determining importance. In Zeeland-Flanders there is a difference between the western part, the 'pull area', with rich marine clay, and the eastern part, the 'push area', with soil of lesser quality.[12] Here we have to do with a variation in fertility despite a generally similar classification of soil (marine clay). Differences in North-Brabant are yet more obvious, where sandy ground makes up the 'push area' south of the line Bergen op Zoom-Geertruidenberg-Den Bosch and marine clay constitutes the 'pull area' north of this line. The same pattern obtains in the provinces of North-Holland and Utrecht: to the east of the line Muiden-Zeist sandy soils as 'push areas', to the west of the line, peat-soils and clay-soils as 'pull areas'. The same is true for the IJssel valley, the Kop van Overijssel, Friesland, Groningen and Ostfriesland and, finally, for the fertile marine soil area of Butjadingen with its hinterland of bogs and sandy soil. In all these places, however, peat-bogs, even when situated near sandy soil, belong within the confines of 'pull areas'.

The north-south dividing line following kind and quality of soil, coinciding with the border between 'pull area' and 'push area', proves remarkably unreliable in places, however. The pattern breaks down especially in the region of the great rivers. There, in the midst of highly fruitful marine and river clay soils, 'neutral areas' suddenly crop up, places to which and from which no appreciable migratory labour occurred. In particular, we can identify as counter-example 'neutral areas' the Krimpenerwaard, the Lopikerwaard, the eastern part of the Alblasserwaard, the Vijfherenlanden, the Land van Heusden and Altena, and comparable areas further to the east (the Betuwe). Here, internally, there were even limited 'push areas' such as the southern dike of the Alblasserwaard (Sliedrecht and the surrounding area) and, on the other side of the water, the northern dike of the Land van Heusden and Altena (Werkendam). These places were renowned for their navvies, like other locations, it is true, in the region of the great rivers.[13] This at first sight anomalous situation in the region of the great rivers merits an explanation later in this chapter.

For the moment I will advance the conclusion that the North Sea coast as 'pull area' *c.* 1800 was characterised, economically, by favourable natural conditions (e.g. type of soil, presence of minerals, i.e. peat, network for water travel) and was more developed than the interior as the result of improvements to the infrastructure (canals, centres of population, harbours).

Characteristics of 'Push Areas' and 'Neutral Areas'

Roughly speaking, the hinterland of the North Sea coast exhibits a number of characteristics in common which can be summarised as the negation of what holds true for the coastal strip: lack of (exploitable) peat-bogs, in general less-fertile soil, less-favourable shipping possibilities and a far less developed infrastructure. It can also be shown that the level of wages in these parts was appreciably lower than it was in the 'pull area'.

These shared characteristics, however, still did not lead to migrant labour everywhere throughout the interior. And where migrant labour did occur, it did not invariably occur with the same intensity. The identified characteristics may therefore perhaps be considered as necessary, but not sufficient conditions for migratory labour. Systematic comparison of 'push areas' and 'neutral areas' will possibly enable us to pin down more specific characteristics of 'push areas', therefore recognising sufficient conditions inducing their inhabitants to search for employment away from home.

First of all, we should consider the 'corridor' already identified previously between the Brabantine-Flemish and the Hainaut 'push areas', as well as the 'corridor' separating the vast area with Osnabrück at its centre and the peninsula Minden/Lippe/Wiedenbrück.

It is striking that both of these 'corridors' which we might designate respectively as the 'Flemish' and the 'Bielefeld', occupy a special, joint place in economic history.

Around 1800 both were pre-eminent centres for the spinning of flax, where linen weaving especially was an important economic activity and source of income. The number of looms per thousand inhabitants was comparable in both 'corridors' (see Table 2.1).

The Flemish 'corridor' raises no conundrums; the very place which apparently disgorged no migrant workers had no less than 50 looms per 1,000 population. One out of four households, in other words, contained a loom.[14]

The Bielefeld 'corridor' displays a similar pattern on the whole, yet along its edges we run into some difficulties. In 1846, according to Von Reden, the following areas were centres of hemp and flax processing: the Münster *Kreise* Tecklenburg and Warendorf, the Minden Kreise Halle, Bielefeld, Wiedenbrück, Herford and Minden, the west of Lippe and the south of the Hannoverian Landrosteibezirk Osnabrück.[16] As far as the western boundary of this area is concerned, statistics from 1816 reveal that the Kreise Ahaus and Koesfeld, each with more than 40 linen looms per 1,000 inhabitants, should be included (see Table 2.1).

Figure 2.3 depicts not only the linen area of the Bielefeld 'corridor' but the 'push area' of migrant labour which interests us as well. A certain overlapping is conspicuous.

Towards the west, 'push areas' and areas of linen manufacture overlap in Kreise Ahaus, Steinfurt and Tecklenburg. Migrant labour was far from as important a phenomenon in Ahaus and Steinfurt, however, as it was in Tecklenburg. Kreis Tecklenburg thus poses the most puzzling riddle: in contrast to other areas, here both phenomena were very much in evidence, the weaving of linen and migrant labour.

At the same time this Kreis, thanks to Gladen's detailed study, offers us the opportunity to look more closely at the relation between the linen weavers and departing workers. One can crudely bisect the Kreis into eastern and western zones: migrant labourers appear to have come from the western half.[18] Linen production

Table 2.1: Number of Linen Looms per 1,000 Inhabitants, First Half of the Nineteenth Century, Flanders, Westphalia, Twente[15]

Year	Area			per 1000 inhabitants Looms Total	Migrant workers of which as secondary occupation
c. 1820	Flanders	: district	Gent	51	
			Aalst	57	
			Oudenaarde	71	
			St. Niklaas	8	
			Dendermonde	25	
			Eeklo	44	
1816	Regierungsbezirk Münster	: Kreis	Ahaus	73	70	11
			Beckum	13	4	0
			Borken	39	36	<1
			Koesfeld	48	40	1
			Lüdinghausen	24	15	3
			Münster-Land	22	15	18
			Recklinghausen. Land	19	10	<1
			Steinfurt	33	23	17
			Tecklenburg	61	60	33
			Warendorf	60	43	6
1835/6	Lippe			42	14
1846	Regierungsbezirk Minden:			30	
	— Gemeinsame Handelskammer Bielefeld/Halle/Wiedenbrück/West-Herford/ Lipper Ämter: Oerlinghausen, Lage, Schötmar, Detmold			28	
1838	— Kreis Bielefeld			27	20
1846				52	
1838	— Kreis Herford			10	9
1846				17	
1838	— Kreis Halle			±31	
1811/5	Twente			13	

and looms appear to have been particularly concentrated in the east of the Kreis. This split, upon further consideration, appears connected to patterns of agrarian activity. Linen weaving was primarily a secondary occupation, a winter pastime when there was relatively little agricultural work to perform. In the western half of Tecklenburg there was a far greater concentration of small farmers who rented their land, the so-called *Heuerlinge*, than in the eastern

Figure 2.3: 'Push Areas' of Migrant Labourers and Areas of Linen Manufacture, First Half of the Nineteenth Century in Westphalia[17]

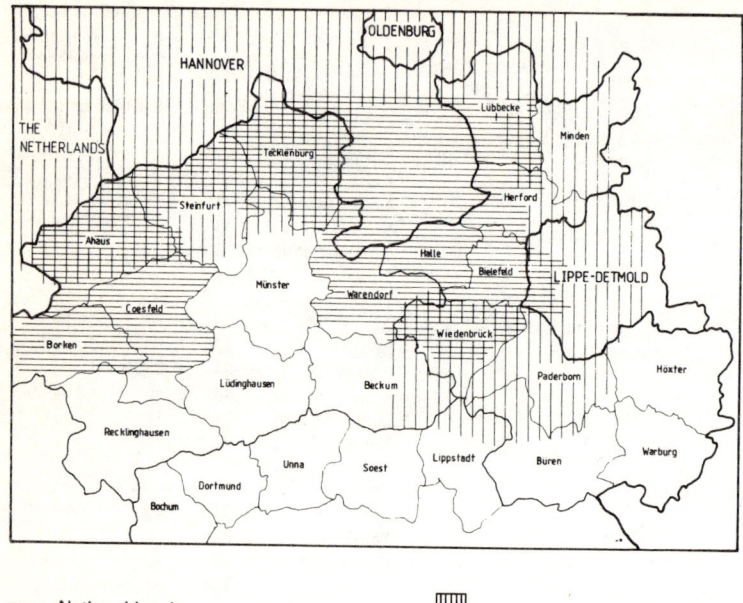

— National border
— Boundary of Prussian *Regierungsbezirke*
— Boundary of Prussian *Kreise*
▓ 'Push area'
▓ Area of linen manufacture

half: from place to place in the west (with the single exception of Brochterbeck) Heuerlinge accounted always for more than 20 per cent of all families, the percentage in Schale rising as high as 43, whereas in the east (discounting Tecklenburg as an exception) Heuerlinge made up but 21 per cent or less of the local population, with a minimal representation of 4 per cent in Lotte. As tenants, Heuerlinge farmed an average of 1.14 ha in the western municipalities in the years 1827-30, but as many as a quarter of them did not even lease holdings of such modest proportions. By contrast in the east there were considerably fewer small farmers, and these, on the average, controlled more land. There seems therefore to be a connection between the incidence of small farms and home weaving on the one hand, and minimal tenant-farming and labour migration on the other. Such a relation does not imply though that the families of migrant workers did not engage in domestic industry.

Spinning, however, was far more likely to have occupied them than weaving. There was a crying need for spinners: for every weaver, four spinners were required. Spinning took place, moreover, primarily during the winter.

Table 2.2 summarises differences between the western and eastern halves of Tecklenburg.

It is not unlikely that further research concerning other areas where both linen production and migrant labour were found would reveal, as in Tecklenburg, an internal line of division.

The overlapping observed in the east of the Bielefeld 'corridor' offers yet a further possible explanation, one different from the explanation for the situation within Tecklenburg. In Table 2.3 certain relevant facts are summarised which pertain to domestic industry and migrant labour in the Regierungsbezirk Minden:

The Kreise Bielefeld and Halle had many a weaver but few migrant labourers. The Kreise Lübbecke and Wiedenbrück, inversely, had many migrant workers and scarcely any weavers, but, and what is more important, plenty of spinners. The Kreis Herford was, just as Tecklenburg, something of a mix: the west conformed with Bielefeld, thus many looms and few departing labourers, the east with Lippe, migrant labour in full swing, few looms. The Kreis Minden, last of all, presents no clear-cut picture: there seems to have taken place little weaving, yet migrant labour was also marginal. It thus makes sense where the production of

Table 2.2: Some Characteristics of the West and East of Tecklenburg, Early Nineteenth Century[19]

	West*	East**
Households 1828	3825	3137
Migrant workers 1811	> 1000	98
Households per migrant worker	< 4	46
Looms as secondary occupation 1827	584	2055
Households per loom	6.4	1.5
Heuerlinge households 1828	1142	611
Heurlinge households as % of total	29.9	19.5

*West: Schale, Halverde, Hopsten, Recke, Mettingen, Dreierwalde, Riesenbeck, Ibbenbüren, Bevergern, Brochterbeck, Ladbergen.
**East: Wersen, Westerkappeln, Lotte, Leeden, Lengerich, Lienen.

Table 2.3: Linen Production and Migrant Labour in Several Kreise of the Régierungbezirk Minden c. 1840[20]

Kreis	Year	per 1000 inhabitants		Spinners		Migrant workers
		Looms/families with looms				
		Primary occupation	Secondary occupation	pri. occ.	sec. occ.	
Lübbecke	1846	few	few	very important		8
Minden	1838	few	few	?	?	1.5
Herford	1838	1	9	0	110	1.5
	1846	17		4	54	1.5
Halle	1838	± 31		4	54	1.5
Bielefeld	1838	7	20	9	77	0.5
	1846	52				
Wiedenbrück	1838	6		62	75	6.5

linen thrived to make a distinction between weaving and spinning. Spinning apparently was easier to combine with migrant labour than was weaving. Spinning could be performed by young and old, male and female; it required little capital and was especially suited to the wintertime.[21]

For Lippe-Detmold it is especially *Amt* Lage that raises questions; there weaving linen took place, but so did labour migration, especially among brick-makers. The western Amt Oerlinghausen supported some weaving, but hardly any labour migration. The eastern *Aemter* featured little textile industry but moderate labour migration, especially of peat-cutters and grass-mowers.[22] If we examine Westphalia as a whole, then it seems that where linen production, especially weaving, went on as domestic industry throughout the entire year, it was more or less impossible to combine it with migratory labour.

In addition to the two 'corridors' just discussed, the large area between the Bielefeld 'corridor' and the Schelde deserves our attention. Within the area, it is true, there were some 'push' islands, but for the most part the whole was characterised by an absence of migrant labour.

Broadly speaking, the area appears to fall into two kinds of regions: those with intensive domestic industry and those where agriculture was practically the only source of income. To the first category belong those places east of the Rhine with extremely active domestic industry. The Prussian *Regierungsbezirke* Arnsberg, Düsseldorf and the *Landkreis* Mülheim — largely co-extensive with the former Mark and Berg — were especially advanced in terms of industrialisation at the outset of the nineteenth century. Together with textiles, metals were a basic part of rural domestic industry here.[23] Further to the west and south the woollen textile industry flourished in the vicinity of Aachen and Verviers, and metal production in Liège and the vicinity.[24] And finally, there was the region of Charleroi, the Borinage and the already strongly industrialised part of the département of Nord round about Lille. Mining in the neighbourhood of Aachen and Liège can be added to this composite picture. For these regions domestic industry and mining may provide an explanation for the lack of migrant labour.

Any such explanation would be invalid, however, for the second category of regions in the area between Bielefeld and the Schelde, those places where agriculture was so dominant (for example, moving from northeast to southwest, in the Regierungsbezirk Münster, the Kreise Beckum, Lüdinghausen, Recklinghausen and Koesfeld and in the Kreise Soest and Hamm[25]) immediately to the south; furthermore, the area between the Rhine and the Maas to the north of the line Aachen-Cologne, the Herve Region and West of the river Maas, above all, most of the Duchy of Brabant).[26]

What, then, is the differences between these agricultural areas and the nearby typical 'push areas' of migrant labour? And is there a plausible explanation for the absence of migrant labour in these areas?

In theory there are two possible explanations for the absence of migrant labour in agricultural areas. The first, and simplest, is that land ownership is divided in such a way that every household possesses enough to be self-supporting and the members of the household can themselves carry out all necessary work. Such a situation, however, appears to have been rather exceptional.

The second, somewhat more complicated explanation is that land ownership may not have been equal, but that the inequalities were such that demand for (seasonal) labour on the part of larger farms could be met locally, or in any event by workers from within the immediate area, because a surplus of labour existed in households with (too) small holdings. At the village, or district level then, no migrant labour would be registered. A precondition for the existence of this situation, however, is that the seasonal peak labour demand for labourers on large farms does not coincide with work needs on small farms. This supposes the cultivation of crops which require intensive labour input at different times.

It is impossible here to prove, or even to make it seem likely that for all the cited agricultural areas in 1811 the conditions existed which would support this second explanation. Yet, for the 'neutral' agricultural areas in Belgium we do have rather extensive information about farm size and a number of indications concerning the difference between large and small farms. On a basis of the agricultural census of 1846, I have divided farms into three size-categories: less than 1 hectare (ha), between 1 and 5 ha, more than 5 ha.

Table 2.4 incorporates information on farm size for all provinces in Belgium. For a number of arrondissements in which migrant labour took place, data in greater detail have been calculated. The degree to which farms of less than 1 ha locally outnumbered those

Table 2.4: Distribution of Belgian Farms According to Size category in 1846[27]

Provinces and arrondissements	Proportion (%)			
	(A) < 1 ha	(B) 1.5 ha	(C) ≥ 5 ha	(A) minus (C)
Luxemburg	31.67	41.88	26.45	5.22
Limburg	42.38	32.62	25.00	17.38
Antwerp	52.15	26.90	20.95	31.20
Namur	52.66	32.92	14.42	38.24
Brabant	51.35	36.20	12.45	38.90
Nivelles	61.89	26.95	11.16	50.73
East-Flanders	54.76	31.50	13.74	41.02
Liège	59.53	25.76	14.71	44.82
Liège	68.15	22.11	9.74	58.41
West-Flanders	64.77	19.21	16.02	48.75
Hainaut	65.45	23.92	10.63	54.82
Tournai	57.82	30.16	12.02	45.80
Thuin	60.51	26.87	12.62	47.89
Soignies	63.47	22.89	13.64	49.83
Ath	62.13	27.24	10.63	51.50
Mons	64.73	24.75	10.62	54.21
Charleroi	79.39	14.08	6.35	72.86

of 5 or more ha appears a reliable indicator for identifying places where a 'push' was exerted on labour: in 1811 the central and northern parts of Hainaut, the south of Brabant and the arrondissement of Liège demonstrate a major expulsion of migrant workers and in 1846 a significant labour 'surplus' in agriculture (column A minus C in Table 2.4). Delatte, in his study of the rural population of the Bishopric of Liège, also emphasises the incidence of extremely small farms in the Jeker valley. He writes: 'Nous nous trouvons en présence du triomphe de la toute petite exploitation'.[28] What is striking is that the 'linen' provinces of East, but especially West-Flanders had every bit as much of a labour 'surplus' as the 'push areas' did.[29]

Let us return to the 'neutral' agricultural regions of Belgium, the core of which was made up of the centre and the north of the Province of Brabant, the south of the Province of Antwerp and the south of the Province of Limburg. Within this territory, moreover, a certain important condition had to be satisfied. Assuming that there were enough small farmers present to help larger landowners during peak labour seasons, then these seasonal peaks should not occur at the same time that the small farmers had work to do on their own farms — in other words, these farmers could be 'missed' to work elsewhere. It seems obvious then that what they chose to plant, and when, would have differed fundamentally from their larger neighbours. Merely the size of their holdings, less than a hectare, supports such a supposition. On such a small surface area, indeed, grain cannot be raised profitably, and grain was the leading crop of the large farms[30]). The small farmers in Brabant ran farms which, according to Vandenbroeke, 'more and more closely resembled market-gardening'. They worked the soil for the most part with shovels. Their main crops were potatoes for home consumption and vegetables for the market. Not only did seasonal peaks occur at different times from grain cultivation, but the division of labour could be timed to differ from the work needs on large farms. Indeed, for a farm of 1 to 1½ ha, a maximum of some 200 work days a year was required. And a portion of the total could be accomplished by women and children.

A description by Arrivabene of the lives of day labourers in Gaasbeek near Brussels clearly depicts the situation on this kind of small farm in 1832/3:

> These people usually own a small house and garden where they

grow vegetables, hops and tobacco. The hops are sold. They also have some animals: a cow, a pig and some chickens. From the age of 14, the children earn wages in the service of a large farmer. When they marry, they buy a plot of 12.5 to 25 *are* [100 m²] and put up a house. It is a wooden shelter with straw roof that can better be called a hut. Some of the day workers, competing keenly among themselves, lease a field to farm, the rest are too poor and don't have a chance to try because the landowners don't trust them. The large farmers are not pleased with tenancy arrangements because it increases the risk that during the harvest there will be a shortage of workers for them. The day labourers work 20 to 30 days a year on their own fields, plus some additional early mornings and late nights. The rest of this work is entrusted to wives and children. The day labourers also try to earn a wage from the large farmers but often they are more or less bound to work for a particular individual whom they owe money or whose plough they wish to borrow or rent.[31]

For the remaining 'neutral' farmlands we have less complete information at our disposal. For the Regierungsbezirk Münster we can demonstrate that the quantity of arable land available per household differed remarkably in 'push areas' from 'neutral areas': in those Kreise with an efflux of migrant workers and in those with domestic industry, average farm size in 1849 was 3.52 ha per house, whereas 5.42 ha per house was the comparable figure in the agricultural Kreise.[32] There is no information as far as I know about the possibility of labour being shared in these locations between large and small farms, nor about possible variations in what was cultivated.

It is, we should note, possible that in some areas which appear 'neutral', migratory labour over extremely short distances took place but was not registered as such. In 1823 in Flanders, for example, in discussing the farmer harvest it was said: 'Our regular servants no longer are content to see our work through to the end, we need to look for help from cottagers, our neighbours'[33]. I imagine that these neighbours were not only small farmers, but linen weavers as well. Similarly, it is possible that the agricultural region of Kreis Soest in the Regierungsbezirk Arnsberg that included an important number of large farms[34] might have been familiar with short-distance labour migration originating from surrounding areas where there were many domestic industrial workers.³⁵

At this point it is opportune to look back at another 'neutral area' encountered during discussion of 'pull areas': the region of the 'great rivers' in the centre of the Netherlands. The area of the 'great rivers' was the most diverse agricultural region in the Netherlands.³⁶ Sharp variations in the quality and composition of the soil resulted in a wide range of extremely different farming activities side by side: agriculture, animal husbandry, fruit-growing and market gardening. In addition to animal husbandry dominant in the west, and the raising of grain dominant in the east, other patterns of agrarian production could also be distinguished. Labour-intensive cultivation of hemp was known in Alblasserwaard, Krimpenerwaard and the Land van Vianen; turning and fertilising the soil before haymaking, and harvesting and further processing of the crop after hay-making provided work for many hands.³⁷ Further south in the Land van Heusden and Altena hops were raised. In the Betuwe to the east, fruit and tobacco farming were common. This considerable variety in cultivation which provided work throughout the year could indeed have created a labour market where supply and demand was rather constant with the passing seasons so that, on the whole, there was no 'push' or 'pull' exercised on workers.³⁸

Such a local labour market, in large part independent of migratory labour, probably entailed a considerable degree of participation by women and children. It is noteworthy that during the evaluation of the early years of compulsory schooling in the Netherlands dating from the beginning of this century, the area of the 'great rivers' exhibited the most absenteeism of school children because of their involvement in farm work.³⁹

Conclusions Concerning Patterns of Migratory Labour at Macro-level

It is possible to distinguish one clear 'pull area' towards which migrant labourers made their way in 1811: the North Sea coast. This elongated coastal strip from Calais to Bremen, never more than 50 km wide, drew workers from a hinterland which stretched inland anywhere from 250 to 300 km. Within this hinterland there were well-defined areas from which migrant workers flowed to the coast, 'push areas', but 'neutral areas' as well, areas where no outmigration to speak of took place.

Central to this chapter has been an analysis of geographical patterns of migrant labour observed at the macro-level in order to discover possible differences in the economic characteristics of 'pull areas' and 'push areas', and furthermore, possible differences between 'pull and push areas' and 'neutral areas'. The 'pull area' appears to have been characterised throughout its length and breadth by its favourable position for shipping and travel, its fortunate endowment with good soils and (exploitable) minerals, and its well-developed economic infrastructure. It can also be shown, moreover, that the level of wages for certain work in the 'pull area' was sufficiently high to attract workers from 'push areas'. The hinterland of the 'pull area', thus both 'push areas' and 'neutral areas', also appears to have had a number of characteristics in common which, speaking generally, can be described as the mirror image of the 'pull area'. Physical geography unsuited to the development of shipping and river transportation, soils of lesser fertility, the lack of exploitable peat-bogs and a rudimentary economic infrastructure appear then to have provided necessary conditions for the emergence of migratory labour — but not in and of themselves sufficient conditions as well. It was the better to understand what such sufficient conditions might be, that we undertook comparison of 'neutral areas' and 'push areas'.

The difference between 'push areas' and 'neutral areas' appears connected to the extensiveness of domestic industry in a given location and to the distribution of farms according to size. Areas with widespread domestic industry, such as the linen-weaving country in Flanders and around Bielefeld and metal-producing areas in the Ruhr valley, do not appear to qualify as 'push areas'. Furthermore, areas with a certain 'balance' between smaller and larger farms do not evince migrant labour, at least not migration covering any considerable distances. In these areas the need for workers on larger farms during seasonal labour peaks would, it is my contention, be eased by optimal use of the entire local work force. During the off-season there should be alternative local sources of income at hand. Agricultural employment would suit this need as well as domestic industry. Smaller farmers could indeed arrange things so that self-employment occupied them on their own land for part of the year: the small size of their farms meant that their cultivation schedule differed essentially from that of their larger neighbours. These differences and the seasonal labour peaks which they entailed were complementary over time.

One may well ask under what conditions employers in the 'pull area' would allow themselves to engage in kinds of production which could not be sustained by the local labour market and demographic structure.

On the other hand, the question arises how it was possible that workers from 'push areas' were ready to leave their homes for work elsewhere just at those very times when the demand for labour in various branches of production in the 'pull area' reached its height. In the coming chapters I will address these, and related questions. To answer the first a more complete description of exactly what kinds of work migrants performed is required. The necessary meso-level analysis is presented in Chapter 4. To answer the question about migrants' readiness to travel from home, we must look more carefully at the sum of the economic activities individual workers and their families performed in the course of the year. Such a micro-level analysis is the substance of Chapter 5. Before embarking on either of these intellectual enterprises, however, let us accompany migrant workers on their bodily journeys from 'push area' to 'pull area', describing this *trait d'union* of theirs in the pages of Chapter 3.

3 MIGRANTS UNDER WAY

Given the elongated form of the 'pull area' involved, the North Sea coast, we cannot speak of a single route which all migrant labourers followed. The journey was a short one from Hainaut Nord towards the coast at Pas de Calais and Nord. From this same point of departure, moreover, many brick-makers and workers with related job experience set out for Antwerp and the surrounding area. Similarly brief was the journey which those from Brabant undertook to Zeeland and South-Holland Islands, and the hayfields of De Langstraat. The brevity of these journeys, which could be accomplished in between one to three days, may explain why we know so little about them.[1] The same holds true for the movements of workers from Liège who went to dig the Grand Canal du Nord.

Further to the north, the heart of the 'pull area', the distance covered by arriving migrant workers was greater, and the stream of arrivals more considerable. We also have more information about their experiences under way. Documentation is once again sketchy, however, concerning the, for the most part, shorter journeys undertaken to Ostfriesland and Butjadingen. At the centre three currents of migrant workers can be differentiated, their choice of alternative routes determined in large part by natural circumstances (see Figure 3.1).

In the text following I will confine myself to describing the journey workers faced who travelled to the centre of the North Sea System. The journey constituted one of the major expenses which a labourer had to meet. Time, under the circumstances, meant money. The best way to save time was to travel as much as possible by ship. Indeed, cross-country travel was invariably far more costly, whether on foot or by coach.[2] The extensive bogs in the east of the Netherlands constituted the most important obstacle to migrant workers from the east. Since workers preferred to travel by ship and the eastern bogs could be crossed only at particular places, a limited number of fixed routes emerged.

Route (A) skirted the Overijssel bogs to the south. Considering the location of the 'push areas' involved, we can assume workers from the vicinity of Ahaus and Steinfurt followed this route. These

Figure 3.1: Most Important Routes Followed to the North Sea Coast by Migrant Labourers

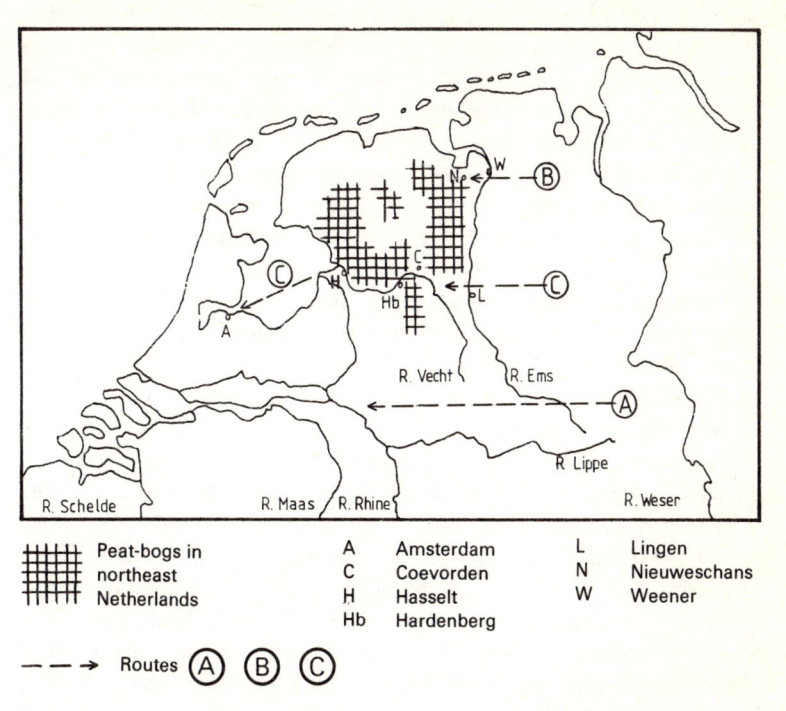

	Peat-bogs in northeast Netherlands	A	Amsterdam	L	Lingen
		C	Coevorden	N	Nieuweschans
		H	Hasselt	W	Weener
		Hb	Hardenberg		

– – → Routes Ⓐ Ⓑ Ⓒ

workers were hardly ever employed in Holland, however, but worked rather in the northern provinces. As a consequence they will have chosen a different path.[3] Only labourers from in and around Wiedenbrück thus remain for route (A). In contrast to their northern neighbours from Lippe, they did work primarily in Holland. If they wished to accomplish as much of their journey as possible by water, they had to locate and reach a navigable waterway close at hand. This may have been the Lippe River. Via the Rhine they were thus able to reach Holland.[4] Annually not many more than a thousand migrants will have selected this route.

Route (B) in the north crossed the narrow strip of land separating the Dollart from the northernmost offshoots of the peat-bogs along the Dutch-German border. This route involved a passage via Nieuweschans and from there southwest towards Winschoten, or northeast towards Delfzijl, a city that could also be reached by ship from Emden.[5] It is likely that the workers who followed this route came first and foremost from the département of Bouches du Weser. They gathered in groups of twenty to a hundred workers at agreed upon locations. Certain trees were favourite meeting places. In Oldenburg such trees remained well known for a long time under the term *Frieseneiche* (Frisian Oaks).[6] From such points of departure groups then pushed on to Weener where they crossed the Ems and continued on to Nieuweschans where they probably boarded a tow-barge.[7] Workers from the département of Ems Supérieur will also have made use of the Nieuweschans bypass. They travelled down the Ems as far as Weener in all probability. All in all not more than several thousand workers will have penetrated the 'pull area' along route (B) in any given year.

The route which remains for consideration, route (C), was indeed the only way possible overland through the bog between Almelo to the south and Nieuweschans to the north. It was a narrow ridge of sand along which the Vecht flowed into Overijssel. Coming from Bentheim county one could follow this ridge north via Coevorden or west via Hardenberg on the Vecht. Those choosing the journey north would primarily have been migrants seeking work in the peat-bogs of Drenthe and Friesland. They came from areas situated along the left bank of the Ems, such as Bentheim county, and from places in the region of Münster further to the south, such as settlements in the vicinity of Ahaus and Steinfurt.[8] The bulk of the workers who took route (C), however — something in the order of 10,000 each year — came from the far side of the Ems, crossing the river at Lingen.

Let us accompany a typical migrant labourer on his journey outwardbound from the heart of a 'push area', from Damme, say, situated in Münsterland in the deep south of Oldenburg (in 1811 Ems Supérieur), to the core of a 'pull area', the peat-bogs, for example, south of Amsterdam. Workers came together on a day in March to start the long journey. Perhaps the scene would have resembled that depicted in the farce *De romanzieke juffer* (The Novel-sick Maid) by Pieter Bernagie (1685), where Hans, in answering the question 'How'd you get here from Westphalia?' replies:

> There were ten of us,
> Farm lads all, at an inn, and we

really got loaded (...)
We set off for Holland[9]

One took leave of wife and children and took to the road with a number of comrades, perhaps to the accompaniment of music or song.[10] It was not easy going, for everyone was laden down heavily with tools and spare clothing, but especially with provisions. Each worker took as much food as possible with him, eager not to have to buy things to eat in Holland, where goods were expensive. Pork, especially smoked pork, was part of the baggage of every worker, as well as bread, flour, tobacco and perhaps a bolt of linen to sell along the way.[11]

En route one met others making towards the same destination. The party will have swollen enormously, for example, at the mammoth, glacier-shifted boulder between Ankum and Ueffeln, the 'Breite Stein', a renowned gathering place for migrant workers.[12] Year after year workers stuck to the same path, pausing at the same places for rest under the same trees, moving west towards the city of Lingen on the Ems. Perhaps under way a number of migrants hired a cart collectively to transport their heavy baggage, or else they lugged it on with bent backs alone.[13] At Lingen, where workers once crossed the Ems on a ferry, a bridge was later built.[14] The mass of migrants, grown by now to thousands, carried on via Neuenhaus and Uelsen in Bentheim county to the Netherlands border at Venebrugge. From there they were soon in the Overijssel town of Hardenberg.

Here the shoving and crowding would have been no joke, each migrant trying to entrust his baggage to expediters or to Vecht helmsmen in order to finish the last stage of the journey in haste.[15] While their freight floated on down the Vecht, the workers themselves headed straight towards the Zuiderzee, sticking to the 'Hessenweg', north of the Vecht towns Dalfsen and Ommen, and just south of the peat-bog.[16] Here too they might become embroiled in the fierce competition prevailing in Hasselt and in Zwolle especially, but also in other towns, to transport them across the Zuiderzee. For this passage Hasselt was most favourably situated and had entered into various contracts with the shipping guild in Amsterdam to achieve a monopoly position with respect to the crossing — at the cost of shipping interests in Zwolle and other places in Overijssel.[17] Zwolle did not take the challenge lying down, but did its utmost to snare migrant workers before they reached Hasselt. Usually, it achieved its purpose by intercepting them along the way at the Berkummer Bridge (also called Noodhaven or Varkensgat), where the Vecht River passed nearest to Zwolle.

In 1733 Zwolle was going to extremes. Her shippers did not hesitate

> to set up signs in the fields near Ommen and Dalfsen with a hand waarop in substanti geschreven stondt dat niemandt sig soude hebben te verstouten een andre weg in te slaan, als dien out and which led to the Berkummer Bridge and from there to Varkensgat, a route posted with similar signs here and there, complete with stated penalties

> (in het veld bij Ommen en Dalfsen Paalen op te rigten met een hand waarop in substanti geschreven stondt dat niemandt sig soude hebben te verstouten een andre weg in te slaan, als dien gem. hand haar aanwees en die op de Barkumer Brugge en vervolgens tot op het verkensgat liep, hebbende mede dusdane bellettries op de gemene passage her en daar aangeplakt alles bij sekre poenaliteit.)

When workers paid no attention, soldiers were brought in to force them to head for the Zwolle ships. Even that failed. In the end the *praam*-shippers of Zwolle and Hardenberg reached a secret agreement that they would not transfer the belongings of the migrant workers as promised to Hasselt, but to Varkensgat instead.[18] In general, the workers will have managed to profit from the keen competition by exacting prices for passage that were lower than the official rates.[19]

We may assume none the less that most migrants proceeded to Hasselt. Leaving Dalfsen to their left they came via the *poepen-* or *pikmaaierspad* (German-path or harvesters' path) and via the small sluice called *poepestouwe* (German stowage) (nowadays along-side the mill 'Streukeldijk') to the high northern dike along the Zwarte Water River. From here one could already spy Hasselt in the distance.[20] Just before entering the city through the Engpoort, on their right travellers passed a spot of special significance for Catholics bound for Holland: the *Heilige Stede* (holy place). This was a small chapel on the 'Island', erected in 1357 and in 1551 endowed with a papal indulgence of 100 days in recognition of miracles which had occurred there. Although the anonymous author of *The Contemporary State of Affairs* in Overijssel in 1803 is of the opinion that

> the power to perform miracles ... disappears during the purification of a religion in the same way that in the past oracles disappeared with the advent of Christianity and all superstitious beliefs will always disappear once viewed in the light of sound intelligence

this enlightened spirit nevertheless notes, 'The uplanders who pass here each year on their way to work in Holland, still do not hesitate in this day and age to demonstrate their respect for miracles by paying a brief visit'.[21]

Fortified, or not, by a visit to the chapel and a stop at a Hasselt inn,[22] workers could board ship — together with their belongings which would have caught up with them. The sea voyage would not have been an undiluted pleasure with 100 workers and their baggage crammed into a ship used at other times of the year to ferry cattle. Via Zwartsluis and Genemuiden the ship traversed the Zwolse Diep and then set out to sea. In his farce, *De zwetser* (The Braggart), from 1712, Pieter Langendijk introduced the simple Westphalian grass-mower Slenderhinke who spoke, as follows, about his sea passage:

> And I went in a ship across wide water, the Zuiderzee, a vast, wide lake, mad white caps that could not be calmed; and my stomach began to growl. I spoke to the skipper and said, you thief, the gallows is too good for you, where are you taking good folk to? Don't you know, you wizard, that I am Slendrinke. Here is no land, no sand, no house, no dung, no trees. Churl, where will you sight to follow a straight course? In all his dread, the wizard stood and sang a song, while the food gushed up out of my belly ... I even spotted something green [bile] and I hadn't eaten anything that colour. Then I fell asleep until morning and saw then for the first time this great Haspeldam, this Amstelholland. That cheered me up. Then I thought, Hinke, you're going to make a lot of money.[23]

After the uncomfortable, but comparatively swift one-day crossing, workers left ship at Amsterdam. Later in the year, men to mow grass would arrive here as well, whether from Hasselt as well, or from a Frisian harbour.[24] Ships from Hasselt, Zwolle and Kampen all docked at the same place: close to the Oude Brug (Old Bridge). Here, as late as 1865, newly arrived migrant workers still had to pay municipal excise duties on whatever meat they brought with them. In the vicinity of the Oude Brug, also called the *Moffenbeurs* (German Exchange), there were many places where migrants could spend the night, eat, and buy tools. As a consequence of all this activity the neighbourhood sometimes had a German air about it. There was even a butcher with special meat for the *hannekemaaiers*, the common Dutch expression for German harvesters.[25]

Thanks to Justus van Maurik's memories of his youth, we are able to form a rather accurate picture of this German sub-culture around 1860. After passing through municipal customs, workers could buy themselves a plate of stew at Ellinkhuizen's 'De portionstafel 't Koningsloo' in the Lange Niezel, or else in another eating-house on the Ouwekerksplein, also called "t Kongingsloo'! At Ellinkhuizen's 5 cents bought a plate of vegetables with potatoes, brown beans with vinegar and apple syrup, onions with carrots and beets, stringbeans with white beans or mashed red cabbage. On the Ouwekerksplein, a hefty portion of rice or groats with apple syrup and a kind of hotchpotch cost only 3 cents. In the evenings, in groups of five or six companions, workers walked along the canals, down the Nieuwendijk, in the Warmoesstraat or along the Buitenkant. Then they would go and sit on a bench in front of the lodgings they had found for the night, or on a neighbour's steps, or even just squat on their heels to watch the people passing by.

A typical lodging was Schirmer's on 't Water, the second or third house from the Ouwebrugsteeg, or the *kruip-in* (crawl-in), the lower part of Lodenkemper's house on the Tesselse Kade, or other *schaftkelders* (dining basements) either on 't Water or the Tesselse Kade between the corner and the Raamskooi. Schirmer and his wife, 'Mutter Minna', let their guests sleep in the few beds which they owned, but also accommodated them on benches in the bar-room and on the floor. In the morning Schirmer put out a few buckets of water on the street in front of the door, each with a towel. Mutter Minna, clapping her hands, would call out in her low-German dialect: 'Allo kiender, hinaus, wasschen!' (Hello, children, out you go, wash up!). And while his guests performed their ablutions outside, Schirmer set up shop inside, displaying his scythes, shovels, bins with whetstones and other tools. Mutter Minna filled large white bowls with coffee and set them in a row on the benches. All the Schirmer's services, shelter and coffee, went for 10 cents. Workers provided their own breakfast from provisions in their kit-bags. Mutter Minna did, however, sell all kinds of sweet, sour and sundry tit-bits.

Lodenkemper, who had at first operated an ordinary schaftkelder, 't Water, now ran his business the way Schirmer did. Justus van Maurik recounts a number of further forms of amusement which the grass-mowers from Germany enjoyed during their stay in Amsterdam. Such pleasures, however, will primarily have been pursued after the working season. First, the peat-dredgers left Amsterdam to earn money, heading south by barge. Grass-mowers, later in the season, primarily went to work in North-Holland above the IJ.

When the season ended, workers returned along the same route they had taken on the way out. Fierce competition for their shipping fares among the skippers of Hasselt and other cities was now concentrated around the Amsterdam docks. During the years around 1725 quarrels were rife, at least according to the testimony of two Amsterdam porters of grain, and a barrow-man employed at the corn market in the neighbourhood of the Hasselt pier. Tension mounted to extremes in 1728. The Amsterdam witnesses just referred to saw how the Hasselt captain Jochem Noes already had a number of mowers on board when rival skippers began to try to persuade them to travel to Zwolle on their ships instead. Probably they quoted a lower price. In any event, some of the mowers were inclined to accept the offer. Jochem Noes, with assistance from his colleague Roelof Grooteboer from Hasselt, endeavoured to convince the mowers to remain where they were, on his craft. This appears to have been contrary to the wishes of the mowers, for one of them

> seized an empty herring tun and another a piece of wood, and with these they bashed a hole in the head of the Hasselt skipper Roelof Grooteboer who was involved in what was going on; his blood gushed out and they in all likelihood would have treated him more brutally still if porters and other good souls nearby hadn't rescued him.[26]

Migrants did not always begin their journey back home in the best of spirits. Some may have saved nothing, or less than they had hoped, their earnings a disappointment either because of illness or failure to find enough work. Frustrated expectations led more than once to migrants' robbing each other. Even murders, we know, took place.[27]

One notorious incident took place in November 1822. Thomas Peeters, nicknamed 'The Lapwing', a resident of Beugen near Boxmeer, left home every autumn for the Zeeland and South-Holland Islands in order to harvest madder.[28] At the end of August, true to habit, he departed once again, leaving behind five children and a wife about to give birth to a sixth. At first he found work near Den Briel on the Island of Voorne, where a fellow worker, Gerard Willesen from Issum near Geldern (in Prussia, less than 40 km as the crow flies from Beugen) convinced him to go along to the Land van Goes on Zuid-Beveland. It was said he could earn more money there, but this turned out not to be true, in part because the price of local madder was so low that year, and consequently wages were low as well, and in part because Thomas Peeters became sick there.

When the season ended in late November, Thomas Peeters had only three *rijksdaalders* in his pocket (7.50 Dutchflorins (Dfl.)) 'as payment for his industry and diligence', whereas his comrade Gerard Willesen had saved Dfl.60. Together they boarded the ship from Goes to Dordrecht and from there took another vessel to Den Bosch. From this point on they went on foot, carrying their madder shovels over their shoulders, heading for Grave and then on to Mill. En route Thomas Peeters was greatly troubled about how he was going to support his family of — by now — six children through the winter. In response, Gerard Willesen offered to lend him half of his earnings, Dfl. 30. According to Thomas Peeters's later statement, at a certain moment Gerard Willesen went back on the offer. That proved to be a fatal change of mind.

On the evening of 20 November 1822, trudging along the main road from Mill with Haps almost in sight — which meant that Thomas was practically home — he bashed in the skull of Willesen from behind with his heavy madder shovel and finished him off with a newly purchased jack-knife. He then stripped the corpse which he buried in a sandpit, of the Dfl. 60 and a silver pocket watch, and proceeded on his way. After his arrest, to mitigate his guilt he asserted that in the eyes of the Almighty he would not be considered so sinful, for through Willesen's death, an unmarried man, neither wife nor children could be made unhappy, but Willesen himself all the sooner would acquire salvation as the reward of his hard work and devout behaviour.

Thomas was condemned to hang.

In addition to limiting a migrant's earning power, illness could cause grave discomfort. Malaria was one of the more serious sicknesses that workers might suffer.[29] Such 'fevers' were generally dreaded by workers heading for Holland. Things reached such a point, indeed, that miners from Tecklenburg who went off to Holland for work throughout the summer could not make any claim on their health insurance fund if they fell ill within six weeks of their return.[30] Sick workers were not popular figures at home. In Holland people wanted them to leave at once; everywhere the public feared added expense to the dole.[31] In 1773 in Zwolle a decision was reached that poor and sick passengers would not be carried free across the Zuiderzee, with one exception:

> Yet as far as foreign workers are concerned who come from Germany to Holland for jobs and there become sick and thus poor and must travel back along their way to their own country — such as these may avail themselves of compassion as necessary as long as they don't stay here any longer than is absolutely necessary and the local authorities are informed of the situation immediately.[32]

The journey sketched in the previous pages will have continued essentially unchanged from the seventeenth until the mid-nineteenth century. Only subsequently did major innovations — trains in Germany and steamboats on the Zuiderzee and on the Holland canals — mean different experiences for workers on the move.[33]

Journeys which did not carry migrants straight from 'push' to 'pull' areas, but involved instead their making their way gradually through an extensive region — as did Wanderburschen, compagnons and pedlars — were very different indeed. Nevertheless, these travels too involved an infrastructure of support services related to the jobs which such itinerant workers performed.[34]

4 MIGRANT LABOUR AT MESO-LEVEL: THE WORK

For proper appreciation of the phenomenon of migrant labour at the meso-level, some idea of the many different kinds of work which migrants performed is necessary.

In this chapter we shall more or less confine ourselves to considering the kinds of work in which more than 500 migrant workers were known to engage at any one time. Certain exceptions will be made, on the grounds that the work involved was almost exclusively the province of migrant workers. The jobs reviewed have been grouped into several sectors: agriculture and forestry; excavation, land reclamation, dredging and cutting peat; industrial jobs; transport; trade; and services.

Jobs which were not — or hardly ever — carried out along the North Sea coast in 1811, or which only later in the course of the nineteenth century became a standard form of employment for migrant workers, have not been included in the following discussion. For this reason, when considering agriculture we omit the weeding and harvesting of sugar beet, for example, and the harvesting of hops. Extensive documentation does not exist, moreover, for all occupations, so that certain kinds of work inevitably receive less notice below than their importance at the time should entitle them to. Whenever possible, in relation to each job examined, I will comment on certain fixed topics: the place such work occupied in the total economy of the 'pull area', earnings involved, the social unit within which the work was performed, employer-worker relations, hierarchic relations involved in performance of the work, and finally, relations between local and migrant workers.

Work in Agriculture and Forestry

Mowing and Hay-making on Dairy Farms

Migrant labourers performed only one kind of job on dairy farms: the mowing of grass and preparation of hay. At least an estimated 12,000 workers came to the North Sea coast in 1811 to do such work, particularly in the area between de Langstraat in North-Brabant, just south of the province of Holland, and Friesland.[1]

Specialised dairy farming in the provinces of Holland and Friesland can be characterised as capital-intensive. Most farmers in the meadowlands, engaged exclusively in raising livestock since the seventeenth century, had stopped other farming. Almost the only kind of animals in which they were interested, moreover, was dairy cattle. Milk was practically all processed into cheese or butter on the farm so that these enterprises also had an industrial nature.[2] In summer the cattle grazed in the grassland, but during the winter had to be stable-fed with hay. Grass for hay was cut during the summer, usually in special meadows where no cattle had pastured earlier during the year. In June the grass was at its longest, and ready for mowing as soon as possible to prevent seed formation.[3] In all regions farmers tried to have the grass of this 'first cut' mown and brought in within six weeks. The climate of the region meant the grass in Friesland was ready for mowing some two weeks before grass in Holland, so that there were mowers who moved on to Holland after completing jobs in Friesland.

Permanent farmhands on a dairy farm could not possibly finish the mowing on time themselves. Indeed, the work of milking, and making cheese and butter had to go on uninterrupted. The farmer therefore needed to take on extra workers for a comparatively short period, and migrant labourers were just what was required. They were recruited in two ways. As a rule contacts grew up through the years between a farmer and a number of mowers whose work pleased him. In any event it is known that during the nineteenth century a farmer would let his regular mowers know in writing when he thought his grass would be full-grown and when he expected them to come to cut it.[4] The Ostfriesland mowers in Friesland, the so-called 'ants', also used an intermediary, the *poepenbode* (German messenger). In April this individual would visit farms to find out when they needed the 'ants' to come. For acting as go-between, he was paid 10 cents by each farmer, and each worker. He carried on a small line of trade as well.[5] There were also workers who journeyed to the meadowlands without pre-arrangements. They went from door to door selling their labour, but also reported to the market of regional centres at certain set times. As a gathering place for mowers the markets of Sneek, Leeuwarden and Joure, among others, were well known — allowing us to speak literally of 'labour markets'.[6]

Grass ready for mowing would have reached a height of some 30 cm, and though the grass was not as tall as grain, we should make no mistake about how heavy the work of cutting was: from one hectare in clayey areas a harvest of 3,000 kg of grain-straw was usual, compared to 5,500 kg of hay.[7] Scythes were used generally to mow the grass. Lucas Rotgans puts it prettily in his 'Boerekermis' of 1715:

> Westphalian heroes who wield the scythe as a spear.
> Grass knights, intrepidly swinging their arms.[8]

The scythe is a cutting implement distinguished by a long handle, a tool designed to contend with the great weight of the crop that had to be moved. The *zwade*, a primitive version of the scythe, is mentioned especially during the seventeenth and eighteenth centuries, but it continues to appear as late as the second half of the nineteenth century. Ostfriesland grass-mowers who went to work in Friesland during the nineteenth century appear to have used a scythe with a shorter shaft.[9]

We know something about the life and work of grass-mowers in Friesland thanks to the diary of Doeke Wijgers Hellema from Wirdum (covering the years 1821-56), and to the recollections of Jacob Hepkes Hepkema in Langweer (*c.* 1865).[10] Upon arrival mowers made a place for themselves somewhere on the farm in the hay. Their baggage consisted of a big sack with tools and, most important, provisions, i.e. meat and bread. They rose as early as possible in the morning, at about 3.00 a.m., and coffee with buttermilk from the farm was brought to them in the fields at about 8.00 a.m. They rested for a while in mid-afternoon, usually in the fields, protected by a crude tent, and in the early evening, at eight o'clock or so, they received a bowl of porridge at the main farmhouse. On such a day, working in teams of two, each mower cleared more than half a hectare of grass, work which earned Dfl. 1.50 in 1811, but more later in the century.[11] After a week or two the farmer summoned a pair of hay-makers, in this case usually from the sandy areas in the east of Friesland. These hay-makers might be of either sex. Usually they came from a lesser distance than the mowers. Their work consisted of turning and finally gathering the grass that the mowers had laid in the 'swathes'.[12] Four weeks after the start of the hay harvest all grass was cut, and another two weeks later, if not too much rain had fallen, the hay was safely stored. For his fifty cows Hellema needed hay from more than 20 ha of meadowland.

Once the mowing was over, wages were paid in cash. Payment was accompanied with simple festivities; the mowers would be treated to a strong drink and pancakes with bacon. Afterwards, on occasion, they helped with other work on the farm. Sometimes they headed on to North-Holland to add to their earnings. Others left for home as soon as the mowing was done. The relationship between mowers and their employer, the 'boss', was rather a personal one. We have already noted that as a rule they worked for the same man year in, year out.[13] The Frisian farmer Hellema describes his bond with a mower eloquently in his diary entry for 6 June 1826. Two days before the diary entry the mowing had commenced once again, but

> with strange mowers, while one of our regular mowers died at home three to four weeks after he left here last year sick. It saddened us to learn the news from the mowers, for he was a good man, although Catholic; he worked for us after the busy season, sat with us at table, would have stayed longer except that he didn't feel well and didn't feel comfortable here any longer, so far from home; therefore he asked permission to depart, which I gave. He went, leaving his cap and wooden shoes behind so that now, if he had come again, he could use them — which he told his close relatives before his death so that a fellow mower from that place here now asked for the cap and wooden shoes which we put in his hands, taking them from the very place where the mower had stored them away last year — which was rather touching. But what can I say! Our lives rest in God's hands and he determines our end, none overstays the time alloted.[14]

The picture of grass-mowing presented here probably applies to North-Holland as well, although it is not clear whether there too a sharp division of tasks was maintained between mowers and hay-makers. A few sources suggest that combined teams of mowers and hay-makers consisted of workers from the same place of origin, the hay-makers at times being women.[15]

Grass-mowing and hay-making in De Langstraat was probably a less personal, large-scale affair. There were no farmhouses here in the vast tracts of grassland, and it is conceivable that workers spent the night in tents. No beverages were brought to the mowers from the 'boss', but instead they paid for drinks from 'providers' who set up a tent in the fields for the hay-making season 'om te tappen voor de hooiers' (to tap beer for the hay-makers).[16]

Not only did grass-mowing take place in June, the so-called 'first cut', but if enough grass grew, in September as well, the 'second cut'. There would then be considerably less grass, however, so that the work, far lighter, was probably not entrusted to migrant labourers but carried out instead by the local workforce.[17] Many workers combined hay-making with jobs in the peat-bogs or on the dikes earlier in the year, or with the mowing of grain and other agricultural tasks later in the year.

The Grain Harvest

In the centre of the 'pull area' there was hardly any milling of grain by migrant workers. Milling did take place, however, in southern and northern extensions of the North Sea coast region. In Flanders, from the département of Nord as far as Cadzand Island and from Groningen/Friesland as far as Butjadingen, several thousand migrant workers took part each year in the harvesting of wheat and rye. Comparatively little grain was cultivated in Holland. All in all along the North Sea coast *c.* 1811 some 6,000 migrant workers found employment as reapers of grain.[18] The crop was ripe in July or August, depending on the type of grain and its exact location. Just as with hay-making, bringing in the grain harvest had, optimally, to be accomplished in a rather short span of time.[19] Grass- and grain-mowers earned roughly the same wages. There were for the rest, however, appreciable differences between the two kinds of labour.

Those who reaped grain worked in much larger groups than grass-mowers. They moved through the region where they came to work in bands of tens and engaged their labour collectively to different farmers for a season. It is probable, although not certain, that the women who weeded grain — their presence is mentioned sporadically during the spring (from April to June) — also worked in this way.[20]

The extensive report of Thomas Radcliff concerning Flemish agriculture, completed in 1819, enables us to picture these particular tasks in more specific detail.[21] His account is probably representative for the southern grain-growing area along the North Sea, and perhaps also for areas to the north. Radcliff described the grain harvest on Cadzand Island in more detail. On an average farm in the area, 67 ha large, approximately 30 ha were planted annually in wheat and tick-beans. To reap and bind these crops and set the sheaves upright against each other, 30-40 workers were needed. They worked in the fields in units of four: two cut, two bound the grain and stacked it. In this way a team could finish the entire harvest of one farm in about four days. Workers occupied a separate small building found expressly for this purpose on every farm, the so-called *Vlaamse keet* (Flemish shed). This shelter, usually detached from the main farm but at times built next to it, consisted of a single room for sleeping and a kitchen that together measured comfortably about 6 m × 3½ m. From the farmer, workers received bean straw as fuel. They prepared their own meals, for which they bought bread, pork and fat, milk and other comestibles from the farmer's wife. Their fare was as a rule utterly simple and frequently consisted of nothing more than home-made buttermilk bread pudding.[22]

Grain could be reaped with various tools.[23] The oldest was the sickle, which was used to cut the grain just beneath the ear. This was for the most part work for women. Later, however, in connection with increasing rationalisation and commercialisation and the growing economic importance of straw, the *zicht* (reaping-hook), twice as efficient, and/or the scythe were widely introduced. These both had longer shafts than the sickle and were wielded only by men. The shaft of the zicht was about 40 cm long, that of the scythe more than twice that figure. In use the zicht was held in the right hand, while the reaper 'steered' the grain with a *pikhaak* (pick) in his left hand. Of these two tools, the zicht was preferred by migrant workers from the North Sea coast. In the British Isles it was not currently in use, and in France it was used only in those northern regions where Belgians came to do the harvesting. In Germany use of the zicht was practically confined to the northwest. Although it was possible to mow as much grain with both tools, about half a hectare a day, the zicht appears to have had a number of advantages over the scythe. [24] The zicht required slightly less physical effort so that a longer working day was possible. It was, moreover, somewhat more suitable for the thicker stubble which grew on heavy clay soils. And finally, the zicht in combination with the pick was better for the job if the grain had been blown flat or drummed down by rain. Most important of all, however, was that with zicht and pick together workers could so neatly arrange the severed stalks on the ground that no raking was necessary to assist the binders. This saved labour. It is therefore probably no coincidence that the zicht is first mentioned in use in the Southern Netherlands (in English the tool is therefore known as the 'Hainault scythe') and was especially popular in the 'pull areas' of the North Sea coast.[25] A farmer who hired enough reapers using zichts could bring in his entire grain harvest in three to four days.[26]

Work relations between grain-cutters and their employers were much less personal than those enjoyed by grass-mowers, in part because reapers worked in a much larger group and in part because their stay on any single farm was far shorter. In addition, within workers' groups hierarchical relationships will have arisen, given that a team leader negotiated with the farmer who employed them. Probably a kind of labour brokerage was in effect practised, but for the period c. 1800 little is known about this phenomenon.[27]

Within a number of weeks the entire grain harvest could, and must, have been completed. Regular workers took over once again to bring in the harvest and plough the fields. Most migrant workers returned home; some stayed behind to help with threshing, ploughing or spreading manure.

The Digging of Madder

Madder is perhaps the best known of the industrial crops harvested by migrant workers along the North Sea coast.[28] Madder was intensively cultivated in an extremely small area: the Zeeland Islands of Tholen, St Philipsland and Schouwen-Duiveland and the South-Holland Islands of Goeree-Overflakkee and Voorne-Putten. We need trouble ourselves no further with Tholen, for there local workers saw to the crop. A total of about 1,000 migrant workers were needed to harvest madder elsewhere.[29] Madder is a crop which demands a capitalistic, commercial-farming approach. From the roots of the plant, once they had been dried, a red textile dye was extracted. The roots were dried in special ovens known as madder-ovens, which were located throughout the islands mentioned above. Madder production required an especially large number of operations. One necessary activity, the harvesting or 'digging', involved migrant workers as well as local ones. The digging began in September and lasted into October and November. Farmers who used migrant workers commissioned foremen who were responsible for the digging of a specified land unit,[30] each foreman gathering a team of men, probably about ten strong.[31] Indeed, if a 'band' of madder diggers had ten members, they could then finish bringing in the crop on an average farm in Schouwen-Duiveland in about four weeks' time. Given the duration of the whole madder harvest season, this meant that two to three farmers could employ such a team each year.[32] If the team were larger, however, of if side by side with migrants local workers dug the crop on the same farm, then of course the travelling band could work for many more employers each harvest season.[33]

Madder had rootstocks that were practically half a metre long. The art of digging was to unearth them intact and undamaged.[34] For this purpose a special spade was used, the *meespade* (madder spade) or *meebeitel* (madder chisel), which had a narrow, unusually long blade of 45 to 55 cm. The handle was reinforced along its entire length with iron. The digger could penetrate all the way under the rootstock with this heavy tool and thus lift it out in as much of one piece as possible. Clinging soil had then to be shaken off and the roots piled in mounds. Towards evening smaller piles were combined into larger ones, and after some days the madder was brought to the closest *meestoof* (madder oven). For their hard work, the diggers could earn about Dfl. 1.50 a day.

These workers probably housed and fed themselves in a fashion similar to the arrangements current for grain-reapers. Practising Roman Catholics, they went to church on Sundays — at least such behaviour is recorded explicitly for the clandestine church of Zierikzee in the eighteenth century.[35] Evidence of group consciousness was reported in 1841 in the form of a harvest custom:

> If someone passed by a field where madder-diggers were at work and shouted '*krootspitters*' [madder-root grubbers], the first two of the diggers to start running chased after him — the rest were not allowed to help. If they managed to catch the challenger who was insulting them, they led him back to the field and, while the other diggers stood by jeering, buried him up to the waist in the earth. He was only released after promising a ransom of drinking money.[36]

Ingeborg Weber-Kellermann, who has studied harvest customs in Germany around the middle of the previous century, describes many comparable rites which were common during the grain harvest under the collective name *binden und lösen* (binding and setting free). She is of the opinion that these rites are indicative of the workers' sense of self-esteem which gave them 'the awareness that during the harvest, because of their labour, they were the true "Lords of the Field" and therefore they dared to claim, without contradiction, their legal rights'.[37]

For most workers the digging of madder will have been their last chance in the year to earn wages. Many will have begun the year's labour on the dikes; in the summer perhaps they then took part in the hay and grain harvests. In connection with these other jobs there were regulations dating from the fifteenth century which stipulated that the madder harvest might not start before September in order not needlessly to jeopardise work on the dikes.[38] After 1870 cultivation of madder in the Netherlands faded rapidly as the result of the discovery and ascension of a synthetic red dye. And with the disappearance of the crop, in the 1870s the migrant madder diggers also vanished from the scene.

The Flax and Potato Harvests

In Bouches de l'Escaut and Bouches de la Meuse, the same départements where madder was dug in 1811 with the help of migrant workers, outside labourers were also employed for the cultivation of flax. Most descriptions of this kind of migrant labour date from the second half of the nineteenth century. It is likely, however, that they are also accurate for the period which concerns us more immediately.[39]

The producers, the flax farmers, came almost exclusively, just as their field hands, from the Hoekse Waard, the Zwijndrechtse Waard and from IJsselmonde. We may consider Ridderkerk and Hendrik-Ido-Ambacht as important flax centres. The flax farmers not only planted their own farms with flax but leased land from others too, in neighbouring municipalities and also further away. At the beginning of the nineteenth century, the *Overmaassche* flax producers rented an estimated minimum of 1,000 ha for their crop in the nearby province of Zeeland. The landowner provided ploughing and harrowing and at times even seeds for sowing, but had nothing further to do with cultivation.[40] The flax farmer organised all the necessary work himself right up to the time when the flax was removed from the fields — and usually sent to his home location for processing. This flax farmer had to arrange for workers both to tend the fields which he may have rented elsewhere and to carry out industrial processing of the flax during the winter months in his own place of residence, processing known as *zwingelen* (swingling). Next to his farmhouse he would have a number of small houses, usually between six and ten, which every year on the first of May he would rent out on terms calling for weekly payment. The family which rented such a house paid a reasonable price and knew, moreover, that when the farmer needed workers for his flax they would be considered first.

For his part, the farmer provided as much work as he could, counting at all times on the full co-operation and effort of all members of his tenants' families aged twelve years or older. He was not obliged, however, to offer work. Such rental agreements enabled the farmer to secure a labour pool of some forty workers from which he could draw at will during the year.

Several weeks after sowing, the first flax shoots appeared. Soon the crop was tall enough to enable flax to be distinguished from weeds. Then the first major task began, weeding, which lasted for six weeks, from April until June. All his adult tenants who were physically able left then for the flax fields. The farmer saw to their transportation. It is not completely clear how the workers arranged the closing of their homes during this weeding period. The smallest children and infants would be sent to stay elsewhere. The household, including children under twelve who came along not to work but because the family's house was temporarily deserted, was then shifted to the fields themselves. It is also possible that such dislocation occurred only during the far shorter harvest time.[41]

A farmer who rented flax land had to provide some kind of shack to shelter his workers where they would live communally for the duration of the work.

The weeding itself consisted of pulling weeds from the earth by hand. The flax plants had to be left as undisturbed as possible. At times the weeders of both sexes would pull socks on over their wooden or other shoes so that any plant injured inadvertently would have a chance to recover quickly.[42]

Once the weeding was done, the families would go back to their houses for some weeks, returning to the fields again in July to harvest the flax. It seems that for the harvest, which lasted two weeks, the house was indeed shut down and the entire family went along. Flax plants were pulled root and all from the earth and placed next to each other in sheaves — *hokken*, (shocks). Once gathered in, the flax was conveyed to the farmer's residence. The workers returned home to begin with rippling and retting the flax: to clear away the seeds with a toothed implement and to soften the flax by soaking it or exposing it to moisture. This continued from the end of July until late September. From mid-October until early April the workers were busy in the swingle-sheds beating the flax and removing the woody parts — a task notorious for the clouds of dust sent swirling into the air.

The variety of tasks involved in raising and processing a crop of flax meant that workers found employment for much, even most of the year. When the flax farmer did not need them, they would hire themselves out elsewhere as fieldhands or even, during the summer, seek work in local brick factories.

The digging of potatoes in the autumn took place in ways similar to worker arrangements for flax cultivation. Owners leased their potato fields to specialised farmers who bore full responsibility for weeding and harvesting. On the South-Holland Islands the harvesting was frequently work for migrant workers. The digging season lasted from August to November, but we do not know more in detail about how the work would have been organised c. 1811.[43]

The Stripping of Oak Trees

The only form of forestry that calls for description in these pages is the stripping of bark from oak trees, not because large numbers were engaged in such work, but rather because it was performed almost exclusively by migrant workers.[44] These migrant workers came from several richly wooded areas in the province of Gelderland. Except for workers from Groesbeek, about whom we know little, most of them came from the northern fringe of the Veluwe, from Nunspeet and vicinity.

Early in May oak-strippers set out for Drenthe, North-Overijssel or South-Friesland, where they had been summoned by the owners of *akkermaalshout* (copses of oak about 8 years old). They crossed the Zuiderzee by ship or went overland with barrows or hooded carts together with their entire families.

A description remains of what the journey was like in May 1840:

> Many carts and wagons covered the road and to be sure it looked like a painting. Men, women and children set out for Elburg with their goods and chattels, with cabinets and chests, with goats, dogs and sheep, in short with everything they

owned. For an outsider such a procession is an imposing spectacle and whoever follows the retinue sees how it comes to a halt at Elburg harbour — everything is unloaded, furniture and household supplies — how each family bivouacs there on the quay and, encircled by their cabinets and coffers, makes itself, as it were, at home: how the mothers nurse their infants openly as if shielded from the eyes of every observer, how every household gathers around a trunk to eat a cold meal.[45]

Upon arrival in the woods, migrants erected a provisional hut or made their homes in the covered vehicles which they brought with them. Their task was not only to cut down the oak trees, but to strip them of bark and to trim them to a size suitable for bundles of firewood for bakers' ovens and other such uses.

Most important of all was the removal of the bark, the so-called *eekschillen* (stripping process). From the loose bark ground in special mills tanning bark was produced, a substance required for turning hides into leather.

The strippers worked standing in square pits which they themselves dug. This saved bending, and enabled them to sit down now and then. With a special small axe which had a dull as well as a sharp edge, they pounded the bark free. The whole family was busy from dawn to dusk. People took care of their own needs entirely, in part by bringing along a milking goat. At the end of the season they were paid according to how much bark they had stripped and how many bundles of firewood they had produced.

On their return journey to the Veluwe, a number of men subsequently went first to mow grass, and then grain, in North-Holland.

Excavation, Dredging and Cutting Peat

These jobs, strictly speaking, do not belong to one single economic sector. Dredging and cutting peat is usually considered to be part of the primary sector. On the other hand, excavation connected to building roads, railways, dikes or canals, is considered a construction activity, thus industrial and part of the secondary sector or even — as government enterprises — the tertiary sector. Considering the nature of the work involved, however, for the purposes of this study we prefer to lump these forms of employment together for discussion. Given the geography of the North

Sea coast, various kinds of excavation and of winning peat provided wòrk for many navvies and peat-cutters, those thanks to whom — in De Zeeuw's words — 'the Republic assumed the mantle of leadership on the path of mankind's economic and social development'.[46]

Even without subscribing to such a monocausal explanation for the economic development of the provinces along the North Sea coast, I find it surprising that so few studies of land reclamation, dredging and related economic activities have appeared. Practically nothing at all is known about the significance of such work for the labour market. More has been written about peat-cutting, especially for the period following the middle of the last century, but for the preceding period the scholarly light that has been shed to date is dim. In sketching how these various kinds of labour were performed I can thus resort only to limited secondary sources and to material in archives. We should not lose sight of the fact, moreover, that specifically during the French occupation of the Netherlands, as the result of the vast expenses of waging war, practically all public works related to drainage had been stopped or were delayed in their implementation. The extent and significance of the jobs we are interested in will not have been consistent throughout this period with earlier and later periods. In the Questionnaire of 1811, indeed, there are only two marshland reclamation projects cited and not a single instance of impoldering. Navvying or ground-work is thus clearly under-represented. Certain kinds of enterprises on the other hand are over-represented in relation to the category as a whole, i.e. activities related to building and maintaining war harbours.

In the Questionnaire we come across some 500 migrant workers engaged in reclamation of marshes in Nieuwveen and Zevenhoven, additional dike-hands in Zeeland, not quite 500 labourers employed to dredge and improve such harbours as Vlissingen, Antwerp, Ostende and Gent, 2,000 plus migrants who worked to dig the Grand Canal du Nord and, finally, some scattered references to workers who paved roads. The total number active in these various related occupations, extracted from analysis of answers to the Questionnaire, amounted to something less that 4,000.[47]

Excavation or Ground-work

In speaking of excavation or ground-work I wish to designate all kinds of labour which involve the moving of earth, unless this happens as part of agriculture or mining. In the area we are considering, ground-work activities usually meant jobs connected to the maintenance and repair of dikes, canals, roads, harbours and fortifications, as well as to the creation of farmland in new polders. Workers who for the most part moved easily from one such job to another, also frequently found construction work of other kinds as well (see under heading 'Industrial Jobs' below). Usually, in addition to workers who shifted earth (the real navvies or *Polderjongens* (polder boys) — as they are called in Dutch), carpenters were needed, and even more in demand were good masons and stone-cutters. Masons and stone-cutters were called on to prepare kinds of artefacts which were practically always required in connection with ground-work, e.g. quay-walls, the brickwork of fortifications, canal locks and related buildings such as the lockkeeper's house. We can, however, distinguish specific ground-work employment with some justification, for separate teams of workers with their own schemes of organisation were clearly hired for carpentry and masonry chores. In the literature, none the less, these construction workers are frequently also designated as polder boys.

Thus, although migrant workers engaged in various kinds of work which involved shifting earth, the labour which they performed and its organisation manifested certain consistent traits.[48] In almost every instance the government or a corporation, such as a polder-board, was instrumental in organising the work. With drainage or impoldering, at times a consortium of private individuals might also run operations with government permission. These differences did not matter much to the workers, however, in any event. They were usually hired on a project basis with control executed by those commissioning the work. The work was invariably delegated in comparatively small segments to contractors who had to accomplish, preferably in a single season, whatever was specified in the plans which they agreed to execute. This simplified control, and reduced the risk involved for those commissioning the work. Indeed, the following season the contractor might once again reach an agreement to carry out a new part of the project. In a number of instances, with the approval of those originating a project, contractors worked with sub-contractors. Sub-contractors and contractors were responsible for acquiring workers and for their performance. Those commissioning the work had nothing to say in these matters, but committed themselves usually to guaranteeing certain kinds of support, such as transportation, or worker control in the form of soldiers.

It is not altogether clear how contractors and sub-contractors managed to secure their necessary labour force. It seems to me that in principle two methods were open to them: they could hire workers from their own neighbourhood, or they could recruit them in places which were known for having a supply of the kind of worker in demand. A variant of the latter approach involved workers who used their own initiative in reporting to the site of major projects in search of a contractor. Hiring locally was perhaps preferable for securing such specialised workers as masons, *rÿswerkers* (fascine-workers) and dredgers. Hiring elsewhere would probably be more suitable for securing workers who could manage a shovel and wheelbarrow properly but from whom not much more skill would be demanded. We encounter contractors recruiting labourers in their own home area especially in the region of the Merwede River, men with experience in fascine-making and dredging. There, on one and the same dike, lived contractors and workers, the so-called *rietbroeken* (reed trousers).[49]

Workers for ordinary digging and hauling came largely from places and regions known for this manpower, such as the banks of the great rivers, West-Brabant, the east of Zeeland-Flanders, and also from Flemish regions further south and areas of Brabant to the southeast.[50]

Fellow villagers usually worked together, offering themselves as a team to a contractor. For this purpose they chose a leader from among themselves, the *putbaas* (the pit-boss, or foreman of a gang of navvies), who would approach possible employers. Alternatively a contractor might select a number of sub-contractors who in turn had to assemble a workforce. Each of these sub-contractors would then also be called putbaas, but in reality they had a different relation with the workers. Their incomes depended indeed on what they could earn by exploiting their workers. The difference between these two kinds of foremen and the two kinds of work teams is an essential one. A sub-contractor's team usually consisted of workers who hardly knew each other, if they knew each other at all. In the literature there is an inclination to describe this kind of loose collection of workers especially, thereby stigmatising all polder boys as a wild bunch of drifters.[51] Such a portrait, as will be made clear below, is inaccurate.

In spring the polder boys set out for the place where they had arranged to work, or where they hoped to be hired. Their baggage consisted of a sack with bedding, some clothes, a piece of bacon or ham, eating utensils and their own tools, a shovel and a *puthaak* (pit-hook). The pit-hook was a stick with a piece of bent metal at the end which was used to shift the planks over which the workers' wheelbarrows had to pass.

At the work site the teams were supposed to find building materials for a temporary shelter, provided by the contractor. Each group, under the leadership of its foreman, set up its own tent or shed. A framework in the form of a tent was erected out of beams. This was covered with reeds and then the side walls were built up out of sods of turf. An opening was left in front and a stoke-hole in the middle. The back part of the interior was partitioned off; here two bunks were made of wood, each able to hold some seven men sleeping next to each other. The front part of the shelter served as a general living space where kitchen goods and food were kept, and where the foreman, assisted by a woman, had his lodgings. The woman might be his wife, or the sister or daughter of one of the others living in the shed. For a price this *keet-vrouw* (shed-woman) brewed coffee, cooked warm meals, cleaned the house and patched the residents' clothing. If the woman had children with her, these too lived in the front room. The toilet consisted of the *papegaai* (parrot), a 'horizontal pole resting on two wooden forks pounded into the ground and covered over with bunches of willow wands or reeds leaning at an angle against each other'; the toilet was set up next to a ditch.[52]

For the duration of the job members of the team thus not only worked together, but also lived as a unit. A number of unwritten rules existed designed to keep disturbances — in the work and living situation — to a minimum. People drew lots for their places in the sleeping berths and at the table. Fines were imposed for a whole battery of transgressions. Even neglect of a weekly bath and change of bedding could incur a penalty.

Ordinarily work was so arranged that a team occupied a designated plot of ground for a season. Here they might be expected to dig a stretch of canal, or dredge it, or erect a section of dike. Usually, a certain set amount of work had to be done each day. The foreman saw to it that each worker in turn dug enough earth to fill a wheelbarrow and then carted it away to a certain point where a fellow worker took over from him and wheeled the load on to the 'dumping place'. Rotation of tasks was necessary because not each part of the operation required an equal effort. In this way a team could accomplish as much as possible collectively. Most contractors hired a number of teams and tried to spur them on competitively. Bonuses were offered for the team which reached the top of the dike first, or first completed some other task. The best groups were better paid for their accomplishments to provide an incentive for other workers to try harder. On the other hand, contractors did not hesitate to hire teams at rates under the going wage. Such practices help to explain why friction was common at the work site.

Tutein Nolthenius has described the lives of the workers who dug the Merwede Canal around 1890. He reports the following daily routine: workers rose and ate their breakfast at 3 or 3.30 a.m.. The 'shed woman' had their coffee waiting. Everyone made his own sandwich — and a sandwich for the first break. Work went on uninterrupted from 5 until 8 a.m., when there was a half-hour rest. Again workers ate sandwiches and drank coffee brought from their shed. Work started and ended with a signal, the hoisting of a *lawei* (flag or basket), or the ringing of a bell. Work continued from 8.30 to noon. Then followed the communal midday meal, in the shelter itself if possible: mashed potatoes and cabbage with cubes of fat, possibly supplemented by an egg or bacon pie which the workers baked themselves. The workers then took a nap until 1.30 p.m., after which they worked until 4 p.m. During the work-break from 4 to 4.30 p.m. a snack of bread with coffee was taken, and finally at 7 p.m. the workday was over.

Back at the shed, the workers washed themselves, ate bread with hot cereal and peeled potatoes for the next day. Then they went to sleep. On Sunday, a day of rest, the men would perhaps call at the sutlers' shanties, which also stood on the work site. In these shanties, adorned with the fanciest of names, drink was served. It was freuqently said that foremen who hired a team them-selves also tapped beer in their own sheds to divert as large a stream as possible of the workers' money into their own pockets.

The ground-work sketched here grew more arduous as the weather turned inclement. Not only was wet earth much heavier to dig and convey than dry, but walking on muddy, slippery planks as workers pushed their wheelbarrows was hazardous. The polder boys' boots were therefore studded with nails. Although various extant calculations display anything but unanimity, we can suppose nevertheless that a good worker could dig up one to one and a-half cubic metres of earth in an hour.[53] The quantity of ground that any team could remove also depended on the distance over which the material had to be trundled off in wheelbarrows. Doing such work, men could earn Dfl. 1.50 a day; after deduction of costs, about Dfl. 1.00 remained.

From among other categories of ground-work, fascine-work and dredging deserve mention here. Fascine-workers braided large mats out of twigs, and small boats towed these to the place where a sea-dike was to be constructed. Once the mats lay in their proper place, floating, workers heaped stones on them to make them sink, thereby providing the future dike with a firm foundation. Dredgers worked, certainly until the second half of the nineteenth century, with a mud scoop. This was a stick some metres long with an iron ring and net fastened to the far end. With this tool the workers scooped up mud into the boat in which they stood.

Most of the tasks which ground-workers performed were dependent on the season. Dike construction and other work along the seashore could only begin in earnest in April; any earlier and the risk was too great that swollen spring tides would destroy whatever had been accomplished. All preparations, such as securing material supplies and enough workmen, should have been completed on time. By the end of June contractors were responsible for achieving the results which they undertook to deliver. Afterwards the chance of flooding either from storm surges or rainy periods with prevailing west winds increased sharply. Work on river dikes began later because the high water levels of the spring had first to subside.

With impoldering, in theory workers had more time, but to avoid problems from too much water they usually did not continue to work beyond the summer. The laying and periodic cleaning of canals, or *slatten* (dredging) as it was called, seems to have been least subject to the vicissitudes of the weather; only when the temperature dropped below freezing did frost slow, or put an end to such work. Indeed, there are numerous reports that when navvies were unable to do the work that was peculiarly their own, they took other jobs. Polder boys from the Merwede region worked during the winter in the willow coppices of the Biesbos, those from Brabant or Flanders usually had small farms of their own. Combinations of ground-work and fishing for herring and seafaring were also known.[54]

It is above all the dependency of ground-work on suitable seasonal conditions which requires us to look askance at descriptions of polder boys as rampaging nomads. To be sure, it seems improbable that year in year out for months at a time thousands of workers reeled about vast work sites in a state of drunkeness. Accounts concerning wild migrants are concentrated primarily in places where the polder boys failed to go home for the winter but stayed on in their team sheds. Here, it might just happen that a foreman, living with his 'shed-woman' (marriage 'over the broomstick' or *puthaak* as it was actually called), exploited his workers by selling them alcoholic beverages, thus driving them deeper into debt. For large projects which were not finished in a single year, the workers' quarters did indeed remain standing throughout the winter. But who lived there then? In the winter of 1829-30 in Moordrecht there stood 34 sheds for migrant workers employed on the impoldering of the Zuidplas. During the census held at this time, the residents of these sheds were included.[55] A hundred and fifty were enumerated, thus an average of slightly more than four to a shed, far fewer than the full working strength of an in-season ground-work team. These 34 sheds, on the Kerklaan and the Sluis in Moordrecht, were at the time occupied almost exclusively by families with children or childless married couples. Only in three instances could one speak of a marriage 'over the broomstick', and in only one shed were there polder boys living who were not related to each other and came from different areas. The make-up of the families does not appear to have deviated from that of the rest of the population. From the children's birthplaces it is indeed possible in a number of instances to tell that the parents simply moved from one major project to another, including, with clear representation, the Groot-Noordhollands Kanaal and the Zuid-Willemsvaart. If the picture emerging from the winter census 1829-30 in Moordrecht may be seen as typical for the inhabitants of project work-sheds throughout the slow winter season, we can attribute a nomadic existence at most to a number of foremen and their families, an extremely small minority of all polder boys. What is more, this group, for the most part, decorously observed the generally accepted conventions of marriage.

The scale of the projects concerned, the vast number of workers and the 'divide and rule' politics of contractors, all meant that a considerable distance separated the polder boys from their employers. This was especially true for ground-workers who chose their own foreman. Among the *rietbroeken*, 'reed trousers', the relationship between workers and their bosses was a different matter; these bosses usually came from the same places of origin as the workers, and only contracted, certainly up until the beginning of the nineteenth century, to carry out rather modest projects. As for workers who were in the team of a foreman who was in fact himself a sub-contractor, although the physical distance between employer and employee was small indeed, there probably was little familiarity or trust between them.

On the other hand, because workers came from diverse places of origin, they did not cohere into a united front. It was thus the nature of the work they did and how it was organised that determined to a large extent the power — or lack of power — which workers could exercise on the labour market. This became manifest above all in the countless strikes which through the years characterised ground-work in the regions in which we are interested. If we consider all strikes in the Netherlands from *c.* 1700 to 1870, it is possible to establish that the majority of them probably could be attributed to ground-workers.[56] In time the 'divide and rule' strategy of employers and, consequently, the competitive struggle among teams of polder boys, especially after the Belgian secession, acquired a national dimension. Fights between Dutch and Belgian workers were subsequently reported with great frequency.[57] The Department for the Maintenance of Dikes, Roads, Bridges and the Navigability of Canals even administered a questionnaire in 1843 among all provincial governors to see whether it would not be possible to use only Dutch workers on public projects.[58] The poor relations between bosses and their workers also had consequences for how the polder boys got along with people who lived in the vicinity of work sites. In general, the polder boys were feared, especially for their thievery of wood and small livestock. In most cases where local residents voiced complaints, however, contractors proved to have been remiss in the paying of wages, or provision of fuel. Troubles, moreover, occurred primarily in the winter when work was at a standstill.

Cutting Peat

Approximately 9,000 migrant labourers worked in the peat bogs. In the area under study there were two kinds of peat-yielding territories: *hoogvenen* (high peat bogs) in Ostfriesland, Groningen,

Drenthe and part of Friesland; and *laagvenen* (low peat bogs) in other parts of Friesland, a small area of Groningen, the Kop van Overijssel, Utrecht and Holland. The distinction between the two kinds depends upon their situation in relation to the water table and therefore upon the growing conditions of the peat. High peat bogs, which lie above the water table, can be drained by excavating canals. The exposed peat can then usually be cut in sods with a shovel. In such bogs an estimated 3,000 migrants found employment in 1811. Low peat bogs could not be drained by digging narrow waterways so their peat had for the most part, to be scooped out in muddy clumps. Under such conditions in 1811 approximately 6,000 migrants were digging peat, most of them in the low peat bogs of Holland-Utrecht.[59]

Until the opening of the coalmines in Limburg on a large scale around 1900, peat was the only mineral extracted from the earth in the Netherlands. Its significance lay on the one hand in its use as a household fuel (especially low peat turf, which gave more heat per unit weight when burned), and on the other hand — and this use was far more important economically — in its application as industrial fuel (above all high peat turf from the bogs in the northeast). As major industrial consumers we should keep in mind distilleries and refineries, soap and salt-winning factories, breweries, bleach-works and brick-ovens. De Zeeuw, who studied the economic significance of peat, considered its exploitation to be an important condition for the flourishing of the Republic in the 'Golden Age'.[60] Up to the present we do not know much about the significance of this sector, so vital for the labour market.[61]

Because of the nature of a bog — and its creation underwater — such marshland areas, especially high peat bogs, were barely accessible at best. Before their exploitation, low peat bogs might be used as grazing-land, but high peat bogs were in general uninhabited morasses. It is obvious therefore that for digging high peat on a large scale, migrant workers or immigrants would invariably be called upon to do the job. In point of fact, this development took place in stages. First some seasonal migrant workers came, followed gradually by immigrants. As the removal of the peat progressed, more and more immigrants followed. After the bog was denuded of peat, the workers started small farms on the sub-soil, which was usually not very fertile.

Such a chronological sequence emerges unambiguously from the observation made for Drenthe in 1840 that most German migrant workers at the time could be found in Oostermoer, fewer in the Smilde bogs and the fewest of all in Hoogeveen. Here we are concerned with the areas where peat cutting took place, respectively, in the nineteenth, eighteenth and seventeenth centuries.[62]

Standard procedures were observed in extracting peat from the high bogs.[63] First of all a set of drainage ditches had to be dug to bring down the water level. It took years to allow the bog to settle gradually. Next, canals were excavated for the transport of the cut peat and migrant (German) workers were pre-eminently those who dug the canals. Several sources suggest that at times they toiled in large crews, as many as 80 or 90 together.[64] But for such *wijkgraven* (canal digging) smaller groups of 5 to 10 men are also cited, as well as for the ensuing task, the commencement of cutting the peat itself. We can assume that on the average a sod of high peat measured 40 × 15 × 15 cm on removal. A worker who was part of a team could cut about 2,000 such sods a day.[65] The first cutting operations on a piece of bog — workplots were defined by the principal canal and two side canals — was particularly difficult because the only place possible for spreading the peat out to dry was at the summit of the marshland. The cut peat had thus to be conveyed to higher ground by wheelbarrow. Because a single bed of peat can be several metres thick, this meant strenuous work; many men were needed for *op het hoog brengen* (mining on top). They worked in teams of two diggers and some eight additional helpers, who saw to it that the peat reached some place where it could dry out. These teams consisted entirely of German migrant workers. Once enough peat had been cut from the bog along the main waterway, as sods were removed they no longer had to be carted to higher ground. The diggers themselves could place the peat on the soil behind them. This meant that the dug peat could be brought *in het laag* (mining at the bottom). This procedure went far more quickly than mining on top, and smaller teams could be used. An example of these smaller crews is provided by the five-man-strong units common among workers from Neuenkirchen in the Oldenburg area (who accomplished the *Nieuwkerker werk* that was named for them). Teams of only two workers were also a frequent phenomenon (they did the *grootwerk* or *waldijkerwerk*). The piece-wages of the teams or pairs who mined at the bottom were far lower than those who struggled on top. Work at the bottom was also performed by local labour. Cutting peat and also, originally, excavation of the necessary canals, was limited to three months in the year, roughly March to June, before which time it was too wet to work in the bog. Peat, moreover, cannot tolerate night frost since it pulverises if exposed to below-freezing temperatures and is no longer serviceable as fuel.

Since peat requires a long drying time, cutting must cease early in the summer. The peat that has been cut wet must be dry as a bone before winter comes. Sods must be put out to dry in piles that allow the wind to blow through them, and must be turned regularly. The many tasks related to processing the peat into turf were carried out by the local population, the new immigrants. Even loading the peat-barges, mostly work for women and children, was not something which migrant workers did.

Organisation of the mining of low peat was a different matter.[66] Low peat was dredged up from under the water with a scoop. Usually a dredger did the work, emptying the net of his scoop into the small boat where he himself stood. Or he might balance on a plank linking the boat to dry land. Part of the marshy polder that was not yet dredged was earmarked for spreading the retrieved mire out to dry. This was known as the *legakker* — the drying field. It was the dredger's team-mate who spread out the low peat and trampled on it in wooden shoes with boards fastened to their bottom. These workers thus functioned as a pair. Only once the muddy peat had dried sufficiently could it be cut into neat sods, after which a further drying period of some months followed. Mining low peat was thus bound to roughly the same seasonal rhythm as the mining of high peat. Although there are reports that migrant workers digging low peat worked in teams of 5 to 8 men,[67] from which we might conclude that they either worked in a few pairs or else also carried out drying operations, the impression prevails, none the less, that foreign migrant labourers confined themselves to dredging, to spreading and to trampling the peat, and that throughout the rest of the year local workers accounted for the remaining tasks.

After employment in the bogs during the spring, some migrant workers went elsewhere in the 'pull area'. They took part in haymaking, or other harvest work for the most part. Others, however, went straight back home. Their earnings from the heavy labour of cutting peat which kept them busy, including work breaks, for sixteen hours a day, were not inconsequential.[68] For diggers of high peat, a special cubic measure called a 'daywork' was used to determine earnings: one full 'daywork' was worth Dfl. 1.00. It was possible, however, to fill more than a single 'daywork' in a day so that wages can have amounted to something between Dfl. 1.50 and Dfl. 2.00 a day.[69] Cutters earned somewhat more than others in the team. The pairs who mined low peat, where a different cubic measure was used, earned as much as the cutters of high peat.[70]

Little is known about the organisation of cutting low peat in the bogs of Holland-Utrecht. Pairs of labourers lived in sheds where some twenty workers were housed. The sheds stood on edges of the bog which were not yet being exploited, usually in remote areas. We can suppose that such sheds became communities with their own way of life.[71]

The social organisation of workers who dug high peat was, in many respects, reminiscent of the polder boys.[72] These peat miners also had specific regulations to determine each man's place both in bed and at the dining table. Even the baking of pancakes was governed by rules. Whoever violated the rules could expect such punishments as *britsen* (flogging): in the presence of his fellow workers the wrong-doer would receive a beating at the hands of an especially appointed 'master'. You could, however, buy yourself free from punishment by handing over drinking money for the others.

The crews that dug ditches had a number of other customs, including an initiation ritual for newcomers, but also for their supervisor, the *veenbaas* (bog overseer).[73] With a measuring stick held in the air to which his handkerchief was fastened as a flag, the overseer had to listen to various speeches and songs from the workmen. These not only reminded him of his duties, but stressed the social difference between labourers and their masters. The ceremony ended with the overseer treating the workers to gin. The even invites comparison to the *Binden-und-Lösen-rite* among madder diggers described above.[74]

The end of the digging season for German Catholic peat-cutters in De Peel was described in verse during the last quarter of the nineteenth century:

The day of departure has now arrived.
Happily they go to the field together.
A huge sod of peat is cut out
Adorned with a wreath and put on display.
A song of thanksgiving is raised to begin with,
Then they fall on their knees in prayer,

Next they spring around the sod three times
Singing and praying each time around.
Then the oldest man steps forward,
He looks at the peat and kneels before it,
There is no more singing, nor prayer,
Suddenly he cleaves the sod through the middle.[75]

Various groups of peat-cutters talked among themselves about wage rates and labour conditions at the beginning and end of the job[76] and yet, just as was true for the polder boys, employers tried to play them off against each other, especially in places where one overseer had a number of teams at work.

Large companies, however, did not dominate the scene — there were many small employers who had only one, or a few teams in their service.[77] These smaller employers kept an eye themselves on how work was progressing, usually without any bog overseer as intermediary.

Small entrepreneurs did, however, try to adhere to a single policy among themselves, as the result of which the teams of cutters, even if employed by different men, also acted in league with each other. The isolated existence which workers led in their remote sheds also probably reinforced their solidarity in dealings with outsiders. Especially at the outset of the peat-cutting season when — with an eye on the market situation — the piecework rate was set, strikes might now and then break out in an attempt by the diggers to extract better remuneration for the whole season.[78]

Industrial Jobs

Around 1811 migrant workers also held positions in certain branches of industry where work was seasonal: in construction, brick-ovens, bleaching plants, and, on an incidental basis, in other kinds of enterprises, especially the textile industry.[79]

There were, moreover, several industries where many foreigners found jobs, although it is not clear whether temporary migrants were hired or if immigrants exercised more or less a monopoly on opportunities. The sugar refineries and cotton-printing plants in Amsterdam are examples of such places.[80]

Considering their importance to migrant labour, we shall consider separately the three industries mentioned initially above: construction, brick-making and bleaching.

Masons, Carpenters and Stone-cutters

According to Knotter, two labour markets in the construction industry should be distinguished: one oriented to maintenance, the second to new projects.[81] It was only as recently as the second half of the nineteenth century that the latter gained ascendancy over the former, at least in Amsterdam. In other parts of the Netherlands this shift may have taken place even later. Migrant workers had no hand in maintenance work; in new construction, however, they occupied a dominant position. In particular, the masons, stone-cutters and stucco workers involved in the construction of new buildings came on a seasonal basis from elsewhere.

In the Questionnaire of 1811 we meet with the following groups of migrant workers in various locations.[82] In the harbour of Antwerp, carpenters were employed on public works. Some two hundred masons travelled to sites in Holland and Groningen. We can also trace almost two hundred carpenters who worked primarily in Groningen and Ostfriesland. For both of these last groups, it is not clear whether they, like the first group, were employed for the most part to help with new cosntruction. In particular, the carpenters at work in the countryside of Groningen might just as plausibly have been busy with restoration.[83] Stucco-workers from Hainaut crop up in the records of French and Belgian départements; remarkably, in 1811 plasterers from Oldenburg, so well known later in the nineteenth century, were not yet mentioned anywhere in Holland or Friesland-Groningen.[84] *Heiers*, travelling workmen who drove piles into the ground, received not a single mention in the entire Questionnaire.[85]

Of the estimated total of more than 1,350 migrant construction workers, the majority held jobs as masons, stone-cutters and pavers on public-works projects. The vocation of mason statistically catches the eye of anyone examining the records. The masons' home areas coincided in part with those of the brick-makers discussed below (Lippe, Bentheim, Liège and Hainaut), and as far as Liège and Hainaut were concerned, were the areas from which ground-workers also came. The same can be said for the masons who were especially well known in Holland: they originated from the vicinity of Den Bosch, an area were polder boys were also recruited. For all areas with the exception of Central Limburg — from which, as far as I have been able to discover, only a small group of construction workers originated — it is true that they supplied not only migrant workers for construction jobs, but for other employment as well. We might suppose that the same workers carried out diverse kinds of work. The idea, however, is not a particularly convincing one, for the different jobs each demanded too much experience for combinations to seem readily feasible. Masons were not so much specialised in putting up simple walls as in the construction of masonry that could be metres thick, such as was required in the building of quay walls and fortifications and certain kinds of foundations — work which in this century is executed primarily in concrete. Masons worked in teams which were paid collectively per 1,000 bricks laid. This explains why masons from North-Brabant who worked on public works were given the nickname *duizendpoters* (millepedes).[86]

Stone-cutters came from areas where well-known quarries were situated, such as Bentheim with its sandstone, and the Brabant-Hainaut area where the blue 'Namur' freestone was quarried. Stones were transported rough-hewn from the quarry to the construction site and there trimmed to size. This was also work which required no little experience to do well. Considering that this type of stone was used not only for the occasional 'grand' house, but also and especially for quay walls, fortifications and public buildings, stone-cutters, like masons, will have worked in teams.[87]

Before cement replaced trass (mortar made from volcanic earth) and lime definitively in the last quarter of the nineteenth century, masons were largely dependent on favourable weather conditions to be able to work. Trass and lime dried far more slowly than cement and could not therefore be used if even the slightest frost was anticipated. In those days, therefore, construction work had to be interrupted for months at a time. During the winter construction workers had to seek other kinds of labour.[88]

Brick-makers

Brick manufacturers on the Oude Rijn complained in 1812 that there was little new construction and that houses which were being built were being made from second-hand bricks.[89] Despite this protest, however, many brick-ovens were then in operation along the North Sea coast. Around 1800 bricks were the most important building material in the area. These were made, reviewing leading centres of production from north to south, on the banks of the Weser, in Ostfriesland, in Reiderland and Groningen, down the west coast of Friesland, in South-Holland in the area of the Oude

Rijn and the Hollandse IJssel, and finally on both sides of the Schelde in Brabant and Flanders.[90] Bricks were also baked on site where major projects were executed, such as the Grand Canal du Nord. After such public works were completed, however the brick-ovens and their clay quarries would be abandoned.[91] Of the brick-ovens enumerated in the above-mentioned areas, those along the Weser, in Ostfriesland, in Reiderland and in Groningen were manned almost exclusively by migrant workers; while those in the region of the Oude Rijn employed non-locals as part of their workforce, and those to the west of the Schelde in the area surrounding Rupelmonde probably hired migrant workers as well. Elsewhere brick-ovens in all likelihood made hardly any use of non-local labour. Brick-making from the Weser to Groningen was a monopoly in the hands of more than 800 Lippe workers; on the banks of the Oude Rijn some fifty brick-makers probably came to work from south of Bentheim and in the vicinity of Rupelmonde an estimated 750, primarily from Hainaut but also from Nord, found employment in brick ovens. All in all, more than 1,800 brick-makers left perennial 'push areas' for 'pull areas' that exercised continuous attraction.[92] We have scant knowledge at best about brick-makers employed in the south, along the Schelde, and in the central coast area along the Oude Rijn. The same holds true for brick-makers coming originally from Liège.[93] Nevertheless, we are well-informed abut those employed in brick-making who came from Lippe; the description below is based on facts concerning this group.[94]

The work of the brick-makers consisted of a number of complementary tasks which meant that workers had to be able to cooperate effectively and rely on each other. Usually local workers had already dug the clay needed for the bricks during the preceding winter, so that the brick-making teams arriving at the ovens in the spring could start to work immediately.

First the clay had to be kneaded, to purify it and make it more elastic. In Groningen and Ostfriesland this was done with a *tonmolen* for roof tiles, and for bricks with a larger *treedeel*. The tonmolen consisted of a barrel (*ton*) in which a vertical axle fitted with knives was set in motion by horse power. The *treedeel* (tread-pit) was a pit, filled with clay, in the middle of which a horizontal beam on top of a pole was erected. A horse either moved paddles connected to this beam or else also circled round itself in the mixing area walking on the clay. The man leading the horse was the *treder* (tread-man), *muller* or *Möller* (miller). From the clay, once it was mixed to the right consistency, the *Aufstecher* (or *Walker* for roof tiles) formed a ball large enough to make one brick, roof- or floor-tile. He passed this mass along to the form-giver. This worker stood inside at a table on top of which he used a wooden mould or framework to work the clay into the right shape. The form-giver then passed the moulded clay on to the *Abträger* (dispatcher), who stacked it away in the drying shed. In this area thus both shaping and drying took place under protection of a roof. Inside the long drying sheds, which could be ventilated through their side walls, the unbaked bricks were first placed flat on the ground, then turned onto their sides, and thereafter stacked. Stacking at times took place in a separate shack. Other products, roof tiles, for example, were not stacked on the ground, but laid on wooden racks to dry. The whole shaping team took part in all activities inside the drying sheds.

Once the unbaked bricks were dry enough, they could then be fired in the oven. The oven in this region was a space surrounded by thick masonry, covered with a dome pierced by a number of smoke holes. In front there was an opening for depositing the bricks to be baked and for removing the finished products. Each side wall of the oven also had three stoke-vents facing each other. The bricks, usually some 100,000 per load per oven, were piled lengthwise in the direction of the facing stoke-vents; between the tiers of brick came the fuel, turf, which could later be replenished at will through the stoke-vents. Once the front of the oven was sealed with clay, the firing began, slowly at first, with little turf. A few days to a week later, the actual firing got under way. Because turf had now to be added constantly, workers had to stand watch by night, too. The entire baking process, under the supervision of the firing master, took three to four weeks; filling the oven and emptying it cost additional time. An oven full of bricks could be fired a maximum of five times a year. If the season began on April first, 100,000 clay bricks could be ready for drying within two weeks. By the middle of May they would be dry enough to go into the oven. By mid-June the first load would have been fired and could be taken out to make room for the second load. If the fifth and final load were placed in the oven towards the end of September, then by the end of October these would be fully baked and in November the team could head for home. From November until March the weather was so unpredictable that hardly any brick-making was possible: too much rain meant that the clay bricks would not dry out sufficiently to be ready for the ovens; and frost could ruin not only the clay, but also the turf used for fuel.

The separate, far smaller tile-ovens required less time for firing. They could produce ten or more loads each season. Tile-makers, who worked in smaller teams than brick-makers, had for that reason to work much more often throughout the night, and yet did not produce as much as the brick-makers: the moulding of the tiles was far more demanding, so that in an average season 300,000 tiles could be made, as compared to 500,000 bricks. Tiles were much more expensive, however, so that the wages of tile-makers and brick-makers were roughly alike. Brick-makers and tile-makers earned about Dfl. 60 a season after room and board and other costs were deducted. Gross wages reached levels between Dfl. 100 and Dfl. 160.[95]

It seems that the Groningen-Ostfriesland area was characterised by small, capital-intensive brick-ovens manned by small teams of migrant workers. Production here was capital intensive because of necessary investments in drying yards, mills and horses to churn clay, and permanent ovens. Brick-yards throughout the remainder of the Netherlands and Belgium, however, while often being larger, were also more labour intensive. Entire families frequently worked in these brick factories, where the labour of women and children assumed a place of importance.

At this period in Groningen and Ostfriesland some ten workers might be employed typically at a brick and tile works, six or seven of them in the brick-making team, the other three or four turning out tiles. They lived in what was called the *tichelkamer* (brick-room), a room near the oven with cupboard-bedsteads in the side walls where workers slept in pairs. In the centre of the room was a table where collective meals were taken three times a day. Members of the work teams prepared these meals themselves, and kept house together. To be sure, brick-makers, like peat-cutters, took pork, groats, flour and other basic foodstuffs with them when they set out from Lippe. Still, they probably purchased most of their food locally, in a number of instances through the owner of the brick-works the *tichelheer* (brick master). In the brick-room, each worker had a cupboard of his own where he could put away his personal belongings. The brick master was responsible for seeing to it that the living quarters and beds were cleaned periodically.

An official messenger maintained contact between the brick-makers from Lippe and their families back home.[96] Since as long ago as the seventeenth century, by virtue of a concession granted by the Count of Lippe, this messenger had exercised a monopoly over the recruitment of brick-makers in Lippe destined for factories in Groningen, Ostfriesland and elsewhere. In this way the government in Lippe could more easily keep its eye on the stream of labour to foreign places. At the time of the Questionnaire of 1811 there were two brick messengers, one for the so-called First District (Groningen and Ostfriesland) and one for the Second (particularly the brick-works on the Weser and in German territories such as Hannover).

During the winter the brick messenger from the First District visited the owners of the brick-yards allotted to him and concluded agreements with them about the number of workers needed for the coming season. In return he received a certain sum of money from the factory owners. The brick messenger for the Second District made such a journey only sporadically, doing most of his business by correspondence. Both messengers negotiated the price per 1,000 bricks. Subsequently, in Lippe, they recruited their firing masters, also in return for a commission from those selected. The messenger informed them where to report to work and how many labourers they should take along with them. The first time a worker was recruited, he paid the messenger a registration fee — or a bribe. The firing masters in turn assembled their teams out of family members, neighbours or others with whom they were familiar. Throughout the season the firing master was responsible for his crew and its labour productivity. In the summer the brick messengers made the rounds of all 'their' brick-yards. At this time they received money from their workers, settled possible differences, saw whether everything was running smoothly, and delivered post. This system of the privileged Lippe brick messengers lasted until 1869.

At the brick-yards, the labourers lived together in what later literature frequently dubbed a 'Lippe Commune'. This is rather idealistically portrayed as a kind of co-operative where whatever happened happened collectively. What the situation in fact amounted to was that the group shared a house in common as described above. At the end of the season household costs were deducted from the total wages which the group had earned, and the rest was then divided. Although costs were spread evenly among all members of the team, net wages were not: a fixed sum was agreed upon beforehand per function (the firing master receiving the largest share, the form-giver the next largest, etc.), and whatever money was left over after division according to this scheme was shared alike among the adult workers.[97]

Modest payment in kind also occurred, such as gin during the firing of the oven, and garden vegetables for the firing master. We can speak of an extremely tight form of social co-operation, one in which various members of the team, including the firing master, depended on each other constantly. By way of contrast, their relation to the *tichelheer* — their employer — could not have been anything but distant. Certainly in Groningen the owner of the brick works was usually a rich man who visited the factory perhaps once a season, if at all. An agent, for example, would provide pay advances, settle accounts at the close of the work season, arrange cleaning and the supply of necessary natural resources. In reality the Lippe workers, from a social point of view, could practically be said to have lived on separate, small islands.

Bleachers

Like brick-works in certain areas, bleacheries in particular places were characterised by the virtually exclusive employment of migrant workers — of both sexes. Indeed, there were two special areas situated along the North Sea coast in 1811 where outside workers were hired for bleaching; one was of primary, the other of secondary importance.[98] The 'Haarlem' bleacheries were the most significant of all, situated among the dunes to the west of Haarlem. The bleacheries of Turnhout in De Kempen were less important. Bleachers who worked in both areas came from the same home region: a number of villages along the border of what today are the provinces of North-Brabant, Belgian and Dutch Limburg. In addition, the Haarlem establishments absorbed a small number of workers from the area of Lingen.

All in all, in 1811 somewhat less than two hundred workers were employed at the Haarlem bleachworks, while about a hundred found similar jobs in Turnhout. Along the North Sea coast, especially in a number of cities in the province of Holland there were certainly more bleacheries where migrant workers were employed, but not in numbers sufficient to merit consideration here.[99] We should realise, moreover, that this branch of industry was then at low ebb. Previously, vastly more workers would have been involved.[100]

Various kinds of things might be bleached: newly woven material, thread or clothing. Each involved different processes, and consequently a different organisation of labour.[101] Traditionally, the bleaching of linen — *lijnwaad* — was of the greatest importance. Bleaching removed impurities from the newly woven cloth that still remained in the fibre, or which during the retting (softening by soaking) or the sizing process (stiffening with a gelatinous solution) clung to it. Through the bleaching — in fact through the frequent repetition of a cycle of bleaching, steeping in lye and washing — the woven material not only turned pure white and supple, but lost approximately a third of its weight at the same time. An average of 50 workers were occupied with these tasks at the Haarlem linen bleach works: 40 women and 10 men. The men's special jobs were wringing out the cloth with the help of treadmills, preparation of the lye and the actual soaking of the linen in the lye-tub, and, finally, sprinkling of the material stretched on the bleaching fields. Women did the remaining work. In particular, the way women washed the linen in pairs, singing while they worked, made an impression on their contemporaries.[102] Bleacheries were capital-intensive enterprises: the 50 labourers accounted for a quarter of total operational costs, raw material (especially ash, soap, milk and turf) for almost half. In addition, among other things, buildings, fires, cauldrons and drying fields were essential. The owner, or master bleacher, left the business of daily supervision to an acting manager called the *loonbaas*, or at times *meesterknecht*. This manager sometimes received a share of the profits in addition to his salary. Usually, beneath him there was an *opperknecht* (headman) — on occasion the same man as the lye-foreman, who kept his eye on the bleachers, the wagon drivers and the cloth wringers. He in turn was assisted by the man who led work on the bleaching fields and by a head bleaching 'maid' especially in charge of women bleachers and apprentices.

Although the way in which bleaching was organised is not always clear (the acting manager, for example, disappeared from the scene towards the close of the eighteenth century), it remains evident that together the workers constituted more or less of a team. They ate together in the 'summer kitchen', a building furnished especially for them. Here, sharing the costs, they did their cooking, in part using provisions such as meat, flour and bread which they brought with them. Here too were the small cupboards where everyone put away his or her own personal belongings. The attics of the bleachery buildings themselves were usually the workers' bedrooms where the women, in any event, slept two by two.[103] Everyone took a turn at guarding the bleaching buildings, primarily to prevent theft. Those on guard duty would stay in a hut, a simple wooden building equipped with a few beds. The notorious bleachers' dogs, and firearms, were at these sentries' disposal.

Workers for a bleachery were probably also hired *en masse*. We may suppose that the 'headman' played a central role in arranging his team's employment.[104] The workers committed themselves for an entire season: from March until September/October. During the rest of the year frost could damage the fabrics, while the sun was not strong enough for the bleaching process. At the close of the season agreements were as a rule concluded for the following year. Per season, after deduction of all expenses, including the costs of the journey, a female apprentice bleacher could wind up with as much as Dfl. 22.50, a female bleacher Dfl. 40, and a male bleacher Dfl. 55.[105]

Bleacheries for thread existed near Haarlem, as well as those for linen. These too were large-scale, capital-intensive enterprises, but nevertheless somewhat more modest than the linen bleacheries. On an average they offered work for 17 labourers, but here with a reversal of the sex ratio observed above, there were 12 male, and 5 female employees.[106] This difference probably had to do with the fact that the threads were considerably less dirty than the linen to be bleached and therefore did not require recurrent washing, but merely rinsing. For the rest, the bleaching process was on the whole the same. A further difference with linen bleach works, was probably the places from which most workers came: men who bleached thread frequently originated from the Lingen area. It is possible, but not certain, that their female colleagues originated from there, too. In any event, *knechten* and *meiden* did not keep house together, but were taken in as boarders by their employer. In general, their work was considered heavier than the work done at linen bleacheries.

Last of all, came the clothing bleacheries: these were really laundries, primarily for dirty household goods with grease stains. In contrast to the other two kinds of bleacheries, these could be established with comparatively modest means. Their owners by no means enjoyed prestige comparable to that accorded the owners of linen or thread bleach works. The number of workers in such a bleachery was small, moreover, usually less than five, with a slight majority of females.

Clothing bleacheries hardly appear in the Questionnaire of 1811, probably because they were not restricted to seasonal operation but carried on right through the winter. Personnel at work in the clothing bleacheries of cities in Holland such as Gouda, Dordrecht, and Rotterdam, and those who held jobs in similar establishments nearby Haarlem, probably came for the greatest part from the region between Eindhoven and Weert.[107] These workers, too, were lodged by their employers. Because the clothing bleacheries were small enterprises and their owners enjoyed no particular social status, it is possible that worker-employer relations would have differed intrinsically from those prevailing at the thread and — most of all — the linen bleach works.

On the whole, the sector of the bleach works is the only one in which women migrant workers found employment on a large scale. They were unmarried, and roughly between the ages of 19 and 40.

Because of competition from bleacheries in Bielefeld and in Ireland, the Haarlem bleach works had gone into a sharp decline already at the end of the seventeenth century. By the second quarter of the nineteenth century, only the clothing bleacheries, or laundries, remained. These, in any event, were then enjoying a period of relative prosperity.[108] Considering the size limits of these businesses, however, we can see that they provided not nearly so many jobs as the earlier, vast linen bleach works once did.

Work in the Transport Sector

In the history of the 'pull area' of the North Sea coast, the migratory labour of seamen was extensive and of great importance for the labour market. Because of the exceptional political relations which obtained during the French Empire, however, in 1811 this group of workers were practically all doing duty in the navy.[109] We might also make mention of cart drivers here, yet they too were scarcely mentioned in responses to the Questionnaire of 1811.[110] From the results of the questionnaire only one extraordinary form of inland shipping emerges as significant: the work of the timber raftsmen. These figure in large numbers in the recorded answers.[111] The timber rafts that floated down river to the North Sea coast were manned by more than 1,500 workers in all. By far the largest contingent was formed of raftsmen who travelled the Rhine and her tributaries, the Mosel, Main and Neckar.[112] Small numbers worked the Maas and the Schelde. Such shipping was a capital-intensive enterprise: at the beginning of the nineteenth century, the fitting out of a large raft cost Dfl. 4,600,000.[113]

Timber-raft shipping as we encounter it in the Questionnaire dates from the second half of the seventeenth century. Until 1650 timber was still transported along the Rhine on ships which were unloaded at Vreeswijk in the province of Utrecht. Thereafter, rafts became increasingly popular — and larger — until at a certain moment after entering the Republic they could no longer navigate the Rhine via Arnhem but had to choose to follow the Waal via Nijmegen. In the eighteenth century the rafts followed this latter route exclusively, and Dordrecht was where they were dismantled. Here, a great part of the wood trade from the Zaan region consequently relocated itself. These rafts were indeed of phenomenal dimensions: they could be as much as 300 metres long and 50 metres wide. For the largest of them, a crew of 500 was required. Most of these had the job of rowing in rowboats or manning the tens of rudders attached to the front and rear of the raft. A few served as cooks, bread-cutters and butchers for the rest of the crew. The owner or shipper who was in charge of such a vast raft, or of a number of smaller ones, had a well-furnished cabin onboard; in addition there were various kitchens, and from 10 to 20 wooden sheds where the crew could sleep. Although I have been unable to discover anything about how the rafting work was organised, we may assume that tasks were carried out in teams.[114]

The work season began for a timber raftsman in March, when smaller rafts were assembled on the tributaries of the Rhine. These were then lashed together into great rafts to the north of Bingen and Koblenz. It was from these two places, indeed, that the large majority of raftsmen originated. It is not known whether they could make more than a single journey a year. Leemans's data disclose that by far the most rafts passed Nijmegen, Tiel and Zaltbommel in July and August, several drifted by in April, and then a somewhat larger number would come along in October/November.[115] Perhaps this is an indication — like the relatively small number of migrant workers in relation to the number of rafts — that raftsmen did indeed go down the Rhine more than once a season.[116]

The prefects of the départements from which the raftsmen came did not think highly of what the raftsmen earned. One arrived at an estimate of 100 French francs per season as a typical wage once costs were deducted.[117] The raftsmen were also responsible for dismantling the rafts in Dordrecht. Once his raft had been taken apart, then the captain transported what remained back upstream by ship: ropes, anchors, kitchens, etc. Whether the workers also returned home in this way, or if they had to walk, I am unable to say.

Work in the Trade and Services Sector

Small traders — pedlars and hawkers in all their variety — constituted the principal form of activity in this sector.[118] In 1811 this group came from a few specifically delineated areas and locations within the 'push areas' of the North Sea System.[119] Moving from north to south, we can first identify a number of places in Ems Supérieur from which at least a thousand *pakkendragers* (packmen) came, all of whom did business in textiles. These places are situated in the north of Tecklenburg, in the Hümmling and in the environs of Lingen, Meppen and Fürstenau. These traders were known by the name of *tüötten*. More than a hundred kilometres further south, an area commences which has a peculiar, elongated shape; it stretches from what today is the southeast part of North-Brabant, by way of Central Limburg and adjacent German territory due south as far as the départements of Meuse and Moselle. Within this strip — never more than 100 kilometres wide and almost 300 kilometres long — there were a number of 'push areas'. These were never far distant from each other and yet had few or no commercial ties. Again, from north to south, first there was the area of the *teuten* in the Kempen and adjoining parts of Central Limburg; then to the east, the area of Breyell; next, in South-Limburg the area of the Groenstraat; further south the département of Ourthe was the source of many kinds of pedlars, as were the départements of Forêts, Meuse and Moselle. This inventory, moreover, omits the villages along the Jeker (Bassenge, Roclenge, Wonck and Glons) from which the sellers of straw hats originated.[120] We cannot accurately calculate the number of *teuten* in 1811, but a conservative estimate of 6,000 hawkers for the entire strip seems in order. Little is known about how these people lived or worked, but a few sources provide the basis for the descriptive discussion which follows.[121]

Up until now I have confined my attention to groups of workers who journeyed to the North Sea coast, but in this instance that is impossible. Packmen not only travelled west, to the North Sea coast, but they were even more inclined to head east, south and north. It is true that the straw-hat makers from the Jeker valley went to a number of cities in the west, to Amsterdam especially. And some Westphalian tüötten worked the North Sea coast. Most pedlars, however, went to Denmark, the centre and east of Germany, Sauerland, the Eifel and France. These destinations, with the exception of the Paris Basin, were not prominent 'pull areas' for other migrant workers.[122]

From the fact that most hawkers sought out these regions to trade in, places which were not among the more economically developed locations in Europe, we might conclude there was a link between the incidence of itinerant vendors and the level of economic development: a weak infrastructure and economically backward conditions would then be seen as attracting pedlars. It is indeed striking to realise what vast distances pedlars were prepared to journey. Consider, for example, the tinkers, ragmen and umbrella salesmen from the Basses Alpes, the *teuten* who trekked as far as Denmark, and the Slovaks who sold spices even in the distant Netherlands.[123] What is also remarkable is how these long-distance routes could be subject to drastic change within a short time. In 1811, for example, it was remarked that tinkers from Auvergne had just recently abandoned the Iberian peninsula to work instead in North France and Belgium. Vendors from Moselle also made a major detour: whereas previously they had headed for southern and southeastern France, after the Coalition Wars they followed the French armies to Holland and Germany as well.

These examples should not suggest that pedlars were at all whimsical about selecting where to go to find work. In general, there were firm agreements among them defining who might cover what territory. Different teuten villages, or the so-called *kompagnieën* (companies) either within such villages or else made up of members from several villages, each had its own work terrain, consisting for the most part of several cities and the surrounding area.¹²⁴ Banding together was typical for packmen. They rarely worked alone. A 'company' usually consisted of two or more 'masters' with a number of apprentices who in time might also become masters. The designation 'master' indicates that a number of the vocations concerned were predominantly or entirely male. Some forms of itinerant trade, however, the selling of straw hats, for example, or of pottery, involved no small number of women.

At the heart of the area where the packmen sold their wares or services, their companies arranged for a depot of goods from a factory or from the migrants' home areas. Here one or more members of the company remained full time to look after the store, handle administrative tasks, carry out possible repairs (e.g. tinkers) or assemble products (straw hats). The masters and their followers then scattered into the countryside and nearby cities to find buyers for their wares. The routes they chose had a number of fixed points — places they lodged, opened shops and stored their supplies.[125]

Hawkers thus did not operate in a 'no man's land'. Their 'infrastructure' of known places of resort may be compared to the arrangements we observed, for example, among mowers who returned each year to the same lodgings, butchers and shops in Amsterdam.

The company mode of business — where risks were shared as well as profits, and business usually took place far from home — involved rigid group norms. Notably, all the trades people discussed here were Roman Catholics.[126] The gifts they made to churches testify to this fact. Many used a kind of secret language which was especially rich in words related to business dealings. There were rules governing behaviour, for the most part unwritten but strict none the less, complete with punishments which primarily involved the fall of whoever violated the rules into disgrace. The situation appears to have been comparable to that among polder boys and construction workers.

It may not seem obvious upon first consideration, yet itinerant selling, although not directly tied to the seasons, had fixed periods of high intensity during the year. Most tüötten returned home twice a year, around Whitsuntide and Christmas. It appears various pedlars also departed twice a year, to judge from the dates on which they applied for passports. At home they frequently prepared or assembled the items with which they carried on their trade. The basis of their economic survival, however, at least for most of them, remained as for so many migrant workers, their own home farms, small or large, in the place of their birth. Because they usually were away from home for long stretches of time, their wives, remaining behind, had to shoulder the brunt of responsibility for running the farm. Strangers who visited Lommel, the centre of the 'push area' of the teuten, expressed surprise to see women walking behind the plough. In other villages bachelors were usually the ones who took to the road with their merchandise. Their goal was to become farmers from the profits of their sales. After ten or fifteen years of journeying, and after turning 30 years of age, a man would contract a marriage. Then, with his savings, if these were ample enough, he would set himself up on farm of his own.

It is difficult to gauge the measure of success achieved by the average pedlar. Histories of the teuten and tüötten especially create the impression that the fortunes of the families *Brenninkmeijer* (of the well-known C & A shops), *Dreesman* and their fellows were typical. Those who in the course of the nineteenth century when this kind of work underwent a rapid decline and attracted the attention of a number of academics were the last survivors of a disappearing breed appear in general to have been among the hawkers who achieved some success, and who therefore contributed to a certain degree to romantic myth-making about the pedlar's way of life. It is also conceivable that a number of teuten families from the Kempen were already prosperous when they embarked on their wandering sales ventures. It has indeed been argued convincingly that a number of successful waggoners who carried freight between Antwerp and the surrounding countryside took up peddling at the end of the sixteenth century.[127]

There are grounds for doubting the general validity of this picture, however. The sheer quantity of pedlars in a number of places, where at times they even constituted a majority of the economically active population, makes it unlikely that all of them belonged to the elite. If we overlook the pedlars who were part of an upper crust, as well as those whose prosperous careers began in penury, the bulk of packmen will in any event have belonged to the lower layers of society.

In summary, we can say that pedlars were in some ways typical of other contemporary migrant workers, and in some ways not. They, like so many of the others, depended on agriculture for the basis of their livelihood; the 'push areas' from which they came were situated to the home areas left by other migrant workers in search of work; peddling, to some extent at any rate, had recognisable seasonal peaks. These itinerant tradesmen differed from other migrant workers, however, in that either they had appreciable financial reserves to begin with, or accumulated them over the years. In addition, they formed unusually cohesive groups, whose closeness was even manifest in the development of secret languages. What is more, the 'pull areas' where pedlars went to seek their fortune did not coincide, for the most part, with the North Sea coast where other migrant workers went for employment.

Summary and Conclusions

Those sectors where migrant workers found employment at the beginning of the nineteenth century were usually modern and capital intensive. Sole exceptions to this rule were the stripping of oak trees — not an important occupation — and some peddling ventures. Yet the reverse of the statement — that all modern, capital-intensive economic activity involved migrant workers — is not true. Nor did migrants invariably dominate those sectors in which they worked. It part the situation simply varied from region to region, but the specific kinds of work which migrants performed also affected the role which they played. Such work was in general characterised by the limited amount of time in which it had to be accomplished — a period determined by seasonal changes in the weather. Speed therefore was of particular importance in the sectors where they were hired. Wages were almost always paid on a piecework basis; gross earnings often reached a high level when computed over time. In bleacheries and on timber rafts workers were not remunerated on a piecework basis as this apparently was not possible; nor were those employed in the flax industry, who received annual contracts which included lodging and work through the winter.

Per work category the size of the units in which workers cooperated differed, but working together in teams occurred frequently.

Teams usually had a leader from their own number, a *primus inter pares*. Only in a few instances, however, was the team leader a labour broker who could consider the team workers as his employees. The team system also commonly entailed communal living arrangements. Earnings were divided among team members in keeping with prior agreements; differences in remuneration derived as a rule from differences in function. Group cohesion was enhanced by a quantity of rules, customs and rituals. The grass-mowers' practice of working in pairs was exceptional, as were pairs of peat-cutters and peat-dredgers. Grass-mowers, moreover, had rather close ties with their employer, even sharing his table at times. It is remarkable in this context that such closeness between employer and migrant worker was possible despite an anonymous market situation, a pattern that on occasion held true for household maids as well:[128] the workers literally stood on the market place to sell their services. Once a price had been agreed upon to mutual satisfaction, however, at the end of the season a new agreement would be concluded for the coming year. Where team labour was involved, it was common for a messenger to negotiate terms, an individual who served as intermediary for more than one team and/or more than one employer.

It is striking that men were the ones who, on the whole, went in search of work. We have evidence to suggest there were only small numbers of female weavers, hay-makers, weeders, bleachers and pedlars. Many migrant workers were, the records indicate, young; but it is questionable whether we should accept their youth as a general characteristic. Indeed, those who stripped oak bark or harvested flax were conspicuous in that they travelled with their entire families.

Relations between employer and employee — with the exception of the grass-mowers mentioned above — were largely impersonal. A worker usually saw his employer seldom, if ever, settling all business with a supervisor or some other employer's representative. In places where various teams worked at the same time to carry out large projects commissioned by rich investors, these employers, or their representatives or (sub-)contractors would pit the workers against each other in competition. Yet there are, on the other hand, also indications that in such situations of insuperable social distance, migrant workers resorted at times to strikes to achieve a measure of conscious collective influence on the labour market. Rituals, too, helped fortify worker solidarity.

Migrants and local workers only sporadically came into contact with each other. To be sure, migrants usually worked in narrowly demarcated sectors within which they carried out, for the most part, specific tasks of a seasonal kind. Although both migrants and local workers cut peat, for example, the two groups performed very different work and had hardly anything to do with each other. Between them, therefore, we should not expect ongoing competition on the labour market.

Who was the migrant worker then journeying along the North Sea coast *c.* 1811? In general, we are dealing with free workers on a strongly segmented and specialised labour market, men who usually worked as part of a team for piecework wages. During the season or seasons of the year when they found work away from home, their earnings could be considerable. Their earning capacity, of course, depended on their sustained good health. Should a migrant worker fall ill, or lose his job for some other reason, the loss was greater than merely a single season's income.

5 MIGRANT LABOUR AT THE MICRO-LEVEL: THE MIGRANT WORKER AND HIS HOUSEHOLD

Introduction

Although many workers left 'push areas' to search elsewhere for work, these large absolute numbers still represented only a small minority of the total population. In the 'push areas' of the North Sea System, per département maximally migrant workers made up 3 per cent of the inhabitants.[1] Supposing that on the average the economically active male population constituted a quarter of the whole, then we can calculate that at most migrant workers made up 12 per cent of the economically active male population. At arrondissement level, along similar lines, we can in places reach as high a figure for migrants as 26 per cent of the economically active male population.[2] If we base calculations on yet smaller units then, in a number of instances, we achieve still higher percentages.[3] This does not detract from the fact, however, that seldom did as many as half the economically active males in a prominent 'push area' who were of an age to take such a step actually depart to seek work.

Why then did Jost but not his neighbour Jochem leave home each year for a job on the North Sea coast? To answer this question location-specific research in detail is, ultimately, necessary. Here I hope merely to sketch a framework within which such research might take place. And in our search for explanations of behaviour, I suggest that the income structure of a migrant worker and his household may prove to be of crucial importance.

The Income Structure of a Migrant Worker's Household

Given the nature of the Questionnaire of 1811 responses for the most part contain little information about the composition of migrant workers' incomes. Fortunately for our purposes, Bütemeister, the ex-*Amtmann* of Diepholz, took the unusual action in December 1811 of sending the Prefect of Ems Supérieur his opinions concerning migrant labour. We do not know in what official capacity he was acting when he did so. In any event, about the people of his canton, he wrote:

> All people from my canton who go to Holland own only a small amount of land which doesn't yield enough to meet rents and duties. They must also choose this secondary work whose advantages, not to underestimate them, are more considerable than any other alternative. Nor is their absence a drawback in the least.
> Those who have travelled out are back by St Jacob's and departure for Holland only takes place after the sowing season. This way workers miss only the hay-making which can be carried out by the female family members who remain at home.
> Because the Holland-goer takes pork provisions with him — from his own slaughtered pig — he realizes the maximum profit from his production and that is an advantage to the state that should be especially taken into account.
> Just so from a statistical point of view it is extremely important that practically every migrant to Holland carries along a piece of linen which on his own, without a middleman, he sells there for the highest possible price.[4]

The journey yielded some 40 *Reichsthalers* (or 160 FF) for the average worker from Diepholz. Bütemeister emphasises yet again that it is impossible to think of any other secondary work — *Nebenwerb* — 'which doesn't interfere with the primary vocation'.

The emphasis which he places on the complementarity of agriculture and migratory labour is striking. Although he does not mention domestic industry explicitly, we may assume that migrant workers from his canton were engaged in such work as well. If they had not indeed woven the linen themselves which they took to Holland, they would certainly have spun flax during the winter. Given the combination of migration and spinning in the *Bezirke* of Wiedenbrück and Lübbecke, we may suppose the same held true for nearby Diepholz.[5]

If we imagine the income earned by a migrant worker's household in Diepholz in 1811 in the form of a circle, and allow segments of the circle to represent the twelve months, we can fill in the year's earnings from different economic activities as follows: winter months, domestic industry; the spring segment, sowing the household's fields; the three months preceding St Jacob's (25

July), the journey to Holland; from St Jacob's to early autumn, harvesting own produce; the autumn segment, slaughtering own livestock. Raising pigs and bringing in the hay in June remain the work of women in this scheme. My preference is to include these tasks carried out on the migrant's own farm in a smaller circle concentric with the first one. This symbolises that such work constitutes the primary work of the household, or, to use Bütemeister's term, the *Haupterwerb*. On the other hand, this manner of portraying the household's activities means that migrant labour because of its situation in the outer circle occupies a large area. We can justify this spatial attribution, however, in terms of the comparatively high incomes that such work abroad generated: the 40 Reichsthalers which the migrant earned in a quarter of a year away from home represented at least an estimated third of the total annual income of his household.[6] The circle drawn as I have indicated, I call the 'work cycle'. This work cycle depicts the distribution of various kinds of work and the respective earnings involved over a typical year (see Figure 5.1).

From scattered data it is also possible to draw up a slightly more complicated work cycle, one which includes various tasks performed by migrants in succession while away from home. The basic principle, however, remains the same.

Changes in the Work Cycle

The work cycle was not identical for all households in the same area. Nor was it necessarily constant for any given household during different phases of the household's development.

Potential sources of income, and accordingly the distribution of the work cycle among its three principle components: farmwork at home, domestic industry and migrant labour, differed from household to household in one and the same location. Production factors — here especially the availability of arable land — were not, after all, equally divided. The more a household could earn from its own farming, the less essential were domestic industry and migratory labour. Relying on Tecklenburg, I have concluded that households where domestic industry, linen weaving in particular, was a significant source of income, probably had more land at their disposal than the households of migrant workers.[8] To subsist entirely on a basis of agriculture, a household in Westphalia had to

Figure 5.1: Examples of the Work Cycle of Westphalian 'Heuerlinge' in the Eighteenth and Nineteenth Centuries[7]

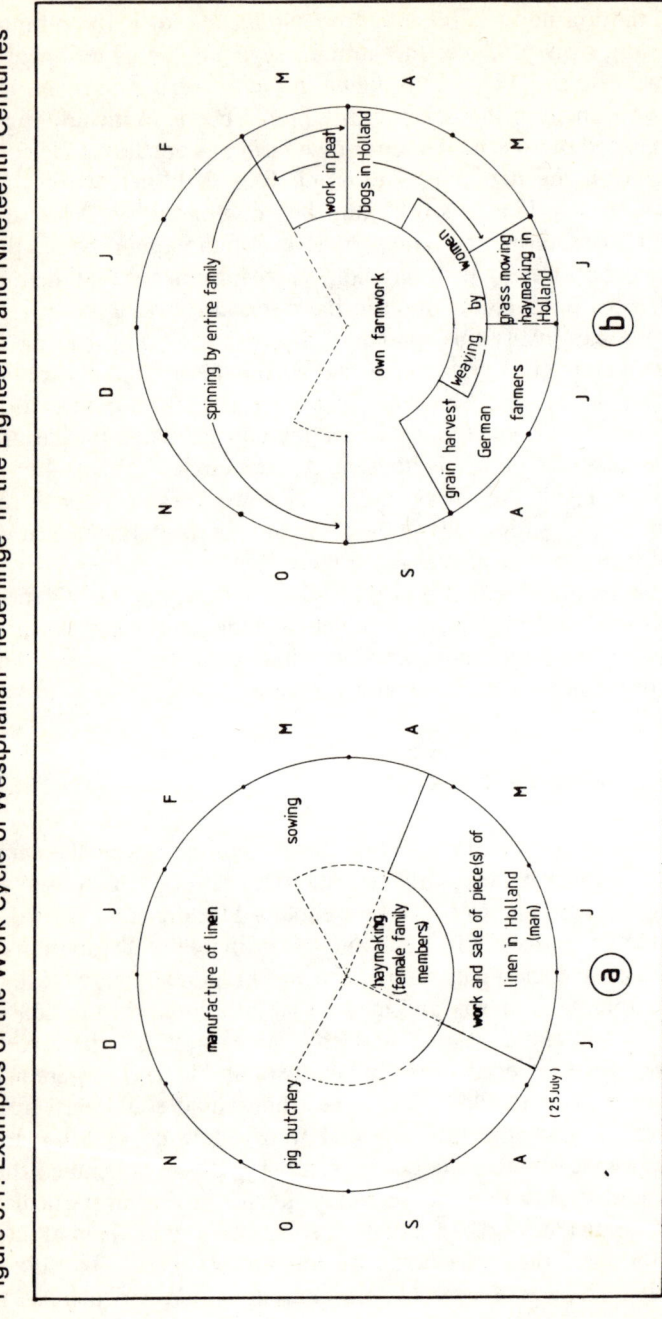

(a) Based on ex-Amtmann Bütemeister of Diepholz in 1811. (b) Based on various sources cited in text.

cultivate at least 5 ha. Migrant workers probably had to manage to earn something from holdings as small as 1 ha.[9]

Over time, however, every household will have undergone its own particular development. Chayanov has traced such possibilities of growth and decline for small farms in Russia in the late nineteenth century.[10] The pattern he identified may, I think, prove illuminating for western Europe as well, especially for the households of migrant workers. A basic premise in any analysis such as Chayanov's remains that every member of a household was both a consumer and a potential producer. Immediately after marriage, a household contains as many consumers as producers: two. The ratio of consumers to producers is one. As children are born the ratio changes, climbing by the fourteenth year of marriage to an average of practically two. As soon as the oldest offspring begin to help out, the ratio dips sharply. The (economically) fortunate situation of a ratio of one, however, never returns, in part because the original partners grow older. If we apply this analytic scheme to migrant workers, two situations, or periods of time are imaginable when leaving home to find work elsewhere will appear indicated as a way to generate supplementary household income: several years after marriage when the ratio of consumers to producers has increased steadily; and during those years when, given the amount of work that has to be done on a small farm, there are consistently too many producers present. The latter will be especially true when a couple has sons 15 or more years old. The prospect of such a youth's being able to earn savings for a future marriage can then act as an added inducement for him to seek a job away from home.

Here, however, we must leave unresolved the question of the degree to which both the factors we have identified — access to means of production and the present stage of household development — actually determine whether or not a household member will leave home to find work elsewhere. Once again, we should allude to the particular role which women played within the household of a migrant worker: we have observed that migrant labour is usually a male phenomenon; a corollary to this fact is that in the absence of the migrant worker his wife had the responsibility for running the farm in addition to continuing her important function in domestic industrial production.[11]

CONCLUSION

Study of the Questionnaire of *c.* 1811 administered in the north of the French Empire, and concerning the phenomenon of migrant labour, has led us to discover clearly differentiable 'pull areas' and 'push areas', terms which denote, respectively, the destination and the points of origin of workers who left home to find employment elsewhere. A number of 'neutral areas' have also been discerned, areas not far from 'pull areas' but from which workers did not depart to search for outside jobs. The interrelated whole of 'pull areas' and 'push areas' I have called a 'system'. The system of particular interest to us in these pages I have identified as the 'North Sea System', one in which *c.* 1811 some 30,000 migrant workers were active annually.

Economic preconditions for the emergence of such a system have been analysed at three levels: at the level of geographical regions (the macro-level), at the level of kinds of work performed in 'pull areas' (the meso-level), and at the level of migrants' households in 'push areas' (the micro-level).

This analytical differentiation into three levels will now be re-integrated into a descriptive whole. The economic conditions underlying the emergence of migratory labour appear to involve the existence, at no great distance from each other, of 'pull' and 'push' areas which meet certain criteria (for the North Sea System in 1811 the 'pull' and 'push' areas were some 200 to 300 km apart). The 'pull area' must have a well-developed infrastructure and be characterised by an economy both modern and capital intensive. This will mean that specialisation has taken place, so that mono-cropping is practised (e.g. grain, flax and animal husbandry), major (public) works are executed, or specialised enterprises co-exist close to one another. Much of the work that had to be done in 'pull areas' was seasonal by nature, so that at peak times there was a shortage of local labour; in discussing the reasons behind this shortage Tydeman, in 1819, advanced the explanation 'wages earned during the harvest were insufficient to maintain workers in our area throughout the winter and the following spring'.[1] What Tydeman meant is that local Dutch workers could not support their families for the whole year only on the wages they earned during harvesting. Apparently, he conceded that in the winter season especially no employment at all for local Dutch workers was available. In fact for more than 150 years before he wrote, the countryside of Holland and neighbouring seaside-provinces were no longer 'push areas' of seasonal labour. Employers in a number of sectors and branches of production in 'pull areas' therefore needed outside labour periodically, and were also in a position to afford them.

'Push areas' were characterised by a large number of small farmers unable to eke out a living for their families from their holdings alone. Should there by no viable '*alternatif*'[2] at hand, neither domestic industry, especially weaving, nor wage labour at some large farm nearby, then to supplement household income the possibility existed that the 'work cycle' would be completed with migratory labour.

The validity of these assumptions, derived from the study of a single system at a particular point in time, remains to be tested by comparison with other contemporary systems, and by an analysis of the emergence and disappearance of migrant labour systems in general. In Part II I attempt the former, synchronic comparison. In Part III the necessary diachronic perspective is introduced.

PART TWO:

The North Sea System in Wider Perspective:
Migratory Labour in Western Europe *c.* 1800

INTRODUCTION

In Part I a number of theses concerning conditions congenial for the emergence of migrant labour were formulated. These derived from an analysis of the North Sea System at the beginning of the nineteenth century. Here in Part II we shall see whether these theses can be shown to hold true as well for migratory labour during the same period elsewhere in western Europe.

The theses will be tested synchronically. A selection of migratory labour systems will be made. A general description of them then follows. And finally, systems with demonstrable similarities will be analysed.

In identifying a migratory labour system, we make use of two basic criteria: the magnitude of labour movement involved; and the interaction of a single set of clearly demarcated 'push' and 'pull' areas. Here, in order not to exclude any systems of possible interest, I propose to use a somewhat arbitrary threshold well below the numbers involved in the North Sea System, so that an annual volume of 20,000 migrant workers within any given system at the beginning of the nineteenth century is the minimum required for including it in the following discussion.

The descriptive passages in Part II will make use of the framework established in Part I, but will be less extensive.

Of central importance to our consideration of 'pull areas' will be the characteristics of economic sectors in which arriving workers found employment. For 'push areas' we shall pay special attention to relations among agriculture, domestic industry and industry. In mapping the flow of labour from 'push' area to 'pull' area and back again, finally, we will discuss the 'work cycle' which embraced the totality of income-generating occupations in which the migrant worker and his household engaged during the course of the year.

The next topic to require attention is the absence of migrant labour in eastern Europe, despite the existence of conditions in a number of regions which would lead us to anticipate considerable movement of workers in search of jobs away from home. This lack of migratory labour helps to reveal reasons for its emergence elsewhere which remained implicit during our previous analysis of functioning systems.

Source material in Part II is less elaborate than in Part I. For Italy, I have made use of the same questionnaire as for the North Sea System, although confining myself to studying it at the départemental level. Secondary sources provided me with information concerning the other countries reviewed: for France, the monumental monograph of Chatelain; for Spain above all Meijide Pardo's compendious article; for Great Britain, an assortment of specialised studies. How I combined and processed the different sources is presented in Appendix 2.

6 OTHER WEST-EUROPEAN MIGRATORY LABOUR SYSTEMS c. 1800

The Existence of 'Pull' and 'Push' Areas

The collection and processing of material about migrant workers in Europe at the start of the nineteenth century provides us with a reasonably clear picture of the location of 'pull' and 'push' areas, especially in western Europe, in central Spain and in north and central Italy. Gaps in the literature mean we have a less substantial understanding of the situation in central Europe, southern Spain, Sicily and the Balkan states. The magnitude of the south German 'pull area' during this period, for example, is uncertain. For the Austro-Hungarian lowlands, Sicily and the Balkans all we know are a number of routes followed by migrant workers; no data are available, however, about how many people were attracted to 'pull area' destinations, nor about the number of workers setting out from distinct 'push areas'.

Figure 6.1 contains a pictorial summary of all migrant labour routes at the beginning of the nineteenth century with which I am familiar. The map prompts a first conclusion: the North Sea System was by no means unique in Europe. We can differentiate some twenty 'pull areas' of significance, places towards which a number of arrows point. It is striking how poorly central and especially eastern Europe are represented among the 'pull areas', a fact to be considered later as a topic in itself. In addition to 'pull areas', we can also make out a number of 'push areas' on the map.

The Major Migratory Labour Systems

Every year about 30,000 workers journeyed out and back again to hold various jobs within the North Sea System. Around 1800 there were another six systems in Europe, each of which involved an annual minimum of 20,000 labour migrants. These have been entered in Figure 6.2 together with 'water sheds' which mark the frontiers between 'push areas' supplying workers to different systems.

Figure 6.1: Currents of Migratory Labour in Europe at the Beginning of the Nineteenth Century[1]

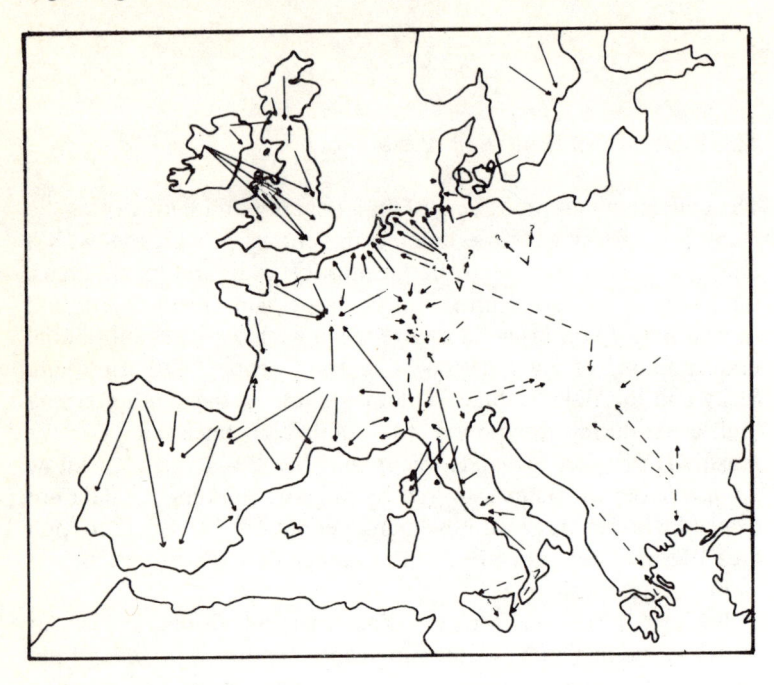

→ direction of migration
--> direction of migration of uncertain date
? unknown destination.

In the north, three regions emerge as distinct. In addition to the North Sea System with which we are already familiar, there are the 'pull areas' of eastern England and of the Paris Basin. In the South we can distinguish four 'pull' areas: Castile, the Mediterranean coast of Catalonia, Languedoc and Provence, the Po Valley and, finally, central Italy, including Corsica.

Every year some 20,000 migrant workers came to work in eastern England. They came to participate in the harvest in Lincolnshire and East Anglia, to garden in the Home Counties and to carry out a thousand and one different jobs, including public works projects, in the capital of London. The overwhelming majority of them came from the far west of Ireland, especially from Connacht. Among their ranks there were Scots, Welshmen and English workers as well.

Other West-European Migratory Labour Systems c. 1800

Figure 6.2: Leading 'Pull Areas' in Europe at the Beginning of the Nineteenth Century

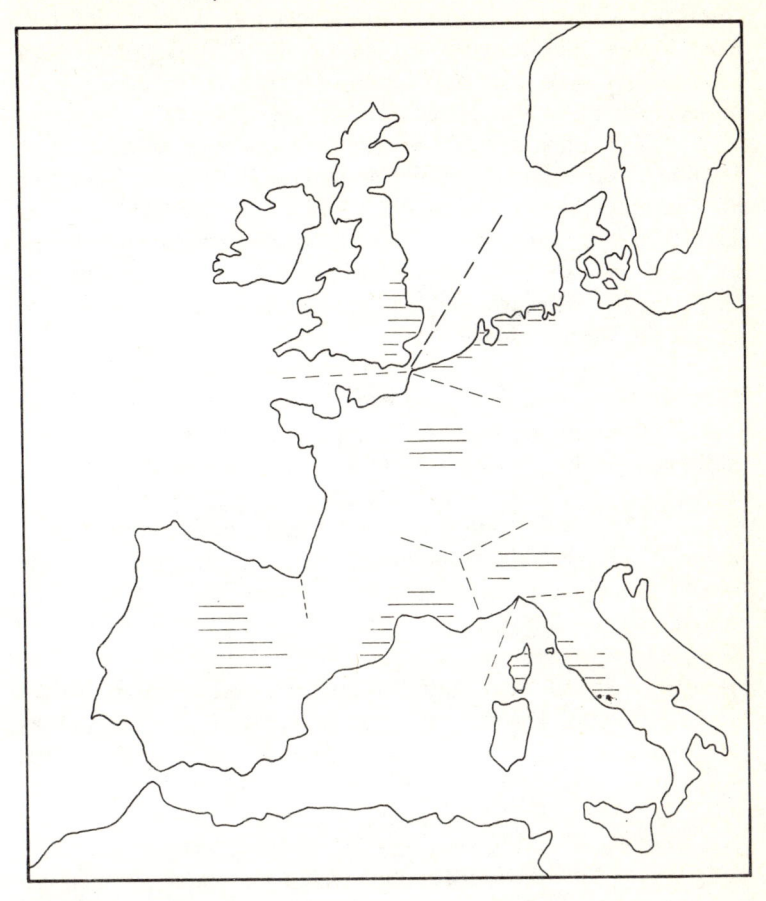

▤ 'Pull areas' attracting more than 20,000 workers annually c. 1800
– – – – 'watersheds' for migrant workers

The Paris Basin drew certainly as many as 60,000 workers each year. The greatest attraction was exercised by the city of Paris itself, where public works, trade and service jobs offered employment. Yet the départements surrounding Paris were also dependent on migrant workers, especially during the grain harvest. The Massif Central was the leading reservoir of workers bound for Paris and vicinity. In addition, the Alps and the west of France supplied no small number of workers.

Castile and its capital Madrid depended each year on the arrival of a minimum of 30,000 workers, primarily from Galicia, but also from other places in northern Spain, such as Asturia, and even from France. The reaping of grain on the Castilian plateau was their leading task; they also found employment on public works projects and in the service sector of the capital.

A total of roughly 35,000 migrant workers came annually to the Mediterranean coast between Catalonia and Provence, primarily for the grain harvest, but to pick grapes as well. The ports of Barcelona and Marseilles did not, however, attract many of these workers. The Alps, but also the Massif Central and in the third place, the Pyrenees, were where the migrant workers lived who set out for the Mediterranean coast.

The Po Valley absorbed each year at least 50,000 migrant workers. Their most important work by far was agricultural: cultivation of rice in the west. Cities such as Milan and Turin drew additional workers to fill jobs in the public works and services sectors, but not nearly on the scale of Paris, for example, or Madrid. Those who came to the 'pull area' to work had permanent homes in the surrounding mountains, from the Bergamasque Alps in the north to the Ligurian Apennines in the south.

The central Italian 'pull area', consisting of the south of Tuscany, Lazio and the islands of Corsica and Elba, attracted approximately twice as many workers each year as the Po Valley, at least 100,000. The harvesting of grain, but of other crops too, provided most arrivals with work. They were also hired for further agricultural tasks. The cities, Rome especially, exercised a strong pull on workers, construction workers first and foremost, but also those who found jobs in the trade and services sectors.

The geographical pattern of the seven major European migrant-labour systems at the beginning of the previous century is portrayed in Figure 6.3. The magnitude of the annual migration within each system is indicated by concentric circles surrounding the centre of each 'pull area'. Each circle represents 10,000 workers. It is possible to distinguish a northern from a southern conglomeration: the southern consisting of a broad base with four systems within which a total of more than 200,000 workers were moving back and forth each year; the northern comprising only three systems, with a total of some 100,000 workers involved. Relations between such conglomerates remain to be explored in future research.

Figure 6.3: The Most Important 'Pull Areas' in Europe at the Beginning of the Nineteenth Century and their Distance from Each Other

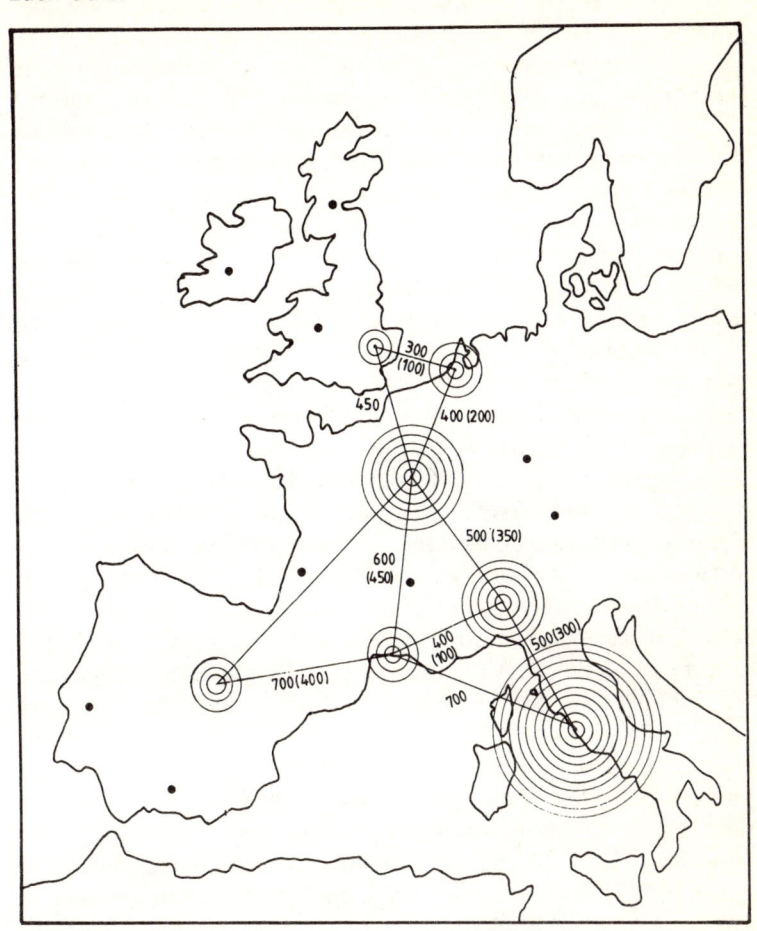

- Smaller 'pull area'.
- Major 'pull area'; each circle represents 10,000 workers.
- 300 Distance in kilometres between the centres of major 'pull areas'.
- (100) Shortest distance in kilometres between the outer edges of major 'pull areas'.

Figure 6.2 also shows the 'water sheds' between migrant labour systems and Figure 6.3 gives the distances which separated different 'pull areas'. The largest numbers in each instance represent the distance in kilometres between the centres of the systems. These distances vary from 300 to 700 km. Since 'push areas' frequently lay spread out between 'pull areas', most migrant workers needed to travel no more than 350 km to reach the heart of a 'pull area'. In practice, for the most part, they travelled less far. Numbers on the map in parentheses indicate the distance between the outermost boundaries of different 'pull areas'. Reasoning along the same lines we used above in calculating travel distance to the centre of migrant-labour systems, we can see that the maximum distance which a migrant worker who came from a 'push area' located between 'pull areas' had to travel was 250 km. These figures agree with observations concerning the North Sea System made in Part I: the farthest workers in this system went to find work was between 250 and 300 km. That any more considerable distance raised difficulties may be deduced from solutions which migrant workers from Galicia were forced to find if they were to manage to work in the rather small 'pull area' of Andalusia. In their case the distance between 'pull' and 'push' area was 500 km. The journey, moreover, passed through mountains and rough terrain. Two choices were possible: a migrant could board a ship in Vigo, for example, or Pontevedra, and travel below deck in a freighter to Cadiz; or he could combine the journey with trade activities along the way.[2] The last option was described by Le Play as part of one of his famous budgets from the 1840s. In Le Play's pages a farmer from Galicia appears who went to work during the winter in the coal mines of Villanueva, 50 km north of Seville. Before beginning his trip on 21 October, he purchased a mule on credit. The beast carried him to the south in ten days. There he sold it for a profit, and from November to May worked in the mines. Before his return journey on 1 June, he used what he had managed to save of his wages — entrusted during his stay to the safekeeping of the mine director — to buy an Andalusian horse at the market in Vilanueva. The horse carried him home, once more in ten days. It too was sold for a profit which enabled the farmer to pay back the money he had originally borrowed to buy the mule.

A number of less prominent 'pull areas' are also designated in Figure 6.3. With a single exception, these appear along the periphery of the northern and southern conglomerates of larger migrant-labour systems. If we start in the northwest and move south, it is possible to distinguish the following smaller 'pull areas': southern Scotland, mid-Ireland, western England, Aquitaine, Portugal, Andalusia, Sicily, and further to the north, southern Germany and the Rhine Valley. Lyon and its environs, wedged in, as it were, among three larger systems, constitutes the exception.

The fact that in general the smaller systems encircled the totality of the larger ones supports the idea that the seven major migrant-labour systems exercised such sufficient labour attraction that no other system could sustain itself in among them.

Now that we have observed how in the beginning of the nineteenth century a number of comparable migrant-labour systems co-existed with the North Sea System, we may proceed to see whether our assumptions concerning the conditions necessary for the emergence of migrant labour — as determined by study of the North Sea System — appear valid for the remaining systems as well. Towards this end I will describe and analyse the other six systems in some detail. In the discussion of 'pull areas', the work which migrants performed there will be the topic of central importance; in the discussion of 'push areas' the structure of the migrant's work cycle will be the focus of the text.

Work and Work Cycle in Major Systems of Migratory Labour

Eastern England[3]

In the 'pull area' of eastern England — at the heart of which were East Anglia and Lincolnshire — the cultivation of grain was the dominant economic activity. In many instances half, or more than half of the arable land was sown with grain,[4] and large to extremely large farms dominated the landscape. The preponderance of grain cultivation meant that there was temporarily an urgent demand for labour during the harvest season, while throughout the remainder of the year there was little work to do. Most of the workers who came to eastern England were Irish, especially from the western counties in Connacht.[5] In Connacht small farms were in the vast majority, and potatoes their leading crop. The rental of small plots of land had risen to exorbitant prices, 'far beyond the real value of the land'. Indeed, the rental fee approached that of the price of the land itself. Irish migrant workers, bringing home earnings of £10 or more at the end of the season, could pay the high rental rate demanded for the ground their households farmed.

Figure 6.4 depicts the work cycle of an Irish migrant worker who went to eastern England to take part in the grain harvest. Income from work abroad accounted for a quarter of the household's total earnings.[6]

Figure 6.4: Work Cycle: Irish Migrant Worker's Household in the Nineteenth Century[7]

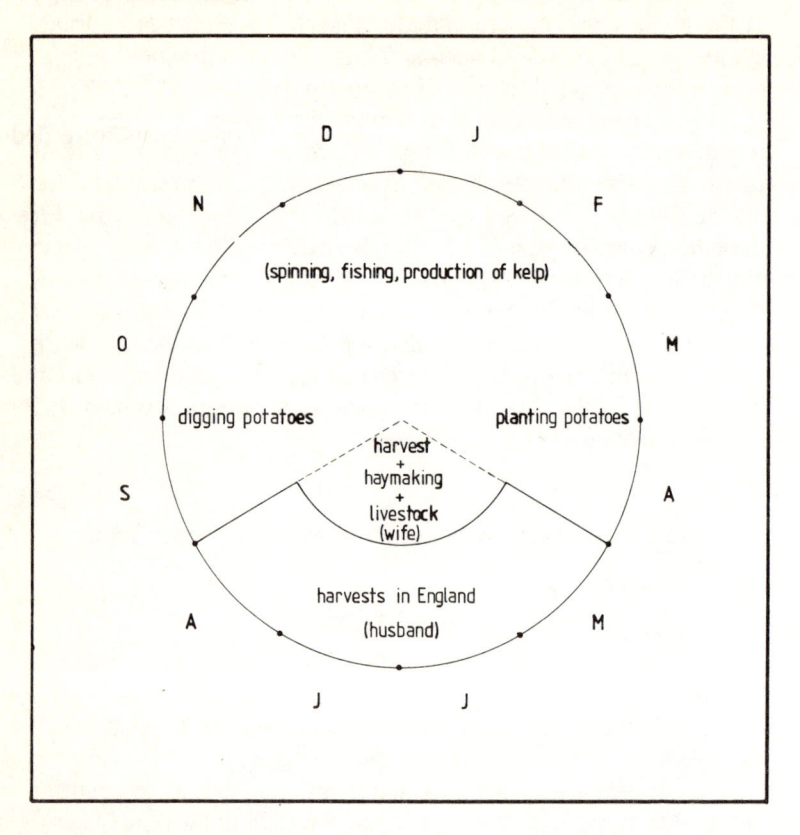

Circular diagram showing months J, F, M, A, M, J, J, A, S, O, N, D around a circle. Labels inside: "(spinning, fishing, production of kelp)" at top, "digging potatoes" on left, "planting potatoes" on right, "harvest + haymaking + livestock (wife)" in center wedge, "harvests in England (husband)" at bottom wedge.

The Paris Basin

Most migrant workers in this region chose Paris as their destination. The situation there will be discussed below as part of a separate treatment of migration to cities. Encircling Paris lay a vast, fertile agricultural area totally oriented to supplying the food needs of the capital. This promoted scaling-up, especially in grain production — just as London's dependence for food on East Anglia did.[8] Here too there arose a sharp demand for migrant workers during the peak harvest season. In response, more than 30,000 migrants came from the Massif Central and from the east and west of France.

Farming in the elevated region of the Massif Central yielded only little grain. What did manage to grow, moreover, was of a poor quality. In addition to dairy products, chestnuts and turnips made good the lack of grain in high altitude areas, whereas at lower levels potatoes had already also achieved popularity.[9]

Castile

The cultivation of grain was more important than other agricultural activities on the Castilian plateau, too. As elsewhere, sparse population density meant that local workers were unable to accomplish all the work there was to do by themselves during high seasonal labour peaks during the summer.[10]

By way of contrast, small farmers from mountainous Galicia and also from the mountains of Léon, from Asturia and from the Basque country were almost always confronted with a shortage of work.[11] Not even half the land in Galicia was under cultivation; in the provinces of Orense and Lugo, for example, the home territory of most migrant workers in this system, only 11.0 and 6.3 per cent of the land, respectively, was being farmed in the second half of the eighteenth century.[12] The greatest part of the land being cultivated, moreover, was in the hands of large landowners, especially abbeys. Small farmers eked out a living on plots of sown land not much larger than half a hectare.[13] It will hardly be surprising that Galicia was obliged to import grain on a large scale. Its own leading products were grapes and other fruit and flax; animal husbandry was not unimportant. Slowly but surely potatoes, introduced into Galicia as early as 1768, had earned themselves a place in the diet of ordinary families, side by side with cornbread. On his *minifundio* (smallholding) the small farmer's hardships were at their annual maximum towards the middle of the year, when grain prices soared and the farmers had to subsist on cabbage soup with a little flour and hardly any fat. This fare might be supplemented with some fruit, a little milk or some carrots.[14] In regions where migrants could find work mowing at this time of the year grain was low in price. The *golondrina* (swallow's flight), as migratory labour was called in Galicia, was therefore a logical solution to the difficult home situation. Every spring the men, and usually a number of single women as well, departed in groups, *cuadrillas*, frequently composed of family members.[15] At the start of the summer the migrants harvested wheat in the vicinity of Madrid, Toledo and Guadalajara. There, in New Castile, the harvest ended on 25 July. This day, the feast of the Apostle Jacob, patron saint of Galicia, was elaborately celebrated away from home. Later the workers moved on to do harvesting in Avila and Segovia, and yet later in Léon more to the north, and in Old Castile.[16]

Meanwhile, back home the farmers' wives kept things running. In addition to working in the fields, they were busy with domestic industry, particularly the spinning of flax.[17] The work cycle of the household in Galicia was intended to maintain the farm: earnings from migrant labour went to pay off land rental fees and family debts. According to Meijide Pardo the entire system had a single goal: shoring up the *status quo*.[18]

Catalonia, Languedoc and Provence

This elongated Spanish-French region also provided migrant workers with work, primarily during the summer grain harvest. The farms were large, just as in the systems already described and in the Italian system discussed below. Braudel summarises the character of the plains in the Mediterranean area — and not merely for the sixteenth century — as follows: 'La plaine appartient au seigneur, et plus encore à la grande propriété' (The plain belongs to the lord, but even more to the big landowner).[19] His statement is illustrated best by the Po Valley and central Italy.

The Po Valley

Cultivation of rice in the Po Valley was the domain of migrant workers. The work involved in this 'Potosi of Piedmont', as the area was dubbed by Davico, was carried out entirely by visiting wage labourers: the sowing, the transplanting, the weeding and, at last, the harvesting. Rice was ready to be cut between the end of August and middle October. The harvest was accomplished in teams, each consisting of six men and six women. Not only did they cut the rice, they also threshed it and saw to it that the full sacks of rice were stored in the granary. Their pay was between $1/14$ and $1/13$ of the yield, which worked out to about 200 litres per person, or, transposed per day, FF 2.50.[20] Braudel points out that for rice cultivation neither the owner's presence nor a permanent work force is required. Workers and owner were on the scene only when the tasks mentioned above had to be attended to. Cavour, the father of Italian unity, is himself a famous example of a rice owner: it was his habit to go himself at the crack of dawn to his rice fields in Léri in order to organise his workers and pay them.[21]

Central Italy

The largest 'pull area' of migrant workers in Europe at the beginning of the nineteenth century, the central Italian coastal plain and the nearby islands of Elba and Corsica, primarily drew workers for the grain harvest. In addition significant groups came for winter jobs such as the cultivating of farmland, the felling and sawing of wood and its processing into charcoal, and the tending of herds of livestock.[22] During the summer more than 40,000 workers would arrive to reap grain in the Roman arrondissements of Rome and Viterbo, the Pontine marshes, the arrondissement of Grosseto in the south of Ombrone and in parts of the département of Trasimène. The Roman prefect wrote that in his arrondissements, which had hardly scarcely any working inhabitants, 500,000 ha had to be harvested. The *latifundia* (very large farms) therefore required migrant labour, workers who came in part from the east (primarily from the Marche of Ancona) and in part from the south (the Roman arrondissement of Frosinone and adjacent Napolitan areas). Workers from this last group in particular failed to make a good impression on the prefect with their old clothes held together by string like the tribesmen of the Hernici portrayed on ancient reliefs. Once the workers arrived, they were assigned a piece of land that a group could mow completely in eleven days. That such work was carried out on a vast scale becomes clear in the Roman prefect's description:

> not seldom one meets six to eight hundred harvesters in the fields, forming a row that goes on for half an hour. From time to time a cry arises that passes down their ranks. Forty to fifty supervisors on horses ride along the row to urge the workers on and to see that they cut the stalks of grain as close to the ground as possible. Mules, laden with wine, bread and cheese, come and go with provisions. At night the workers sleep in the fields.

Although the scarcity of labour meant high wages — according to the prefects of Rome and Ombrone migrant workers netted 2FF per man per day — the prefect of Trasimene recognised serious disadvantages connected with this kind of work. According to him, the workers ran a great risk of falling ill, partially because of the fevers which prevailed during the summer in the Maremma, the coastal plain (comparable to malaria along the North Sea coast), and partially because of the strenuous nature of the work. Treacherous too were the changes in temperature which the workers had to contend with, sweating by day in the heat, shivering by night in the cold under the open skies. In the opinion of this prefect it was therefore also apparently illogical that his people nevertheless should set out to work near Rome. To explain their departure he could only say that they were 'seduced'. He wrote:

> It so happens that wealthy landowners or leaseholders from the Roman Campagna have agents in this département who take advantage of the miseries of winter by advancing a supply of grain to farmers in need. In repayment they merely require that their debtors come to the Roman Campagna for the harvest and in this way pay back part or all of their loan. These persons entrusted with the hiring of workers bear the title of 'caporale'. From the landowner, in addition to a double day wage, they receive a bonus of 25 FF for each worker they take on. These workers in turn were given food and a sum of FF 4 for every work day, half of which they had to give back to pay off their debt to the landowner. Free of debt, a worker would ordinarily be able to take 25 to 30 FF home with him.

The prefect of Arno confirmed that for the mountain dwellers in his arrondissement, Pistoia, it was absolutely necessary for them to find work away from home, because although all the households in the mountains owned some farmland or woods, their holdings were only enough to provide them with support for four to six months out of the year.[23]

During the winter most of the work performed had to do with caring for the land: clods of soil were broken up, the irrigation system repaired, vineyards tended, terraces patched up, walls built, and drainage ditches dug or improved. Work in the woods was also of importance during this season: trees were felled or trimmed and boards cut from the wood; the so-called *carbonari* prepared charcoal. The prefects of Golo and Liamone[24] described activities on Corsica. Workers from Lucca and the surrounding area arrived there in the fall in units of six to ten workers known as *camerate*. One worker was the 'caporale', *primus inter pares*. In the presence of the other workers he negotiated the work to be done and the wage to be paid — net earnings for the period from roughly October to May were estimated at 125 FF for Golo, 200 FF for Liamone, and 260 FF for Elba. An employer was obliged

Other West-European Migratory Labour Systems č. 1800   119

to provide food, and to meet this obligation he distributed 1½kg chestnut flour to each worker every day, or in Liamone, the same amount of ground maize. From this ration the workers cooked *polenta*. When the polenta cooled off it was cut into pieces with a string and eaten three times a day. This basic diet was sometimes supplemented with meat, cheese or dried fish. Water was practically the only thing the workers drank; wine was scarcely ever on hand. This simple, limited fare had to sustain the workers throughout their winter labours.

During the winter herdsmen also descended to the plains where they rented pastureland. In Ombrone 50 herdsmen paid no less than 70,000 to 80,000 FF for grazing-rights, approximately 1,500 FF per shepherd or flock. This expense had to be earned back through the sale of wool and some of the animals. A *chef berger* (head-shepherd) could expect to clear 250 to 400 FF for his efforts, an ordinary herdsman some 18 to 50 FF.

A herdsman began to learn his occupation at the age of 6, looking after lambs. Next he was entrusted with dogs and sick animals. Between the ages of 12 and 14 he assumed responsibility for the first time for a flock of some 60 to 80 sheep. In the course of time he managed to acquire several lambs of his own, from which he could raise an entire flock. The head herdsman, the *vergaro*, began his career with the sale of lambs and the supervision of cheese-making (*buttaro*). He could end up as an important sheep dealer, settling in the Roman Campagna.[25]

The Relationship Between 'Pull' and 'Push' Areas

Writers who have occupied themselves with the history of migrant labour in various countries have, not inaccurately, pointed out that workers came primarily from mountainous regions and journeyed down to the plains in search of work. It is by no means certain, however, how we should interpret this observation. Is there really any essential difference between migratory labour systems in which workers for the most part come from the mountains and systems, such as the North Sea System, where this is not the case?

We can investigate this problem in some depth for the Italian 'push' areas in the Alps, the Apennines and the Abruzzi, which wound around two major 'pull' areas in the form, as it were, of an S. The number of migrant labourers from some of these mountainous areas was extremely large, not only in absolute terms, but proportionately as well. The arrondissement Biella (in the département of Sésia), for example, had a population of 89,000 in 1810, 9,000 of whom (14 per cent) were migrant workers; in the arrondissement Bobbio (in the département Gênes), a third of the inhabitants travelled out to find work elsewhere; and in the arrondissement Novi (also in Gênes) it was reported that even half the population departed seasonally to find jobs.[26] Nowhere to the north did I come across comparably high percentages. Here, however, not only did grown men migrate, as in most systems, but also women and children in large numbers.

As far as Novi was concerned: 'Throughout the winter, there remain in our village only the elderly, a few women and some young children.' Particularly in bad years, when the mountain harvest failed, as happened in Stura in 1810, the following winter the volume of migration frequently would increase two or three-fold. In normal years, however, the obvious purpose of the mountain people was to better their position through migrant labour. From their savings, smiths and tinkers from the Aosta valley in the département of Doire bought small plots of land at home, because, as the prefect of the département of Sésia put it so poetically: 'these men, though cosmopolitan by necessity, still cherish the spot where their cradle stood'. In the prefect's way of thinking there lurks a danger that crops up constantly during interpretations of the seasonal migration habits of workers from the mountains. To cite the prefect of Sésia once more, on this occasion speaking in sentimental terms about the trek of almost ten thousand workers from his own arrondissement, Biella:

> the displacement of surplus inhabitants appears to accord with the wisdom of a Providence which wishes to forge social bonds between distant peoples through an exchange of services, assistance, labour and wages. Their mutual dependence brings them closer, unites them and establishes an equable balance of prosperity between diverse regions.

Not only this prefect, but contemporary historians too exhibit an inclination to regard seasonal migration from the mountains to the valleys as a natural law. Braudel, for one, complementing his description of the capitalistic character of the plains which encircle the Mediterranean Sea, delineates the mountains as follows: 'A factory of people for the use of others: that's what the mountains really are'.[27] Yet it is incorrect to present the phenomenon of migratory labour as the manifestation of any natural law — and certainly such an interpretation of permanent migration is mistaken. A closer look at mountainous areas reveals that from one upland valley workers streamed below to the plains to find seasonal employment, but from the neighbouring valley with exactly the same natural features, they did not. Sella has made this point tellingly and also offered an explanation for why it happened.

Areas in the mountains from which workers did not depart were characterised by local industries — in metal, for example.[28] A mountain dweller was, to be sure, not by definition poor. It is evident, of course, that the fertile plains were better suited to the development of capitalistic monocropping. As a result, two complementary economics could exist: that of the plains where workers were required on only a temporary basis, and that of the mountains where climatic conditions made workers temporarily superfluous. Yet workers from the mountains did not invariably want to relocate permanently on the plains; this would mean relinquishing part — probably the most important part — of the source of their incomes, their own upland farms. In Sella's words:

> it is in the country of their birth, through subsistence agriculture, that migrant workers possess the resources which are indispensable for complementing their insufficient wages: theirs is an unsettled existence, divided between two economies, between two worlds profoundly different which contain, in the final analysis, their lives.[29]

In point of fact, 'push areas' in mountainous regions do not essentially differ from 'push areas' anywhere else, including those within the North Sea System. Preconditions for the rise of migratory labour are the same: a large part of the population faces extremely limited possibilities for economic gain at or near home. At most, we may venture to say the chance that a mountainous area will become a 'push area' is greater because natural factors there interfere with the development of jobs related to agriculture, industry or growing urbanisation — at least they are likely to interfere with such development more than do natural factors in non-mountainous 'push areas'. This is not to deny, however, that other forms of (secondary) employment, such as domestic industrial activities, can exist to a substantial degree in mountainous 'push areas', offering an alternative to migratory labour.

The Drawing Power of Large Cities

Comparison of the North Sea System with other western European migratory labour systems yields in each instance one remarkable difference: in other systems large cities also exerted an important pull on labourers from 'push areas'. In the North Sea System even such a city as Amsterdam offered only a modest number of job opportunties to migrants. Paris, on the other hand, according to an estimate by Chatelain, was offering seasonal employment c. 1800 to more than 20,000 workers annually. Such work fell mostly within three sectors: construction, masonry in particular; a number of specific crafts; trade and services. Construction work was dominated by migrants from Limousin; they especially controlled new bricklaying.[30] Such work at the turn of the nineteenth century was still clearly seasonal. Migrant workers who found work as craftsmen appear to have been employed primarily in the metal sector. Much greater, however, was the number of non-Parisians who came to work for part of each year in the trade and services sector. Chatelain groups these jobs together as 'métiers de la rue' (street trades) and cites Mercier's *Tableau de Paris* (1789) in which those who engage in such occupations are attributed with a sensitivity to the seasons which was just the opposite of what was usual: 'Like birds driven by cold to a temperate place, these people flee the snow which covers the mountains for eight months out of the year'.

Thus, the seasonal needs of the 'pull area' were not decisive, but rather climatic conditions in the 'push area'.[31] Every year these migrants returned home to hand over their earnings, to conceive a child — another of Mercier's observations — but above all to replenish their supply of saleable goods. These goods were of local manufacture, prepared perhaps even by the migrant's own household. In any event, back home such goods could be purchased far more reasonably than in the 'pull area'. Throughout the period under study, in any event, ties which bound the migrants to their 'push area' of origin, for all groups, were still very strong. In most instances it is impossible to speak of permanent migration.[32] For

Paris Chevalier has demonstrated, for example, that masons from Limousin actually began to settle in the city from the 1840s, when sharper competition on the labour market meant that workers could no longer permit themselves a winter visit home or on returning to the city early the next spring they would find all the available jobs were taken.[33]

We also have information about migrant labourers in other major European cities, especially in the south: Lisbon, Madrid, Milan, Turin and Rome.[34] The Prefect of Rome, for example, wrote that in addition to workers in construction and groundwork, some 300 Genoans worked in his capital city as porters. They waited for employment on the city's bridges, and also carried on trade in the goods which reached Rome along the Tiber. The men who cleaned the intestines of slaughtered cattle came from Leonisse in the Abruzzi; inn-keepers came from La Matrice in the Abruzzi as well; 130 porters on the grain market were migrant workers from the Lake Como area; butchers' assistants came from Vercelli; bakers were Venetians or Bavarians and fishermen were Neapolitans. The prefect ended his report with a lament: 'One might well ask what the Romans themselves did and I'd be hard pressed to say; it is at least true that few of them devote themselves to useful work'.[35] His remark may well have been exaggerated; but it in no way detracts from the fact that in Rome, as well as in the other major cities mentioned above, migrant workers were an integral part of the scene, carrying out an array of occupations.

It would be premature to attempt to draw firm conclusions here concerning differences in the intensity and function of migratory labour on the labour markets of a number of cities. Available material does suggest, however, that there were essentially three kinds of labour markets, each involving migrants in a different way:

(1) an urban labour market, comparatively open, where local workers participate; at best migrant workers may hope to find employment on projects if major new construction is undertaken;
(2) an urban labour market where the trade and services sector is dominated by migrant workers who arrive in groups from a definite 'push area' to find work in what can be considered 'their' 'pull area';
(3) an urban labour market within which crafts particularly are dominated by co-operative societies of workers (*compagnies*

travelling brothers or *Wanderburschen*) who travel a fixed circuit including a number of cities.[36]

No single city in all its parts will have featured only one of these three kinds of labour markets. The typology may be helpful, however, in characterising various cities. Amsterdam and London would appear to belong primarily to the first type, for example; Paris, Lisbon, Madrid, Turin, Milan and Rome to the second; and French cities such as Marseilles, Lille, Mulhouse and Lyon to the third. To whatever extent the typology may prove serviceable in further analyses, we must realise that relations between these types of labour markets within any one city would have changed over time. Thus, Chevalier points out that the transition from migrant labour to permanent, settled labour among construction workers in Paris was in part a consequence of fierce competition which arose between migrant workers and compagnons — strife which led ultimately to the defeat of the latter.[37]

7 THE ABSENCE OF MIGRATORY LABOUR SYSTEMS IN CENTRAL AND EASTERN EUROPE

The Situation *c.* 1800

At the start of Chapter 6, I observed that in central and eastern Europe at the beginning of the nineteenth century there were no major migratory labour systems. If we posit that this observation is sound and not based on an insufficiency of evidence or on misinterpretation of fact[1], then the situation becomes one of extreme theoretical interest. The region involved, known at that time too as 'the granary of Europe', was indeed characterised by massive cultivation of grain on large to very large farms. Especially in Germany, to the east of the Elbe, in Poland and in west Russia, this monocropping must have meant that a vast number of workers were needed at seasonal peaks, particularly at harvest time. Grain was exported traditionally via Baltic ports to western Europe, especially Amsterdam.[2] Since an important number of conditions for the emergence of a migratory labour system appear to have been met in these places — conditions derived from analysis of the North Sea System and its comparison with other western European systems — we would expect to find seasonal shifts among the working population. An explanation as to why apparently no migratory labour system arose here, however, may put us in to the track of conditions for the emergence and spread of migratory labour which up to this point have remained implicit in the text.

I will concentrate on those regions where the combination of large land holdings and massive, monocultivation of grain for sale coincided in 1800. Of central importance is how large landowners secured manpower during seasonal peaks when many workers were needed to carry out certain tasks in a short time. If these workers were not seasonal migrants, the landowners must have been able to rely on the services of small farmers or land tenants to accomplish the necessary work.

In the regions we are considering there did indeed exist an extensive group of small farmers who had to eke out a living from agriculture. Their relation to large farmers, however was entirely different from that encountered at the same time in western Europe. Between the end of the fifteenth and the beginning of the sixteenth centuries, 'second serfdom' was introduced in central and eastern Europe. In this period of mounting grain prices, the nobility managed to bind small farmers to them legally.[3] They were not successful everywhere,[4] but this system of 'serfdom' was established in much of the region east of the Elbe which was then under cultivation.

Under this system of serfdom, the large estates (also called *Gutswirtschaften*) had a number of farmers at their disposal who were obliged to carry out personal services for them.[5] Next to the house where the owner or estate manager lived, there were sheds and stalls for livestock; most striking, however, on such extensive farms, was the virtual absence of draught animals and accommodation for workers. In neighbouring villages, on the other hand, which were the property of the landlord, small farmers lived with their draught animals. These farmers had fields too, but their 'master', the landowner, was entitled, for example, to let his cattle graze on all stubble, including that which grew on the plots cultivated by the farmers. His holdings, moreover, were tended by farmer-serfs from the village. Every evening the estate steward would assign work for the following day, telling each man whether he was expected to work with his hands (as during the harvest), or to provide a team of animals (e.g. for ploughing). In autumn and winter the farmer-serfs had to thresh the grain and carry it to market using their own teams of animals. This description, borrowed from Knapp, who was describing Germany east of the Elbe, is accurate as far as the main points go for Poland and western Russia as well.[6]

Consequences of the Abolition of Serfdom

The system of serfdom that eliminated the need for migrant labour as a source of manpower where monocropping prevailed was, however, around 1800, on the point of dissolution in large parts of central and eastern Europe. Serfdom was legally abolished in the Kingdom of Prussia in 1807, soon thereafter in the Grand Duchy of Warsaw, and finally in 1861 throughout the Russian Empire. In actuality traces of serfdom lingered on for decades, however, after its official abolition. It only disappeared in Prussia, for example, towards the middle of the nineteenth century.

The first consequence of the end of serfdom was the further extension of the already far-advanced pattern of vast estates.[7] In particular, the area of land under cultivation increased: in Prussia and Poland crop acreage doubled. A combination of crops and agricultural techniques which were labour intensive meant an increasingly urgent demand for manpower. This need was met in Prussia east of the Elbe by the '*Instleute*' system: workers leased themselves contractually to farmers for an entire year. The clearance of new farmland in combination with the *Instensystem* led to a rapid growth of the population. Ipsen, who describes this process, is of the opinion that growth tapered off around 1865.[8]

Once grain prices began to climb in the decade 1830-40 and extremely labour-intensive crops such as sugar beet were introduced, migratory-labour systems also grew up in central and eastern Europe. Particularly spectacular was the growth of the 'pull area' between Donau and Don: Moldavia, Bessarabia, Cherson, Tauria, Ekaterinoslav and the Don region. Here after 1850 farmers abandoned extensive animal husbandry and began to raise wheat. By 1900 this area, too, was attracting upwards of 5 million migratory workers. Here, however, serfdom had hardly existed if at all.[9] In other Russian areas, where serfdom had been known, the phenomenon of migratory labour flourished as well, and at the turn of the century as many as a few million workers were already involved.[10]

CONCLUSION

Comparison of the North Sea System with six other major systems of migrant labour in Europe has confirmed the general validity of earlier conclusions, and brought new understandings to light as well. To begin with what we have learned: an essential condition for the rise of migrant labour appears to be the existence of a free labour market. Where sources of manpower are guaranteed by systems of serfdom or slavery, migrant workers are not needed. In addition, migratory labour appears not to be a phenomenon confined to rural areas; significant numbers of migrants worked in various groups in major cities. Finally, however impressive the number of workers who participated in the North Sea System might be in itself, compared to other systems, especially in the south of Europe, the North Sea System was not exceptionally large.

Discussion in the preceeding chapter has largely confirmed what we observed earlier about relations between 'pull' and 'push' areas, and between employers and their workers. 'Pull areas' offered a favourable opportunity to combine available means of production, culminating accordingly in large-scale capitalistic enterprises characterised by the production of a single crop. As the result of seasonal peaks of labour demand spread unevenly throughout the year, migrant workers were in great demand. 'Push areas' were everywhere characterised by the predominance of small farms where, in addition to periods when cultivation required the intensive input of labour, there were periods when the manpower available was in excess of what was needed. It was through migratory labour that small farms were able to protract their survival, or even to flourish and multiply. The rational self-interest of employers in 'pull areas' and of workers in 'push areas' thus served to conserve both poles of the single system.

PART THREE:

The Rise and Fall of Systems of Migratory Labour

INTRODUCTION

In Parts I and II we have recognised the conditions necessary for the emergence of migratory labour in a static situation. In Part III, applying a diachronic test, we will consider the rise and fall of systems of migratory labour. If one expects conditions derived from a (static) situation to have something more than incidental validity, then the occurrence of these conditions should lead necessarily to the appearance of the phenomenon under study, in this instance migratory labour. The same holds true for the disappearance of the phenomenon in question. Here, concretely, such reasoning means that we may anticipate the rise of migrant labour:

(a) if there is a free labour market;
(b) if there are two regions within reach of each other where wage and price levels differ sufficiently;
(c) if in one of these regions — a potential 'pull area' — capitalistic projects or single crop cultivation involve seasonal peaks in the demand for labour;
(d) while in the other region — the potential 'push area' — there is a large class of small farmers who are unable to guarantee their annual income by engaging in domestic industry.

It is possible to summarise these conditions as follows: if in potential 'pull' and 'push' areas a need for workers in the former coincides with a need for employment away from home in the latter, then one can expect migratory labour to answer both needs. Only the concurrence of the entire set of conditions will lead to the anticipated consequences as soon as the fourth and last condition is fulfilled. Each essential condition can arise independently of the others; e.g. a free labour market may come into existence in a potential 'pull area' (condition a) for reasons having no connection whatsoever to do with changes in the situation of cottage industry in a 'push area' (condition d). We should, however, take into account that under the influence of an external factor more than one condition may be met at the same time. Fluctuations in the economy, as will be made clear subsequently, may be regarded as one such external factor.

Introduction

The ideas sketched here in short will serve as a guideline for the description of historical developments in the text below. The choice of which period to study was determined primarily by the destiny of the North Sea System. As will be recounted hereafter, this system arose in the seventeenth century and vanished in the nineteenth. As a result, this diachronic test of the conditions we have identified as necessary for the emergence of a system of migratory labour will span the years, roughly, from 1600 to 1900.

8 THE RISE OF SYSTEMS OF MIGRATORY LABOUR: A CASE STUDY OF THE EMERGENCE OF THE NORTH SEA SYSTEM

The description of the birth of systems of migratory labour which follows involves three distinct geographical settings[1]. First and foremost we shall examine developments at the core of what became the North Sea System, considering the situation in Holland, a 'pull area', and in Westphalia, a 'push area'. Secondly we shall deal with the northern and southern extremities of the North Sea coast. Thirdly, we shall turn our attention to the remaining major European systems. In conclusion we shall concern ourselves with the relationship between economic fluctuations (trade cycles) and the rise of systems of migratory labour.

Conditions for the Rise of Migrant Labour from Westphalia to the Province of Holland, the Heart of the North Sea Coast

Development of the Population and the Labour Market in Holland: 1500-1800

In different parts of Holland very different patterns of population development can be distinguished. After a presentation of regional population statistics, we shall discuss separately the state of the labour markets both south and north of the IJ.

We can trace demographic development in the province of Holland globally, on the basis of information presented in Table 8.1. Population growth was robust north of the IJ until *c.* 1650; although even there, in rural areas outside the Zaan region a rapid decline took place until *c.* 1750, followed by a slight recovery. In contrast, the population of the Zaan region continued to expand until *c.* 1750, after which it fell off somewhat. To the south of the IJ the turning-point can be dated somewhat later: growth until *c.* 1680 and then decline. Here too we can differentiate by subregion: in the second half of the eighteenth century the population of the area to the south of the Lek River and Delfland continued to increase; the area between the Lek and the Haarlemmermeer exhibited a stable pattern or some slight increase; on the other

Table 8.1: Population Developments in the Province of Holland 1514-1795 (in 1,000s)[2]

	1514	1622	c. 1650	c. 1680	c. 1750	1795
North of the IJ						
7 cities	22	64	70	70	35	35
Zaan region	7	20	24	26	28	25
Other places	52	106	117	92	65	68
Sub-total	81	190	211	188	128	128
South of the IJ						
12 cities	105	299		470	440	427
Rural areas	89	183		225	215	228
Sub-total	194	482		695	655	655
Total	275	672		883	783	783

hand, rural areas immediately south of the IJ and the city of Amsterdam saw their populations decrease, their losses consistent with developments in the Zaan region to the immediate north.

According to Van der Woude, population decreases after 1650 in the north and after 1680 in the south can be attributed primarily to a falling birth-rate.[3] This may have been a response to economic hardship in the form of shrinking means of subsistence. Although we know little about job opportunities at this period in rural Holland, I will try to summarise the principal information available, distinguishing the situations that prevailed north and south of the IJ.

In considering the labour market in Holland north of the IJ we should realise that demographic growth in the first half of the seventeenth century coincided with a vast increase of arable land area acquired by land reclamation. Of the new polders then formed the Purmer, Wormer, Beemster and Schermer are the best known. It is even not beyond the realm of possibility that population growth and extension of land under cultivation kept pace with each other, which is not to say that new farmland was as densely settled as old.[4]

It is not altogether clear whether, with the exception of the Zaan region and Schermer Island, rural industry was of major importance. In any event, the rural population outside the areas specified above worked for the most part in agriculture and fishing; the digging of peat took place only in Assendelft.

Figure 8.1 opposite represents the work cycle of small farmers and

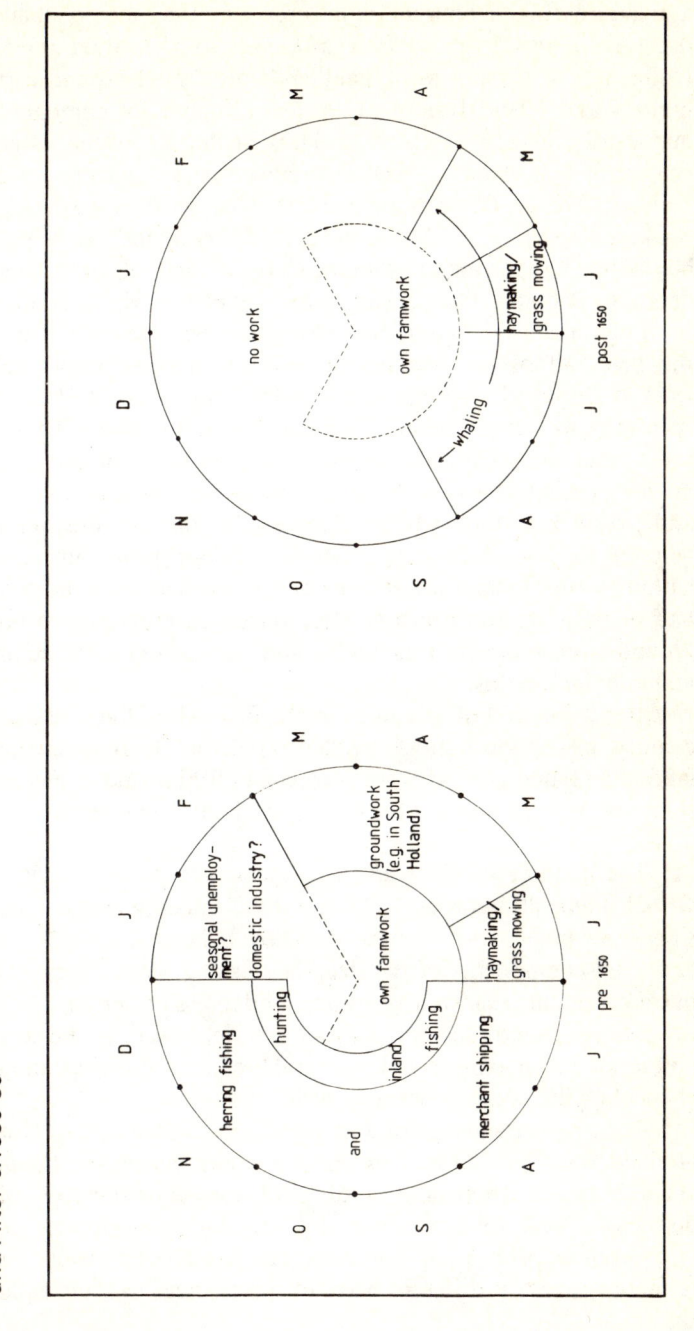

Figure 8.1: The Work Cycles of Labourers and Small Farmers from Certain Rural Areas in North-Holland, Before and After c.1650-80

agricultural wage labourers in this area. Omitting the possibility of domestic industry, we should regard the rural population of North-Holland as a composite of fieldhands and small groundworker-hunters and inland fishermen. A few examples of combinations may clarify this characterisation. Thus, at the end of the sixteenth century it was Andries Vierling's advice to put an end to dike building 'before the coming harvest because then most of the workers depart'. In addition, he cites the combination of polder boy-seaman, reporting that there is a large number of North Hollanders at work on the dikes, usually sea-going people who have already begun to take leave to join the herring fleet and merchant ships. In the first half of the seventeenth century North-Holland sailors worked during the spring in South-Holland as polder boys and then took to the sea again in the summer and autumn. Two centuries later the combination farmer-seafarer was still common in West-Friesland. It was said: 'They were content with as much land and livestock as their wives could manage through the summer. Winters they were farmers'.[5] Migrant labour from outside and within North-Holland has thus been documented since the second half of the sixteenth century. Men journeyed especially to major ground-work projects in the spring and went to sea in the summer and autumn months.

After the period of expansion in the first half of the seventeenth century, job opportunities dwindled rapidly in clearing new farmland and related ground-work projects, in fishing and in merchant shipping. We can account for the cut-back in several ways:

(1) The building of dikes and construction of polders came to a virtual standstill; between 1644 and the nineteenth century only a single new polder was drained (see Table 8.2).

(2) Vital components of the deep-sea fishing sector, such as the herring fleet, also showed symptoms of depression. From 1630-40 to 1680 the rate of decline, slight at first, increased. In the second half of the seventeenth century several branches of European merchant shipping began to wane as well.[7]

(3) After a protracted period of prosperity, agriculture in North-Holland was characterised by sinking prices during the hundred years between 1650 and 1750. All the consequences of a depression were soon manifest, not only for grain-growing areas but, certainly after 1680, for dairy farming areas as well. There farmers reacted in different ways to the changes in their circum-

Table 8.2: Land Reclamation and Dike Construction on the North-Holland Mainland 1600-1800 (in km²)[6]

	Impoldering	Dike building
1600-20	78.6	2.6
1620-40	153.7	—
1640-60	10.2	—
1660-80	—	—
1680-1700	—	—
1700-20	3.3	—
1720-1800	—	—

stances. In the first place they tried to save on permanent labour costs by introducing labour-saving technology, such as churning machines, and by converting from dairy farming to livestock farming (especially) to feeding, and fattening of young livestock and/or to (increased) sheep-farming. In addition, farms scaled up, especially in exclusive cattle-raising areas, often at the expense of smaller farms.[8] *Greppelen* — the cleaning and deepening of drainage ditches — work primarily carried out by individual labourers, also took place at longer intervals during periods of depression.[9]

(4) The improvement and maintenance of dikes, the building of fortifications, the enlargement of cities and the installation and care of harbours: all such projects were kept to an absolute minimum. Extension of the canal network, used for barges, also came to a halt.[10]

(5) As a result of the creation of new polders, there were also fewer jobs to be had in fishing in inland waters, hunting birds, mowing reeds and doing similar work connected to lakes and inland seas.[11]

In summary, with the exception of the Zaan region, after *c.* 1650 there were far fewer jobs available in the following sectors throughout the rural areas of North-Holland: permanent (year-long) farm work, ground-work (spring), herring fishing (June to December), hunting and inland fishing (summer and autumn), cleaning ditches — and perhaps domestic industry (winter). Thus, the work cycle was shattered in all its various quadrants. North-Holland retained its livestock, however, and therefore its demand for hay. The mowing of grass and making of hay in June and July also continued without pause. Since such work requires completion in an extremely short time span, an acute need for manpower existed during this seasonal peak period. If, as I hypothesise, the local population was so drastically in decline as the result of the breaking up of the established work cycle, there would now be scope for seasonal migratory labour from outside the area. There was one occupation where jobs increased during these generally hard times: whaling from North-Holland in the second half of the seventeenth century. As we might expect, this work, which lasted more or less from May to August, was therefore performed almost exclusively by workers who came from considerable distances away.[12] Developments in the work cycle in North-Holland before and after *c.* 1650-80 are depicted in Figure 8.1. The labour market in Holland south of the IJ displayed different features. Following 1650 there was no dramatic decrease in the population inhabiting the countryside of South-Holland; a decline was registered after *c.* 1680, but this was far less consequential than the drop in population in rural areas north of the IJ (with the exception of the Zaan region where population was still rising). The previous strong growth of population can only in small part be explained by the expansion of cultivated land area. Land reclamation through the building of dikes on the islands of South-Holland proceeded only on a limited scale in relation to population growth. Impoldering of former turf bogs in the centre of Holland can hardly be considered to represent a net gain of land, moreover, for these bogs in the past had been deducted from the arable land total when they were put to use for digging peat.[13]

The increase in population throughout the countryside of South-Holland in the seventeenth century led thus to greater population density. There are no indications that prior to *c.* 1680 large-scale seasonal labour migration occurred here.

Let us at this point see whether after 1680 the same tell-tale signs of economic crisis appeared in South-Holland as north of the IJ.

(1) As we observed in discussing Holland north of the IJ, large numbers left that area to move south within the province, bound primarily for major embankments, certainly during the period *c.* 1570-1650. After *c.* 1650, however, impoldering activities on the islands of South-Holland slowed drastically; the drainage of marshes in central Holland came to a halt somewhat later, around

1670. Although impoldering on the islands of South-Holland never again assumed significance, in the course of the eighteenth century marsh reclamation underwent a strong revival (see Table 8.3). As far as peat-mining activity is concerned, I only have statistics pertaining to the area under the administration of the *Hoogheemraadschap van Rijnland* (Rhineland Polder Board), and then only for post-1680. It is well known, however, that during the sixteenth century peat was removed from the bogs of South-Holland on a large scale; the same was probably also true for the bogs of neighbouring Utrecht.[14] Perhaps such mining continued in all its vigour into the early seventeenth century; what happened subsequently remains rather obscure. Statistics from Rhineland indicate in any event that from 1680 on, and perhaps from somewhat earlier, cutting peat increased until *c.* 1700. Activity then declined until 1735. A recovery at this period turned out to be only a brief reprieve. After 1765 the peat industry here spiralled downwards until 1814 when things began to improve. Activity in the three South-Holland sectors sketched above is summarised in Table 8.3. Because we have no way as yet to know how many workers were used on an average per km^2 of dike construction, land reclamation or peat mining, we cannot compare the number of jobs represented by these different activities. It is possible that in the centre of Holland in particular, an increase in jobs in land

Table 8.3: Ground-work and Peat-dredging in Holland South of the IJ. 1600-1800 (in km^2)[15]

	Land gains on the Islands of South-Holland (20-year totals)	Impoldering by Marsh reclamation (20-year totals)	Average area of bogs being mined for peat in the Hoogheemraadschap van Rijnland (annually)
1600-20	37	5	?
1620-40	28	21	?
1640-60	56	10	?
1660-80	2	20	?
1680-1700	2	2	3.9
1700-20	4	13	3.5
1720-40	0	26	2.6
1740-60	5	15	3.0
1760-80	6	108	2.8
1780-1800	7	66	1.7

reclamation compensated, more or less, for declining work opportunities in the bogs and other ground-work projects (see below).
(2) In South-Holland fishing, especially for herring, fell off. The relative importance of this development for the labour market here, however, was less than it was north of the IJ.
(3) For livestock areas in the middle of Holland the situation was identical to what was happening in livestock areas to the north. Even farms growing commercial crops on the islands of South-Holland (just as in Zeeland) replaced full-time workers with seasonal manpower; wage labourers also began to carry out their work on a contract basis, especially in the rapidly expanding business of madder cultivation.[16]
(4) Observations about a decline in maintaining and improving dikes, building fortifications, expanding cities, building and improving harbours apply just as well to areas south of the IJ as to areas north of the IJ — perhaps for the south, they are even more applicable as far as work on cities and ports is concerned. In the south, too, the cessation of building barge-canals had even more repercussions for the labour market.[17]
(5) Jobs in hunting and inland fishing will have been less important in South-Holland than in the north.
(6) After 1650 we hear nothing more of the domestic industry which was so common in rural areas in the sixteenth century and which clearly lasted into the seventeenth century (witness constant complaint stemming from cities about shameless competition from cottage industry). Yet we hear all the more about rural industry in Twente and Brabant, relocated there from earlier addresses in Holland by employers influenced in their choice of new settings by the low labour costs prevailing in these regions.[18]

It will be evident that we encounter greater difficulty in drawing conclusions concerning labour-market developments in Holland south of the IJ than we did when examining the situation in the north of the province. Greater economic diversity in the south complicates the picture.

Migratory labour from North-Holland to the polders of South-Holland probably stopped after *c.* 1650. The decision of the northern polder boys to stay away may in part have been induced by the fact that with a decreasing number of jobs on the market the local labour supply was sufficient to fill them — and in this way the workers of South-Holland could manage to keep at least part of their standard work cycle intact. Yet the weakening of various components of the work cycle can certainly be demonstrated. Such erosion of work opportunities locally from 1680 to 1750 — if we keep in mind the drop in population registered during these years — may have culminated in a new impetus for season-related labour migration.[19] Certainly this was true for the region directly south of the IJ in the second half of the eighteenth century.

Least comprehensible of all remains what happened in the area between Lek and the Haarlemmermeer. The local labour supply in this peat country does not appear, on the whole, to have responded either to the increase or the reduction of peat-cutting activities — judging, at least, by demographic developments. If we take a closer look at a number of typical bog villages, it then appears that peat-cutting and population — ups and downs — correspond with each other for the period 1680-1795 in a number of extremely different ways. Parallel development of mining activities and number of inhabitants occurred in Oudshoorn, and before 1747 in Zegwaard and Benthuizen. After 1747, however, in these last two villages and in Ter Aar for the whole period with which we are here concerned, there was an inverse relation between population figures and the quantity of cut peat; and in Aarlanderveen, finally, the relation is altogether unclear.[20] Changes in the work cycle in South-Holland at this time are summarised in Figure 8.2

Development of Population and Labour Market in 'Push Areas', Especially in Westphalia

If we accept that especially in the 'pull area' of North-Holland a possibility existed after 1650 for outside workers to find jobs during set seasons of the year, nevertheless before migratory labour could actually begin to take place, 'push areas' would have to exist as well. I will answer the question whether such areas existed which, given their demographic and labour-market development, were in a position to deliver migrant workers, by referring to developments in areas with which, *c.* 1811, we are already familiar as 'push areas': areas with sandy soil in the east of the Netherlands and the neighbouring German region to the west of the Hamburg-Kassel line. Already during the seventeenth and eighteenth centuries these same places were repeatedly identified as 'push areas'.[21]

Both Twente and adjacent territory in Westphalia suffered from

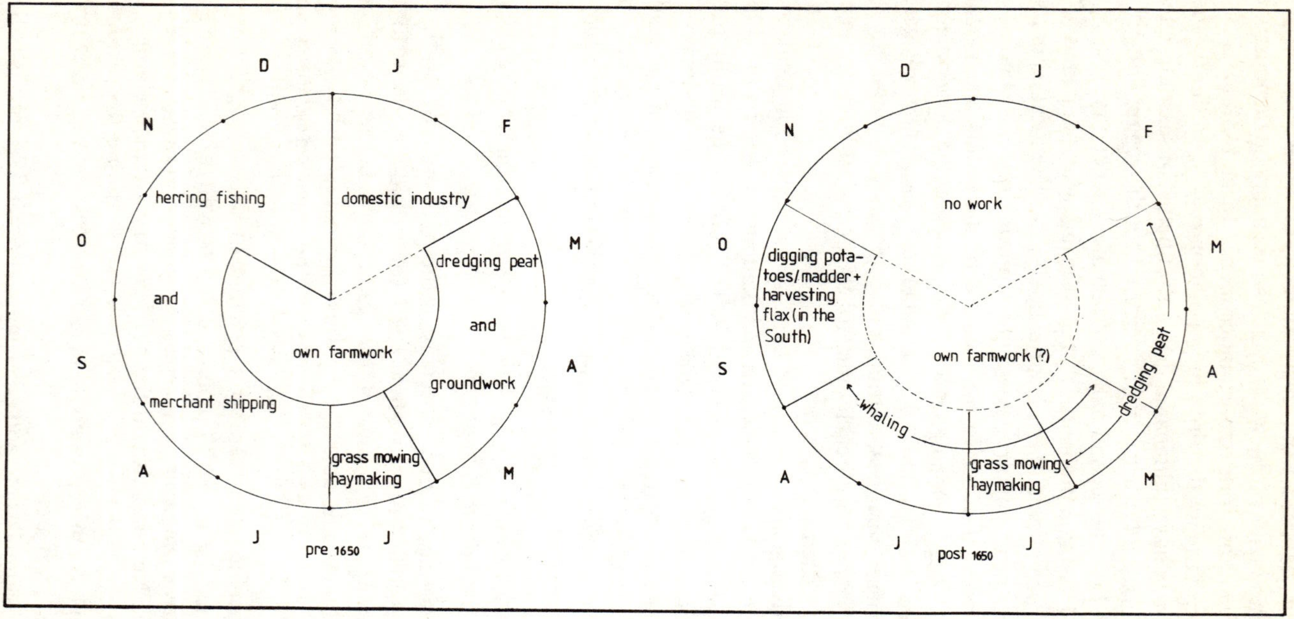

Figure 8.2: Work Cycles in Rural South-Holland Before and After c. 1650-80

warfare in the first half of the seventeenth century: in the Netherlands the Eighty Years War and in Germany the Thirty Years War meant that no population increases were recorded; losses were more the order of the day. Here, the consequences, however, were less severe than disasters undergone in German areas further to the east and south. Once these wars ended, rapid population growth followed. Table 8.4 summarises population statistics for four 'push areas' in the North Sea System.

This population expansion led to a marked increase of rural inhabitants without property of their own who were unable to subsist on their earnings from small leased farms. These farmers acquired the name *Heuerlinge* in many parts of northwest Germany. This trend is clearly illustrated in the bishopric of Osnabrück by the increase of so-called *Nebenfeuerstätten* (farms worked by small tenant farmers or cottagers) in relation to *Hauptfeuerstätten* (full-size farms) (see Table 8.5).

It was not permitted to split large farms up among different heirs, so that the number of such farms remained more or less constant, certainly during the period of sinking grain prices (*c.* 1650-1750) when there was little motivation to clear new land to expand acreage under cultivation. During this period of low prices farmers were inclined to accord a place of greater importance to the raising of livestock, curtailing the raising of crops to some extent. This diversification eased their manpower requirements. Other labour-saving methods were also used.[23]

Table 8.4: Population Development in Four 'Push Areas' of the North Sea System 1600-1800[22]

	Twente	Ravensberg	Minden	Lippe
1616				40,220
1648				25,955
1675	18,000			
1685		47,000	35,000	
1700				36,329
1722		93,000		
1723	29,100			
1748	49,104			
1764	47,200			
1776				58,324
1787		81,000	68,000	
1795	53,072			
1807				70,540

Table 8.5: Hauptfeuerstätten and Nebenfeuerstätten in Osnabrück 1663-1801[24]

	1663	1667	1670	1718	1772	1801
Hauptfeuerstätten[a]	5710		5969	5788	6350	6968
Nebenfeuerstätten[a]			3605	5624	6718	6688
Nebenfeuerstätten[b]		4422	4664		9164	9547

Notes: a. numbers excluding towns and the Aemter of Osnabrück and Iburg.
b. numbers excluding the towns of Wiedenbrück, Quakenbrück and Iburg.

Growth of the population, and of the number of heuerlinge in particular, was accompanied by the rise of the rural textile industry.[25] Indeed, a strong increase in the number of heuerlinge was only possible thanks to this proto-industrialisation. As we have already observed, in the first half of the nineteenth century minimal farms, domestic industry and migratory labour could be readily combined within a work cycle. Consequent population growth, coupled with the rise of domestic production which we can establish took place in those areas which appear to have been 'push areas' in 1811, opened up the possibility of workers journeying for seasonal employment to Holland as early as the second half of the seventeenth century — at any rate after *c.* 1670 at the latest. It is probable that such migrant labour was stimulated by the inclination of large farmers to keep local wages low.[26]

It is indeed of relevance here to point out that not every arbitrary combination of small farming, domestic industry and migratory labour is feasible. With Tecklenburg as an example, we earlier affirmed the idea that where farmers cultivated something more than subsistence acreage, and where domestic weaving went on without interruption for virtually the whole year, members of the household were not so quick to depart to find work away from home. They were needed where they were. The same may also have held true for spinning as a form of domestic industry, as maintained by Mager for the village of Spenge.[27] (For the combination of these three sources of income, see again Figure 5.1, p. 98 above.)

Differences in Wage and Price-levels Between 'Pull' and 'Push' Areas

Without hesitation we can give a positive answer to the question whether or not there was a great enough difference in the standard of living between Holland and its hinterland to make it lucrative — at least theoretically — for workers to leave their homes in search of work further west. Wages in Holland for agricultural work during the summer, for example, were twice those paid in Twente and the Achterhoek, and even three times as much as wages in Tecklenburg further to the east.[28] The differences also become clear when we realise that a Westphalian migrant worker around 1800 was in a position to earn fully a third of the annual income of his household in a comparatively short time.[29] This was possible, in part, because of the great price difference between 'pull' and 'push' areas. To increase their savings capacity migrants took with them as much non-perishable food as possible (salted meat, flour, groats), thereby avoiding the considerable expense of purchasing such provisions along the North Sea coast.[30] Migrant workers also managed to be economical about lodgings away from home.[31]

In Holland during the last quarter of the seventeenth century, both immediately to the north and south of the IJ, we may conclude that conditions were favourable for the emergence of a labour 'pull area'; at the same time in regions to the east conditions existed which were conducive to the development of a 'push area'; there existed between the two regions, moreover, substantial differences in wage and price levels.

The Actual Development of Labour Migration from Westphalia to Holland

Research Method

Ideally, one would attempt to measure the dimensions of this phenomenon by counting either the number of workers who left the 'push area' or the number of workers finding jobs in the 'pull area', or combinations of both. Such statistics, unfortunately, hardly exist for the seventeenth and eighteenth centuries. As a result, imperfect source material will have to be used, the representativeness of which is difficult to establish. There are two references dates between which I will attempt to trace developments: the first is the presumable beginning of migratory labour from Westphalia to Holland, the second is 1811, the year of the Questionnaire.

The trek in which we are interested appears to have begun early in the seventeenth century. I am unaware of any positive evidence that might confirm the existence of migratory labour between Westphalia and Holland at an earlier date. During the first decades of the seventeenth century, on the other hand, reports about *Hollands-* and *Frieslandsgängerei* surface at the same time in various parts of Westphalia including Lippe, Osnabrück and Münster.[32]

At the time of the Questionnaire of 1811, 15,000 migrants were journeying annually to the 'pull areas' of the départements of Zuiderzee and Bouches de la Meuse.[33] The question then is how the migration of labour between Holland and West Utrecht, on the one hand, and areas further to the east on the other, grew from nothing in 1600 to 15,000 workers a year in 1811.

An earlier attempt of mine to describe the quantitative growth of this system involved me in considerable difficulties. Since that time scarcely any new data have come to my attention.[34] Here, I have chosen to approach the subject in a number of steps.

The first step consists of an analysis of regional differences in the spread of migratory labour throughout Holland and West Utrecht. On a basis of the differences which I ascertain among regional labour markets in Holland, we may indeed suppose that in 1811 migratory labour took place with varying degrees of intensity.

The second step involves discussing what value we should attach to registered numbers of migrant workers in 1811. In reviewing source material in the Introduction to this study, I have already observed that in 1811 migrant labour was at a low ebb.

The third step entails our taking a closer look at the quantitative data which are available. Because information concerning 'pull' and 'push' areas is scanty as well as scarce, here we will concentrate on the development of large-scale transportation of migrant workers across the Zuiderzee.

The Regional Distribution of Migrant Workers in 1811

Figure 8.3 presents, per arrondissement of the départements of Zuiderzee and Bouches de la Meuse, the relation between number of migrant workers and the total rural population. The greatest concentrations of migrant workers appear to have found employment in the grasslands of Holland north and immediately south of the IJ and in bogs along the Holland-Utrecht border. This is consistent with what we would expect from demographic patterns and

Figure 8.3: Proportion of Rural Population in the Arrondissements of Zuyderzee and Bouches de la Meuse Made Up by Migrant Workers 1811 (in per cent)[35]

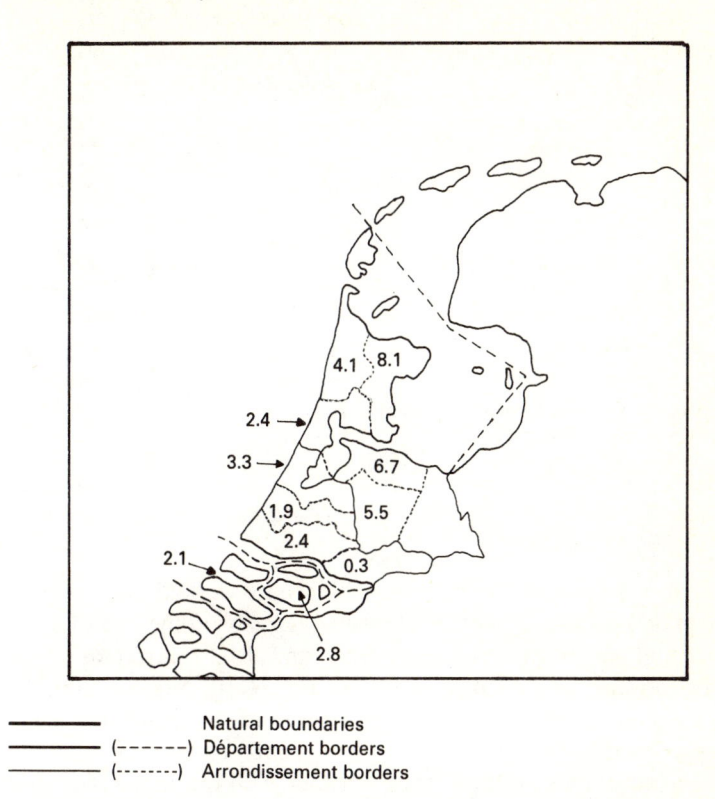

```
——————          Natural boundaries
—————— (------) Département borders
—————— (-------) Arrondissement borders
```

developments in the labour market between, roughly, 1650 and 1750. This also implies that the structure of labour markets here did not undergo substantial change between 1750 and 1811.

The Long-term Applicability of Statistics from 1811

It is definite that in 1811 seasonal labour migration to the North Sea coast was at its nadir.[36] We cannot be sure, however, to what extent it had already begun to taper off before 1811. Table 8.6 presents diverse quantitative data of relevance to our interest in mapping this decline through the years immediately preceding the Questionnaire.

The picture that emerges from Table 8.6 is not an unambiguous

Table 8.6: Development of the Number of Migrant Workers in Several Locations and Regions of the North Sea System 1806-11[37]

		1806	1807	1808	1809	1810	1811[a]	1811[b]
Turf-diggers:	Weesperkarpsel	306	188	179	164	97	105	±140
Grass-mowers:	Watergraafsmeer	36	36	47	17	7	13	13
	Graft	28	19	8	11	2	19	10
	Schoorl	13	18	21	12	14	11	24
	Oudorp	15	44	27	27	12	34	6
	Velsen	30	18	15	16	1	29	20
	Sub-total	122	135	118	83	36	106	73
	Heilo	—	—	—	—	45	48	70
	Akersloot	98	77	—	—	—	—	19
	Buiksloot	16	13	18	9	11	—	11
Bleachers:	Velsen	50	69	56	61	68	58	66
	Bloemendaal	—	—	114	80	75	80	80
Migrant workers from:	Arr. Roersmond	2000	800	800	800	460	—	—
	Canton Roermond	300	300	180	120	80	20	—

Note: For places in Holland, data for 1806-1811a derive from licensing records; data for 1811 are from the Questionnaire of 1811.

one: it is true that fewer migrant bleachers worked each year in Bloemendaal, but the decline depended largely on the fate of a few particular businesses. Between 1807 and 1810 each year fewer grass-mowers found employment in the North Sea System; the drop, in fact, was more than 50 per cent in six of the eight locations included in the table. Letters from a number of *maires* in the vicinity of Osnabrück leave a reader with the impression that such a decrease in employment opportunities for grass-mowers was indeed typical of the times.[38] Statistics for these years from the arrondissement of Roermond, and from the canton of Roermond as well, reveal a decline of the same order of magnitude; if we include figures for 1806 and 1811, then the falling off was even more precipitous still. All we can affirm here is that the number of migrant workers who came to Holland must have grown between 1600 and 1800 by more than our original notion of from zero to 15,000. Perhaps we should be thinking of a maximum closer to 30,000 workers.

Transport of Migrant Workers Across the Zuiderzee, 1600-1800
For this period, as pointed out above, we have no census or

registration of migrant workers to rely on. Reconstruction of the development of migratory labour based exclusively on limited, random information is unsatisfactory. However, there is in my opinion a reasonably reliable indirect method that can enable us to trace this development — as least broadly. Indeed, in describing the journeys undertaken by migrant workers on their way to find employment, I mentioned that workers who came to Holland from the east embarked at Hasselt to reach Amsterdam by ship.[39] If a large majority of migrants made regular use of ships that commuted between Hasselt and Amsterdam during the period which concerns us here, then information about the relevant transport activities may provide us with an indication of the volume of migratory labour to Holland. As far as it is possible to tell, in the seventeenth century Hasselt did indeed manage to monopolise the transport of seasonal workers bound for Holland. Other places tried to break the monopoly time and again, Zwolle above all, but invariably in vain. Hasselt defended its position with determination; in 1728 the ferrying of workers was spoken of as 'the leading support of this city'. If we take the development of scheduled shipping from Hasselt as our point of departure in this analysis, then we must try to determine what proportion of this shipping activity directly involved migrant workers. There are but limited quantitative data relevant to this question at our disposal. We know how much money skippers from Hasselt had to pay in 1728 and 1729 to their guild for specific kinds of transportation; these specifications together with frequencies of voyages are presented in Table 8.7. In addition to three regularly scheduled ships every week, additional crossings were made as well, including vessels to convey migrant workers to Amsterdam. For all such voyages skippers were obliged to pay a contribution to their guild: considering the amounts reported, it would appear the contribution probably amounted to $1^1/_2$ *stiver* (stuiver, i.e. Dfl. 0.05) per worker, 10 stiver for a shipload of pigs, 6 stiver for a shipload of oxen.

From the total payment to the guild per category of transport it emerges that conveyance of migrant workers constituted the leading source of income earned by skippers on the Hasselt-Amsterdam route.

In addition to voyages with only migrants aboard in March and April (turf-cutters) and in June (grass-mowers), the usual scheduled trips in these months also appear to have had more

Table 8.7: Voyages from Hasselt and Fees Paid by Skippers from Hasselt to their Guild per Voyage, May to December 1728 and March to April 1729[40]

	Regularly scheduled voyages	Extra voyages with			Total
		migrants	cattle	other goods	
May 1728	13	—	—	—	13
June	13	23	12	3	51
July	14	—	5	—	19
August	13	—	1	—	14
September	13	—	—	—	13
October	13	—	2	—	15
November	13	—	—	—	13
December	13	—	—	—	13
Date unknown	2	—	—	—	2
March 1729	14	39	5	—	58
April	13	13	37	—	63
Total number of voyages	134	75	62	3	274
— registered voyages	114	75	62	3	254
— voyages for which guild fees were paid	110	70	61	3	244
Fees in Dfl.	235.50	331.75	28.35	1.20	598.80
Average fee per voyage in Dfl.	2.14	4.74	0.46	0.40	

passengers than at other times. The average fee paid to the guild, Dfl. 2.14 for a voyage (see Table 8.7), was surpassed specifically in March (Dfl. 4.33), April (Dfl. 2.50), May (Dfl. 3.96) and June (Dfl. 3.35). In the first two months yet additional turf-cutters probably made the crossing with regularly scheduled ships and extra grass-mowers will have crowded these standard voyages during the latter two months.

The question now arises whether the situation sketched for 1728-9 was typical of the entire period under study. Here again, we have only little information. First of all the fact that in 1728-9 fourteen skippers made 274 voyages, and in 1812 eleven skippers made 194 voyages, yields approximately the same ratio of skippers and trips. The transport of people was by far the most important source of business for these ships. In 1754 it was written that 'the passage of mowers and workers or other passengers is at present still the sole support of shipping traffic'.[41] Furthermore, the competitive struggle between Zwolle and Hasselt continuously revolved around the conveyance of migrant workers. Other persons and livestock were far less an issue.

If we may now suppose that the transport of migrant workers from Hasselt to Amsterdam during the entire period constituted the single most important source of revenue for skippers from Hasselt, then the growth and decline (albeit the decline would probably be delayed) of regular shipping services based in Hasselt may be regarded as a broad indicator of the growth and decline of migratory labour to Holland. Figure 8.4 presents the history of shipping development in Hasselt from 1617 to 1812.

Two pronounced increases in the number of skippers are visible from the graph. The first took place around 1630-40, after which stagnation and decline set in until 1665. Subsequently, a second period of strong growth followed which exceeded the previous peak in 1680, climbing to its greatest height shortly before the turn of the century.

The eighteenth century reveals a mild decline, but primarily the state of shipping stayed more or less constant. In the first decade of the nineteenth century things took a sharper turn for the worse. Trends in the amount of fees paid by Hasselt skippers, the so-called *Ensergeld*, which we may regard as an indicator of the development of shipping, also suggest this same pattern of growth and decline.[43]

During the eighteenth century the number of skippers voyaging regularly from Zwolle to Amsterdam in competition with Hasselt also remained more or less constant. Zwolle failed thus to make any appreciable gains at the expense of her rival in transporting migrant workers.[44]

On the basis of the suppositions set forth, we may venture to describe the development of the shipping capacity of ferries from Hasselt, and therefore of the annual number of migrant workers journeying from the east to Holland, as follows: an initial period of growth in the first half of the seventeenth century; a second, more rapid spurt of growth in the second half of the century; stagnation throughout the eighteenth century; and finally retrogression in the first decade of the nineteenth century.

This summary portrays the overall development of the volume of labour migration from the east to Holland. Estimation of the numbers who came involves more problems and requires some closer interpretation of sources. Our point of departure is once again the year of the Questionnaire, 1811. In that year, according

Figure 8.4: Transport of Migrant Workers from Hasselt to Holland, Estimated as a Function of the Number of Hasselt Skippers Making Regular Journeys to Amsterdam 1617-1812[42]

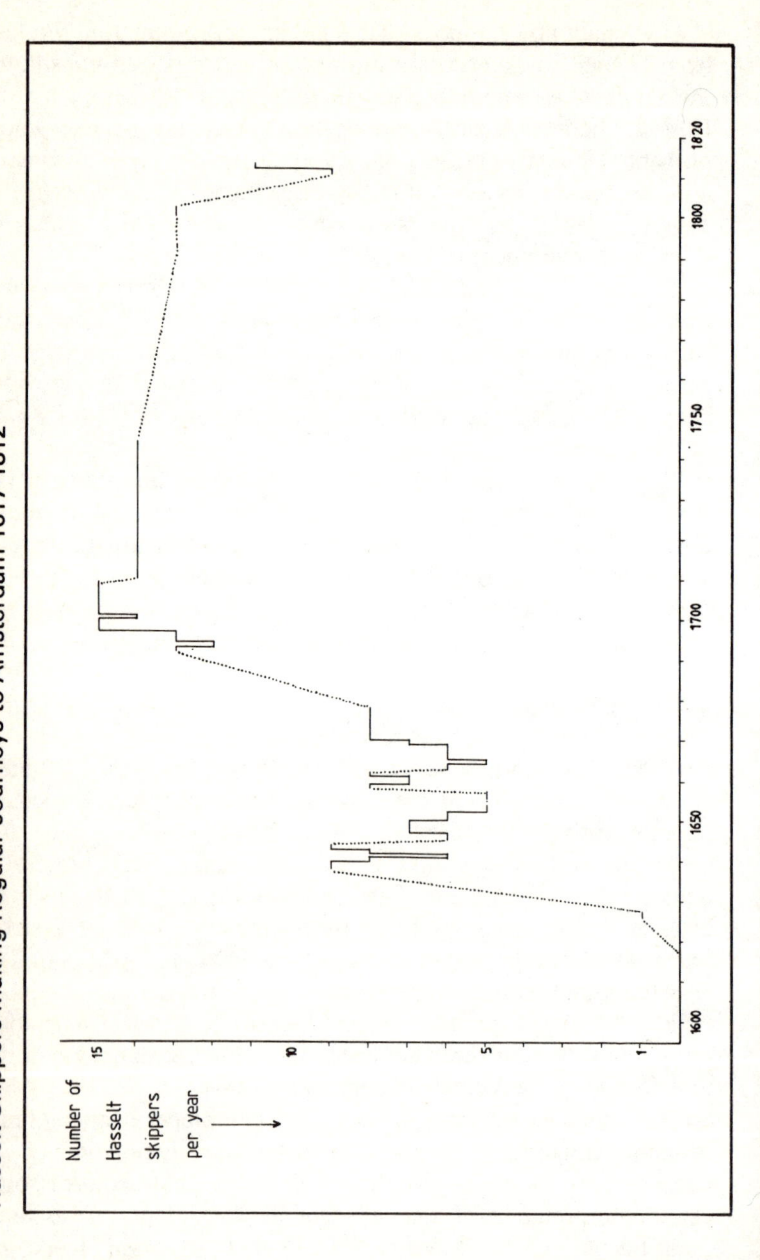

to my calculations, nine skippers from Hasselt carried some 10,000 workers to Amsterdam. Thus, each skipper transported roughly 1,100 outwardbound migrants.[45] In 1728/9 14 skippers were regularly sailing this same route — at 1,000 workers per skipper, this would have meant about 15,000 migrant workers were transported. At that time there were an extra 75 voyages with only migrant workers as passengers; were all these boats full,[46] 6,000 workers could have made the crossing in them. If we then add the usual scheduled voyages of March/April and June, we arrive at a maximum of 10,000 workers. The remaining migrants would have had to be transported on non-registered crossings from Hasselt, or on the ships of competitors. Clearly, these numbers derived from shipping records may only be used with appropriate caution.

Data from 'Pull' and 'Push' Areas, 1600-1800

We have no general enumeration or registration of migrant workers which predates 1811, neither for 'push areas' nor 'pull areas'. Incidental data exist, however, in primary as well as secondary sources for certain periods and regions. The question that concerns us at this point is to what extent such data are consistent with the reconstruction of the development of migratory labour which we have just attempted by using information about voyages across the Zuiderzee.

As far as 'push areas' are concerned, only the Bishopric of Osnabrück really offers us a starting point for discussion. Here, in 1608 migrant workers 'nach Friesland und sonst ausserhalb Stiftes' ('to Friesland and to other places outside this bishopric') are mentioned for the first time, and in 1620 Holland is first specified as a destination. It was then also affirmed that since 1608 the trek to Holland had increased sharply.[47] Subsequently, silence prevails concerning labour migration until 1648; in 1656 numbers of workers are cited for the first time,[48] and in that year 925 *Hollandsgänger* were counted.[49] The next total to appear in print dates from around 1780: J.E. Stüve claimed at this time that there were 6,000 migrant workers from Osnabrück.[50] And for 1811, culling Questionnaire responses, I arrive at a total of 4,672 Osnabrück migrant labourers.[51]

From these scattered references we can conclude that after initial growth between the beginning of the seventeenth century and 1656, accelerated expansion occurred between 1656 and c. 1780 followed by a radical decline right up until 1811. To judge

Figure 8.5: Political Division of Several 'Pull' and 'Push' Areas within the North Sea System from the Seventeenth to the Nineteenth Centuries

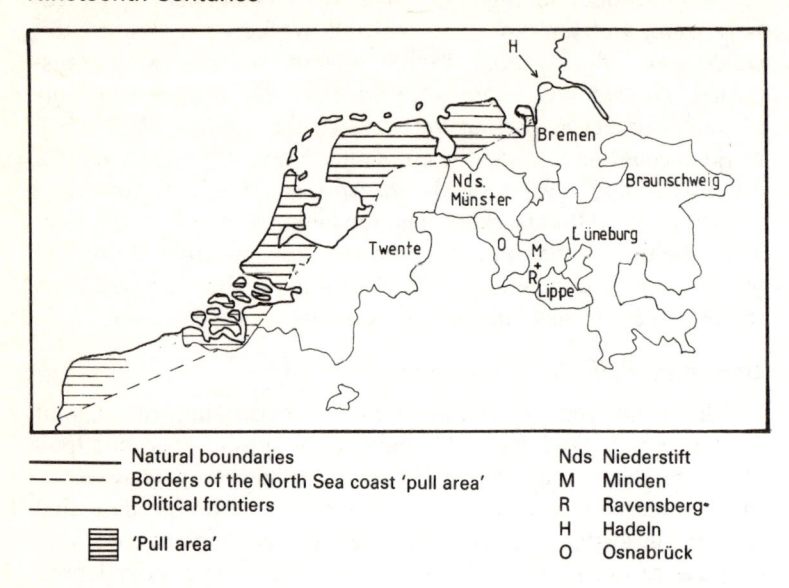

———— Natural boundaries	Nds Niederstift
– – – – Borders of the North Sea coast 'pull area'	M Minden
———— Political frontiers	R Ravensberg
▨ 'Pull area'	H Hadeln
	O Osnabrück

from remarks made by a number of Osnabrück maires in 1811, this last decline must have taken place for the most part only shortly before 1811.[52] Data from Osnabrück are least satisfactory for the long stretch between 1656 and 1780 because we are unable to break this period down into shorter units of development. At best, using data from nearby Amt Syke in the principality of Brunswick-Lüneburg, we can hypothesise that a surge of migration had already taken place before c. 1720.

Table 8.8: Labour Migration from Amt Syke 1718-1808[53]

Year	Number of migrant workers
1718	357
1767	150
1775	205
1777	206
1778	193
1793	144
1808	69

It will be obvious, however, that on the basis of this data we can say no more than that migration grew faster during the period 1656-c. 1780 than during the first half of the seventeenth century, and that perhaps this accelerated growth took place already during the years between 1656 and 1720. Nor does statistical information from other German areas justify any farther-reaching conclusion.[54]

For the 'pull area' we have only a single piece of quantitative data prior to 1811: comments attached to the total of able-bodied men enumerated in South-Holland in 1747. Since the interpretation of these comments is extremely complex, however, especially with respect to the nationality of the migrant workers who were counted, I have chosen to make no use of this material here.[55]

Summary

The actual development of the migration of workers from Westphalia to Holland can be reconstructed on the basis of data concerning the development of shipping between Hasselt and Amsterdam, in broad terms, as follows:

- growth from c. 1600 to c. 1650
- accelerated growth from c. 1670 to c. 1700
- stagnation in the eighteenth century
- rapid decline in the first decade of the nineteenth century.

For the periods 1600-56 and 1780-1811 this reconstruction is confirmed by data about migratory labour migration from the Bishopric of Osnabrück. For the rest, information which is available does not contradict the reconstruction.

The Development of Non-seasonal Labour Migration to the North Sea Coast

Now that we can accept that conditions for the emergence of migratory labour — as set forth in the first section of this chapter — in reality also led to migratory labour — as shown in the subsequent section — we can ask ourselves what the disruption of his work cycle meant for the local worker in Holland; this is an inquiry into the alternatives from which he might choose. Such alternatives must be sought for in work that was not bound to a specific season.

The most important non-seasonal forms of employment which

drew workers to the North Sea coast — usually for a period of some years — were service in the army, and shipping out beyond Europe.[56] The number of soldiers from abroad is not known. As for intercontinental voyages, the VOC (Dutch East Indies Company), which captured an ever increasing part of the labour market for seamen in the course of time, was by far the leading employer of sailors who came from outside the maritime provinces, and of foreigners especially.

Figure 8.6 represents the relative strength of Dutch and foreign personnel working for the VOC to the extent that they were on a company ship or other company property. It shows how during periods of prosperity more foreigners were in service, and in times of recession more Dutchmen. In interpreting this extraordinary finding, we need to emphasise the special nature of the work involved as a VOC sailor or soldier. It was the worst imaginable alternative for someone seeking employment: low wages, years of separation from home, a good chance of dying en route or in the Far East. We need have no hesitation about claiming that most of the men who joined up could think of no other solution to their problems. Therefore, we should not be surprised at the large number of foreigners, men from countries which lagged behind the Dutch Republic economically during the 'Golden Age'.

The remarkable interest of Dutchmen during the second half of the seventeenth and the first quarter of the eighteenth centuries in work that was valued so lowly was related to the economic crisis already discussed in this chapter. This statement gains in conviction because we can demonstrate that the VOC during this period concentrated its recruitment of workers primarily in the maritime provinces. I believe I can establish this fact by contrasting the number of workers hired by the VOC in the maritime provinces of Holland and Friesland with the arrival of newcomers on the labour market (see Table 8.9).

Given that the first (maximum) estimate of total population c. 1650 is more probable,[59] we may conclude that in the maritime province of Holland and Friesland an ever larger proportion of local workers during the hundred-year period 1650 to 1750 were obliged to resort to the worst kind of work which could be found. On the other hand, between c. 1660 and 1700, VOC recruitment of foreigners, Germans in particular, declined. Apparently, the VOC recruiters, once the economic crisis meant that they could choose, preferred their own countrymen to foreigners.

Figure 8.6: Reconstruction of Recruitment of VOC Personnel, Dutch vs Foreigners, by Decades during the Period 1630-1795[57]

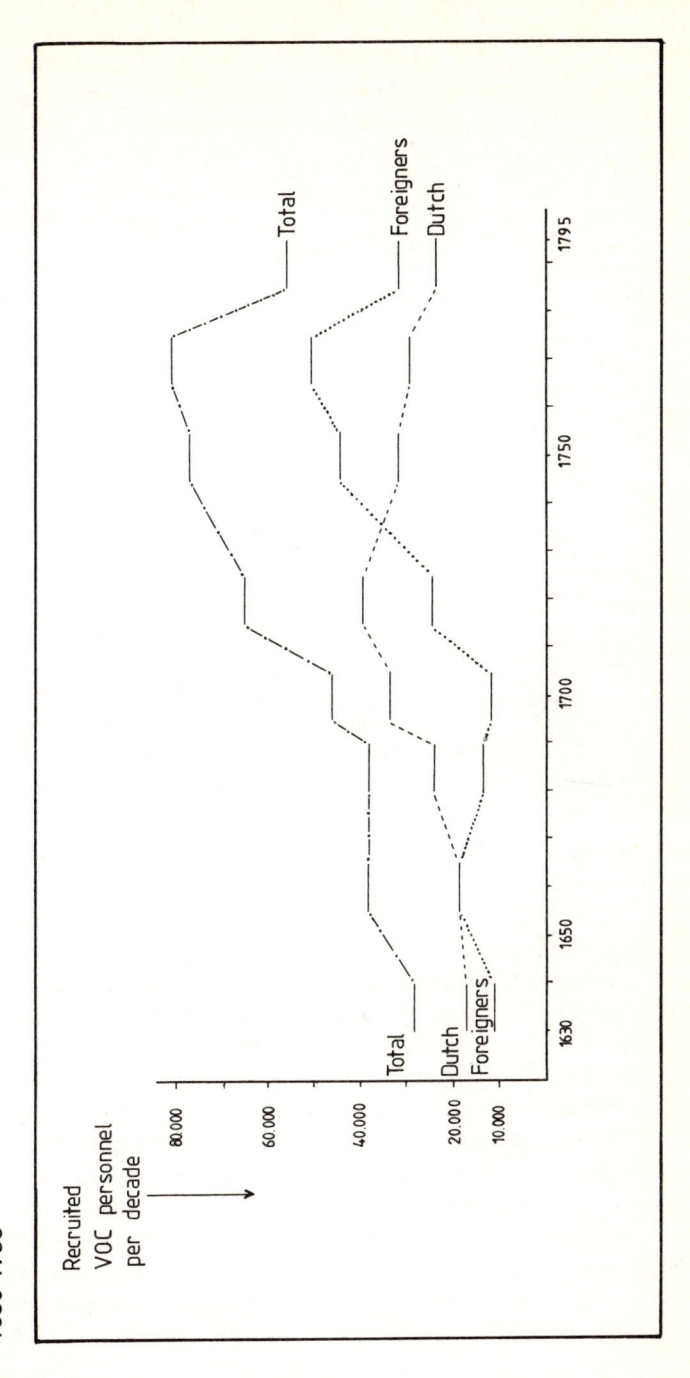

Table 8.9: Annual Hiring of VOC Personnel from Maritime Provinces Compared to the Annual Increase of Provincial Manpower Supply on the Non-agrarian Labour Market in Holland and Friesland c. 1650-1795[58]

	c. 1650 (a)	(b)	c. 1680	c. 1750	c. 1795
Population of Holland and Friesland	1,100,000	800,000	1,012,000	918,000	940,000
(A) Annual number of new arrivals on the non-agrarian labour market	6,875	5,937	6,330	5,740	5,880
(B) Annual recruitment of soldiers and sailors by the VOC in the maritime provinces	1,210	1,210	1,430	1,320	1,050
(B) as % of (A)	17.6	4.2	22.6	23.0	17.9

Notes: (a) maximum estimate based on a population of 900,000 in South-Holland; the total population of Holland would then be approximately 1.1 million.
(b) minimum estimate based on a population of 600,000 in South-Holland; the total population of Holland would then be 0.8 million. The annual number of male newcomers on the non-agrarian labour market was calculated to be 1/160 of the total population by multiplying ½ (the non-agrarian population) × ¼ (the economically active male population) × 1/20 (the number of years a person was considered to be economically active). The final products were rounded off.

Development of Labour Migration to the Extreme Ends of the North Sea Coast

The North

In the preceding paragraphs I have traced the similarity of developments post-1650 in Friesland and Holland. With respect to the emergence of migratory labour, there is an indication that Friesland should be compared especially with North-Holland. Just as North-Holland, at the beginning of the seventeenth century Friesland was probably rather a 'push' area than a 'pull' area. In the journals of the Frisian farmer Dirck Jansz, under the entries for 1607, we find one which reports how many Frisian *hoeijmaeijiers* (hay-mowers) that summer were turned away and came back from Holland because 'het Lant onder stonde' (the land was under water) — in other words because the grass was much too wet to cut. For the first time two years later, in 1608, Friesland is cited by

Osnabrück as a 'pull' area, but the reference might actually be to the German Ostfriesland instead. In any event, the trek to Friesland, just as the trek to Holland, will have started already in the first half of the seventeenth century. As a separate factor which can have stimulated this trek, the vast expansion of Frisian grassland acreage also deserves mention — an expansion achieved primarily through impoldering and improved drainage.[60]

In one of the northern offshoots of the North Sea System, Ostfriesland, other factors were at work. There, migrant workers were primarily employed in mining peat and in making bricks. The history of these two sectors has been documented with reasonable thoroughness so that the contributing role of migrant workers can be sketched.

According to the Questionnaire of 1811 it was especially the bogs which provided work for outside workers. The first large-scale peat-cutting operations in this region took place in the first half of the seventeenth century.[61] Between 1633 and 1660 six companies to mine peat were founded; afterwards there was no development for a long time. In 1673 even the independent production of the important 'Grossfehngesellschaft' came to an end. Only in 1736 was a new company established, followed by the state enterprise 'Spetzerfehnunternehmung' in 1746, which passed into private hands in 1751. The great increase, however, took place only later, in the twelve years between 1768 and 1780 when five new firms were set up. At the same time, the investment level in building canals went up: from the start of peat mining only 15,000 Reichsthaler had been spent in digging canals prior to 1770, but 168,000 Reichsthaler went into canal construction during the decade 1770-80. It is my impression that before this period cutting peat had been a small-scale, rather crude affair. Migrant labour was not yet part of the industry during this early period. This probably changed after 1770-80. If we compare the development of the population in the Ostfriesland bogs with how much turf was produced there, a discrepancy appears to have arisen in the period between 1770-80 and c.1820: turf production grew at a faster rate than the local population (see Figure 8.7). It was within this very period that the Questionnaire of 1811 was administered.

In neighbouring Groningen the production of turf ran a course parallel to that in Ostfriesland.[63] For the remainder of the nineteenth century a balance appears to have been reached between

Figure 8.7: Development of Turf Production and Population in the Ostfriesland Bogs 1748-1900[62]

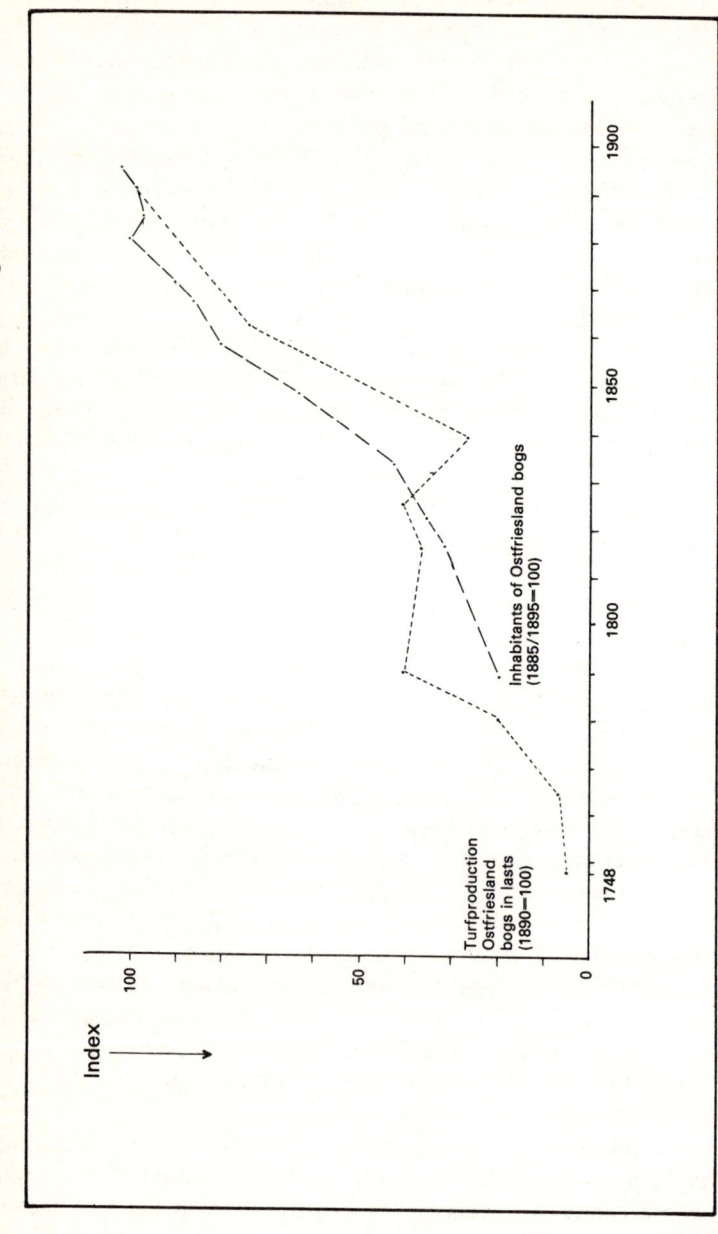

Index

Turfproduction Ostfriesland bogs in lasts (1890=100)

Inhabitants of Ostfriesland bogs (1885/1895=100)

local population and production, although a drop in production between 1820 and 1850 will have entailed extreme hardship for the bog inhabitants.

We may infer from Figure 8.7 that migrant labour arose in response to a sudden increase in economic activity in the bogs, and therefore of job opportunities around 1770-80. Only after about half a century were population and jobs in this bog region once again in equilibrium.

Brick-ovens in Ostfriesland also offered employment to migrant workers.[64] The brick-works were situated on both banks of the Ems. On the left bank, in Reiderland, they stretched out one after the other along the Ditzum sea-dike in the north via Jemgum and Bingum as far as Weener. On the right bank most were in the neighbourhood of the port of Emden. Originally, the ovens in Reiderland were probably the most important; it is here one learns of migrant workers from the Principality of Lippe already in the late seventeenth and early eighteenth centuries. It is not impossible that Lippe workers had already monopolised brick-making on the left-bank of the Ems in this period, and that hardly any local people any longer worked in the brick-works. On the right bank, particularly in the vicinity of Emden, a boom in brick-making took place in the second half of the eighteenth century. Tens of factories sprang up and at the same time the number of workers from Lippe multiplied. In 1780 there were a total of 285 brick-makers in Ostfriesland, 91 of them from Lippe; they were primarily employed in the bricks-works of Reiderland. In 1811, however, of the 300 brick-makers at work on the right bank of the Ems, 285 came from Lippe: their monopoly was established there. The rise in the number of migrants from Lippe must have occurred during the last two decades of the eighteenth century, as happened also in the province of Groningen. At this point the question arises whether the local inhabitants were unable or unwilling to do this work. Probably they were unwilling. The number of workers involved — absolutely — was not great, far fewer in fact than worked in the bogs. During the period 1770-1810, moreover, the entire Ostfriesland economy was flourishing. Prosperity was a consequence not only of rising agricultural prices, but especially of extraordinary political circumstances. Prussia managed to maintain neutrality during both the American War of Independence (1776-83) and the Coalition Wars until 1806; as a result Prussia, and especially Ostfriesland as part of it, reaped profits at the expense of the Republic. Many ships from Holland sailed under an Ostfriesland' flag and Emden became a bustling port. In addition to trade, herring fishing (the 'Heringsfischerey-Compagnie' of 1769) and industry, including brick-making, expanded vigorously.[65]

Migratory labour to Ostfriesland (and Groningen) arose thus in a different period from migratory labour to Holland and Friesland. In Holland it began, certainly, in a time of economic expansion, the first half of the seventeenth century, but initial major expansion of migratory labour occurred when the economy was in recession during the second half of the same century. In contrast the emergence of migratory labour and economic expansion coincided in eighteenth-century Ostfriesland and seventeenth-century Groningen — with the possible exception of the trek of workers to the tile-works in Reiderland on the left bank of the Ems. As far as the tile-workers are concerned, we may speak perhaps of a pattern more closely resembling events in Holland.

The South

Available data about the southern part of the North Sea System are less ample than data about Ostfriesland, so that it is not possible to present a coherent account of the emergence of migratory labour to the coasts of Zeeland and Flanders. There are indications in support of the assumption that migratory labour was able to develop primarily during periods of economic expansion. This is especially clear in relation to the construction of dikes. As we have had occasion to observe earlier, the building of dikes and polders are activities which are highly sensitive to the fluctuations of the economy.[66] With agricultural prices rising, investment in new farmland was lucrative so that projects to create dikes and polders were popular. When prices dropped, however, such activity came to a virtual standstill. Considering that the winning of new land proceeded by means of vast enterprises which commonly called for thousands of workers, we can realise that local populations could seldom meet the manpower needs involved, and that such undertakings by their very nature entailed the use of migrant workers. This is made clear, for example, in the *Tractaat van dijckagie* (Treatise on making dikes) by Andries Vierlingh.[67] He describes the construction of dikes in southwest Netherlands in the sixteenth century. The workers seem to have come in great numbers not from Zeeland itself, but primarily from Holland. Regulations concerning the earliest permitted date for beginning the harvesting of madder also point in this direction.[68] To prevent dike workers from deserting their tasks for agricultural jobs, the authorities had repeatedly to draft measures which stipulated when, at the earliest, the digging of madder might begin.

The rise of migratory labour to harvest crops in southwest Netherlands is poorly documented. The first reference to migrant workers who went to mow grain in Zeeland-Flanders, in Cadzand Oostburg, Wulpen and other seaside places and who came originally from Brabant, Zeeland, Holland, and the South of Flanders dates from 1561.[69] Their motives were explained: 'seeing that no workers lived in Zeeland-Flanders and along the seaside to do the daily work'. This need for migrants to bring in the grain in Zeeland-Flanders appears to have remained constant thereafter.[70]

The harvesting of madder by migrant labourers who were specialists had already been known since the fifteenth century.[71] The numbers of migrants involved in the trek differed strongly from place to place. On Schouwen-Duiveland the madder was dug in large part by workers from the Antwerp region, whereas on Tholen to the west local workers managed the harvest themselves. In all probability such differences were connected to cod-fishing expeditions which sailed from Zierikzee. It was precisely in the autumn when the madder roots had to be lifted that many men from Schouwen-Duiveland went to fish for cod. Nor was merchant shipping from this island insignificant. On Tholen, on the other hand, merchant shipping and fishing were of no great importance, so that enough local workers were at home to harvest the madder; these workers even had a reputation which extended beyond the island for their special skill in processing madder.[72]

The rise of migratory labour to the dikes in the southwest of the Netherlands was directly related to the construction of these embankments and therefore came in a period of economic expansion. This trek has, in any event, been documented for the second half of the sixteenth century. The same may possibly be said for the mowing of grain. For the rest, however, data concerning the southwest of the Netherlands and Flanders do not enable us to draw any evident conclusions.[73]

Before moving on to discussion of the development of other systems of migrant labour in the seventeenth and eighteenth centuries, I will first venture some provisional conclusions about the emergence and development of migratory labour on the North Sea coast.

Seasonal demand for migrant workers during periods of economic prosperity appears to have characterised projects to build dikes and polders in southwest and west Netherlands (c. 1550-1650), the mining of peat in Groningen (first half of the seventeenth century) and Ostfriesland (c. 1770-1820), the grain harvest in Zeeland-Flanders (second half of the sixteenth century) and brick-making in Ostfriesland (end of the eighteenth, beginning of the nineteenth century).[74]

Seasonal need for migrant workers during periods of economic crisis appears to have increased sharply in the sectors of grass-mowing and whaling in Holland (second half of the seventeenth century).

The Emergence of Other Systems of Migrant Labour

The origin or development of migratory labour in four European systems about which I have been able to secure some facts will be sketched here. We will then see whether their histories can be elucidated by the set of conditions conducive to migratory labour identified earlier in this text.

Eastern England

In England during the second half of the eighteenth century both 'industrial' and 'agricultural' revolutions took place. The industrial revolution began in the textile industry, which was radically modernised, particularly in Lancashire. As a consequence, domestic weaving and spinning in other parts of England, including East Anglia, faded.[75] The agricultural revolution in England meant the major expansion of land under cultivation and the use of more intensive techniques, especially in crop production. In the east of England, under the influence of rising grain prices during the second half of the eighteenth century, farms scaled up in size considerably.[76] Hobsbawm and Rudé maintain that the work cycle of farm labourers was disrupted by the one-sided ascendancy of grain.

Fieldhands who had known permanent employment became casual workers. As grain prices rose, payment in kind was replaced by cash wages, and the length of time a man was employed shrank from a year to a number of months or weeks, even to a single day, and in Suffolk to contracts by the hour.[77] The largest growth of

Plate 1: An Official, Completed Questionnaire Form for Bouches de la Meuse, Arrondissement Rotterdam, Mairie Nieuwerkerk aan den Ijssel, 6 December 1811

Note: In most départements no ready-made forms were used.
Source: ARA; GB 1807-15: 920.

Plate 2: Prins Hendrikkade in Amsterdam *c.* 1870

At the time the street was still known as the Tesselse Kade. The side street to the left is the Raamskooi, the bridge to the right crosses the Martelaarsgracht. Lodgings and sleeping-basements for German migrant labourers who came to work in North and South Holland were concentrated in this neighbourhood. The small hotel of the widow A.J. Gusteloo, for example, was located on the Tesselse Kade, as was, originally Lodenkemper's inn, later moved to the Raamskooi. (See 'Adresboekein' of Amsterdam and Van Maurik 1901.)

Drawing in charcoal by A. Goedkoop: GA Amsterdam, Topografische Atlas.

Plate 3: Ostfriesland *Mieren* (Ants) Mowing Grass Early in the Twentieth Century

Two by two the mowers cut the grass with short scythes, then lay it in swathes. They work in their long underwear and carry a scythe-stone in the waistband to sharpen the blade of their tools regularly. In the background is a tent-like shelter where mowers took their noon meal and rested. To the left, in the distance, hay has already been tossed into stacks.

Photograph of a drawing by Ids Wiersma: Rijksmuseum voor Volkskunde 'Het Nederlands Openluchtmuseum', Arnhem, Documentation Collection.

Plate 4: Workers Turning the Hay, Friesland, Early Twentieth Century
These workers, stretched out in a long line, are turning the hay with rakes. Probably they came from the east of the province to *de greidhoek* (green belt). Their clothing differs from that of Ostfriesland mowers (see Plate 5).
Photograph of a drawing by Ids Wiersma: Rijksmuseum voor Volkskunde 'Het Nederlands Openluchtmuseum', Arnhem, Documentation Collection.

Plate 5: Grain Reapers, Probably in de Liemers, c. 1930
Six reapers in a row are busy harvesting what probably was wheat. With their right hands they swing the zicht, while with their left they guide the grain with a pick.
Photograph: Rijksmuseum voor Volkskunde 'Het Nederlands Openluchtmuseum', Arnhem, Documentation Centre.

Plate 6: Madder-diggers in Zeeland 1830
The diggers use a spade with a long blade to remove the madder roots from the ground. The madder was cultivated in beds.
Engraving: Provinciale Bibliotheek van Zeeland, Midelburg, J.A. Verplancke, 'Beschrijving der werkdadige landbouwkonst van de meekrap voor de ingezetenen van de beide Vlaanderen' (Description of how to raise madder profitably for the inhabitants of the two Flanders, Gent, 1830.

Plate 7: Oak-strippers in Drenthe c. 1940
In the background is the oak copse being felled. Trees, cut to size, are passed on to the three strippers. They stand in a shallow pit. To the left lies the bark which they have already pounded loose with the dull back edge of a small axe. The denuded slender trunks are tossed onto a pile (lower right) and sold for firewood. The oak bark is ground finely into tanning bark for use in tanneries.
Photograph: Rijksmuseum voor Volkskunde 'Het Nederlands Openluchtmuseum', Arnhem, Documentation Collection.

Plate 9: Workers Digging Low Peat in the Bogs of South Holland and Utrecht *c.* 1850 (opposite page)

In this school print which derives from examples dating from the eighteenth century, all four of the most important tasks involved in cutting peat are illustrated. In reality, however, a single team of two men performed the tasks sequentially. In the foreground, left, stands the dredger in his high boots. (He stood either on a plank or in the boat.) With his scoop he pulls the peat out of the water and drumps it into the boat. The dredger's mate spreads the wet turf evenly on a drying bed and then tramples it down — as shown on the right hand side of the print. Next he cuts the dried peat into the desired shapes, as the worker can be seen doing in the centre of the print. Finally, in the background, the peat has already been stacked in readiness for further drying.

Lithograph, Wolters Noordhoff Groningen: Rijksmuseum voor Volkskunde 'Het Nederlands Openluchtmuseum', Arnhem, Documentation Collection.

Plate 8: Turf-diggers in a High Peat Bog in Drenthe, Nieuw-Amsterdam *c.* 1910-20

In the foreground a worker cuts peat; in the background his mate wheels the sods away. The workers functioned as a pair while the peat was dug; this was different from the nineteenth century technique when German crews did this work.

Photograph, edition R. Mande, Nieuw-Amsterdam, No. 2612 LRV: Rijksmuseum voor Volkskunde, 'Het Nederlands Openluchtmuseum', Arnhem, Documentation Collection.

Plate 10: Female and Male Bleachers, the Haarlem Dunes *c.* 1615

This print portrays certain key tasks, stripped to essentials, which were carried out at a linen bleachery. Actually almost ten times as many workers would be employed at such an establishment as are pictured here. To the left the 'maids' are washing the cloth; in the middle others are spreading it out on the bleaching field while a guard with a staff sees to it that the linen will not be fouled by the birds, nor stolen by thieves; to the right two workers are bending over the lye-tub.

Anonymous etching (the original edition of *Deliciae Batavae* from which this etching comes appeared in 1615 at Leiden, printed by Jacob Marcusz): Atlas van Stolk, Rotterdam 1027 III-45.

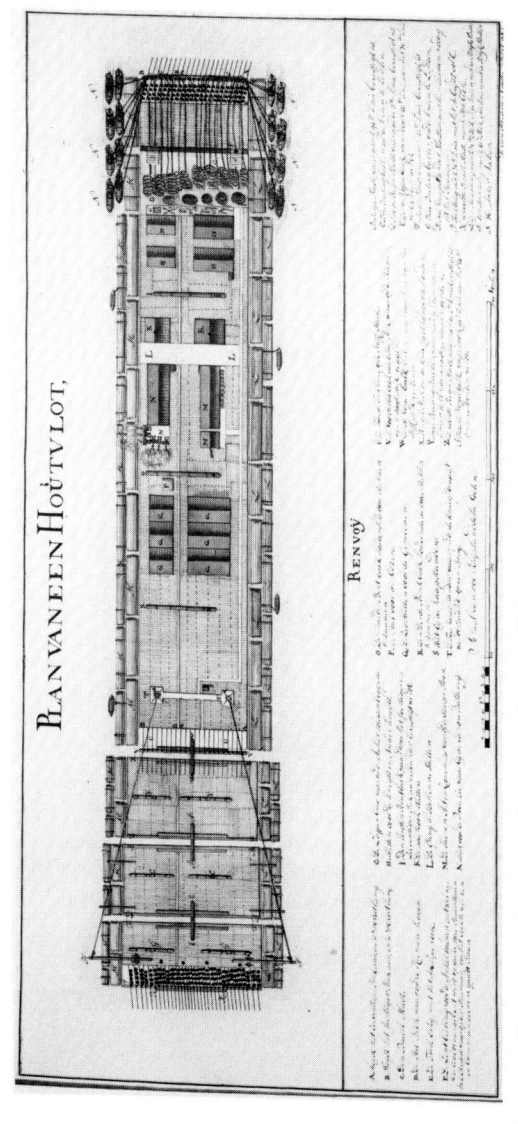

Plate 11: Aerial View of a Timber-raft on the Rhine, 1782

According to the text below the illustration, the raft was about 1,000 Rhineland feet long, i.e. some 300 metres. To the right are four cabins for the hands and the anchor-men (H); to their left are two cooking huts (K); again to the left and down is 'The Master's cabin and summer house from which the flags fly' (M); above this is the pantry (N); left of the most central lateral joist is 'the stall for the oxen' (P), with 'The six cabins for the common people' (Q) next door. Fore and aft are 22 and 33 rudders for the 'Working people'. If we consider that four points have been drawn beside each, then 220 workers were required — to man the rudders alone.

Drawing by A. van Hoeij van Oostzee: RA Arnhem, Gelderse Rekenkamer 813, vol. I (transactions of the tax collector from Nijmegen, H.G. Verkerk).

Plate 12: Itinerant Tinker at Work in Front of a House Somewhere in the Province of Holland, First Half of the Nineteenth Century

With his left foot he plies a bellows while repairing a kettle on an anvil. A woman offers him a broken *snuiter* (oil lamp) to fix. Behind him his back-pack full of kettles leans against a tree. The man is probably meant to be a 'teut' from the Brabant — Limburg area.

Anonymous etching: Atlas van Stolk, Rotterdam, 5660, vol. III.

Plate 13: A Slovakian Vendor of Medicinal Herbs in Front of the Inn 'De rustende jager' (The resting huntsman), First Half of the Nineteenth Century

These Slovaks with spices and herbs for sale put in regular appearances in the Netherlands during the last century.

Anonymous etching, colour added: Atlas van Stolk, Rotterdam 5660.

Plate 14: Mowers' Market in Hungary, 1943
Here, as in many Frisian towns, a number of mowers stand waiting until they are hired by a farmer. It is quite possible that the women carrying sacks are part of the team, either as hay-makers or binders. The blades of the men's scythes are tied tight to the shaft which makes it easier and safer to carry them. As early as the nineteenth century there are indications that the Hungarian lowlands attracted a flow of migrant workers.

Photograph: Rijksmuseum voor Volkskunde 'Het Nederlands Openluchtmuseum', Arnhem, Documentation Collection.

De Beeldjes-koop.

Deez Beelden-koopman is Italies schoone streken,
De vruchtbare Appenijn en d' Arno-vloed ontweken,
Om in ons Vaderland zijn koopwaar aan te biên.
Zijn kleine galerij kunt ge op zijn draagplank zien.
Zijn beelden zijn zeer fraai, natuurlijk, naar het leven,
Zoo als hij u vertelt, goedkoop wil hij ze u geven.
Hoe vreedzaam ziet gij kat en uil en baviaan
En andre beeldjes meer, hier door elkander staan.

Plate 15: Sale of Statuettes from Lucca in a Dutch City, 1846

This popular illustration shows a vendor who sold plaster figures. He carried his merchandise on a tray on his head, where stood not only 'cat and owl and ape' as the rhyme below tells us, but Napoleon as well. It is remarkable that he had no religious images for sale.

Text of Print: 'The Sales of Statues'

This salesman of statues has left Italy's beautiful regions, the fruitful Appenines and Arno River valley to offer his goods for sale in our fatherland. You can see his small gallery on the platform he carries. His statues are very attractive, natural, life-like. As he himself says, he will let you have them cheap. How peacefully you can see cat and owl and ape and other images.

Woodcut from G. van Sandwijk, *Prenten-magazijn voor de jeugd* (Illustrated magazine for youth) 5, 1846 (printed in Purmerend by J. Schuitemaker): Atlas van Stolk, Rotterdam, the cited book and 5852[VII], no. 109: 5.

Ik maai met mijn fcherp geweer
(Zegt hans van Weftfalen,)
Weelig Gras opveld ter neer,
Eer 't den Boer kan halen.

Plate 16: *Hannekemaaier* (Migrant German Mower), of the End of the Eighteenth Century

The Hannekemaaier in this primitive children's illustration holds a kind of scythe in both hands. The poetic text involves punning on a popular idea about the etymology o the word hannekemaaier, that it was derived from the name Hans. Indeed, the phrase *scherp geweer* (sharp weapon) in combination with Westphalia is reminiscent of Lucas Rotgans' poem from 1715 mentioned earlier in the text.

Text of Print:

With my sharp weapon I mow down the abundant grass, says Hans of Westphalia, before the farmer brings it in.

Woodcut, detail of children's print no. 103, from J.C. Vaarberg of Weesp, entitled *Der Boeren en der Herdren leven* (Lives of farmers and shepherds), distributor J. Noman of Zaltbommel: Atlas van Stolk, Rotterdam, 5857a.

Plate 17: The 'Kamper Steiger' (Kampen Jetty) in Amsterdam, Seen from the Nieuwe Brug *c.* 1765

Here ships anchored, including those from Hasselt, which according to schedule sailed back and forth from Amsterdam over the Zuiderzee to ports in Overijssel and Friesland.

Engraving by H. Schoute in *Nieuwe atlas van de voornaamste gebouwen,* published by Changuion and P. den Hengst 1783 (Fouquet) no. 40: GA Amsterdam, Topografische Atlas.

Plate 18: Savoyards in Rotterdam, Second Half of the Eighteenth Century
This engraving for children shows a boy with a guinea pig (left), and a man with an organ hanging against his stomach and a *camera obscura* on his back (right). According to the poem printed beneath the illustration, the man would be invited to enter peoples' homes. For Savoyards with such occupations, cf. Appendix 2.3.

Coloured woodcut, signed H. Numan (at work in Amsterdam, 1759-88), distributors Gebrs. Van Kapel, Rijswijk: Atlas van Stolk, Rotterdam, 5830 [VIII] h.

Plate 19: *Hannekemaaiers* Under Way, Friesland, 1896

These three men are probably grass-mowers ('mieren', 'ants') from Ostfriesland or Aschendorf *en route* to their work in Friesland. Pastel drawing by C.W. Allers; according to the original owners of the drawing the artist, originally from Hamburg, was staying in Friesland when he sketched this group portrait.

Rijksmuseum voor Volkskunde 'Het Nederlands Openluchtmuseum', Arnhem, Print Collection.

Plate 20: Polish 'Beet-Girls' in the Fields of Søby Søgård on Funen Island, Denmark, in the Spring of 1913

The women, dressed in their own native clothing, hold weeding-hooks in their right hands, which they used to thin out the sugar-beet. At least one of them worked in bare feet. According to Nellemann, the face of the Danish foreman was intentionally blotted out because he was unpopular. (Nellemann 1981: 69.)

Photograph: Nationalmuseet, Kopenhagen.

population therefore did not take place in the east, but in the north and west of England where the industrial revolution began in earnest. For a very long time to come, English industrial workers there continued to combine work at the loom with chores on the land during harvest peaks.[78] In the west, to be sure, in addition to crop farming there was a great deal of animal husbandry. The combination of industry, crops and livestock in the middle and northwest of England explains why with respect to migratory labour these places remained 'neutral areas'.[79]

We can thus posit that in the northwest of England the work cycle was enriched, while in the east of England it became doubly impoverished — through the demise of domestic industry and, above all, through the mounting economic difficulties of small farms. The urgent seasonal demand for grass-mowers in the east was met by Irish migrants;[80] and this trek for the Irish came into its own in the second half of the eighteenth century. That it was the Irish from the western counties in Connacht who were in a position to absorb migratory labour to eastern England into their work cycle can be explained by the nature of the many small farms in the region. As a result of the introduction of potatoes in Connacht, such small farms quickly multiplied; the Irish population practically tripled between 1785 and 1841.

The Paris Basin

Less is known about the emergence of labour migration to the Paris Basin in order to assist with the grain harvest; its origins can be dated at the end of the sixteenth or beginning of the seventeenth century, according to a study by Jacquart.[81]

By studying the development of Hurepoix, the area due south of Paris, Jacquart establishes that as a consequence of the rise of grain prices in the second half of the sixteenth and the first decades of the seventeenth centuries, there took place a strong expansion of medium-large and very large farms where grain was raised exclusively. At the same time, especially in the west of this area, small wine-growers and *manouvriers* disappeared. This last group combined a small vineyard with domestic production of cloth and with working in the fields of large farmers during the summer harvest months. In connection with the religious wars of the later sixteenth century and the changing relation of grain and wine prices — grain steadily gaining in value — the position of many of these small labourers became untenable and they departed in large numbers. Whole hamlets disappeared or were absorbed into a single, vast farm. A slight recovery in the early decades of the seventeenth century was once again followed by devastation during the Fronde (1648-53) and later years.

The citizens of the city of Paris reaped the most benefits from such dispossession and concentration; either city dwellers managed to acquire country property, or large landowners from Hurepoix moved to the capital. The village of Avrainville in 1688 offers us a clear example of the processes at work.[82] Of the total 650 to 700 ha which the village held, four farms owned 460 of them. Then, trailing far behind the giants, there were five farms, each with an average of 10 ha, and three others with 6 to 9 ha. For the rest, the village was inhabited by 21 *manouvriers*, 2 *jardiniers*, 4 *artisans*, only one wine-grower and a number of widows. It would scarcely have been possible for these 21 workers, even assisted by gardeners and craftsmen, women and children, to bring in the harvest of the four 'coqs du village' on time. To accomplish this, many seasonal workers from elsewhere were required.

Jacquart refers to seasonal workers for the first time in 1612; they came from La Perche (in what later became the départements of Orne and Eure et Loire) to harvest grain. From marriages and persons left behind Jacquart concludes that the migration of workers from the west had already begun during the final decade of the sixteenth century, and since that time had continued without interruption. As late as 1811 a large part of the migrant workforce recruited for the Paris Basin came from these same places.[83]

During the Napoleonic era far larger numbers of migrant workers came from the Massif Central to the Paris Basin. The first who came, at the start of the seventeenth century, were masons from Limousin. A more sizable trek from this region should probably be dated sometime early in the eighteenth century. At this time in Auvergne land holdings were being split into smaller and smaller farms and the price of land rental was rising.[84] In the second half of the eighteenth century and especially post-1770 when wine prices plummeted, the terms of trade deteriorated to the disadvantage of places in this region: the prices of local products, especially livestock and wine, went down, but the price of grain, not cultivated in the Massif Central in sufficient supply, went up.[85]

In 1770 the potato came to Auvergne. According to Le Roy Ladurie, this innovation was not confined to Auvergne, but was introduced in Gascogny and Haut Languedoc as well.[86] Perhaps from these pieces of information we may conclude that the rising grain prices of the sixteenth and early seventeenth centuries culminated finally in the concentration of land ownership, the advancement of grain cultivation and the depopulation of the Paris Basin. As a result, migratory labour started up out of the west of France. In the next period of climbing grain prices, the second half of the eighteenth century, migrant workers in large numbers also began to pour out of Auvergne. In both instances we can establish a deterioration of the terms of trade of 'push areas' with respect to 'pull areas'.

Castile

Although the trek of Galicians to Castile can be documented as early as *c.* 1710, major expansion of this migration took place only much later.[87] It is significant that in 1761 a law was enacted in which it was forbidden thereafter to interfere with migrant workers on their way from Galicia to Castile and to impress them into the army. These migrant workers also acquired explicit permission to have their wives, sons and daughters accompany them.[88] The interests of the grain harvest in Castile thus superseded those of the army.

Galicia, just as the 'push areas' of the Paris Basin, also witnessed a deterioration in the terms of trade during the second half of the eighteenth century: the price of local goods, such as livestock produce, wine and fish, declined, while the price of grain — which had to be imported in large quantities — rose.[89] The consequences of this shift for the diet of the Galician population have already been discussed (p. 115). Mounting grain prices and, in response, expanded grain production in Castile, coupled with deterioration of the terms of trade in grain-importing Galicia, probably stimulated the '*golondrina*', migratory labour between these two areas.

The Po Valley

At the end of the eighteenth century rice, already cultivated for centuries, gained greatly in desirability as a result of the rising price of grain. Vineyards on the other hand, especially small ones, were put under pressure because at this same time the price of wine kept falling. On the one hand small, specialised wine-growers saw their position eroded;[90] on the other hand, investors who lived in the cities forged ahead with enlarging farms planted in grain and rice. Sharecropping, or *mezzadria*, where a labourer who rented land exchanged half his harvest for seed and tools, was abandoned as widely as possible. Large landowners preferred to hire their workers instead.[91] The consequence was a decline in population because there was no longer work to do the whole year round. Davico, who confirms such a population decrease between 1789 and 1806, attributes it primarily to the high mortality rate, especially in rice-growing areas; he cites a report from the Société d'Agriculture of the département of Sésia: 'Il paraît que les rizières devraient dévorer la population entière dans l'espace de deux siècles' (It looks as though the rice fields swallowed the whole population in the span of two centuries).[92]

Here too we can observe an increasing gap between the price of grain and other commodities, the so-called 'scissors-effect'. Plains where grain was cultivated were drained of population by the concentration of farmland in a few hands, and mountain dwellers, who depended in part on the cultivation of grapes, were keen to discover ways to supplement their income.

Migrant Workers and Drifters

In connection with the developments described above, we should also reconsider our thinking about the phenomenon of drifters. These were reported not only in northern Italy, but also in France and England.[93] Such figures did not move back and forth between clear-cut 'push areas' and 'pull areas'; instead they seemed to have earned their living without any place of permanent residence, in part by begging and in part by helping with the harvest during seasonal peaks.

When we discussed ground-workers in the North Sea System above, we noted that some remained on the work site throughout the winter; these too were drifters of a sort — a phenomenon probably vastly exaggerated by moralistic writers of the nineteenth century, and by later commentators. The existence of such wandering groups is undeniable, but it is unlikely that they originated from the mountains or from other poor regions as has been suggested. They should therefore not be mentioned together in the same breath with migrant workers without further qualification.[94] Probably they were expelled from more prosperous areas as the result of the scaling-up of farms that went hand in hand with the introduction of capitalistic monocropping. Some lost their own farms, others could only find work locally during the peak summer season and were obliged for the rest of the year to seek some other way to subsist.

Thus, Collins is convinced that the large number of Scottish drifters did not originate from the Highlands, the traditional home of migrant workers.[95] He makes no explicit remarks concerning the precise places of origin of the tens of thousands of Irish 'navvies' about whom he writes, but in this context it is certainly striking that the pronounced fall in population registered in Ireland during the nineteenth century did not occur in that part of Connacht from which the majority of migrant workers came. In precisely this area the population managed to remain stable, even in the wake of famine, and landholdings necessarily continued to be divided into ever smaller units. The change in population was centred in the fertile middle and east of Ireland. It was indeed *to* part of this region, to the counties of Limerick, Clare, Tipperary and the north of Cork, that thousands came to find work — migrant workers from the poor areas of Kerry, Cork and Galway.[96] It appears, although more research on this topic is desirable, that the depopulation of a region may be accompanied by the attraction of migrant workers. In this instance, local workers may be worse off than migrant ones.[97] This holds true as well for industrial areas in England from which many drifters also have originated during periods of economic recession.[98]

Migratory Labour and Economic Fluctuations, 1600-1800

In the introduction to Part III conditions for the rise of migratory labour were summed up — in hypothetical fashion. On a basis of the discussion in Part II, the first two conditions specified — a free labour market and a negotiable travel distance — could in fact be considered to have already been met in the region under study during the seventeenth and eighteenth centuries.

The last two conditions — the simultaneous demand for seasonal work elsewhere in a 'push area' and for seasonal workers in a 'pull area' — also appear to have been fulfilled in the English, French, Spanish and Italian systems of migratory labour here reviewed. In the Introduction the possibility was also raised that a number of conditions could be fulfilled at the same time under the influence of what may be regarded as an external factor. From the preceding text it has become clear that long-term shifts in prices may have indeed exercised just such an influence.

Since Simiand's research in the 1930s, economic historians have distinguished long-term price movements (*secular trends*). According to this concept, prices and population figures have a tendency to develop in a specific, predictable fashion: first they rise together and then they fall together, successive upward or downward trends, lasting a century or more, alternate in succession.[99] For the years with which we are concerned, a positive secular trend (secular = approximately a century long) has been identified stretching from the end of the fifteenth century until c. 1650 (also called the Age of the Price Revolution) followed by a negative secular trend spanning the hundred years c. 1650 to c. 1750 (also called the Crisis of the Seventeenth Century), followed in turn by an upswing again which began c. 1750 and lasted at least until the end of the Napoleonic wars.

A basic characteristic of these long-term fluctuations is an inverse relation between the price of grain and the prices of other products. This derives from the fact that for the majority of the population during the *ancien régime* budgets were so tight that any increase in the price of grain — pre-eminently the staple food of the lower classes — meant that immediately people could afford to purchase less of other products. In such a case the demand fell, for example, for livestock products and wine. This limited spending capacity that prevailed during the *ancien régime* had as its consequence the 'scissors-effect' on prices established above.

Given that most 'push areas' described were characteristically short of grain, and indeed specialised in other products, in these places during periods of rising grain prices a need arose to find sources of supplementary income, for example, in the form of outside employment. At the same time in 'pull areas' the cultivation of grain as monoculture was vigorously expanded. On the one hand, this caused depopulation, and on the other, a yet stronger seasonal demand for labour at harvest time.

In eastern England, the grain-growing region of the Paris Basin, Castile and the Po Valley, this link between the 'scissors-effect' of rising grain prices and the falling prices of other commodities on the one hand, and on the other, the emergence of migratory labour indeed seems credible. For the North Sea System, however, there exists no such unambiguous connection. An explanation for this fact must be sought in the enormous variety of sectors within which migrant workers found jobs along the North Sea coast. Different sectors reacted differently to economic fluctuations.

Major infrastructural projects, for example, brick-works in Ostfriesland and grain cultivation in Zeeland-Flanders, responded consistently with what happened elsewhere in Europe. For other sectors the connection was more complicated. In any event things were not nearly so simple that the centre of the North Sea coast, an area specialised in the production of commodities other than grain, experienced unqualified prosperity at times of falling grain prices. The successful mercantile policy of other major European states, jealous of the power and wealth of the tiny Republic, was already in itself sufficient to prevent this.

In particular, the seasonal migration of workers to the grasslands of Holland, above all prior to 1650, presents us with analytic difficulties — for this and other reasons. This trek has already been described as being far less the consequence of rapidly expanding job opportunities in a 'pull area' than the result of the decline of the local workforce. If we consider that this grassland was indeed a 'push area' prior to *c.* 1650 — with workers departing particularly to find jobs on public works projects, so sensitive to economic fluctuations — then the succeeding crisis in the work cycle of the migrant worker from North Holland does fit in with the scheme of declining prices and its repercussions. The subsequent attraction of workers to places which previously were 'push areas', however, must consequently be interpreted as a secondary effect.

It is perhaps in order to point out here that through detailed examination of the labour market in Holland it has been possible to avoid too easy a coupling of the secular trend and the rise and fall of the labour migration systems. We have been able to devote far less attention to other systems than to the North Sea System. We should therefore not exclude the possibility that further, more detailed study of other systems would also reveal a more complicated relation between long-term price movements, such as the secular trend, and the migration of workers.

9 THE DEMISE OF THE NORTH SEA SYSTEM AND CHANGES IN OTHER EUROPEAN SYSTEMS OF MIGRATORY LABOUR

Should my hypotheses be accurate concerning the constellation of conditions that must exist in order for a system of migratory labour to emerge, then the later cessation of such a system should also be explicable in terms of the disappearance of one or more of these conditions. What changes among the conditions necessary for the continuation of the North Sea System, for example, can account for the disappearance of this system in the second half of the nineteenth and first half of the twentieth centuries? We can omit several of these conditions from consideration: there is no trace, for example, of any essential change in the free-market system; nor can travelling distances — i.e, obstruction of traditional routes between 'push' and 'pull' areas — contribute to our understanding of the system's decline. Indeed, as will appear below, in this period potential migrants enjoyed much greater latitude of movement. Thus, I shall concentrate on other, remaining conditions, the modification of which may help to clarify why a system of migratory labour comes to an end:

- a change in job opportunities (or, to put it more generally, new ways to earn sufficient income) within 'push areas' which makes it no longer necessary, or at the least no longer attractive, for former migrant workers to travel out in search of work;
- a change in (seasonal) employment possibilities in 'pull areas' which makes it no longer necessary to attract outside manpower.

This second diachronic test will be applied below to developments within the North Sea System during the nineteenth century. Global comparisons with other major systems of migratory labour, and intervening changes in patterns of labour movement and economic prosperity and recession will provide a basis, finally, for evaluating the broader validity, the representativeness, of the fate of the North Sea System in the nineteenth century.

A Statistical Description of the Waning of Migratory Labour in the North Sea System

If we compare migration within the North Sea System in 1811 to the situation in the same area a century later, we discover that by then the system had virtually disappeared. During the preparation of his book which appeared in 1902, Tack, very like an anthropologist practising participant observation, visited migrant workers on their way to Friesland to mow grass.[1] He travelled in the company of the German preacher Voss, who made it his business to look up his Ostfrisian parishioners during the summer where they were working away from home. Tack confirmed that at the time there were only a few hundred German migrant workers who still went to the Netherlands. These men originated from the south of Ostfriesland and the region of the Ems further south. Around 1900 there was also some migration, as will be demonstrated below, from the sandy regions of the Netherlands to the North Sea coast.[2] This was but a ragged vestige, however, of the previous North Sea System.

The question is, at what pace did the North Sea coast lose its allure for migrant workers; what possible explanations exist within 'pull' and 'push' areas for this decline?

The most obvious way to try to trace the developments in which we are interested would be to attempt a quantitative analysis similar to the one carried out in the preceding part of this book in relation to the rise of the North Sea System. As far as the 'pull area' is concerned, however, statistics for the nineteenth century are scarce as well. We only know, on occasion, how many migrant workers were employed in a number of bogs. Yet bogs have an extremely variable production capacity so that the number of migrant workers in any one specific bog region is anything but representative of the presence of migrant workers employed in digging peat on the whole; nor can work in bogs be considered representative for developments in all sectors of the North Sea System.[3] A second possibility, analysing developments along the water route Hasselt-Amsterdam, is not satisfactory for the post-1840 years. To begin with, the paving of a road via Staphorst and Rooveen diverted a great deal of traffic from Hasselt. For migrant workers this probably meant that some of them bound for the south of Friesland no longer boarded ship in Hasselt but reached their destinations on foot. Yet others could be ferried across from

Meppel to Amsterdam.[4] The municipal report of Hasselt in 1842 mentions that fewer migrants were now passing through than the ten to twelve thousand who could be expected in previous years. In 1845 the total was down to six to seven thousand.[5] A second important and conclusive blow to Hasselt's role in the transportation of migrant workers was the opening of the steamship line Zwolle-Amsterdam. The steamship from Zwolle carried migrant workers for the extraordinary fare of Dfl. 0.75.

Repercussions were soon apparent in Hasselt: by 1849 there was no longer a single regularly scheduled weekly crossing to Amsterdam.[6] We are unable to trace the decline of Hasselt shipping in detail, but we may perhaps conclude that it remained more or less constant in volume until *c.* 1840. And as for traffic from Zwolle, I am aware of no statistical data and can therefore venture no further conclusions.

For the rest we are entirely dependent on quantitative data from German 'push areas'. Although such data are a good deal more abundant than for previous hundred-year periods, it is nevertheless impossible to carry out anything resembling a rigorous statistical analysis. Available information has been collected per region in Appendix 3. To the extent that data are available for the period before *c.* 1825, we may deduce that the decline in migrant labour established for the years immediately preceding 1811, the year of the Questionnaire, was quickly made good again thereafter.[7] In the early 1820s the levels of the first years of the century may indeed have been once again attained. The question to be discussed below may therefore be formulated as how the phenomenon of the German worker who came for employment to the Netherlands faded — from a workforce of some tens of thousands in the 1820s to several hundred by the turn of the next century.

The statistics in Appendix 3 do not lend themselves to any straightforward graphic presentation that might reveal at a glance how the flow of migrant workers dried up. We are able, however, to distinguish three principal developments:

I. A stabilisation of the number of migrant workers from 1820 to 1860, after which a precipitous decline followed. Variants of this pattern can be observed in the Prussian *Regierungsbezirk* Minden[8] and in *Kreis* Tecklenburg. It is uncertain whether developments followed a course similar to those in Kreis Tecklenburg in neighbouring Kreis Münster. The same pattern is demonstrated within the Kingdom of Hannover in Kreis Lingen and *Landdrostei* Hannover, although statistical information from Kries Diepholz confuses the picture somewhat. This is even more true for the important Kreis Bersenbrück. Even if we consider the hundreds of itinerant textile vendors separately, there is a perceptible cut-back in out-migration here already prior to 1860. None the less, migratory labour from this area continued for an extremely long time — so that we cannot say that developments in this Kreis conformed with the pattern prevailing for the following group of locations. Perhaps it is best to see Kreis Bersenbrück as something of a transitional area midway between I and II.[9]

II. A rapid decline in the first half of the nineteenth century, so far-going that by the 1850s migratory labour had largely, or entirely disappeared. We encounter this pattern in the southern Prussian Kreise Steinfurt, Koesfeld and Ahaus — with parallel developments in Warendorf and the less important Kreise Lüdinghausen, Borken, Recklinghausen and Beckum. This probably obtains also for the Hannoverian Kreise Wittlage, Osnabrück, Iburg and Melle. In the north we can descry the pattern against in the Hannoverian Landdrostei Stade and in part of Oldenburg — in this last instance, however, plasterers continued to migrate in force and, quite probably, migratory labour from the south of Oldenburg carried on without severe losses.[10]

III. A rapid increase in migratory labour until 1870 at least, and perhaps in a number of instances yet later; here decline set in only in the last quarter of the nineteenth century, and workers continued to seek employment away from home until the early years of the twentieth century. This pattern is exemplified by Ostfriesland (the Hannoverian Landdrostei Aurich), and the adjacent Kreis Aschendorf. Migration among plasterers from Oldenburg and brick-makers from Lippe also thrived until a late date.[11]

The development of migratory labour in a number of locations — especially the Kreise Sögel, Meppen and Bentheim — is difficult to categorise along any of the alternative lines sketched above, although there are reasons to maintain Bentheim as adhering to pattern I.[12]

The distribution of patterns I, II and III is depicted in Figure 9.1. Figure 9.1 does not enable us to derive any totals for the number of workers who left these various 'push areas' during the time

176 *The Demise of the North Sea System.*

periods concerned. Figure 9.2, however, is a help in this direction.

Until 1870 the total number of migrant workers who left these areas each year was determined by the relation between the absolute numbers of workers from locations where patterns III (increased, possibly, by those of Ia) and II prevailed. The increase in pattern III areas — at least as far as the trek to the Netherlands is concerned — amounted at most to several thousands, roughly equivalent to the maximum decreases registered in pattern II areas. Thus, these two patterns of development worked counter to each

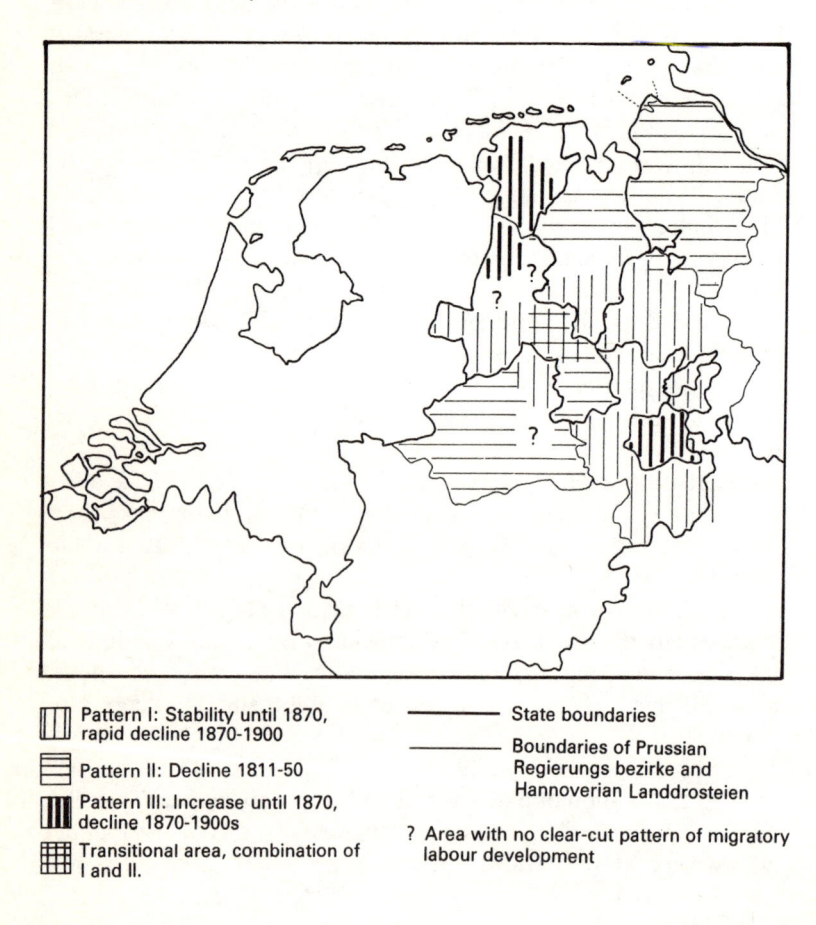

Figure 9.1: Development of Migratory Labour from a Number of German 'Push Areas' in the North Sea System during the Nineteenth Century

Pattern I: Stability until 1870, rapid decline 1870-1900

Pattern II: Decline 1811-50

Pattern III: Increase until 1870, decline 1870-1900s

Transitional area, combination of I and II.

——— State boundaries

——— Boundaries of Prussian Regierungs bezirke and Hannoverian Landdrosteien

? Area with no clear-cut pattern of migratory labour development

Figure 9.2: Comparative Development of Migratory Labour from German 'Push Areas' to the North Sea Coast during the Nineteenth Century[13]

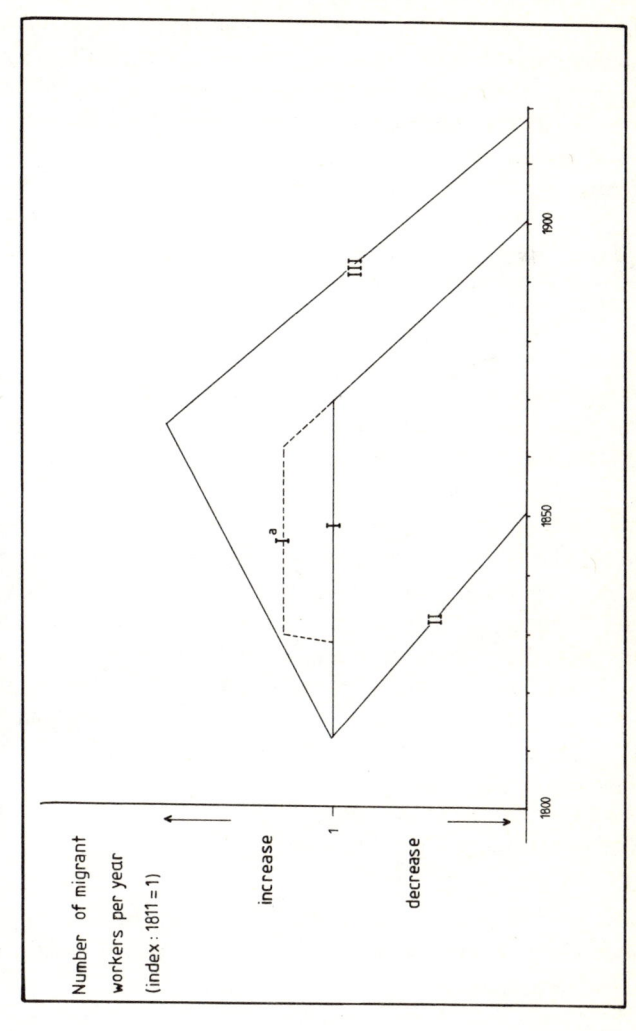

I, II and III are patterns of development of migratory labour as described in the Key to Figure 9.1. Ia represents possible developments in the Regierungsbezirk Minden.

other as far as the total of migrant workers was concerned so that from year to year little net loss or gain might be recorded. That the picture which emerges suffers from a certain positive distortion derives from what happened in areas where developments were less clear cut, e.g. the Kreise Münster, Meppen, Sögel and parts of Oldenburg; between 1820 and 1870 all in all probably several thousand fewer migrant workers left annually from these areas to seek employment elsewhere. On the whole, however, we can say that until 1870 labour migration to the Netherlands from German 'push areas' remained rather constant, only to plunge drastically thereafter — with the exception of a few areas such as Weener/Aschendorf and of a few occupations fulfilled by workers from Diepholz, Lippe and Bentheim — ultimately terminating sometime near the start of the present century.

Developments in the Labour Market in the 'Pull Area' of the North Sea System as a Possible Explanation for Declining Migratory Labour

In an attempt to understand the patterns of labour movement sketched above, I wish to direct attention first of all to events in the 'pull area' involved. Can we identify specific reasons why German worker became, sooner in certain places and sectors, later in others, but ultimately everywhere on the North Sea coast, superfluous? Only when we have arrived at a satisfactory answer to this question; can we look for possible causal explanations in 'push areas' — keeping in mind, naturally, the major different patterns of migrant labour development just described.

Three factors in the 'pull area' might have been responsible for the decline of migrant labour from Germany:

(1) the jobs for which the workers came can have disappeared without their being replaced by other seasonal employment opportunities;
(2) the work itself may have remained, but employers in the Netherlands may have preferred new methods for carrying it out, opting for mechanisation instead of manpower, and in so doing eliminating the seasonal nature of certain jobs;
(3) the work itself may have remained, employers may have con-

tinued to hire muscle instead of investing in machines, but for one reason or another at the same time they may have decided to hire local or migrant workers from within the Netherlands instead of from Germany.

These three possibilities deserve scrutiny in succession, with special attention to the far-reaching changes which took place around 1870.

Not every kind of work will be examined in depth; emphasis must be accorded to those sectors where most migrant workers found employment. Agriculture therefore assumes the place of most prominence in this review.[14] Despite innovations in cultivation schedules under the influence of economic change — temporary and structural — there was little loss of employment in such jobs as grass-mowing and hay-making, the reaping of grain and also the weeding and harvesting of industrial crops. More intensive methods were introduced for raising most crops, moreover — while degree of mechanisation remained constant — so that employment opportunities could actually increase. Certain crops underwent drastic expansion or curtailment: flax production increased in the north of the country; after 1870 madder rapidly lost ground; sugar beet, an especially labour-intensive commodity, was a newcomer to the scene. Indeed sugar beet could have had a pronounced influence on the pattern of migratory labour from Germany, but there are no indications that German migrant workers were employed in its cultivation.[15] All in all, it can be asserted that those jobs which German migrant workers used to perform as part of traditional agriculture in the Netherlands remained stable during the entirety of the nineteenth century.

The mining of peat presents a less unambiguous picture.[16] The cutting of turf is by its nature finite. During the nineteenth century commercial activities in many Dutch bogs came to an end. This holds true especially for the most important bogs where German workers held jobs: large-scale mining operations in the vicinity of Dedemsvaart which began around 1810, terminated around 1860-70; cutting peat near Smilde and Assen had also by then entered its final phase, just as work in the bogs close to Hoogeveen; somewhat later turf production in the vicinity of Stadskanaal and in the east of Friesland tapered off sharply.

In the east and southeast of Drenthe, on the other hand, turf production beginning in the second half of the nineteenth century continued to offer work to many hands until after the World War I. In the south of the Netherlands at the same time major mining of peat commenced in the Peel Bog along the border between Brabant and Limburg, attracting many workers from Ladbergen and Valdorf, villages which during the previous fifty years had provided workers for Dedemsvaart and the surrounding area.[17] In the west of the Netherlands, last of all, the mining of low peat certainly abated, although a considerable number of jobs remained available well into the beginning of the twentieth century, primarily in the bogs due south of Amsterdam. Although thus from region to region turf production alternately expanded or contracted, we should nevertheless take into consideration that the sum of job opportunities in this sector, particularly during the final quarter of the nineteenth century, showed shrinkage. Without adequate statistical material, however, I dare not venture to try to quantify the extent of this shrinkage.[18]

For polder boys work opportunities through the nineteenth century were not always constant, but there was certainly no downward trend. Many polders, dikes and canals were constructed. Here we need only recall the Zuid-Willemsvaart, the Groot Noordhollands Kanaal, the Voorns Kanaal, the Zuidplaspolder, the reclamation of the Haarlemmermeer, the digging of the Nieuwe Waterweg, the Noordzeekanaal and the Merwedekanaal. We should add here as well a totally new activity for such groundworkers that began in the 1830s: laying beds of earth for the railway network.[19]

Branches of industry for which we already have established that migrant workers were employed in 1811, e.g. bleach-works (in Haarlem) and brick-ovens (in Groningen), also underwent an expansion of job opportunities: laundries (the so-called 'clothing-bleacheries') multiplied, and the production of bricks increased considerably after 1840.[20]

Cumulative evidence therefore encourages the supposition that employment in those sectors which had already been dominated for generations by migrant workers, especially workers from Germany, suffered little attrition, if any, during the course of the century. In the last quarter of the nineteenth century only, some jobs were lost in turf production.

The second possible explanation for the decline of migrant labour which calls for further examination here is the one which would single out mechanisation as the underlying factor: the mechanisation of work formerly carried out by migrants, especially the harvesting of grass and grain, the cutting of peat and the execution of ground-work projects.

Although harvesting machines were invented already early in the nineteenth century, the introduction on a large scale, certainly in the Netherlands, followed only much later. A machine to mow grass, a potential source of formidable competition for the 'hannekemaaiers', begins to receive mention starting around 1860.[21] The number of such machines rose until *c.* 1875, fell again, and then beginning in the 1890s, rebounded and climbed steadily. Nevertheless, at the beginning of the twentieth century much less than 10 per cent of typical grassland farms owned such a machine.[22] If we keep in mind that the yield of grass rose in the nineteenth century,[23] then perhaps we may say mechanisation emerged as a rival to manual mowers, but certainly not a serious one. Yet we must still face a 'Which came first, the chicken or the egg?' question, for just at the time more and more German workers renounced their journey to the Netherlands, grass-mowing machines became popular. Did the migrants stay home daunted by competition, or did Dutch farmers resort to mechanisation only once their trusted fieldhands were deserting them? In the reports of a well-known Dutch agricultural society, an enthusiastic proponent of mechanisation, repeated stress is laid on the indecently high wages which workers demanded — the only escape from which for their employers lay in the use of machines.[24]

In the pages of the report of this society for 1862, the large-scale farmer Bosker from Wieringen describes the troubles he had with his workers at the start of the hay-making season in June 1861. His clover was in fine condition and he expected compliments from his mowers, but they only remarked: 'what a lot is growing there! Ya, I won't say ... it can be mowed, but ...' and 'so, so ... that's job! How much are you paying per hectare?' Bosker offered too little and the mowers refused to work for that amount. To their surprise Bosker conceded nothing, but bought a mowing machine and alleged that it saved him Dfl. 68/ha, or 45 per cent compared to manual-labour costs. He concludes his account with a sigh: 'Look after your working people, yet never let them put the squeeze on you'. Complaints concerning the high level of wages paid to seasonal workers — attributed to the scarcity of manpower on the labour market — were common in the 1860s and early 1870s. The fact that rising wages and mechanisation coincided, to be sure, already pointed in this direction. Only after the great agricultural crisis began to drag on did the supply of labour increase somewhat. Then one also hears of mowing machines which were purchased ten years earlier being left to stand idle. Consequently, in 1893 Dutch farmers used only two thirds as many grass-mowers as they had a decade earlier. Rising wages and mechanisation went hand in hand — sinking wages and demechanisation, too. The decision of some workers to stop migrating to the grasslands was thus the cause, and mechanisation the partial consequence. The fact that comparatively so few farmers opted for machines indicates that the replacement of foreign with Dutch workers also played a role. In part, this entailed further involvement of Dutch migrant workers — especially for hay-making — who came from areas with sandy soils (Gelderland, Brabant, Overijssel, Drenthe and the east of Friesland); in part too, although this is more difficult to pinpoint, more work became available for local workers.[25]

The work cycle of these Dutch migrant workers is accurately depicted in the following passage from 1891:

> The situation here in Drenthe is of such a totally extraordinary nature that it can almost not be compared to that of other provinces. Certainly here in Beilen it is impossible to distinguish clearly between actual labourers and small farmers — for every worker is in a certain sense also a farmer, yes, a limited land owner. For 10 to 50 or 100 guilders one buys one or more hectares, clears them oneself and builds a house there of sods and a roof. The next year, upon returning from Holland or Friesland after the mowing season, one raises a façade of brick and later improvements are made depending on the energy and thrift, primarily of the wife but in a certain sense, of both man and wife.
>
> The life of these people is primitive and more than stark, and their houses and beds are sometimes a horrible sight. If they're careful, however, and the wife is frugal and tidy, then despite their simple style of life they know no poverty. They pay no rent for their quarters, no money for fuel (which is everywhere at hand sufficient and costs only the trouble of collecting it!). They grow their own rye (their bread thus and porridge and pancakes) and potatoes (with pancakes and porridge as practically their sole repasts). Most have one or more pigs, some sheep and

goats, but most, especially those with large families, can butcher no pigs but must sell them. On the whole the situation here is certainly better than that in other places even if workers in Friesland would turn up their noses at such houses etc. You'll understand, however, that living as they do there is no such thing as a budget. They take in little money, almost only during the harvest in Holland and Friesland and when they sell some livestock or butter ... Poor relief here, however, costs practically nothing.[26]

The number of Flemish workers in the Netherlands also increased in the second half of the nineteenth century; they penetrated, moreover, far further north than in 1811. While at the beginning of the century they were reported no farther north than the Islands of Zeeland, or perhaps those of South-Holland, a half-century later one encounters them in the Haarlemmermeer and even as far north as the Anna Paulownapolder in North-Holland. This situation perpetuated itself far into the twentieth century.[27]

The story of grain-mowing is an analogous one.[28] In peat production, mechanisation came very late, on a major scale in any event only after the years in which we are interested here (c. 1870).[29] The same holds true for ground-work projects, which expanded significantly.[30]

In general then, we have arrived at answers to our three principal questions concerning possible developments in the 'pull area' of the North Sea System which might account for the decline of labour migration to the North Sea coast. And all three answers are negative: migrant workers did not disappear from the Netherlands because there was no more work for them to do, nor because the work became mechanised, nor because Dutch workers crowded them out of the labour market. On the contrary, we are able to ascertain that German migrant workers remained in increasing numbers at home, and therefore adaptation to the new situation on the labour market was necessary either through the new introduction of machines or the attraction of Dutch and occasionally Flemish workers. The ultimate explanation for the demise of the North Sea System must accordingly be sought for in developments which took place within its 'push areas'.

Development of the Labour Market in 'Push Areas' of the North Sea System

In the preceding discussion of migratory labour from Germany to the Netherlands during the nineteenth century, we distinguished three patterns of development (see p. 174) which will serve here as guidelines for continuing our analysis of the decline of the North Sea System.

To begin with, it is striking that it was in two important areas far distant from each other, one in the north and the other in the south of the 'push area', that migratory labour first ceased. The areas concerned in the north were in the vicinity of Bremen and Hamburg. Tack associates the slow-down in migration directly with the development of both these ports.[31] The first time he affirms this connection is during the American Revolution, a war from which Bremen especially profited. We are to imagine that as a result of the war and the port's growth, an increase in jobs on the docks and aboard ship offered alternatives to the journey to find employment in the Netherlands. Exactly the reverse development happened during the Coalition Wars, in particular when the French Empire absorbed Bremen and Hamburg both. Once the French withdrew and the sea was free once more, a definitive end came to the century-long trek to the North Sea coast in the decades between 1820 and 1850-60. One implication of this appraisal of events is that a work cycle during which the principal breadwinner was away for part of the year was either exchanged for permanent employment, or else that jobs in and around the harbour and on ships were also seasonal in nature and therefore could readily be substituted for the segment of the old work cycle that previously was taken up by seasonal migration to the North Sea coast. Exactly what was happening in the north must remain unanswered for the time being; for the south, however, we are able perhaps to provide a more complete answer. It was in the south we observed an initial decline in labour migration from the Prussian Regierungsbezirk Münster, at first with the exception of Tecklenburg. After approximately 1860, workers began to follow suit who came from the Regierungsbezirk Minden and from most areas of Hannover, leaving Ostfriesland and the adjoining Kreis Aschendorf on one side and Lippe-Detmold on the other as still-functioning 'push areas' of importance. From this geographical pattern it is tempting to deduce that the closeness of the Ruhr valley and the industrialisation which took place there at an accelerated pace after *c.* 1840, drew workers from the nearby Münster Kreise and subsequently also from Minden and more distant locations. Emigration statistics from these areas to the Ruhr valley do, in any event, suggest as much.[32] The same question must be posed here which we previously asked with respect to the 'pulling' power of Bremen and Hamburg and how it affected earlier work cycles. Two possible answers present themselves:

(1) the trek to the Ruhr valley took place at the same season(s) of the year as migration to the North Sea coast;
(2) one of the other segments of the work cycle was so undermined that seasonal migration to the North Sea coast could not generate sufficient income to compensate for the losses involved; this in turn meant that the family breadwinner had to look for a full-time job, or at any rate for employment that was not severely seasonbound.

Clearly, given the nature of modern industry, the second possibility deserves primary consideration. The next thing we need to know is what part or parts of the extant work cycle might have been so gravely threatened. There is nothing to indicate that this might have been the worker's own farming activities — these, to be sure, hardly depended, if at all, on the state of the market. The most likely candidate for threatened work-cycle sector would be domestic industry, specifically spinning and weaving. Not long after English home-weavers had to concede defeat in their competition with mechanised industry, it was the turn of major continental centres of domestic industry to fight their last battle for survival, either against the British, or against new, local textile factories.[33] For Germany it was above all the Silesian weavers who were hard-pressed; the vast Westphalian linen territory suffered the same lot. In the process an essential component of the traditional work cycle dropped out, both for those workers in the 'Bielefeld corridor' who, as we have noted before, managed to live almost entirely from their weaving, as well as for those in adjoining areas who combined farming, domestic industry and migratory labour. It is not evident which group was the first to turn its back on domestic industry, yet ultimately both in large part resorted to upcoming industrial areas, the Ruhr valley especially, in their search for new work to replace the old. Events here invite a short comparison with what went on in that other 'corridor' with which the Bielefeld corridor was compared in Part I (p. 30): the linen-producing area of Flanders.[34]

In 1811 Flemish home weavers depended almost entirely on their earnings from domestic industry; there was hardly any labour migration across appreciable distances. When domestic industry collapsed here in the years after 1820, a mass search for new sources of income also was necessitated. Although certain industrial areas, such as the Borinage, were not too distant, a different alternative was actually seized: migratory labour to France, especially to areas where the cultivation of sugar beet was gaining rapidly in popularity, but also in search of other possible jobs in agricultural, and later also industrial regions. The previously mentioned increase of Flemish migratory labour to the Netherlands also took place in this context (see p. 183). Although we need more precise information about fundamental shifts in local labour markets, using the examples of Westphalia and Bielefeld it is possible to portray schematically several changes in the work cycle (see Figure 9.3).

The journey of the Flemish to France, so colourfully portrayed by Stijn Streuvels in his famous novel *De Oogst* (*The Harvest*),[35] meant a radical realignment of the 'watershed' between the North Sea coast and the Paris Basin. The North Sea System was eroded not only in the centre through the decline and at last the virtual discontinuation of German migration to the Netherlands, but also in the south. Let us return to the waning Westphalian 'push area'. There is no way to describe the demise of the North Sea System more vividly than by emphasising not so much the end of the trek from east to west but the rise of a trek in the opposite direction! After the Franco-German war, from the inception of the so-called *Gründerzeit* when the German economy grew explosively, workers began to migrate from the Netherlands to find employment in Germany. From questionnaires administered at the very time this was happening by the *Maatschappij tot Nut van 't Algemeen*, we are able to follow this process for the first time.[36] From the entire east of the Netherlands, from Bellingwolde in the north to Roermond in the south, the start of migration to Germany is annotated. It began in 1870. In Borculo (Gelderland), for example, until 1870 the labour market was calm, but

later a large number of workers temporarily removed to Essen,

The Demise of the North Sea System 187

Figure 9.3: Changes in the Work Cycle of Various Workers Active in Domestic Industry and of Migrant Labourers — Changes Brought About by the Mechanisation of the Textile Industry in the Nineteenth Century

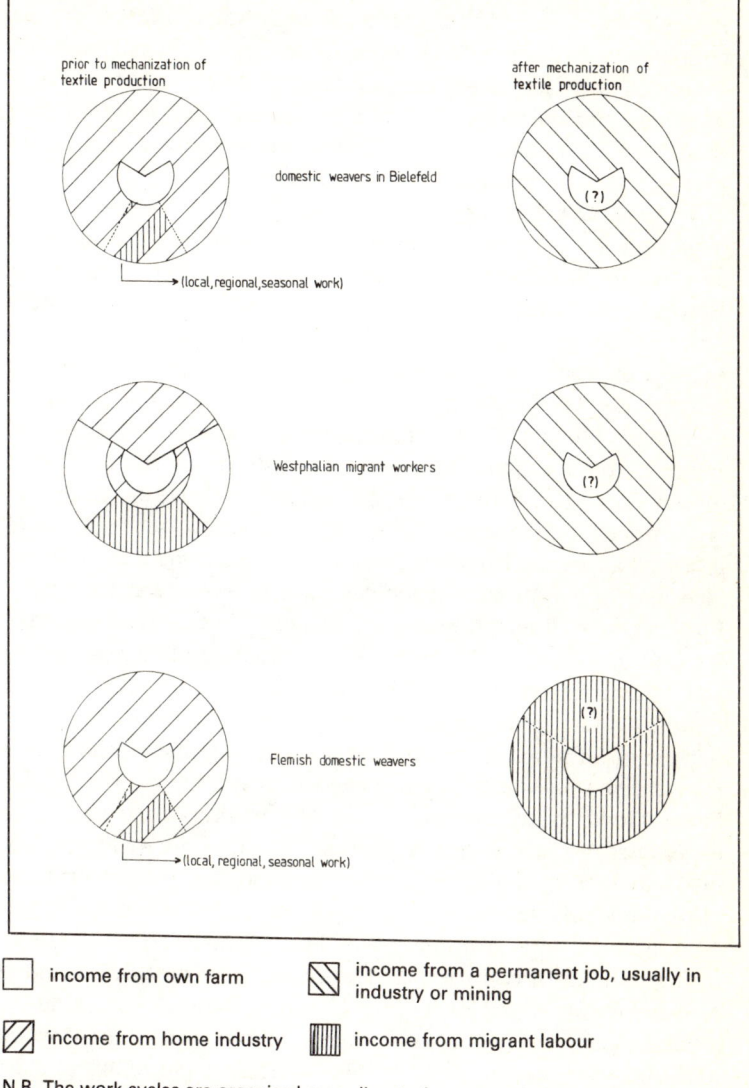

prior to mechanization of textile production

after mechanization of textile production

domestic weavers in Bielefeld

→ (local, regional, seasonal work)

Westphalian migrant workers

Flemish domestic weavers

→ (local, regional, seasonal work)

☐ income from own farm

◧ income from a permanent job, usually in industry or mining

▨ income from home industry

▥ income from migrant labour

N.B. The work cycles are organised according to the same principles followed in Figures 5.1, 6.4, 8.1 and 8.2

Oberhausen and other Prussian places because of the much higher daily wages there so that, especially in the spring and during the harvest time, there was a shortage of workers.

Deventer's story sounds very similar. Lobith and Bellingwolde reported yet an extra reason why the trek to Germany grew so strongly. In addition to the extremely high wages offered, Prussian compulsory education of children to the age of 14 played a role. Although this law meant that German children might no longer work in the factories, in their places Dutch children were employed. It is, however, not clear how significant this participation in labour migration by children was.

Despite the Great Depression of the 1880s, the volume of labour migration to German increased, as we can read from many answers to the agricultural questionnaire of 1886.[37] Responses from Limburg particularly emphasised this trek. In the spring of 1889 the agricultural instructor Corten from Limburg wrote that each year from this province at least 20,000 men and women crossed the border to find work in Belgium, but especially in Germany. We can deduce the existence of a work cycle from his remark: 'many a small farm owes its existence or maintenance to money earned in foreign places'. Migration drove up both local land prices and wages. With the temporary set-back which followed after the Gründerzeit, here too there came a slight about-face and 'grain-mowing machines [which thus were acquired in Limburg as well at the beginning of the 1870s — JL] once more fell into disuse'. In 1889, however, the situation of 15 years earlier was re-established. The farmer Beekers from Oirsbeek in South Limburg refers to the same phenomena and complains: 'the whole decline of farming can be attributed to the fact that workhands, at the very season when they are needed, leave the country'.[38] The Frisian Imke Klaver is one of the few workers to have put his experiences as a migrant worker in Germany in writing.[39] Like many men from the southeast of Friesland, he worked primarily during the winter months in the Ruhr valley when there was nothing to be done at home. In the late summer of 1899, together with a number of companions, two of his older brothers included, he set out for Düsseldorf. For 15 weeks they did all kinds of ground-work, and came home again in December. In May the following year they headed for Düsseldorf once more, this time for a longer period. In the succeeding years until 1908 he went to

Germany again a number of times to work. Imke Klaver was one of many.[40] How many, however, it is difficult to make out, for the statistics at our disposal are often not consistent.[41] Generally speaking, we may suppose that around 1910 there were some 100,000 workers from the Netherlands who held more-or-less temporary jobs in Germany, particularly in the Ruhr valley. This number, compared with the number of migrants who came to the North Sea coast from Germany in 1811 to find work, is in itself a sufficient indication of how the former 'pull area' was supplanted by the new one. The importance of this new 'pull area', however, did not solely depend on the flow of Dutch workers. They constituted by a small percentage of the total number of migrant labourers who found work there. This emerges indeed from several passages in Imke Klaver's lively account: in 1899, among his adventures he worked as a helper to a couple of street-pavers. They were French-speaking Belgians. As far as that goes they weren't much use to me. But at first the work suited us all right.' In 1901 he came across a foreman from Roermond at work with thirty labourers, Frisians, Poles and Croatians, and although the foreman knew five languages he couldn't understand any of his workers. Later that year Imke Klaver worked with the only five Frisians among a group of Italians; this time the foreman came from Zeeland.[42] For Germany as a whole around 1910, estimates concerning the number of foreign workers exceed a million. Table 9.1 shows the distribution of these workers according to country of origin.

These new developments, however, do not indeed mesh completely with the definition of migratory labour which we have been

Table 9.1: Foreign Migrant Workers in Germany *c.* 1910 by Country of Origin[43]

Poles from Russia	380,000
Poles from Austria	200,000
Italians	150,000
Ukranians from Austro-Hungary	90,000
Belgians and Netherlanders	60,000
Germans from Austria	50,000
Hungarians	30,000
Germans from Russia	20,000
Danes, Swedes, Norse	10,000
Other nationalities	40,000
Total	1,030,000

using up to now. On the one hand, foreign workers settled for years, or for good, in Germany; on the other hand, hundreds of thousands of German migrant labourers, particularly in the east, were not included in government statistics because they did not cross a national frontier in their search for work away from home.[45] The share in the statistics of workers from central and eastern Europe is striking, with Poles in the lead. Prior to World War I the total number of Polish migrant workers alone was already estimated at 650,000 to 660,000.[46] The abolition of serfdom, as described earlier, (p. 126) and the termination of domestic industry several decades later, as in Silesia, helped to swell the ranks of workers journeying forth from this 'push area' to find jobs elsewhere. Turbulent economic growth in industry and mining, but in agriculture as well, account for the drawing power of new 'pull areas'. The growth of production in the east of Germany as the result of the triumph of single-crop agriculture, culminated in addition to depopulation here.[47] In the wake of these developments there was such a scarcity of manpower to harvest sugar beet that between 1889 and 1891 farmers in Prussia, West-Pomerania and Silesia even seriously considered importing Chinese coolies.[48]

Before concluding this discussion of the demise of the North Sea System, we should comment upon the third pattern of development of migratory labour which we have observed: the pattern obtaining for the two 'push areas' Ostfriesland/Aschendorf and Lippe. From these areas throughout certainly the first three-quarters of the nineteenth century, migratory labour rose steadily, plunging only later, first in Ostfriesland and then some decades later in Lippe (cf. Figure 9.2). Migratory labour of some significance from these 'push areas' survived into the twentieth century.

We encounter the least difficulty in explaining what went on in Ostfriesland and its southern neighbour Aschendorf. Migrant workers came from places where during the preceding centuries bogs had been stripped of their peat. As was also the situation in the northern provinces of the Netherlands where resources eventually were depleted by sustained turf production, once mining operation ceased there was a critical shortage of local employment during the spring season.[49] Agriculture could not adequately replace digging peat in the standard work cycle. Indeed, the area was not especially fertile, and farms which sprang up were usually of modest dimensions. Ex-turf cutters who settled there did so aware of the prospect that to fill out their annual work cycle they would be obliged to travel out for part of the year to find work elsewhere. In this respect, migrant workers from the south of the Reiderland in Ostfriesland and workers from Aschendorf and the immediate vicinity were similar to those from the east of Friesland, from the boglands in Drenthe and Groningen.[50]

The enduring vitality of migratory labour from Lippe is more difficult to explain. Not only did the trek continue for so long, but in addition it assumed proportions unequalled in most parts of northwestern Europe. Figure 9.4 portrays the statistical development of migratory labour from this unique 'push area'. If we compare Lippe-Detmold to other German areas, what is at once striking is how closely the fate of peat-diggers and grass-mowers here ran parallel to developments elsewhere: migration holding steady until roughly 1870 and then plummeting until, at the turn of the century, it can no longer be said to exist. For brick-makers what is immediately apparent is that developments in the 1st district differed a great deal from developments in the 2nd to 4th districts. In the 1st district, the traditional destination of brick-makers from Lippe since the eighteenth century, an increase may have taken place until around 1860, but after 1870 the number of workers dipped sharply. The reasons why Lippe-Detmold deviated from other Westphalian areas remains to be sought in the trek of brick-makers to the 2nd to 4th districts, i.e. to all areas outside Groningen and Ostfriesland. Broadly, developments can be sketched as follows:[52] during the first half of the nineteenth century it was above all the brick-ovens along the Oste and the lower reaches of the Elbe that grew so tumultuously; the rapid growth of the economy of the North German coastal strip described above (cf. p. 184), with the cities of Bremen and Hamburg attracting workers with the most force, ushered in a hectic period of construction. The great fire that ravaged Hamburg in 1842 was yet an additional goad to building activity. When several years later construction activities in Hamburg returned to normal proportions, workers from Lippe cast about for other job possibilities.

They found work above all in Schleswig-Holstein, and after 1847, in the Kingdom of Denmark too. Even brick-ovens in Sweden and Norway began to hire workers from Lippe. Lippe migrants pushed farther to the east as well, as far as Poland and Russia. In the south they reached as far as Bohemia, the Ruhr valley and a number of southern German factories. Towards the close

Figure 9.4: Numbers of Three Leading Categories of Migrant Workers Originating from Lippe-Detmold 1811-1923[51]

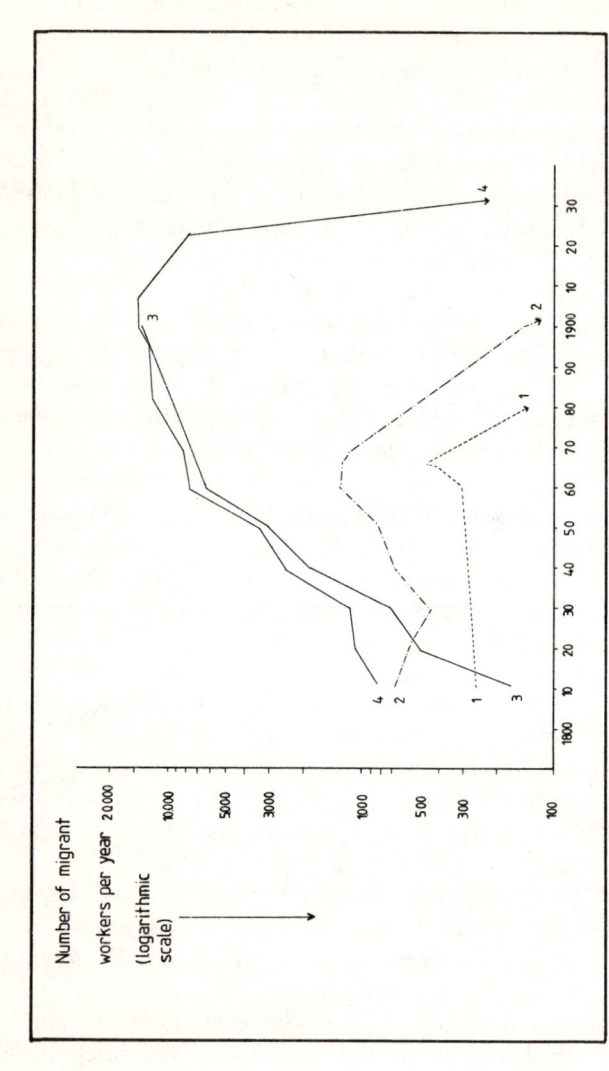

Key:
1. Grass mowers and peat-cutters who went to the Netherlands and Ostfriesland
2. Brick-makers who went to the Netherlands and to Ostfriesland (1st district)
3. Brick-makers who went elsewhere (2nd-4th districts)
4. Total number of brick-makers

of the nineteenth century, however, brick-makers from Lippe began to confine their activities increasingly to within the borders of the German Empire, and by the twentieth century migrant labour abroad has dwindled to insignificance.

Apparently, these migrant workers managed to locate jobs in the brick-making industry which was flourishing throughout Europe. But why was it that especially workers from Lippe seized such opportunities *en masse*? First and foremost, factors within Lippe itself which contributed to the large-scale exodus of labour deserve our attention. In contrast to other Westphalian workers, brick-makers did not leave home for a few months only, primarily in the spring and early summer; their working season lasted instead from early spring until late autumn. The manpower of these migrants was missing therefore at the time that all essential chores had to be carried out on their own farms. Wives and children would have had to see to this work practically unaided. It seems obvious in our concern to find underlying reasons for the pattern of migrant labour development here, that we should consider carefully the size and nature of small farms in Lippe in contrast to those in the rest of Westphalia. Unfortunately, uncertainty at present prevails on this point, and further research is needed before we can be in a position to draw conclusions with any confidence.[53] Nevertheless, Steinbach for one has marshalled evidence which suggests we might hope to find a solution for the behaviour in which we are interested in the unusual combination of agriculture and migrant labour which prevailed here. In Lippe-Detmold mini-farms accounted for an uncommonly high proportion of agrarian enterprises. The farms I mean were less than a single hectare in area; potatoes, since the second half of the nineteenth century, were their leading crop.[54] For the rest, two goats, which grazed along the shoulders of the road, were usually raised. In Lippe these goats were dubbed *Zieglerkühe*, a term rife with meaning: 'brick-cows'. The small farms for the most part rented their land from larger farmers. Highly intensive cultivation — using techniques which resembled vegetable gardening more closely than agriculture — probably meant that grain was seldom grown. We can postulate that the brick-maker himself may at most have turned the soil, leaving his wife and children to carry on from there. In the nineteenth century winters were still a time for domestic spinning; and beginning with the second half of the century there would also have been work for a number of men in the sprawling local forests. Other production at home, of wooden shoes, for example, also took place during the cold months.

Which came first though in this homeland of migrant brick-makers, constant partition of farms into smaller and smaller units, or migratory labour? The former is perhaps more probable, given that the rise of migration led to a sharp rise in the rental price of land, above all for small plots. As a consequence of these processes, medium and large farms in Lippe from the 1840s onwards wrestled with labour shortages at peak seasons. At first they were obliged to hire workers from the neighbouring Westphalian part of Prussia. By the 1860s they were attracting migrants from as far away as Poland. It seems that brick-makers found it preferable to be away from home for eight or nine months at a stretch than to have to work for their more wealthy countrymen during the summer months.

Conclusion: the Disappearance of the North Sea System

The rise of a powerful new 'pull area' close by, the Ruhr valley, tolled the death knell of the North Sea System of migratory labour in the second half of the nineteenth century. Not only did this new 'pull area' offer attractively higher wages, its drawing power was enhanced above all by the variety of jobs it could provide: seasonal work in summer and in winter, but full-time year-round employment as well. 'Push areas' that had previously supplied labour to the North Sea coast were now drawn into the sphere of the 'Ruhr System' and other systems (such as that of the North German ports and the greatly expanded system of the Paris Basin). One might say that labour 'watersheds' shifted distinctly closer to the North Sea coast. The old system was put to the test: it had to find replacement labour for the migrants who had stopped making the annual trek from the east. Mechanisation might be a solution, or the hiring of local manpower, or a realignment of economic activities.

Developments in Other Systems of Migratory Labour 1800-1900

The fate of the North Sea System in the nineteenth century has enabled us to observe several new aspects of the phenomenon of migratory labour:

- first, there is a possibility that one system (emerging or growing stronger) supplants another;
- secondly, the nature of migratory labour may change, becoming more permanent, less seasonal;
- thirdly, migratory labour can exhibit extraordinary growth, both absolutely, and comparatively.

Both the shift of migratory labour towards permanent employment and its capacity for vital expansion have been illustrated summarily during discussion above of the emergence of systems of migratory labour late in the nineteenth century in the Ruhr Valley and eastern Germany.

Comparison with other major western European systems of migratory labour as they functioned c. 1800 should include reference to these three new aspects of the phenomenon. For France above all there is ample source material available. In addition, what we know about systems of migratory labour at the time in England and in northern Italy will enable us to increase our understanding of developments elsewhere. Finally, in brief, basing discussion on events in Germany, we shall consider the rise of new systems of migratory labour in Europe, facilitating a broad comparison of the situation in 1811 with the state of affairs a hundred years later.

France

Thanks to the study of Chatelain, it is possible to present a broad outline of the development of migratory labour in France during the previous century.[55] As our point of departure, we can compare the situations that existed around 1800 and 1900. C. 1900 'pull areas' which could be distinguished a century earlier still all existed; their relative importance, moreover, was more-or-less unchanged. First and foremost was the Paris Basin, followed by southern France, whereas the regions of Lyon and Bordeaux-Toulouse also attracted many workers. The volume of migratory labour to these destinations, however, was far greater than it had been around 1800. In southern France, with Marseilles at its heart, not only did far more workers gravitate to growing cities than during the French Empire, construction workers above all, but more migrants found employment in agriculture as well. Just as in 1800, the grain and grape harvests created vast numbers of jobs, and during the first half of the nineteenth century the cultivation of olives and chestnuts gained in importance. Commercial farming of flowers and trees near Nice and in Provence grew vigorously and drew labourers.[56] It was primarily the perfume industry that raised flowers. In 1912 about 18,000 workers, mostly migrants from Italy, were engaged in the flower fields. From the province of Cuneo, for example, many came to pick jasmine in July, August and September.

It is in general difficult to express the increase in migratory labour in the nineteenth century numerically; for the leading French 'pull area', the Paris Basin, we do, however, have enough information available to reconstruct the order of magnitude of the trek c. 1900, enabling us to compare it in global terms to the situation in 1811. First of all Paris itself. At the beginning of the nineteenth century, according to Chatelain, the city was attracting 30,000 to 40,000 workers annually; a century later fourteen times this number were coming.[57] The principal occupations involved, as formerly, were construction work and trade and transport.

In discussing migrant labour to large cities c. 1800 (see p. 122), we have already established that Paris and a number of cities in South Europe drew comparatively large numbers of workers. The same holds true for Paris a hundred years later. It should be noted, however, that during the intervening period the nature of the jobs that workers came to perform changed significantly. In this regard, workers from Auvergne have been studied by such writers as Chevalier, Chatelain and Girard.[58] There are various phases in the transition from migratory labour to permanent resettlement which we can distinguish:

- in the beginning, primarily men went to Paris for certain seasons, e.g. construction workers during the summer and others, employed mostly in trade, during the winter. Wives, children and parents cared for the farm back home.[59]
- in the next stage, probably in the course of the first half of the nineteenth century, mainly self-supporting small tradesmen took the trek to Paris, their wives going along with them. Should a child be born while they were away, it would be returned to Auvergne and entrusted to the care of grandparents or other family members. Only when big enough to work in the store, did the child

come back to his or her birthplace, Paris. The tradesman and his wife struggled to save enough so that the time would come, after 10 years perhaps, or 20 or 30, when they could resume farming in Auvergne on the farm of their parents, or even perhaps begin a new farm there of their own.[60]

- yet later, probably in the course of the second half of the nineteenth century, young children remained with their parents in Paris, visiting their relatives in Auvergne only during school vacations. Parents worked towards eventual return to the Massif Central, but sooner for retirement than as farmers. One wished, in any event, to die at home in Auvergne. A native wrote proudly in 1883 that no one from Auvergne sat in an old people's home in Paris, no beggars from Auvergne wandered the city. And most important of all: Auvergnians did not die in a hospital, but 'we the Auvergnians, we are different, we will end our days peacefully in the shade of the old tree which embowered our infancy, and perhaps our first loves as well.'[61]
- the final phase, which commenced after World War I and for many 'Parisian' Auvergnians continues still, is characterised by permanent settlement in Paris, although Auvergnians continue to feel strong bonds with thier 'old' homeland.[62] Such sentiment is obvious in the columns of *L'Auvergnat de Paris*, a newspaper which this group has published since 1882.

Not only the city of Paris, but also the surrounding départements which together make up the Paris Basin witnessed a formidable increase of labour migration between 1800 and 1900. Here, new crops, sugar beet above all, but also hops, which spread rapidly, and market gardening required a great deal of manpower. The development of sugar beet cultivation in northern France closely resembled what took place in eastern Germany: not only did raising sugar beet demand far more labour than the traditional cultivation of grain, it also led to the scaling-up of farm size and, consequently, to an efflux of the rural population.[63] For the département of the Oise it has been demonstrated, for example, that the expansion of sugar beet and depopulation were closely connected. In certain municipalities the local population decreased by as much as a third, or even a half.

Traditional 'push areas' were no longer able to supply enough workers for the enlarged needs of the Paris Basin. New ones emerged. The first major group of new migrant workers were the

Belgians who began to come to help with the grain harvest about 1820. Once the Flemish linen industry collapsed in the 1840s, the number of migrants rose steadily, and from this time on they worked to an increasing degree in the booming sugar beet sector. Around 1900 the number of Belgians who crossed the French border as migrant workers was estimated at 50,000 annually.[64]

Later still, inhabitants from the area around Cambrai and from Picardy joined the flow of workers. In and around 1800 these workers from the eastern arrondissements of the départements of Nord and Pas de Calais still journeyed to the North Sea coast as described earlier (see p. 26), but by 1900 the Paris Basin had become their journey's end. More than 35,000 workers would have been following this trek by then.[65] Among migrant workers from inside France, we should here also mention the Bretons, although their numbers were not so large.[66]

The migration of workers from Poland to France provides evidence that the need for workers in this area was extremely urgent. In 1906 the first contact was established between Nancy and Galicia in southern Poland. The next year the first contingent of 400 migrant workers arrived, and by 1913 there were already 20,000 Poles coming to work in France.[67]

We can with confidence estimate the total number of migrant workers who came to the Paris Basin at the beginning of the twentieth century at half a million. Thus, in a single century the number of migrants increased fourteen fold, an expansion which was matched perhaps in other French 'pull areas' as well.[68]

Great Britain

The development of migratory labour in Great Britain between 1800 and 1900 is much less well documented. Nevertheless, we can detect certain changes in the pattern of labour migration. The most important 'pull area' that can be distinguished in Great Britain at the beginning of the nineteenth century was in eastern England, with London in the south and the Humber in the north. The foremost group of migrant workers who came there for jobs were Irish, 15,000 to 20,000 strong. As the century aged, the trek from Ireland to England grew: in 1841 57,651 harvest workers were counted making the passage by boat from Ireland to England.[69] Ó Gráda has good reasons for contending that in the middle of the nineteenth century and in the twenty five years following a hundred thousand migrant workers were in fact crossing the Irish Sea each year.[70] This surge was on the one hand attributable to perennial Irish famine, and on the other, to the ever more pressing demand for workers in England. In England more land was being brought under cultivation; the planting of grain in particular kept expanding.[71] In addition, the labour-intensive raising of root-crops, hops and market vegetables was important, although in England sugar beet claimed no dominant position as in Germany and France. Not only did seasonal demand for migrant workers increase, in 'pull areas' the supply of local workers also dwindled. The industrial revolution crushed domestic industry so that the long-standing combination of agriculture during peak seasons and home industry during slack seasons was no longer viable for rural workers.[72] In the second half of the nineteenth century a new factor meant that the need for migrant workers gradually tapered off: the mechanisation of agriculture, especially the introduction of mowing and threshing machines made it less and less necessary to attract outside help to work on large English farms. During the fourth quarter of the nineteenth century a drop was thus recorded in the number of Irish migrant workers who came to England: by 1900 during the harvest season only some 32,000 Irish workers were registered in eastern England, a total that subsequently shrank further.[73] Of course there were other English migrant workers, but we know nothing about their number. Usually, during seasonal peaks many individual workers from English cities found employment south of London in market gardens, fruit orchards and hop-gardens.[74]

As far as temporary migration of labour to major English cities is concerned, I remain largely in the dark. It may be true that many Irish workers emigrated in the course of the nineteenth century to settle in English urban areas, London above all, but it is unclear whether they maintained close relations with their places of origin for any length of time, as, for example, the Poles did in Germany and the Auvergnians did in Paris.[75] It is therefore difficult to say to what extent such shifts involved migration of labour as we have been studying it.

As a final group of migrant workers we have yet to mention the 'navvies'. They worked primarily laying railways, and their ranks swelled dramatically from about 1820 until 1870. According to Terry Coleman, in 1845 200,000 workers participated in laying 3,000 miles of new track: between 1822 and 1900 such navvies accounted for construction of a total of 20,000 miles of railway in

Great Britain and a great deal more outside it. Still, by 1870 the great expansion of the railway network in England was an accomplished fact, and around 1900 there were only approximately 10,000 navvies currently employed.[76]

Of the smaller 'pull' and 'push areas' which could be differentiated in the British Isles around 1800, a century later a few such as the 'pull area' in the east of Ireland, still existed; others, in Scotland, for example, had disappeared. The trek from Wales probably ceased for the most part during the first half of the nineteenth century, just as the one from the middle and south of Scotland. At first the latter 'push area' was replaced by islands off the Scottish coast.[77]

Thus, the large 'pull area' in the southeast and east of England, with London as an important centre, was able to maintain its position throughout the nineteenth century, certainly in comparison to other 'pull areas' in Great Britain. The volume of migrant labour to this area in 1900 was also vastly greater than it was around 1800. Nevertheless, we can note important ways in which developments differed from those in Germany and France. Until 1870 the growth of the number of migrants in England continued at the same pace as in France and was perhaps at first even more rapid; in the last quarter of the century, however, there was a clear downwards trend in England, whereas the major French 'pull areas' continued to draw ever larger numbers, and in Germany new 'pull areas' emerged and demonstrated an increasing drawing power. Certainly, while the early mechanisation of English agriculture will have made itself felt on the labour market, it can hardly be accepted entirely on its own as a satisfactory explanation for developments. Lack of clear data concerning English migratory labour around 1900 prevents us from venturing any farther-reaching conclusions.[78]

Italy

From the research of Marchetti and Förster, it is apparent that migratory labour in Italy grew significantly during the nineteenth century.[79] Marchetti cites a questionnaire concerning migratory labour in agriculture in 1910. No fewer than 559,434 Italians were involved — not only in 'pull areas' with which we are already familiar, northern and central Italy, but in southern Italy as well. In addition we need to include some six to seven thousand brickmakers, primarily in northern Italy, and an unknown number of masons, silk workers (female), charcoal-burners, wood-cutters and fishermen.

It is striking how the internal trek has increased within the northern and central Italian System. Corsini already established that the trek was at its lowest ebb in 1811, with respect to both preceding and ensuing periods.[80] And yet the pattern of migratory movement about 1900 remains the same as it was a hundred years earlier. Clear proof of this assertion comes from comparing the prefect's description of the Roman grain harvest in 1813 (see p. 117) with Marchetti's account dating from 1914:

> It is an extremely typical spectacle one takes in when, at the start of summer, one crosses the Roman Campagna by train or car. One sees whole multitudes of men in large straw hats mowing the ripe grain under the burning sun while women carefully glean the ears. These workers spend the night under the open skies or quickly pitch tents or else they seek shelter in the hospitable caves which are so numerous in this region, so richly endowed with tuff. They eat with restraint and know how to save practically all the wages which they earn.[81]

In addition to the increased volume of migration, however, there are also of course some changes to be observed. Corsica, for example, from 1850 onwards can no longer be considered part of the central Italian 'pull area', but on the contrary, the island from this point in time should be rather seen as a 'push area' releasing workers for southern France.[82] From the founding of the French Second Empire onwards, there are references in ever-increasing number to Corsicans who migrated to southeastern France to work there for years at a stretch. As the century drew to a close, the preferred route of the migrants shifted, primarily in the direction of the Paris Basin. When this trek commenced, fear spread on Corsica that at the same time migration to the island from Italy would suffer and grave labour market problems might arise. The Corsican prefect was apprehensive in 1861 that favourable economic developments in northern Italy would put a swift end to this region's former 'push area' function.[83] It is uncertain how accurate his prognosis proved to be.

In addition to these two well-known systems, large-scale migratory labour also took place in southern Italy, especially to

Basilicata and Calabria, but also to the islands of Sardinia, and particularly Sicily.[84]

Although in 1811 few Italian workers crossed Italy's frontiers to seek work, in the second half of the nineteenth century they began to leave in droves. Here we are entering the prickly region of Italian emigration statistics — so skilfully analysed by Förster.[85] Förster has demonstrated that while Italy saw millions depart, other millions returned.

Thus, at the beginning of the present century some 250,000 Italian workers departed annually for destinations to the north or ringing the Mediterranean Sea. Some 90 per cent of them, after a long or short sojourn, made their way back to Italy.[86] In reality, migratory labour was involved, especially from northern Italy to France, Austria, Hungary, Switzerland and Germany — to name the most prominent countries involved. Construction workers, brick-makers and navvies were strongly represented, but so were traditional salesmen of statues and ice-cream vendors, a new phenomenon.

Migration overseas, which also reached appreciable levels at the beginning of the twentieth century, fluctuating between a quarter and half million workers a year, should also actually be regarded, for more than half, as migratory labour.[87] Destinations of choice were the United States and the Rio de la Plata (Argentina and Uruguay above all) — usually for several years, but in many instances for only a single season. Workers left, for example, in October with the advent of the Italian winter when the job supply dwindled, and went to Argentina to take part in the harvest; in spring the workers were back to resume employment near home. Many Italians also went between March and May to the United States, coming back, however, between October and December. Around 1870-80 this transoceanic labour migration was almost exclusively undertaken by northern and central Italian workers, but by the early 1900s southern Italians overshadowed them. On the whole, one may estimate Italian migratory labour $c.$ 1900 to have involved in the order of one million workers, an extremely large increase when compared to the figures for 1811.

New 'Pull Areas' in the Nineteenth Century

Up to this point we have been comparing the disappearance of the North Sea System with the ups and downs of other major systems of migratory labour which already existed at the beginning of the nineteenth century. In this way, however, we do not glimpse the full picture *c.* 1900. The emergence of several new German 'pull areas' has already been discussed above (see p. 189). At least one more 'pull area' of significance arose during the nineteenth century: migrant labour to Switzerland began in the 1850s.[88] Around 1800 Switzerland was still a 'push area', notably for the plains of North Italy. Around 1850, however, considerable immigration into Switzerland began. By 1888-1900 the country had a positive immigration balance, one which was to grow even more quickly during the twentieth century. In the same period, moreover, a seasonal trek of increasing importance commenced, especially supplying workers for construction and roadbuilding.

At this time many more smaller systems of migratory labour also came into being. Denmark, for example: here in the second half of the previous century a 'pull area' was established via three successive waves of migrant workers from different countries of origin. The new trek to Denmark began with brick-makers from Lippe who first came there to work in 1847. In 1857 this migration reached its height with approximately 2,000 workers. Subsequently, their number decreased gradually, and Lippe brickmakers had probably stopped coming by the end of the century. This does not mean, however, that at this time only local workers were employed in the Danish brick-works. Those from Lippe were in part replaced by Swedes.[89] From Sweden too came fieldhands in the years 1874-1900, above all women and girls to work in the prospering sugar beet sector in Denmark.[90] In turn these Swedish migrants were replaced little by little by Poles, once again primarily women and girls. By 1914 already 13,000 were making the journey to Denmark annually, especially to the vicinity of Maribo on Lolland-Falster. The Poles too, however, later ceded to others: workers from Jutland [91] took their place so that by 1929 migratory labour from Poland to Denmark had ceased.

Summary

Careful consideration of the development of the North Sea System brings to light three new elements of migratory labour in Europe in the nineteenth century:

- rapidly growing systems of migratory labour compete with each other for workers from 'push areas'; at times this competition can lead to the defeat of one system, its extermination by another; in the case of the North Sea System, its fate was sealed by the ascension of new 'pull areas';
- the new system of the Ruhr Valley far outstripped any previously known system of migratory labour in the region, both in the absolute and the proportional number of workers who participated;
- at the same time the nature of the work which migrants performed changed, becoming with time progressively less seasonal in nature.

For a number of other European systems of migratory labour in the nineteenth century, the scale grew enormously and the nature of the work involved changed.[92] (Even though in Great Britain in the last quarter of the century the system appears to have entered into decline.) By tracing the way in which the migration and work habits of Auvergnians who found work in Paris changed over time, I have tried to illustrate the process by which, especially in urban areas, migratory labour as we originally defined it in this book turned into a different kind of affair.

As far as competition between systems of migratory labour is concerned, it is difficult to demonstrate such forces at work outside the North Sea System. Only for Corsica has it proved possible to show a development analogous to the erosion through rivalry undergone by the North Sea System.

The shortage of 'victims' from competition is somewhat surprising when we realise that a number of old and new 'pull areas' grew as well, both territorially and in the number of migrants which they required to fill available work vacancies. What happened, quite simply, is that workers were recruited, or attracted, over greater distances than before. The presence of Poles in northern France and Denmark bears witness to this fact.

Migratory Labour and Economic Trends: the Kondratieff, 1800-1900

I have explored above the relation between migratory labour and the prevailing state of the economy during the seventeenth and eighteenth centuries. In general, a positive connection appears to have existed between a rising phase of the 'secular trend' and migratory labour, even if in every instance it is not an easy matter to establish direct causality.

For the nineteenth century too we can ask ourselves how migratory labour and economic trends were related. Economic historians have discarded the concept of the 'secular trend' for post-1800 developments; it was essentially a descriptive tool applicable to trade cycles in an agrarian society. Instead, they have adopted a theoretical framework which anticipates more rapid shifts between good times and bad, with alternating ups and downs of 25 years each, and not of centuries. This framework is often called after one of the eminent economists, Kondratieff, whose career was devoted to studying the economic cycles with shorter periodicity which characterise the industrial age.[93]

The nature of the connection between the Kondratieff — which works as a kind of barometer of economic activity — and the state of the labour market is a complicated one. Here, we can simply establish some facets of the interrelationship between migratory labour and the Kondratieff, without attempting anything resembling an analysis.

The rise of the German system of migratory labour coincided with an economic upswing, the 'hausse' of 1850-75. In various places I have already alluded to the Great Depression of c. 1875-95. A marked increase in the number of migrant workers, above all since 1890 when the economy began to recover, also thus took place at the same time as a 'boom'. During this expansive period activity in most economic sectors thrived and the only possible short-term response to the demand for workers in European economic centres was a demographic one: population growth.

For the present century too there are indications that the mobilisation of migrant workers began only in earnest during periods of economic growth.[94]

CHANGES IN SYSTEMS OF MIGRATORY LABOUR: SUMMARY AND CONCLUSION

The diachronic testing of conditions for the emergence of migratory labour has in part confirmed earlier conclusions, and in part has generated new understanding of the processes involved.

The conditions which must be met by potential 'pull' and 'push' areas were confirmed: the rise of capitalistic monocropping and intense economic activity coupled with strong seasonal peaks of labour demand did indeed culminate in the attraction of workers from regions where many small farmers were entangled in economic problems.

Study of possible connections between migratory labour and the 'secular trend' has enabled us to make a number of discoveries: in its expansive phase the pronounced scissors-effect of rising grain prices on the one hand, and the falling prices of other agricultural commodities on the other, led to an urgent need for manpower in places where grain had displaced all other crops, whereas elsewhere jobs became increasingly scarce. The scaling-up of migratory labour in the course of time also became evident as we traced its history, in the nineteenth century above all, yet probably also already in the second half of the eighteenth century. With migratory labour systems achieving new dimensions as the nineteenth century ended, competition became fierce for sources of labour. Therefore new, more-distant 'push areas' were exploited, and former 'push areas' grew in extent.

Finally, we have had occasion to observe that the nature of migratory labour changed during the nineteenth century. Certain kinds of work performed traditionally by migrant labourers became less and less restricted to set seasons. Concomitantly, as generation followed generation, the distinction became blurred between migratory labour and permanent settlement in a 'pull area'.

SUMMARY AND FINAL REMARKS

The phenomenon of migratory labour is the subject of this book: work performed far enough away from the labourer's home so that he is unable to return to his household each night. Such work may mean a man sees his family only once a week, or less. Often the job involved will be seasonal, so that the migrant is separated from his home situation for the whole season concerned.

Migrant Labour in Europe 1600-1900 contains three parts. Part I presents a description and preliminary analysis of migratory labour attracted to the eastern part of the North Sea coast around 1800. In Part II conclusions from Part I are tested synchronically: patterns emerging along the North Sea coast are compared to movements of labour in other parts of western Europe at the beginning of the nineteenth century. In Part III conclusions from Parts I and II are tested diachronically: conditions necessary to migrant labour, derived from the study of a static situation, are examined dynamically; an attempt is made to see whether the rise of migratory labour and its decline and disappearance can be explained by hypotheses formulated from analysis of migratory labour *c.* 1800.

Part I depends in large part on a study of the results of a questionnaire adminstered during the First French Empire. This survey took place not only within France itself, but also within conquered areas of what today have become Belgium, Luxemburg, the Netherlands and Germany. The Questionnaire was designed to trace the movements of workers within this sizable portion of Europe. The geographical pattern which emerges from survey results has prompted me to introduce certain basic concepts helpful in understanding the behaviour of migrant workers: a 'pull area' — a place which attracts labourers in search of work away from home; a 'push area' — a location from which the inhabitants in appreciable numbers set out to search for outside employment; a 'neutral area' — a region where migratory labour does not appear to have been at all significant; and, finally, a 'system' of migratory labour — the combination of related 'pull areas' and the 'push areas' from which the workers they attract originally come. The North Sea System, for example, consisted of a 'pull area' — a strip along the coast that extended several tens of kilometres inland and stretched from Calais in the south to Butjadingen, not far from Bremen, in the north — and a 'push area' made up of a number of locations including Westphalia, the northwest reaches of Brabant, the Liège and Hainaut/Picardy region and, last of all, parts of Eifel and Hunsrück. In the years immediately before and after 1811, some 30,000 workers were moving back and forth between their homes and places of temporary employment within this North Sea System, their annual migration for the most part conforming with seasonal labour opportunities. The families of these workers remained behind in the 'push area', supported in part by the earnings amassed by members at work for some of the year in the 'pull area'.

The North Sea System is analysed at three levels. At the most abstract level the geographical pattern of labour movement is examined more closely. The 'pull area' appears to have exhibited a number of characteristics typical of the capitalist mode of production. On the one hand, there was such a configuration of means of production in the 'pull area' that monocropping could emerge; and insufficient labour was on hand locally to satisfy demands during peak seasons. On the other hand, the configuration of means of production enabled employers in the 'pull area' to offer wages high enough to lure workers from elsewhere to abandon their homes for a season.

'Push areas' are analysed primarily in comparison to 'neutral areas'. These 'neutral areas' were neighbouring regions up to some two to three hundred kilometres from 'pull areas'; few if any workers, however, were enticed away from 'neutral areas' in search of employment. In determining what became a 'push area' or 'neutral area', three components of rural incomes, or rather the relative importance of these components, appears to have been decisive: whether or not and to what extent the family farmed land of its own; the degree to which domestic industry could be practised; the level of earnings accruing from the migrant labour of one or more family members. Places where weaving or metal processing were done at home and generated a large share of family income throughout the year or during much of it, proto-industrial areas thus, did not supply any considerable number of migrants to 'pull areas'. This was true for Flanders, the area surrounding Bielefeld and the Ruhr valley. What is more, there appear to have been agricultural regions where it can be convincingly argued that the labour needs of large and small farms were so attuned that the only wage labourers employed were of local origin. We can recognise such a situation in Belgian-Brabant, Hesbaye and the region due north of the Ruhr valley. For the region in the Netherlands known as 'between the great rivers' (roughly from Arnhem to Rotterdam), neutrality can be attributed to the rich variety of crops produced there and the distribution over time of peak labour needs. For us to be able to penetrate to the heart of the phenomenon of migratory labour, however, the initial treatment of 'pull' and 'push' areas at the regional level depends too largely on aggregate data.

The second, less abstract level of analysis in Part I, entails description of sectors which provided employment for migrants and of the actual work which they performed: grass-mowing and reaping grain, the harvesting of such industrial crops as flax and madder, land reclamation, dredging and cutting peat; industrial jobs such as construction, brick-making and bleaching, the floating of logs down major rivers; and finally peddling and vending. For each occupation I take into consideration the particular time of year when most jobs were available, the level of capital intensity involved, how the work was organised, what procedures had to be carried out, and what was the nature of relations between employer and worker, and among the workers themselves. Many migrant workers appear to have hired themselves out as groups on a piecework basis and to have set up communal households for the duration of their employment. Readers should be able to form a concrete image of migratory labour in the early nineteenth century from passages in the text concerning the workers' travels and day-to-day work schedules.

Conclusions at this level of analysis are consistent with findings at the first level. Detailed descriptions, it is important to emphasise, make it possible within a given 'pull area' to differentiate between sectors which typically employed migrant labourers and those which did not. Indeed, whereas in one region or sub-region a certain occupation might mean jobs for migrants, elsewhere the same occupation might be closed to them.

At the third level of analysis, that of the individual worker, the core questions we need to answer are: 'Who chose to travel out for work and why?' It was rare indeed in the North Sea System for all able-bodied, economically active males to leave any given village or 'push area' and become migrant workers. To help clarify matters I have introduced here the concept of the 'work cycle': the work cycle depicts how within a given family the various jobs which members perform to generate household income are divided among the months of the year. Work on the family farm is the core of the work cycle. Family labour resources that from time to time are not utilised on the land become available for domestic industry or migratory labour, activities intended to produce supplementary income. Shifts among these various income components, or changes in the economically active membership of the household, can lead to additional participation in the system of migratory labour. In 'push areas' the work done by the wife and children on the family farm is important. In 'neutral areas' it is striking to realise that women and children have found jobs for which they receive pay. At the level of the individual migrant worker, however, research, both in general and in these pages as well, remains largely in preliminary stages.

The findings of the analyses at three different levels which I have undertaken in Part I complement each other and suggest a set of conditions prerequisite for the rise of migratory labour. The validity of these results — achieved by examining and describing one particular system at a particular point in time — is subsequently tested by two comparisons.

Part II presents a synchronic comparison of systems of migratory labour. In addition to the North Sea System, were there any other comparable self-contained systems of labour circulation in Europe at the beginning of the nineteenth century? As criteria for a system, I adopt the conjunction of a distinct 'pull' and 'push' area and a minimum number of 20,000 workers who annually left home to find work. Available literature, and, for Italy in particular, study of relevant responses to the 1811 Questionnaire, reveal no less than six such systems in addition to the North Sea System, all of which were active during the period in question. These were located, respectively, in eastern England between London and the Humber; in the Paris Basin; in Provence, Languedoc and adjoining Catalonia; in Castile; in Piedmont in northern Italy; in South Tuscany and Lazio in central Italy, in combination with Corsica offshore. All these European migratory labour systems appear to have been demarcated rather precisely by 'watersheds': imaginary lines running through a 'push area' which indicate towards which 'pull areas' workers who live there will migrate; those on one side of a 'watershed' flow out in one direction, those on the other side flow out in another. The geographical pattern of the seven coexisting systems and their 'watersheds' appears not to have tolerated any neighbouring and thus competing systems. A new element to be observed, especially in England, France and Italy, is the volume of migratory labour to large cities. In the North Sea System cities exercised only a moderate pull on migrant workers.

The absence of systems of migratory labour in central and eastern Europe requires explanation. Indeed, the essential conditions for emergence of migratory labour were amply fulfilled in a number of regions without workers actually taking to the road on any scale worth mentioning. Clarification for this situation lies in the serfdom which still prevailed in these regions: the work force was legally bound to obey the wishes of local landowners. It would appear thus that forms of serfdom or slavery impede the development of systems of migratory labour, or to state the issue slightly differently, that migratory labour can only arise once serfdom and slavery are abolished.

Conclusions drawn from study of the North Sea System in Part I gain further confirmation from comparison with other European systems of migratory labour in Part II.

Part III entails diachronic comparisons: the origins and history of the North Sea System are explored. To the extent that available information permits, the emergence and development of other European systems of migratory labour also enter into discussion. Subsequently, the decline and demise of the North Sea System, once more with reference to other contemporary systems wherever possible, is anatomised. It proves possible to demonstrate how during the first half of the seventeenth century in the west and north of the Republic of the United Netherlands, the heart of the later North Sea System, an absolute shortage of labour provided the incentive for a tidal wave of immigration, but also for incipient migratory labour as well. Under the influence of declining economic welfare in the late seventeenth and early eighteenth centuries, the labour market underwent a restructuring which consequently led to basic modification of the pattern of migrant labour that then obtained. The shattering of the long-established work cycles of small farmers in North-Holland as the result of a profound reduction of employment opportunities in a number of sectors, culminated in a new increase of non-seasonal migratory labour (on the ships of the Dutch East Indies Company) and to a decline in population. Since certain seasonal jobs remained, especially the mowing of grass, migrant labour from Westphalia to the North Sea coast was stimulated significantly. Periods of major economic expansion and contraction in Europe prior to 1800 and the relation of such cyclic fluctuations to migratory labour are discussed separately. It appears that during phases of economic growth systems of migratory labour could arise, promoted in no small measure by the scissors-effect of the prices of grain and other commodities. During periods of economic difficulty systems of migratory labour do not fade altogether, but they may change essentially in their character. The development of the North Sea System between 1650 and 1750 illustrates the differential impact of 'boom' and 'bust' periods. We can further postulate that crisis phenomena at the time of economic decline prompt an outpouring of workers from 'push areas'. Income from outside labour helps to preserve the small farms which they leave behind in the care of their families. The contrasting development of 'pull' and 'push' areas can in this way continue.

Erosion of the North Sea system appears to have taken place at a brisk pace during the last quarter of the nineteenth century, although the number of workers involved had already diminished earlier. There was an external cause responsible for the dissolution of this centuries-old system. New 'pull areas' began to exercise a powerful attraction over workers from the North Sea System 'push area': Bremen and Hamburg, the Paris Basin and above all, the Ruhr valley diverted long-established patterns of labour circulation into new channels; from the east and south of the Netherlands, migrants now set out towards the east instead of the west.

Close comparison with other systems of migratory labour in operation around 1800, suggests that in certain respects the North Sea System was atypical. At least four of the other six major systems expanded during the nineteenth century, a growth that was both absolute, and relative in respect to population increases; the 'pull areas' of these systems, moreover, spread and drew workers from greater distances. At this point, just as earlier the link between migratory labour and economic fluctuation was examined, the connection between developments in systems of migratory labour and periodic cycles of prosperity and recession during the nineteenth and twentieth centuries becomes a topic for discussion. It is possible to observe that the emergence of new systems of migratory labour and the expansion of certain established systems coincide in large part with the growth period of the trade cycle formulated by, and named after, the economist Kondratieff.

The remarkable growth of migratory labour in the past two centuries, coupled with the expansion and diversification of the 'push areas' from which migrant workers come, demonstrate that systems of migratory labour do not merely fulfil a short-term transitional function, but rather constitute a basic and integral part of the economic and social development of Europe. During the twentieth century migrant workers have been drawn to the European 'pull area' from 'push areas' in neighbouring Asian and African countries. At the same time, however, the essence of migratory labour has altered to a great extent: it is no longer a seasonal affair; the duration of workers' separation from home is now commonly a matter of years; ultimate relocation, family reunion in Europe instead of eventual return to the worker's homeland is no longer exceptional.

The difference between migratory labour and permanent resettlement, so clear-cut in past centuries, has grown vague. The blurring of the distinction is important for other reasons, too. The concept of the migrant worker embodies a relation between various economic developments in 'push' and 'pull' areas. In essence, a migrant worker is a small or tenant farmer able to maintain his farm and meet the basic needs of his household only thanks to extra income earned away from home. Thus the work done abroad is of significance for both the 'pull' and the 'push' area, although its significance in the two places differs fundamentally.

If we approach the concept from this perspective, it then sheds new light on many instances of apparent migratory labour which, retrospectively, we can see were in fact no less than permanent migration. Some workers leaving home to find jobs elsewhere, especially since the nineteenth century, have ultimately changed their places of residence. This does not imply, however, that they have severed connections with their regions of origin. They may well continue to save money, or even to invest it in their former home areas or countries, nurturing the hope that they will return one day to live and work there. It may cost them years before they are able to accept themselves as emigrants. Indeed, such acceptance may never occur.

An understanding of systems of migratory labour, their rise and fall, and their present-day metamorphosis, helps us follow the historical development of the mentality of European labourers.

216 *Summary and Final Remarks*

The migrant worker, to be sure, stands with one foot squarely in the world of agrarian self-sufficiency and with the other in the world of hired labour. It has often been maintained that the individualistic mentality of farmers conflicts with collective, modern proletarian consciousness. If this assertion contains a grain of truth, which way of seeing the world will be dominant among migrant workers?

APPENDIX 1
Migratory Labour in the North of the French Empire in 1811. Responses to the Questionnaire of the French Minister of the Interior and Statistical Reports from the Principality of Lippe-Detmold

Introduction

This appendix is a condensation of Bijlage 1 in the original Dutch text of this book.[1] The reader interested in the details of migratory labour to and from the départements and regions mentioned below, should consult that text. Here, I will confine myself to describing my work methods, to indicating the principal source or sources for each area covered, and to rendering the final outcome of the reconstruction of migratory labour which I have attempted for the North Sea coast based primarily on answers to the Questionnaire of 1811.

In the Dutch version of Appendix 1 as much data as possible concerning migratory labour in 1811 are presented per département. In the first place, facts from the responses of officials are arranged département by département. In the second place, these facts are compared with those from other départements which reported either migrant workers from or migrant workers bound for the particular département concerned. In many instances the data thus compared are not wholly consistent, but at times downright contradictory. Where differences appear significant, I attempt to determine why the differences in reporting may have arisen, beginning with the possible influence of administrative procedures. In many cases the fact that the trek of certain workers is omitted from a report can be attributed to administrative errors. Such errors may have to do with a too hasty, and therefore not sufficiently careful answer to the minister's inquiry; or they may involve a mistaken interpretation of the Minister of the Interior's intentions.

From the totality of data available, as reliable an answer as possible has been reconstructed. A note of caution is in order here: not every piece of information thus acquired is as reliable as the next. Notes recur frequently in the text which raise the question of the accuracy of particular figures. In general, perhaps we can venture to say that data from the more southern départements which are treated here are the least impeachable, for no adequate possibility to control their validity was at hand.

Two kinds of data are most prominent: as far as numbers are concerned, the order of magnitude; as far as categories of work are concerned, as inclusive a listing as possible. The attempt at such inclusiveness — even when only extremely small numbers may have practised certain occupations — is motivated by a wish to communicate as wide a variety of treks as I can. Further research may well disclose that a particular trek which at present appears to have involved but trivial numbers of workers was in fact of broader significance. On the whole, data from départements which provided each other with migrant workers are complementary, with the exception of those départements where the persons reporting were vague about where workers from outside came from and where local workers departing to find jobs were bound for. Most importantly, such lack of specificity characterises reports concerning the timber rafts that went down the Rhine. The destination of the workers involved could have been given as Bouches de la Meuse, for it was in Dordrecht, by and large, that the rafts were dismantled.

In the original Dutch text of Appendix 1, data for all areas under examination are presented in keeping with the following division:

A. Sources and administrative procedures.
B.1. Complementary information from the reports of other areas.
B.2. Complementary information from internal or other criticism.
C. The trek to the département (number of workers, kinds of occupations, départements of origin). Here sub-totals by kind of work are added together, even if one and the same worker may have performed two different jobs sequentially. This has been done since the same duplication in effect is allowed when one worker has found employment in two different départements. Such cases, however, are repeatedly alluded to in connection with attempts to balance reports of workers departing from 'push areas' with those of workers employed in 'pull areas'.
D. The trek from the département (number of workers, kinds of occupations, départements of destination).
E. Intradépartemental migration (as far as is known; the Minister of the Interior did not inquire into such internal treks, yet on occa-

sion they are included in responses).

F. More detailed information about the trek to the département (in particular further specification of where migrants came from and where they found work).

G. More detailed information about the trek from the département (in particular further specification of where migrants came from and where they found work).

H. Conclusion — in the form of a quotient: $\dfrac{\text{trek to } \chi}{\text{trek from } \chi}$

Statistics are rounded off to the nearest 100. Internal treks are taken into account by indicating them, in numerator and denominator as well, within parentheses.

Where no numbers are available, I designate the treks concerned *pro memoria* (PM).

Départements and Regions Studied

From the original Dutch Annex 1, here I simply reproduce the essence of A. and B.2. for non-Dutch-speaking areas, and only the heading of the relevant annex section for Dutch-speaking localities.

1.1: Département of Bouches de l'Elbe, Capital City Hamburg

AN F 20 434 (in the Ems collection, together with Ems Oriental and Ems Occidental), 26/8/1812 Response from Hamburg to Paris. Considering the speed of the answer, we may assume it was more probably formulated by the prefecture (only the trek from the département).

1.2: Département of Bouches du Weser, Capital City Bremen

AN F 20 435, 25/11/1811 Request for information from the prefect to sub-prefects; 7/12/1812 Response from Bremen to Paris; SAB 6.2 (F.2.a and F.3.a): correspondence concerning migrant workers' passports.

1.3: Department of Ems Oriental, Capital City Aurich

AN F 20 434, final draft 19/12/1811 from Aurich to Paris, presumably compiled in the prefecture on the basis of data contained in the archives of the 'Kriegs- und Domänenkammer'; ARA, BZ 1796-1813: 842-3 (statistical data concerning Ostfriesland at the time of its incorporation within the Kingdom of Holland in 1806); idem: 1062 (peat mining in 1811); idem: 1121 (copy of final draft); idem: 1193 (peat mining 1812).

1.4: Département of Ems Supérieur, Capital City Osnabrück

AN F 20 435 (final draft); SAO, Rep 240 OED 751 (copy and rough draft of prefect's response, 11/1/1812; original answers from the maires of arrondissement Osnabrück (final draft sub-prefect Quackenbrück, final draft sub-prefect Lingen, final draft sub-prefect Minden, final draft former Amtmann of Diepholz).

1.5: Département of Lippe, Capital City Münster

AN F 20 435 (final draft, 31/1/1812); ARA BZ 1796-1813, 1121 (copy); SAO, Rep. 250 Neuenhaus A 17 (rough draft Arr. Neuenhaus); idem and SAO Rep. 250 Lingen II: 144 (original answers from the maires of arrondissement Neuenhaus, respectively those of the cantons Neuenhaus, Nordhorn and Bentheim and those of the cantons Wesuwe and Rhede).

1.6: The Principality of Lippe-Detmold, Capital City Detmold

Since 1778 a twofold administration of migrant labourers had been in effect within the principality.[2] On the one hand, a list of the names of persons was kept to whom passports had been disbursed; on the other hand, there was the institution of the brick-messenger who had his own registration system. The brick-messenger was a person officially appointed by the state whose task it was to serve as employment agent for the inhabitants of Lippe wishing to work outside the country as brick-makers. Every year the brick-messenger had to submit to the government a list of those persons for whom he had found work. By 1811 there were in fact two such brick-messengers. The one from the so-called First District acted on behalf of workers heading for Groningen and Ostfriesland (then Ems Occidental and Ems Oriental), the one from the so-called Second District on behalf of those journeying to other 'pull areas', in this case Bouches du Weser and perhaps also Ems Supérieur, Bouches de l'Elbe, the Kingdoms of Denmark and Westphalia, and the département of Lippe.

Both lists overlap each other in part. For 1811 they can be

found in SAD, L77A 4738; SAD, L77A 4722, no. 6 (report from 1830).

1.7: Département of Ems Occidental, Capital City Groningen[3]

1.8: Département of Frise, Capital City Leeuwarden

1.9: Département of Bouches de l'Issel, Capital City Zwolle

1.10: Département of Issel Supérieur, Capital City Arnhem

1.11: Département of Zuyderzee, Capital City Amsterdam

1.12: Département of Bouches de la Meuse, Capital City The Hague

1.13: Département of Bouches de l'Escaut, Capital City Middelburg

1.14: Département of Deux Nèthes, Capital City Antwerp

1.15: Département of Bouches du Rhin, Capital City Den Bosch

1.16: Département of Meuse Inférieure, Capital City Maastricht

1.17: Département of Roër, Capital City Aachen

AN F 20 435, 16/6/1811; HSAD Roer-Département 2841 (concerning the arrondissement of Cologne); GA Helden, 447 (response from the maire of Helden to Kleve inquiry).

1.18: Département of Rhin et Moselle, Capital City Koblenz

AN F 20 435, 16/3/1811.

1.19: Département of Sarre, Capital City Trier

AN F 20 435, 25/3/1811 (containing only data about the trek out of the département); 20/6/1811: Inquiry from Paris concerning the trek to the département, but the response from Trier in answer could not be located.

1.20: Département of Mont Tonnerre, Capital City Mainz

AN F 20 435, 7/11/1811; Chatelain 1976:795, maps I-1/2, II-16/17 and 19 (Bas Rhin).

1.21: Département of Lys, Capital City Bruge

1.22: Département of Escaut, Capital City Gent

1.23: Département of Jemappes, Capital City Mons

AN F 20 435, 19/4/1811; Chatelain 1976: 161, 168, 188-9, 449, 795, 928.

1.24: Département of Dyle, Capital City Brussels

AN F 20 435, 17/9/1810; Chatelain 1976: 795; ARAB, Dyle 1245 (passports April/May 1809).

1.25: Département of Sambre et Meuse, Capital City Namur

AN F 20 435; idem, F 20 147. In F 20 L 435 there is merely an allusion to 'un supplément au grand memoire'. In this *grand-mémoire*, compiled around 1805 and contained in F 20 147, there is again a reference to the chapter about emigration and immigration, this time in the same ink and handwriting as the initial reference in F 20 435. Emigration and immigration, however, are not the same as migratory labour.

1.26: Département of Ourthe, Capital City Liège

AN F 20 435, 6/4/1811 (based on passports issued in 1808-10). The average of the years 1808-10 probably provides an accurate picture of the magnitude of the trek from Ourthe. Comparison with other départements which report statistics from 1811, however, is problematical.

1.27: Département of Forêts, Capital City Luxemburg

AN F 20 435, 20/6/1811; Chatelain 1976: 795.

1.28: Département of Nord, Capital City Lille

AN F 20 434 (the badly damaged response from Lille, 12/12/1811, stored, indeed, under Manche); Chatelain 1976: 778, 788, 795, 928. As the result of an erroneous interpretation of data from Dyle, Chatelain (1976: 795) expresses his surprise (unfounded in my opinion) that there is no trace of information about these workers in the report from Nord. The copy-response can not be traced in the départemental archives in Lille.

1.29: Département of Pas de Calais, Capital City Arras

AN F 20 435, 12/3/1811; Chatelain 1976: 448, 449, 795.

1.30: Département of Ardennes, Capital City Mézières

AN F 20 434, 3/4/1810; Chatelain 1976: 417, 448.

1.31: *Département of Meuse, Capital City Bar-le-Duc*

AN F 20 434, 13/11/1811; Chatelain 1976: 431; Mauco 1932: 59.

1.32: *Département of Moselle, Capital City Metz*

AN F 20 434, 11/2/1809 and 14/3/1811: specified by arrondissement; Chatelain 1976: 431, 448, 485, 778, 795, 797, 808, 857; Mauco 1932: 14, 60. In 1809 the migrant workers are said to have been 2,000 strong, in 1811, 200. Mauco and Chatelain accept the figure 200, as do I, deferring to their authority.

1.33: *Other Départements in the Empire (in so far as they entertain relations with the North Sea System)*

Chatelain 1976: 448 (Aisne); 449-50 (Somme); 422-3, 443, 454 (Cantal and Puy de Dôme); 442, 472 (Basses Alpes). Mauco 1932: 22, 46 (Cantal); 29, 67 (Seine et Oise). The trek from south to north was negligible. The trek from north to south, for actual labourers, was extremely limited; for certain kinds of hawkers and traders from départements in South Netherlands or northern France, however, in several instances migration took place on a considerable scale. Here, I have Meuse in mind, and Forêts and Ourthe as well, and perhaps even Dyle.

1.34: *Areas North and East of the French Empire*[4]

Based on Appendices 1.1, 1.4, 1.6 to 1.9, 1.11, 1.12, 1.16 to 1.20, 1.26, 1.27, 1.32, 2.4, 2.5, 3.1, 3.2 and 3.5; GA Amsterdam, GA Weesperkarspel 225 (licenses foreign workers 1806-11) and idem, GA Watergraafsmeer 67/70 (licenses foreign workers 1806-11).

The trek from areas covered in Appendices 1.1 to 1.32 to areas east of the Empire consisted primarily of timber-rafters from the region of the Mosel who first went to the Spessart and the Schwarzwald to collect wood and build rafts in order subsequently, as rafters, to re-enter the 'pull area' of the North Sea coast. The second major group of migrants here were itinerant vendors, both those from Westphalian territory (especially Mettingen) and those from the Brabant-Limburg border (the 'teuten'), as well as tradesmen from the Ardennes and neighbouring mountain regions. Lastly, the group of agricultural labourers who journeyed to areas further north is striking. They are considered in Appendix 2.5.

The most important group which can be distinguished among migrants who trekked to the French Empire were the agricultural and bog workers. The smallest group of these workers, those from the vicinity of Darmstadt in the Grand Duchy of Hesse, crossed the Rhine to find work in the environs of Mainz. The largest group of all, however, comprised workers from the Kingdom of Westphalia and, to a far lesser extent, from the Grand Duchy of Berg and the Grand Duchy of Hesse who went to find jobs in the North Sea area, above all in Holland. Primarily by consulting the license records of Weesperkarspel and Watergraafsmeer, it is possible to determine the places of origin of these migrant workers more specifically; these turn out in particular to have been the Kreise Wiedenbrück, Paderborn and Büren in the Prussian Regierungsbezirk of Minden. In addition, they also came from the Westphalian corridor between the French Empire and the Principality of Lippe: portions of the later Kreise Minden and Herford (see Figure 2.3, p. 32).

Summary of Appendices 1.1 to 1.34

In conclusion, the results of Appendices 1.1 to 1.32 are summarily presented in Figures A1.1 to A1.4.

Table A1.1: Migratory Labour in the North of the French Empire in 1811[5]

Area		Migrant workers To	Migrant workers From	Inhabitants 1811	Migrant workers as % of the population To	Migrant workers as % of the population From
1.1	Bouches de l'Elbe	100	400	375,976	0.03	0.11
1.2	Bouches du Weser	500/600	2,000/2,100	327,175	0.15/0.18	0.61/0.64
1.3	Ems Oriental	2,100	100	128,200	1.64	0.08
1.4	Ems Supérieur	100/PM	12,000/PM	415,018	0.02	2.89
1.5	Lippe (département)	PM	3,000/PM	339,355	—	0.88
1.6	Lippe (principality)	—	1,200	70,540	—	1.70
1.7	Ems Occidental	3,000/3,100	800/900	191,100	1.57/1.62	0.42/0.47
1.8	Frise	4,600	100	175,400	2.62	0.06
1.9	Bouches de l'Issel	900	600	145,000	0.62	0.41
1.10	Issel Supérieur	100/200	700/800	192,700	0.05/0.10	0.36/0.41
1.11	Zuyderzee	10,000/10,200	200/PM	507,500	1.97/2.01	—/0.04
1.12	Bouches de la Meuse	4,700/4,800	300/400	393,600	1.19/1.22	0.08/0.10
1.13	Bouches de l'Escaut	1,200	—	76,820	1.56	—
1.14	Deux Nèthes	1,100	1,200	367,184	0.30	0.33
1.15	Bouches du Rhin	100/1,100	1,400/2,400	257,584	0.04/0.43	0.54/0.93
1.16	Meuse Inférieure	PM	800/PM	267,249	—	0.30
1.17	Roër	2,400	600	631,094	0.38	0.09
1.18	Rhin et Moselle	PM	1,100	269,700	—	0.41
1.19	Sarre	200	400	277,596	0.07	0.12
1.20	Mont Tonnerre	800/1,500	600/1,300	342,316	0.23/0.44	0.17/0.38
1.21	Lys	200/PM	300/PM	491,143	0.04	0.06
1.22	Escaut	1,200/2,200	200/1,200	636,438	0.19/0.35	0.03/0.19
1.23	Jemappes	PM	2,000	472,366	—	0.42
1.24	Dyle	100	200	431,969	0.02	0.05
1.25	Sambre et Meuse	PM	PM	180,655	—	—
1.26	Ourthe	PM	3,600	352,264	—	1.02
1.27	Forêts	—	600	246,333	—	0.24
1.28	Nord	300/2,700	1,100/3,500	839,833	0.03/0.27	0.11/0.35
1.29	Pas de Calais	600	PM	580,457	0.11	—
1.30	Ardennes	PM	100	275,792	—	0.03
1.31	Meuse	PM	4,000	284,703	—	1.40
1.32	Moselle	100	200	413,260	0.03	0.06
1.34	(Regierungsbezirk Minden)	—	1,227	340,614	—	0.36
				±11,000,000		

226 Appendix 1

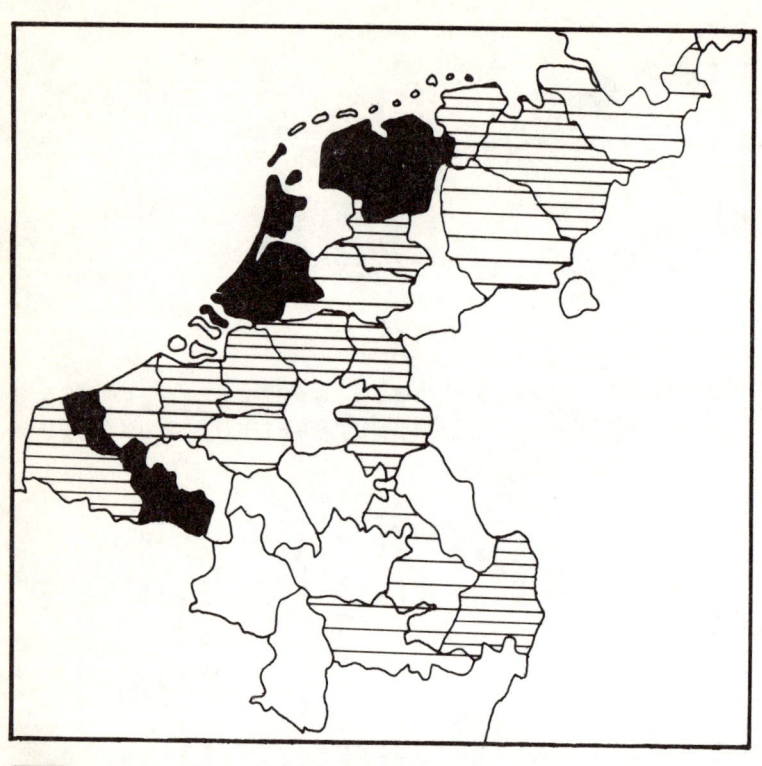

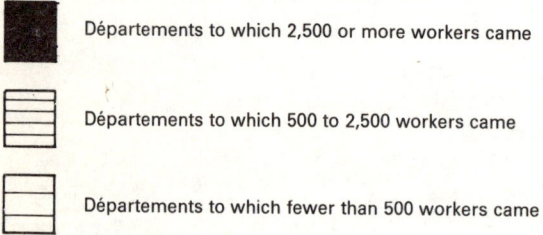

Figure A1.1: 'Pull' of Workers in 1811 per Département in Absolute Numbers

■ Départements to which 2,500 or more workers came

▤ Départements to which 500 to 2,500 workers came

▢ Départements to which fewer than 500 workers came

Appendix 1 227

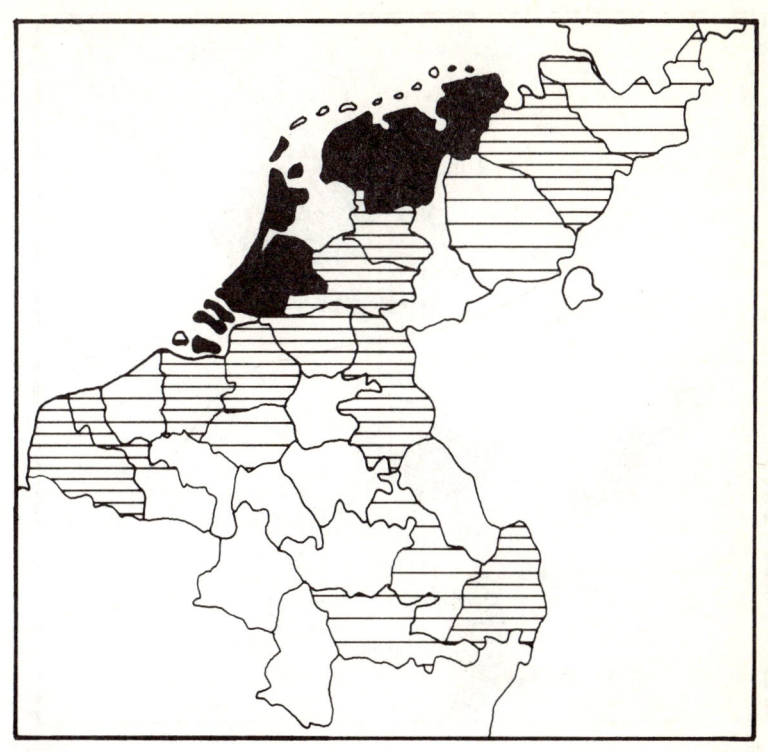

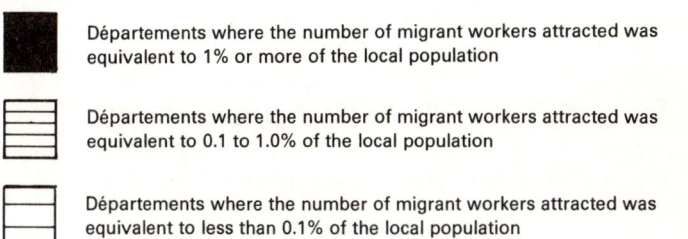

Figure A1.2: 'Pull' of Workers in 1811 per Département, Related to Number of Inhabitants

▪ Départements where the number of migrant workers attracted was equivalent to 1% or more of the local population

▤ Départements where the number of migrant workers attracted was equivalent to 0.1 to 1.0% of the local population

☐ Départements where the number of migrant workers attracted was equivalent to less than 0.1% of the local population

228 *Appendix 1*

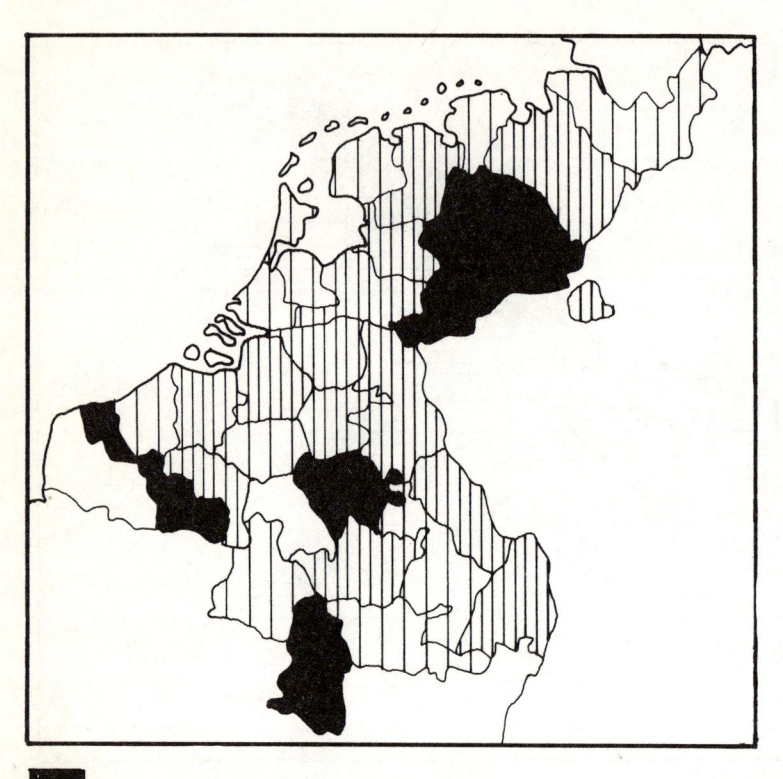

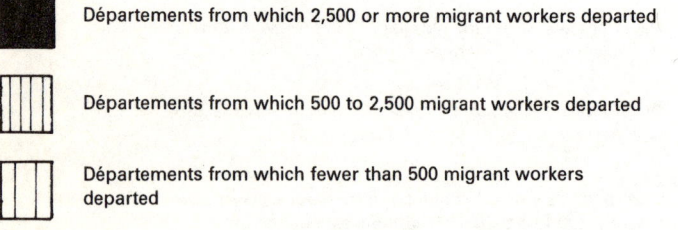

Figure A1.3: 'Push' of Workers in 1811 per Département in Absolute Numbers

■ Départements from which 2,500 or more migrant workers departed

▥ Départements from which 500 to 2,500 migrant workers departed

▥ Départements from which fewer than 500 migrant workers departed

Appendix 1 229

Figure A1.4: 'Push' of Workers in 1811 per Département, Related to Number of Inhabitants

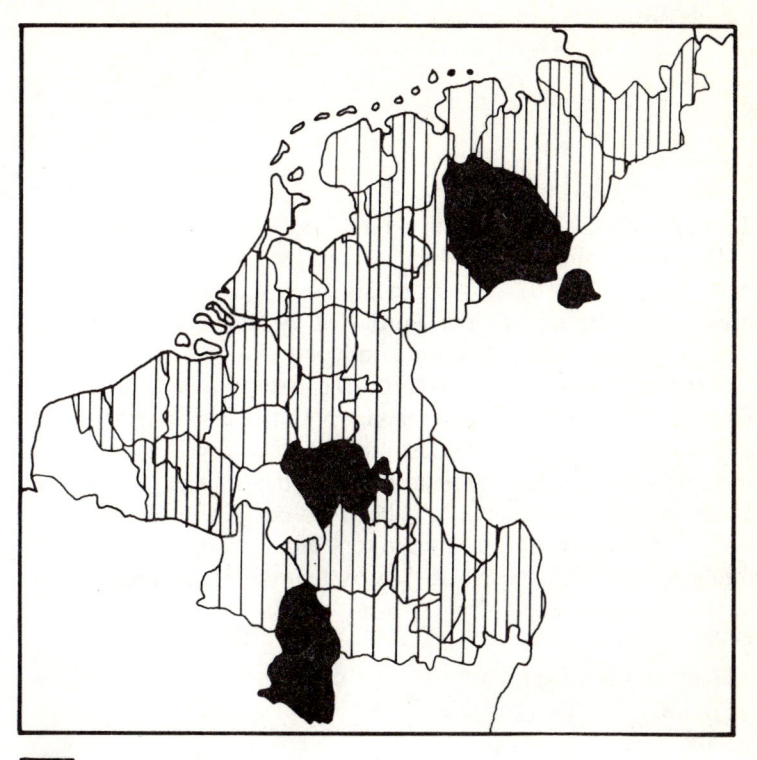

■ Départements from which 1% or more of the local population left as migrant workers

▥ Départements from which 0.1 to 1.0% of the local population left as migrant workers

▥ Départements from which less than 0.1% of the local population left as migrant workers

APPENDIX 2
Migratory Labour in Western and Southern Europe Outside the Northern Sea System at the Beginning of the Nineteenth Century

Introduction

The scope of this appendix is a limited one. An attempt will be made to determine whether there were migratory labour systems of some size, that is to say embracing several thousand workers, active in Europe outside the North Sea System c. 1800, systems attracting labour annually to the same 'pull area'.

For most of the countries considered, study of the migratory labour situation is confined to secondary sources; for northern and central Italy, however, a modest amount of archival research has been undertaken. Eastern Europe[1] and the Balkans,[2] with the exceptions indicated below, have been left out of consideration.

The appearance of major migratory labour systems on a scale commensurate with the North Sea System will be investigated in the following regions:

Spain and Portugal
France
Italy
Germany, Switzerland, Austria and Hungary
Scandinavia (including Schleswig-Holstein)
Great Britain and Ireland

2.1: Migratory Labour in Spain and Portugal at the Beginning of the Nineteenth Century[3]

At the beginning of the nineteenth century on the Iberian peninsula it is possible to differentiate four principal currents of migratory labour.

The first stream flowed in the direction of Catalonia and adjacent territories.[4] Although as a consequence of the Napoleonic Wars the trek at this time diminished markedly, we can nevertheless think in terms of several thousand French workers who journeyed annually to Spain, and to Catalonia in particular. The most conspicuous group was 1,200 tinkers from Haute Garonne who went, among other places, to the region of Pamplona in Navarra. Furthermore, several hundred of their colleagues from Auvergne and an unknown number from Ariège and the French Pyrenees. Of more importance from this last area are the five to six hundred charcoal burners who travelled to North Catalonia; they were joined, moreover, by a number of smiths. From French Basque territory construction workers, foresters and tanners went to Spanish Basqueland. From Aveyron and Puy de Dôme sawyers, some hundreds at most c. 1811, came to Catalonia and, last of all, vendors from the Basses Alpes are reported in Barcelona.

Although this trek recovered after the war, especially the labour flow from Auvergne and the French Pyrenees, a total of 10,000 was probably never again surpassed.[5] What is more, in the course of the nineteenth century the trek from Spain to France commenced in earnest.

Catalonia and nearby regions border on an important French 'pull' area: the French Mediterranean sea coast consisting of Provence and Languedoc. It is together with these two places, therefore, that Catalonia will be treated.[6]

The second current of migratory labour headed in the direction of Castile, and towards the east of León as well. According to most writers French workers were the ones primarily involved. Already for centuries a trek had existed from Auvergne and the French Pyrenees to Spain. After a decline at the outset of the eighteenth century, this trek probably reached its greatest proportions later in the century. We are at a loss, however, to say with any exactitude how many workers took part and where the leading 'pull' area was situated. The frequently quoted total of 20,000 Frenchmen in Spain is too unreliable to be applied without qualification to a specific period — not to mention totals several times as large.[7]

Probably much more important than the French trek and in any event more verifiable is the stream of migratory labour from northwest Spain to Castile and the east of León. The workers who took part came from the west of Asturia and the far north of Portugal, but also in large part from Galicia, in particular from the provinces of Orense and Lugo.[8] The statistics in Table A2.1 have been derived from Meijide Pardo's well-documented article concerning this trek.

For the period under consideration we must estimate the number of workers drawn to the Castilian 'pull' area as 30,000 at a mini-

Table A2.1: Number of Migratory Workers from Galicia to Castile and the East of Léon 1767-c. 1900[9]

1767	>25,000
1769	40,000
1775	>40,000
end 18th century	60,000
1804	30,000
c. 1900	25,000

mum. This only includes the 'Gallegos', not Asturians, and not possible French migrant workers.

The third 'pull' area that requires attention is Andalusia. According to Meijide Pardo, however, this region was of secondary importance even though thousands of 'Gallegos' certainly headed there. Yet considering the importance of this pole of attraction in the second half of the nineteenth century, we should bear in mind here the possibility that Meijide Pardo has underestimated the number of workers involved.

The 'pull' area of central Portugal, especially the harbour cities of Lisbon and Porto was of significance — yet it remains for research to determine the actual number of migrant workers who participated.[10]

In conclusion, we can state that Castile certainly belonged to the major European migratory labour systems operative in the early nineteenth century; Catalonia should be considered as part of the French Mediterranean sea-coast system; and pending further study both central Portugal and Andalusia may temporarily be relegated to systems of secondary rank, as may also have been the case with Valencia.[11]

2.2: *Migratory Labour in France at the Beginning of the Nineteenth Century*

Thanks to Abel Chatelain's great posthumous work, *Les Migrants temporaires en France de 1800 à 1914*, we are able to distinguish five major 'pull areas' in France c. 1800 without much further research:[12]

(a) The Paris Basin. This area was by far the most important 'pull area' in the whole of France. Although Chatelain provides no explicit total, we may fix the number at a minimum of 60,000

incoming workers.[13] The city of Paris itself provided the largest share of jobs for these arrivals, attracting 30,000 to 40,000 workers. Here, we should think especially of construction workers, water-carriers and all kinds of small tradesmen and labourers employed in the services sector. Yet within a considerable radius of Paris agriculture also required a great many hands. The cultivation of grain led all other farming activities (départements Seine et Marne, Eure et Loire and Seine et Oise),[14] followed a considerable distance behind by grape-growing (département Yonne).[15] This system was separated from the North Sea System by the départements Oise, Somme, and Pas de Calais, a 'neutral area' where at most only very little labour migration took place.[16]

(b) The Mediterranean Coast. In comparison to Paris, five times its size, Marseilles was of comparatively little significance as a 'pull area'.[17] Yet the need there for harvest workers was similar to the Paris Basin. All in all, the French Mediterranean coast will have required something in the order of 20,000 migrant workers to reap its wheat crop.[18]

In Provence, Bouches du Rhône drew by far the most workers, followed by Pyrenees Orientales and Hérault. To the north of these locations, Lozère and Aveyron deserve mention. At this time southern France was the second most important wine-producing region in the country after the region of Bordeaux. The labour needs in this sector should therefore be estimated to have run into several thousands.[19]

All in all, the Mediterranean coast provided employment for 30,000 migrant workers. This area, moreover, bordered on the Spanish 'pull area' of Catalonia — which will have boosted its total to perhaps 35,000.[20] As a boundary to the south, therefore, not the Pyrenees but the Ebro should be taken, and in the east while Var may be included as part of the system, the Alpes Maritimes fall outside it. It is a matter of definition whether or not one also chooses to consider Corsica as part of this system — thousands of workers came annually to the island from the Italian mainland in connection with the labour needs of Corsican viticulture.[21]

(c) The Bordeaux Region. The wine-growing area of Bordeaux, where Gironde and Charente Inférieure needed thousands of workers,[22] was extremely small in comparison to the migratory labour systems in France mentioned above. With the exception of

work in the vineyards, only the cultivation of grain in Charente Inférieure offered employment for outsiders. A total of more than 8,000 migrants were attracted to Aquitaine.[23]

(d) Alsace. In order of magnitude, this area was equivalent to the Bordeaux system, only here harvesters for grain, not grapes, were needed in the départements of Bas Rhin and Haut Rhin.[24] Even if we opt to fuse this area with the 'pull areas' of Mainz, Speier and Frankfurt, thus making a unit of the Rhine Valley, the total number of migrant workers involved will in all likelihood not have exceeded 10,000.[25]

(e) The Saône-Rhône Region. Approximately 6,000 migrants came there to participate in harvesting grain and vineyards.[26]

At the time practically all migrant workers in France came from 'push areas' within national frontiers. With Chatelain's study to assist us, we can now differentiate these as well. Six regions recur prominently:[27]

(i) The most important encompasses the départements of the Massif Central. For the 15 départements of the Massif Central Chatelain arrives at a total of 61,000 departing workers, which he considers a minimal estimate. The largest share of workers was provided by the départements of Creuse and Puy de Dôme, but Haute Vienne and Cantal, each with practically 10,000, do not lag far behind. The remaining départements, especially in the south of the Massif, each yielded several thousands. Most of these migrants set out for the Paris Basin, yet Languedoc and Gironde were also popular destinations. Some, primarily tinkers and hawkers, left the country, crossing into Spain and the Netherlands.[28]

(ii) A second important 'push area' was formed by the Alps and the Jura, from which perhaps some 40,000 migrant workers descended into French 'pull areas'. Ain, Montblanc, Alpes Maritimes and then Isère, Hautes Alpes and Basses Alpes were sources of the majority of workers. Provence and the area around Lyons drew the largest number of these, yet not unappreciable numbers journeyed on to the Paris Basin.[29]

(iii) As a third 'push area' we can distinguish several regions in western France: Maine (above all Mayenne), Normandy (primarily Calvados and Orne), Brittany (especially Morbihan) and the

Vendée). These locations constitute far less of an entity than (i) or (ii) above, and the number of workers from these home locations, an estimated 18,000, while respectable, is a good deal smaller than the numbers who left (i) or (ii) to search for work. The Paris Basin was their principal destination once again, although some trekked south.[30]

(iv) In the northeast, between the 'pull areas' of the Paris Basin and the Rhine Valley, a number of départements yielded annually some 10,000 migrant workers or more: Meuse, above all, but also Haute Marne, Aube and Côte d'Or and Yonne as well. These départements adjoined the southeastern 'push area' of the North Sea System but labour flowed from them in a different direction so that we can speak of a 'watershed' dividing distinct systems.[31]

(v) The Pyrenees probably did not exceed an annual efflux of 10,000 workers, most of whom came from Ariège and from Basses Pyrenees and Rousillon. Garonne, farther to the north, was part of this 'push area'. Aquitaine and the Mediterranean coast, on opposite sides of the Pyrenees, were leading centres of employment for these workers, as was, to a lesser extent, Spanish Basque and adjacent territories.[32]

(vi) Just as in the northeast, in the northwest we can identify a 'push area' separated from the North Sea System by a 'watershed' running east to west. To the north of this imaginary division lies Nord and also Ardennes; to its south, Aisne and Oise. Indeed, this smallest of all 'push areas' will not have supplied more than 5,000 workers a year to the 'pull area' of the Paris Basin.[33]

2.3: Migratory Labour in Italy at the Beginning of the Nineteenth Century

The questionnaire that was administered throughout the French Empire between 1808 and 1813, not only for all of France but also for Belgium, Luxemburg, the Netherlands and the west of Germany, and which has proven inestimably valuable for the reconstruction of migratory labour, was also administered in parts of Italy and Switzerland. In Switzerland the département of Simplon belonged to the French Empire. Similarly, in the northwest of Italy nine départements (Doire, Sésia, Stura, Pô, Montenotte, Marengo, Gênes, Taro and Apennins, an area coextensive in large part with the older entities of Piedmont, Liguria, and Parma) and in the centre another five départements (Arno, Méditerranée, Ombrone — these three comprising the former Tuscany; Trasimène and Rome — these two part of the Papal States) were part of the French Empire. For the rest, Italy consisted of states that were friendly to France and to a strong degree under French influence, e.g. the Kingdoms of Italy, Naples and Sardinia, the Principalities of Lucca and Piombino, the island of Elba and the Kingdom of Sicily. The political situation is represented in Figure A2.1.

Figure A2.1: Political Geography of Italy in 1810

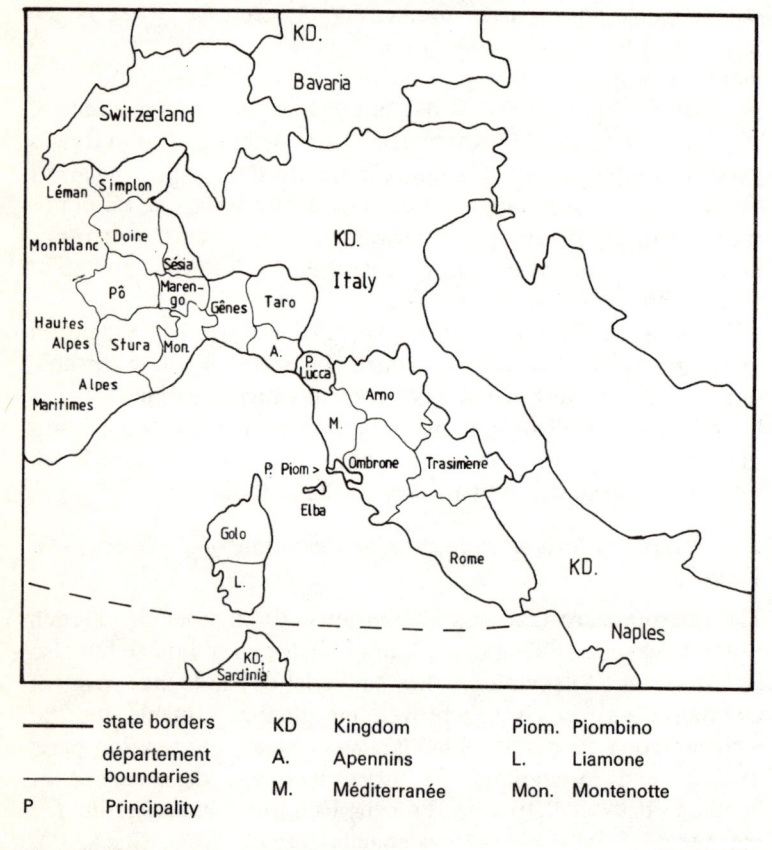

———	state borders	KD	Kingdom	Piom.	Piombino
———	département boundaries	A.	Apennins	L.	Liamone
P	Principality	M.	Méditerranée	Mon.	Montenotte

Quantitative results of the questionnaire, specified by département, have previously been published, in part, by Corsini.[34] Since his findings differ rather substantially here and there from mine, my reconstruction of migratory labour in Italy in the early 1800s has been reproduced here in its entirety, with as much attention as possible to points of disagreement with Corsini.

Questionnaire results are presented in a uniform, concise format below. As for political entities outside the French Empire, direct information is also available concerning Lucca and Piombino, whereas for the remaining states some data can be derived indirectly from questionnaire responses in French départements. The départements of Corsica and the island of Elba have been included in this survey because of their relations as far as labour is concerned with the facing Italian coast. By reviewing data from several départements in France (Isère, Alpes Maritimes, Hautes Alpes and Léman; I was unable to trace responses from Montblanc) I tried to cross-check information from the French départements in Italy.[35]

In the presentation of what follows, I adhere to the following system:

(A) Where and when primary data were encountered, and of what they consist (unless stipulated otherwise such data are in the form of letters from prefects to the Minister of the Interior in Paris).
(B) Location of other data not present in the source reported sub-A. Areas appear in alphabetical order. Italy, Naples, Bavaria and other such designations invariably refer to political divisions as they then existed.
(C) A sketch of the trek of workers to the area, specifying vocational categories and places of origin. Groups of less than 100 are not mentioned separately.
(D) Sketch of the trek from outside the area.
(E) Sketch of the trek within the area.
(F) Conclusion (as in Appendix 1, see p. 219).

The data which follow reproduce in summary, standardised form the content of the original (prefects') responses to the questionnaire. In general, for example, no attempt is made here to differentiate such administrative sub-divisions as arrondissements and cantons, even when such differentiation is made in the sources.

Supplementary data from other départements (sub-B) have only been processed when they involve no ambiguities. That the questionnaire was administered throughout the entire 1808-13 period helps explain why certain information at times appears inconsistent when cross-checked. Responses from Golo and Liamone, for example, pertain to the situation in 1808, from Méditerranée, Apennins, Sésia, Gênes and Doire to the situation in 1809, from Montenotte, Taro, Stura, Marengo, Ombrone, Pô and Simplon to the situation in (1810) 1811, and from Arno, Trasimène and Rome to the situation in 1812.

A second complication is the frequent use of antiquated administrative and political units such a Tuscany, Piedmont, Roman States and Liguria.

Départements examined have been grouped from north to south, followed by the remaining Italian states.

Review of Départements and States

2.3a Département of Simplon

(A) AN F 20 435, Sion 2/4/1812.
'Pull' and 'push' per canton.
(B) —
(C) The trek to Simplon included workers with the following occupations from the following places of origin:

road-workers and workers employed at the 'hospice du Simplon'	1,000
agricultural labourers from Léman, and also Montblanc	224
vineyard workers from Montblanc	200
masons from Italy	113
others (tinkers and flax workers primarily from Piedmont, Pô and Switzerland)	59
	1,596

Sion (arr. Sion) and Monthey (arr. St Maurice) can be designated as leading destinations (except for the 1,000 road-workers whose place of employment is not given).

(D) The trek from Simplon included workers with the following occupations headed for the following places:

agricultural and forest labourers bound for Doire, Montblanc, Pô and Léman	350
others (shepherds to Doire, Italy and Piedmont and timber traders to Léman)	85
	435

The leading place of origin for these migrants is the canton of St Maurice in the arrondissement of the same name.
(E) The internal trek within Simplon involved 700 to 1,000 agricultural and vineyard workers from the high valleys who descended to work in the Rhône valley. I will work with the number 1,000.
(F) Conclusion:

$$\frac{\text{Trek to Simplon}}{\text{Trek from Simplon}} : \frac{1{,}596\ (2{,}596)}{435\ (1{,}435)} \text{ or, rounded off, } \frac{1{,}600\ (2{,}600)}{400\ (1{,}400)}$$

2.3b Département of Doire

(A) AN F 20 435, Ivrea 22/5/1810.
'Push' per canton, 'pull' per occupational group.
(B) Pô, Sésia, Simplon, Stura
(C) The trek to Doire included workers with the following occupations from the following places of origin:

masons from Sésia, Italy and Switzerland	240
sawyers from Italy and Bavaria	150
charcoal burners from Sésia	100
others (primarily shepherds from Pô, casters from Italy and weavers from Pô and Sésia)	229
	719

Although workers from other areas mentioned under (B) above are likely to have come to Doire, lack of specific data prevents their number from being added to the total of 719.
(D) The trek from Doire included workers with the following occupations headed for the following places

agricultural labourers bound for Montblanc, Pô, Sésia and Italy	620
tinkers bound for Italy, Pô, Stura, Sésia, Doire and Tuscany	570
flax-combers bound for Pô and Sésia	500
miners bound for Pô, Montblanc, Isère and Italy	410
hawkers bound for Italy, Pô, Stura, Sésia, Doire, Tuscany and France	370
chimneysweeps bound for Pô, Stura, Sésia and Doire	300
masons bound for Montblanc, Léman and France	280

sawyers bound for Pô and Sésia 140
others (primarily cloth tradesmen bound for Switzerland
and Bavaria) 110
3,300

The most important arrondissement from which workers departed was Ivrea, followed by Aosta.
(E) See sub-(D).
(F) Conclusion:

$$\frac{\text{Trek to Doire}}{\text{Trek from Doire}} : \frac{719}{3,300} \text{ or rounded off, } \frac{700}{3,300}$$

2.3c Département of Sésia

(A) AN F 20 435, Vercelli 12/3/1810, complete text in Corsini 1969: 146-7.
Only the 'push' from the arrondissement of Biella (per canton) is given.
(B) Doire, Marengo, Montenotte, Pô, Rome, Stura
(C) The trek to Sésia included workers with the following occupations from the following places of origin (only the 'pull' exercised on shepherds from Italy is mentioned by the prefect; the remaining data come from other areas):

workers in the rice fields of Vercelli from Marengo
(<6,500), Montenotte (250), Pô (205) and Stura 7,000

Although many additional hundreds of workers may well have journeyed to Sésia, above all from Doire, but also from Stura, other reports concerning migrant workers are not specific enough to be included in the calculations of this annex.[36]
(D) The trek from Sésia included workers with the following occupations headed for the following places:

masons bound for many destinations, including
Marengo, Montenotte, Pô and Stura 3,500
roadsmen and navvies for other public works 2,000
stonecutters and miners bound for Pô, Doire and
Alpine roads 1,200
brick- and tile-makers bound for Pô, Stura, Doire
and Marengo 1,000

weavers bound for Pô, Marengo, Stura and Doire	900
street-pavers bound for Pô, Doire, Montblanc and Italy	350
pork-butchers bound for Pô and Rome	>200
plasterers bound for France	160
charcoal-burners bound for Doire	100
others bound for Pô, Doire and Italy	160
	>9,570[37]

The overwhelming majority came from the arrondissement of Biella; only the pork-butchers (probably from Vercelli) and the charcoal-burners appear in the reports of other prefects and thus may have originated from other arrondissements.

(E) —

(F) Conclusion:

$$\frac{\text{Trek to Sésia}}{\text{Trek from Sésia}} : \frac{> 7,000}{> 9,570} \text{ or rounded off, } \frac{7,000}{9,600}$$

2.3d Département of Pô

(A) AN F 20 435, Turin 18/12/1811.
'Pull' per municipality, 'push' per canton.
(B) Alpes Maritimes, Doire, Hautes Alpes, Sésia, Simplon, Stura.
(C) The trek to Pô included workers with the following occupations from the following places of origin:

harvesters (including some shepherds) from Doire, Marengo, Sésia, Stura, Switzerland and Italy	2,005
masons from Sésia, Doire, Switzerland and Italy	904
pork-butchers from Sésia	200
street-pavers from Sésia	200
carpenters, wagon-makers and smiths from Doire, Marengo and Italy	200
the above occupations combined with others (e.g. sawyers and straw-hat vendors)	379
	3,888[38]

The vast majority went to the city and arrondissement of Turin.

(D) The trek from Pô included workers with the following occupations headed for the following places:

| street-pavers bound for Montblanc and Montenotte | 672 |

242 *Appendix 2*

> schoolmasters and flax-combers bound for neighbouring
> départements including Alpes Maritimes   250
> harvesters bound for Sésia   205
> others (including flax-combers bound for Pô and
> Doire, and shepherds bound for Doire)   170
>   _____
>   1,297[39]

Among the category 'others' are 82 workers extracted from the data for Doire (70 shepherds, 12 furriers). The trek primarily involved migrants from the arrondissements Turin and Pinerolo (40 per cent each).

(E) Within the département Pô, within the arrondissement of Turin, 1,472 agricultural labourers went from the canton of Viù to Turin and the surrounding area. Some of the flax-combers listed under (D) above should actually appear here as participants in the intradépartemental trek.

(F) Conclusion:

$$\frac{\text{Trek to Pô}}{\text{Trek from Pô}} : \frac{3{,}888\ (5{,}360)}{1{,}297\ (2{,}769)} \text{ or rounded off, } \frac{3{,}900\ (5{,}400)}{1{,}300\ (2{,}800)}$$

2.3e *Département of Marengo*

(A) AN F 20 435, Alessandria 28/11/1811, complete text in Corsini 1969: 146-7.

'Pull' and 'push' per occupational group.

(B) Montenotte, Pô, Sésia, Stura.

(C) The trek to Marengo included workers with the following occupations from the following places of origin:

> masons and brick-makers for the fortifications of
> Alessandria, from Sésia and Italy   1,200
> grain-harvesters from Montenotte   800
> sawyers from Arno and Taro   260
> tinkers, chimneysweeps and pewterers, primarily from
> Doire and also from Naples   150
>   _____
>   2,410

The grain-harvesters were not reported by the prefect of Marengo, but rather by his colleague from Montenotte.[40]

(D) The trek from Marengo included workers with the following occupations headed for the following places:

rice harvesters (2,500 of whom earlier sowed the rice)
bound for Sésia, and Italy   4,000
threshers bound for Stura $>$ 100
    $>$4,100

Not the prefect from Marengo, but his colleague in Stura reported the threshers.

(E) —

(F) Conclusion:

$$\frac{\text{Trek to Marengo}}{\text{Trek from Marengo}} : \frac{2{,}410}{>4{,}100} \text{ or rounded off, } \frac{2{,}400}{4{,}100}$$

2.3f Département of Stura

(A) AN F 20 435 (with Pô), Cuneo 20/7/1811.
'Pull' and 'push' per arrondissement.

(B) Doire, Hautes Alpes, Pô and Sésia.

(C) The trek to Stura included workers with the following occupations from the following places of origin:

masons from Sésia, Marengo, Italy and Switzerland   270
threshers from Marengo $>$100
others (including tile-makers from Sésia)   61
    $>$431

The majority went to the arrondissement of Savigliano.

(D) The trek from Stura included workers with the following occupations headed for the following places:

day labourers (especially for the rice harvest, and also for hay-making and the olive harvest) bound for Piedmont, Liguria and France   5,800[41]
olive-harvesters in Liguria   400
flax-combers bound for Pô, Doire and Sésia   300
olive-oil production in Provence   200
others (bound for work in the ports of Toulon and Marseilles)   50
    6,750

Most of these migrants came from the arrondissements of Mondovi (2,400), Cuneo (1,500/2,000), Saluzzo (1,350) and

Alba (more than 1,000). No one left the arrondissement of Savigliano.
(E) —
(F) Conclusion:

$$\frac{\text{Trek to Stura}}{\text{Trek from Stura}} : \frac{>431}{6{,}750} \text{ or rounded off, } \frac{400}{6{,}800}$$

2.3g Département of Montenotte

(A) AN F 20 435, Savona 4/4/1811.
'Pull' per occupational group, 'push' per occupational group (and various administrative units).
(B) Pô.
(C) The trek to Montenotte included workers with the following occupations from the following places of origin:

masons from Sésia and Italy	150
others (including tinkers from Naples and roadworkers)	20
	170

(D) The trek from Montenotte included workers with the following occupations headed for the following places:

grain-harvesters bound for Marengo	800
rice-harvesters bound for Sésia	250
sawyers bound for Gênes, Marengo, Alpes Maritimes and Apennins	150
others (glass-blowers) bound for Taro, Tuscany and Italy	60
	1,260

Most migrants came from the arrondissement of Acqui, and also from the arrondissement of Savona.
(E) —
(F) Conclusion:

$$\frac{\text{Trek to Montenotte}}{\text{Trek from Montenotte}} : \frac{170}{1{,}260} \text{ or rounded off, } \frac{200}{1{,}300}$$

2.3h Département of Gênes

(A) AN F 20 435, Genoa 24/4/1810.

Only 'push' reported for the arrondissements Novi, Genoa and Bobbio.
(B) Elba, Golo, Liamone, Montenotte, Rome, Taro, Trasimème.
(C) The trek to Gênes was only reported by the prefects of Montenotte and Taro, without, however, specification of the numbers of workers involved. Thus, for this appendix, we can only enter PM (*pro memoria*) to represent the total number of workers attracted.[42]
(D) The trek from Gênes included workers with the following occupations headed for the following places:

agricultural labourers (especially for the rice fields) combined with charcoal-burners bound for Taro, Golo, Liamone, Elba, Tuscany and Italy	30,200
porters bound for Rome	300
	30,500

Porters were cited solely by the prefect of Rome. The most important arrondissements of origin were Novi (16,000), Bobbio (12,000) and Genoa (2,200).
(E) —
(F) Conclusion:

$$\frac{\text{Trek to Gênes}}{\text{Trek from Gênes}} : \frac{\text{PM}}{30,500}$$

2.3i Département of Taro

(A) AN F 435, Parma 22/5/1811.
'Pull' and 'push' according to arrondissement, geographical features (plains, hills, mountains) and municipalities.
(B) Arno, Gênes, Golo, Liamone, Marengo, Montenotte, Ombrone.
(C) According to the prefect of Taro, 64 workers came, primarily from Italy. Data from Montenotte and Gênes are insufficiently specific to be incorporated here.
(D) The trek from Taro included workers with the following occupations headed for the following places

agricultural labourers bound for Italy, Lucca, Piombino, Golo, Liamone, Gênes and Tuscany	3,776
sawyers bound for Golo, Liamone and Italy	810

246 *Appendix 2*

> charcoal-burners/wood-cutters, bound primarily
> for Italy   144
> sawyers and wood-cutters, bound primarily for Italy 115
> others (especially hawkers, helmsmen and shepherds),
> bound primarily for Italy   234
>
> 5,079

In total 715 migrants went to French départements and 4,364 to Italy. Arrondissements of origin were Parma (2,699), Piacenza (1,363) and Borgo San Donnino (1,017). Or, from a geographical perspective, 1,272 workers left homes in the plains, 394 from homes in the hills, 3,413 from homes in the mountains.

(E) —

(F) Conclusion:

$$\frac{\text{Trek to Taro}}{\text{Trek from Taro}} : \frac{64}{5{,}079} \text{ or rounded off, } \frac{100}{5{,}100}$$

2.3j *Département of Apennins*

(A) AN F 20 435, Chiavari 28/7/1809.

Information concerning this département comes from responses to an enquiry concerning the economic relations between the principality of Lucca and neighbouring French départements; questions 7 and 8 of the enquiry were about migratory labour (cf. 2.3l below for the same questionnaire).

(B) Arno, Golo, Liamone, Montenotte.

(C) The trek to Apennins involved only sawyers from Montenotte and the makers of plaster images from Lucca; no specific numbers were reported.

We will refer to the number of workers arriving annually in Apennins during this period as PM.

(D) The trek from Apennins consisted of workers bound for Lucca (workers for the lime-kilns, agricultural and forestry labourers), sawyers going to Arno and agricultural, forestry, and ground-workers with employment in the Corsican départements of Golo and Liamone. This last group, originating from the arrondissements Pontremoli and Sarzana as well, and which also went to Ombrone, brought back a net amount of 15,000 to FF 20,000. Using remuneration for comparable work in Ombrone and in Golo — FF 100 and FF 125 per worker per season, respect-

ively — it is possible to calculate that some 200 men took part in the trek.[43]
(E) —
(F) Conclusion:

$$\frac{\text{Trek to Apennins}}{\text{Trek from Apennins}} : \frac{\text{PM}}{200}$$

2.3k Département of Arno

(A) AN F 20 434, Florence 1/9/1812; Corsini 1969: 143 (text of Paris question 13/11/1811), 144 (further administrative history). 'Pull' per occupational category, 'push' per arrondissement.
(B) Marengo, Ombrone, Rome, Trasimène.
(C) The trek to Arno included workers with the following occupations from the following places of origin:

masons, chimneysweeps and chestnut-roasters from Italy and Switzerland	300-400
sawyers from the départements in the Apennine mountains and from Taro	50-60
	350-460

In addition, Trasimène reports pork-butchers from the mountains of Norcia and porters who went to Florence. Although no numbers are specified, the citation induces me to round off the total trek to Arno at 500 migrant workers.

(D) The trek from Arno involved 5,000 to 6,000 agricultural, forestry and industrial labourers and shepherds who went to Rome, Ombrone, Méditerranée and Piombino. Since this trek is confirmed not only for Ombrone and Rome but for Marengo as well, I have chosen to fix the total at 6,000.

Workers came from the following arrondissements: Pistoia (4,800), Arezzo (900), Modigliana (300) and Florence (almost nobody).

(E) —
(F) Conclusion:

$$\frac{\text{Trek to Arno}}{\text{Trek from Arno}} : \frac{500}{6,000}$$

2.3l Département of Méditerranée

(A) AN F 20 435, Livorno 26/9/1809.
Information concerning this département derives from the response to a questionnaire concerning economic relations between the Principalities of Lucca and Piombino and neighbouring French départements (cf. appendix 2.3j).
(B) Arno, Piombino, Trasimène.
(C) Arno merely reported an unspecified number of agricultural and forestry labourers; Trasimène did the same for porters. Consequently the trek to Méditerranée is represented here as PM.[44]
(D) The only known groups of workers departing from Méditerranée were agricultural labourers from the arrondissement of Volterra, and shepherds; both groups went to Piombino. Their trek too can only be indicated as PM.
(E) —
(F) Conclusion:

$$\frac{\text{Trek to Méditerranée}}{\text{Trek from Méditerranée}} : \frac{\text{PM}}{\text{PM}}$$

2.3m Département of Ombrone

(A) AN F 20 435 (under Méditerranée), Sienna 9/12/1811.
'Pull' of arrondissement Grosseto per occupational category.
(B) Apennins, Arno.
(C) The trek to Ombrone included workers with the following occupations from the following places of origin:

harvesters from Trasimène	3,000
ditch-diggers from Naples	500
sowers and wood-cutters from Italy and Taro	1,000
grass-mowers and sowers from Lucca	200
workers in the iron-forges (origin uncertain)	450
others (shepherds from Arno and Italy, craftsmen from Arno)	80
	5,230

Reports from Apennins and Arno could not easily be incorporated in this total. All migrants were bound for the arrondissement of Grosseto.
(D) No workers left Ombrone.

Appèndix 2   249

(E) —
(F) Conclusion:

$$\frac{\text{Trek to Ombrone}}{\text{Trek from Ombrone}} : \frac{5{,}230}{0} \text{ or rounded off,} \frac{5{,}200}{0}$$

2.3n Département of Trasimène

(A) AN F 20 435, Spoleto 24/12/1812, complete text in Corsini 1969: 154-7.
'Pull' and 'push' per arrondissement.
(B) Ombrone and Rome.
(C) The trek to Trasimène included workers with the following occupations from the following places of origin:

harvesters agricultural labourers	from Naples, Italy, Rome, Arno and Ombrone	6,940 1,312
sawyers		350
wool-carders from Naples		299
chimneysweeps and scissors-sharpeners from Italy and Bavaria		144
others (96 Neapolitan and Genoan tradesmen; 50 Italian tinkers)		146
		9,191
Roman harvesters (extremely probable)[45]		8,000
		17,191

The 9,191 migrants to Trasimène found work in the following arrondissements: Foligno (2,992), Perugia (2,756), Spoleto (1,923) and Todi (1,520).
(D) The trek from Trasimène included workers with the following occupations headed for the following places:

agricultural labourers bound for the Roman Campagna or Tuscany	8,113
shepherds	980
pork-butchers bound for major cities (e.g. Rome, Florence, Venice)	524
castrators and stone-cutters bound for all Italy and Europe	222
coopers	171

Appendix 2

wool-carders	132
others (83 silk-spoolers, 47 hackle-makers, etc.)	361
	10,503

These workers came from the arrondissements of Todi (4,085), Spoleto (2,314), Perugia (2,315) and Foligno (1,789). We can deduce from the prefect's report, moreover, that 150 charcoal-burners set out to work in Rome, as well as the same number of migrants who sold chicory and other vegetables.

(E) Harvesters who returned from Rome competed in the fields of Trasimène with Roman migrant workers who came at the same time. This trek is incorporated here as PM.

(F) Conclusion:

$$\frac{\text{Trek to Trasimène}}{\text{Trek from Trasimène}} : \frac{17{,}191\ (\text{PM})}{10{,}803\ (\text{PM})} \text{ or rounded off, } \frac{17{,}200\ (\text{PM})}{10{,}800\ (\text{PM})}$$

2.3o Département of Rome

(A) AN F 20 435, Rome 7/1/1813, complete text in Corsini 1969: 151-3.

'Pull' per occupational group.

(B) Arno, Trasimène.

(C) The trek to Rome included workers with the following occupations from the following places of origin:

harvesters from Naples, Italy, Tuscany and Trasimène	32,000
agricultural labourers (ground-work, weeding, viti-culture) from Naples, Italy and Trasimène	30,000
shepherds from Naples and Italy	4,300
roadmen and ground-workers from Naples and Italy	4,000
grass-mowers from Naples and Italy	3,000
wood-cutters/charcoal-burners from Arno, Tuscany, Italy, Naples	1,500
sowers from Naples	1,200
masons, street-menders and quarrymen from Naples	600
porters from Gênes (300) and Italy (130)	430
	77,030

For the city of Rome the prefect reported yet additional occupations, without, however, specifying any numbers. The 'pull' effect was strongest in the arrondissement of Rome (the city of

Rome and Civitavecchia), the arrondissement of Viterbo (Corneto, Toscanella, Canino and the city of Viterbo), the Pontine marshes and Montalto.
(D) According to the Roman prefect, no workers left Rome; the prefect of Trasimène, however, stated that 8,000 harvesters came to his département from Rome.[46]
(E) The harvest in Rome was brought in also in part by migrant workers from the same département. The prefect provides no numbers; he merely reports on one occasion that workers from the arrondissement of Frosinone made up part of the 32,000 harvesters listed as migrant workers.
(F) Conclusion:

$$\frac{\text{Trek to Rome}}{\text{Trek from Rome}} : \frac{77{,}030 \text{ (PM)}}{8{,}000 \text{ (PM)}} \text{ or rounded off, } \frac{77{,}000 \text{ (PM)}}{8{,}000 \text{ (PM)}}$$

2.3p Département of Golo

(A) AN F 20 434, Bastia 29/8/1808.
'Pull' per occupational group.
(B) Apennins, Taro.
(C) More than 1,600 workers came to Golo during winters to restore the fields and vineyards to order, to cut wood and to make charcoal. They originated from Taro (minimally 250), Gênes, Apennins, Tuscany and Lucca.
(D) No migrants left Golo.
(E) —
(F) Conclusion:

$$\frac{\text{Trek to Golo}}{\text{Trek from Golo}} : \frac{1{,}600}{0}$$

2.3q Département of Liamone

(A) AN F 20 434, Ajaccio 26/9/1808.
'Pull' per occupational group.
(B) Apennins, Taro.
(C) The trek to Liamone consisted of 400 workers, most of them from Lucca, who restored order to fields and vineyards during the winter, felled trees in the forests and prepared charcoal.
(D) Hardly anybody left Liamone to look for work elsewhere.
(E) —
(F) Conclusion:

$$\frac{\text{Trek to Liamone}}{\text{Trek from Liamone}} : \frac{400}{0}$$

2.3r The Kingdom of Italy

(A) —

(B) Alpes Maritimes, Arno, Doire, Elba, Gênes, Hautes Alpes, Marengo, Montenotte, Ombrone, Pô, Rome, Sésia, Simplon, Stura, Taro, Trasimène.

(C) The trek to the Kingdom of Italy included the following groups of workers arranged according to place of origin:

from Doire: tinkers	300
others (70 hawkers, 50 agricultural labourers, 30 miners)	150
from Gênes: a large part of the 30,200 agricultural labourers for the rice fields, and wood-cutters, estimated by me to number at least	25,000
from Marengo: a part of the 4,000 agricultural workers for the rice fields, estimated by me to number at least	1,000
from Montenotte: some of the 60 glass-blowers	PM
from Sésia: some of the 70 carpenters and 350 road repairmen	PM
from Simplon: shepherds	15
from Stura: workers for the rice fields	PM
from Taro: primarily agricultural labourers but also sawyers/wood-cutters and such	4,364
from Trasimène: some of the 300 pork-butchers	PM
	30,829

Considering the uncertainty of the estimates, I believe a total of 30,000 is on the safe side. The most important group of migrants, the agricultural labourers, reported as their destination the Italian départements along the Pô:Agogna, Olona, Haut Pô, Mincio and also Crostolo.

(D) The trek from the Kingdom of Italy included the following groups of workers arranged according to their destinations:

Alpes Maritimes: sieve repairmen and other craftsmen	100
Arno: some of 300-400 masons/chimneysweeps and of 50-60 sawyers and chestnut-roasters	PM

Doire: some of 240 masons, 150 sawyers, 25 straw-hat vendors	PM
others (including 50 casters and 20 makers of wooden grain vats)	82
Hautes Alpes: some of 200 masons/stone-cutters and several tinsmiths	PM
Elba: a small part of 260 agricultural labourers/pedlars	PM
Marengo: some of 1,200 masons/brick-makers and several basket-makers	PM
Montenotte: some of 150 masons	PM
Ombrone: part of 1,000 sawyers/sowers etc. and of 150 shepherds	PM
Pô: some of 1,200 agricultural labourers, of 200 carpenters/wagon-makers/smiths, and of 180 harvesters/shepherds	PM
others (50 sawyers, 10 workers, 8 masons)	68
Rome: some of 32,000 harvesters, of 30,000 agricultural labourers, of 3,400 shepherds and of 1,500 charcoal burners	PM
porters bound for the city of Rome	130
Sésia: shepherds	PM
Simplon: some of 25 masons	PM
masons and two others	90
Stura: part of 270 masons and 9 sawyers	PM
Taro: diverse occupations	64
Trasimène: workers (including 144 chimney-sweeps/scissors-sharpeners)	10,091
	10,625

Given the many groups of workers represented here necessarily by PM, the total 10,625 will be lower than the actual number of migrant workers involved in the trek from Italy. Of more importance are specifications of areas of origin. We can distinguish two principal source areas:

- the Alps (in particular Tirol, Bergamo, Trento, Lake Maggiore and Lake Como are cited),
- the Apennines (in particular the départements Crostolo and Panaro are mentioned, and in addition Urbino, Sassoferrato and the Marche of Ancona).

(E) —
(F) Conclusion:

$$\frac{\text{Trek to Italy}}{\text{Trek from Italy}} : \frac{30{,}000}{>10{,}625} \text{ or rounded off } \frac{30{,}000}{>10{,}600}$$

2.3s The Principality of Lucca

(A) See 2.3j and 2.3l.
(B) Apennins, Elba, Golo, Hautes Alpes, Liamone, Marengo, Méditerranée, Ombrone, Pô, Rome.
(C) Only a small but unknown number of lime-kiln workers, foresters and agricultural labourers from Apennins made the trek to Lucca (recorded as PM).
(D) The trek from Lucca included the following groups of workers arranged according to their destinations:

Apennins: several makers and sellers of plaster statues	PM
Elba: some of 260 agricultural labourers/small traders, estimated by me at	100
Golo: some of 1,600 agricultural and forestry labourers	PM
Hautes Alpes: makers of plaster statues	10
Liamone: a large part of 400 agricultural and forestry labourers, estimated by me at	300
Marengo: makers of plaster statues	PM
Ombrone: grass-mowers/sowers	200
Piombino: grass-mowers/sowers	PM
Pô: makers of plaster statues	30
Rome: olive-pickers	PM
	640

Considering the uncertainty of the number of workers from Golo and Piombino, we should realise the actual total of migrants in the trek from Lucca will have been appreciably higher.

I have consistently interpreted 'plâtriers' and 'ouvriers en plâtre' to conform with the description provided by the prefect of Marengo, 'fabricants de figures en plâtre', and thus translated all alike as the makers of plaster statues — influenced in this choice by awareness of the fact that the inhabitants of Lucca were renowned for this specialisation in the nineteenth century.[47]

(E) —
(F) Conclusion:

$$\frac{\text{Trek to Lucca}}{\text{Trek from Lucca}} : \frac{PM}{>640} \text{ or rounded off, } \frac{PM}{>600}$$

2.3t The Principality of Piombino

(A) See 2.3j and 2.3l.
(B) Arno, Méditerranée and Ombrone.
(C) The trek to Piombino involved 2,000 workers annually, primarily agricultural labourers. They came from the French départements Apennins, Arno, Méditerranée, Ombrone and Taro, the Italian département of Crostolo and from Lucca.
(D) No one left Piombino to find work elsewhere.
(E) —
(F) Conclusion:

$$\frac{\text{Trek to Piombino}}{\text{Trek from Piombino}} : \frac{2,000}{0}$$

2.3u Elba

(A) AN F 20 435 (under Méditerranée), letter from Galeazzini, Commissaire Général de l'Isle d'Elbe et dépendances, Portoferrajo 7/9/1808.
(B) —
(C) The trek to Elba included workers with the following occupations from the following places of origin:

agricultural labourers and (in increasing numbers) small traders from Tuscany and Lucca, and some from Gênes and Italy	260
fishermen from Naples	200
	460

(D) No mention is made of any trek from Elba.
(E) —
(F) Conclusion:

$$\frac{\text{Trek to Elba}}{\text{Trek from Elba}} : \frac{460}{0} \text{ or rounded off, } \frac{500}{0}$$

Appendix 2

2.3v The Kingdom of Naples

(A) —
(B) Alpes Maritimes, Elba, Hautes Alpes, Marengo, Montenotte, Ombrone, Rome, Stura, Trasimène, the Kingdom of Sicily.
(C) Trek to the Kingdom of Naples is not mentioned anywhere.
(D) The trek from the Kingdom of Naples consisted of the following groups of workers arranged according to their destination:

Alpes Maritimes: Calabrian tinkers	100
Elba: Neapolitan fishermen	200
Hautes Alpes: tinkers from both Sicilies	25
Marengo: several Calabrian tinkers, chimneysweeps and tinsmiths	PM
Montenotte: Calabrian tinkers	25
Ombrone: ground-workers from the Abruzzis	500
Rome: sowers from the Abruzzis	1,200
masons, street repairmen and quarryworkers from the Abruzzis	600
some of the 32,000 harvesters, 30,000 agricultural labourers, 4,000 road and canal-construction workers, 3,400 shepherds, 3,000 mowers and 1,500 charcoal-burners from the Abruzzis	PM
Stura: some Calabrian tinkers	PM
Trasimène: some of 9,191 workers from Naples	PM
of whom wool-combers from the Abruzzis	299
Sicily: harvesters	PM
	>2,949

Because of the lack of any reasonable certainty concerning the number of migrant workers bound for Rome and Trasimène, the total here has little significance. In reality it might well have been ten times greater. The most important area of origin was without doubt the Abruzzis. The hundreds of Calabrian tinkers also catch the eye.

(E) —
(F) Conclusion:

$$\frac{\text{Trek to Naples}}{\text{Trek from Naples}} : \frac{0}{>2{,}949} \text{ or rounded off, } \frac{0}{>2{,}900}$$

Appendix 2 257

2.3w The Kingdom of Sardinia

(A) —
(B) Montenotte.
(C) Before 1811, 1,000 tuna fishermen from Montenotte came to Sardinia yearly; afterwards, however, this trek came to an end.
(D) —
(E) —
(F) —

2.3x The Kingdom of Sicily

(A) Aymard 1974: 140-2.
(B) —
(C) From Calabria in the Kingdom of Naples, workers journeyed out to harvest grain on the plains of Catania; to harvest olives, work in vineyards, and to do construction work they travelled to the environs of Palermo. From southern Italy migrants were attracted to the vicinity of Messina for work.
(D) —
(E) —
(F) Conclusion:

$$\frac{\text{Trek to Sicily}}{\text{Trek from Sicily}} : \frac{\text{PM}}{0}$$

2.3y Summary

The number of migrant workers who participated in the treks listed in this appendix are summarised in Table A2.2.

The seasonal shifts of labour described can also be presented in map form as in Figure A2.2.

In attempting to present a summary of the preceding statistical information, complemented by references to leading secondary sources, we remain most in the dark about what went on along the lower reaches of the Pô, to the south of Naples, and on the islands of Sicily and Sardinia.[49]

Two 'pull areas' emerge pre-eminently:

(a) The Pô-Valley: especially the western part of the Pô valley. The trek to Doire, Sésia, Pô, Marengo, Stura and (as far as we can learn) this part of the Kingdom of Italy involved about 46,000 migrants. To this sum we must still add migrant workers from

Table A2.2: Migratory Labour in Italy c. 1810, in Absolute Numbers and Related to Number of Inhabitants[48]

District		Migrant workers to	from	Inhabitants in 1811	% of population to	from
2.3a	Simplon	1,600/2,600	400/1,400	126,000	1.27/2.06	0.32/1.11
b	Doire	700	3,300	234,822	0.30	1.40
c	Sésia	7,000	9,600	202,822	3.45	4.73
d	Pô	3,900/5,400	1,300/2,800	399,237	0.98/1.35	0.33/0.70
e	Marengo	2,400	4,100	318,447	0.75	1.29
f	Stura	400	6,800	431,438	0.09	1.58
g	Montenotte	200	1,300	289,823	0.07	0.45
h	Gênes	PM	30,500	400,056	—	7.62
i	Taro	100	5,100	376,558	0.03	1.35
j	Apennins	PM	200	214,746	—	0.09
k	Arno	500	6,000	599,750	0.08	1.00
l	Méditerranée	PM	PM	318,725	—	—
m	Ombrone	5,200	0	162,795	3.19	0
n	Trasimène	17,200/PM	10,800/PM	300,000	5.73	3.60
o	Rome	77,000/PM	8,000/PM	586,000	13.14	1.36
p	Golo	1,600	0	112,348	1.42	0
q	Liamone	400	0	62,354	0.64	0
r	Italy	30,000	>10,600			
s	Lucca	PM	> 600			
t	Piombino	2,000	0			
u	Elba	500	0			
v	Naples	0	> 2,900			
w	Sardinia	—	—			
x	Sicily	—	—			

Figure A2.2: Migratory Labour in Central and Northern Italy at the Beginning of the Nineteenth Century

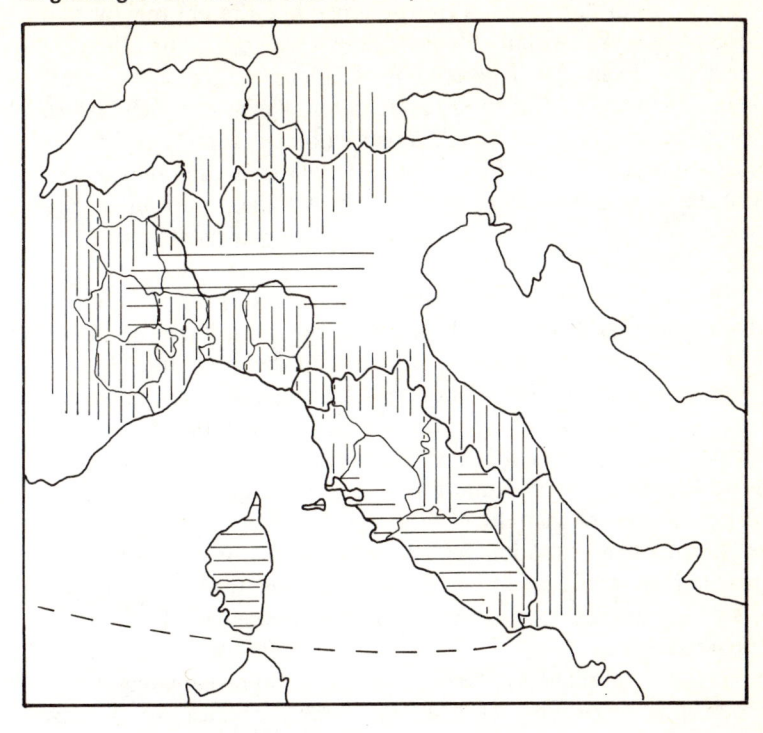

—————— state borders
—————— départemental borders

||| 'push area'

≡ 'pull area'

Switzerland, and the Bavarian and Italian Alps who came to work in the Italian portion of the Pô valley, so that all in all a total of 50,000 workers for this system appears conservative.

In the far west rice cultivation attracted many workers (Vercelli); the care of other crops was dependent on migratory labour as well.[50] In addition the cities as well, Turin and Milan in particular, and perhaps Venice were important employers.[51] Perhaps construction and public works were leading sources of job opportunities, but the services and small-trade sectors were also not negligible. Workers bound for the Pô valley originated from the surrounding mountains: the Ligurian Apennines to the south, Piedmont to the west, the Alps to the north. Different regions and different valleys within them yielded workers with different specialities. From the département of Gênes came many workers for rice cultivation, from Doire and Sésia, the most northwestern départements, came, above all, construction workers, stone-cutters and road-workers, and from Domodossola came chimneysweeps — to mention a few examples.[52] As far as Italian 'push areas' are concerned, their 'watersheds' remain to be indicated here — at least to the extent that this is possible.

Workers from Piedmont certainly also left for France, although those who did are unlikely at the time to have yet been numerous.[53] Thus, in the west of Piedmont there will have been a 'watershed', above all in relation to the French Mediterranean sea coast. In the south there was perhaps a 'watershed' running between Parma and Genoa.[54] In the north we can trace a line from Mont Blanc to Mont Saint Bernhard, on either side of which workers departed on treks in different directions.[55] Last of all, in the northeast the situation was more complicated: it appears as if workers from a large portion of the Dolomites were also attracted to Venice, but their trek was primarily oriented to the Austro-Hungarian plains.[56]

(b) The coastal plane of Piombino as far as, approximately, Cape Circeo, thus Lazio and the southern reaches of Tuscany. To this 'pull area' we should also allocate the islands of Corsica and Elba. For these islands and the principality of Piombino, and for the départements of Ombrone, Trasimène and Rome, 104,800 workers left their homes; a round figure of 100,000 for participants in this system will not exaggerate its dimensions. Here, above all, agriculture needed workers, especially for the cultivation of grain, but viticulture too.[57] In addition the major cities, first and foremost Rome, drew many navvies, construction workers, tradesmen and people employed in the services sector.[58] Such migrant workers came in the first place from the Abruzzi, and in addition from the Apennines, from Umbria and even Calabria.[59]

In closing, we should note that various prefects commented in their responses that at the time of the questionnaire the volume of migratory labour was much lower than it had been previously.[60]

2.4: Migratory Labour in Switzerland, Germany, Austria and Hungary at the Beginning of the Nineteenth Century

Of all the countries treated in this study, I grope most in the dark when attempting to describe the situation in German-speaking states east of the French Empire. Since the researches of Mannhardt in 1865 and of Von der Goltz in 1872, there has existed something of an overall picture of migratory labour in the largest part of these lands, at least for the years mentioned. Yet there are strong indications that immediately prior to the research being undertaken, far-reaching changes in the extent and nature of migratory labour took place so that Mannhardt's and Von der Goltz's material can be used only with the utmost caution in attempting to reconstruct the situation early in the nineteenth century.[61] In so far as earlier information is available, it does appear clear that there were a number of 'push areas', but the existence of demarcated 'pull areas' is less conclusively established. The evidence does not allow us to claim more than three 'pull areas' of more than short-range significance: one in the Austro-Hungarian plains (a), one in southern Germany (b), and one in the Rhine valley (c).

(a) Although I know of no numerical documentation of the trek, in a striking number of instances I have come across mention of labour migration from widely scattered points of origin to the Austro-Hungarian plains. From the variety of 'push areas' tapped and from the distances workers were prepared to travel, we may, however, posit the existence of a — numerically significant — 'pull area'. Workers are reported arriving from the Carpathians, the Tatra (origin of the Podhalian people) and from Venice and Friuli.[62]

(b) Although far less a variety of 'push areas' is reported for the south of Württemberg and of Bavaria and workers came from shorter distances, in one instance larger numbers of migrants have been reported. The workers in this region come on the one hand from more northern places such as Schwarzwald, Alb and Bayerische Wald, and on the other hand, and to a far greater extent, from the eastern Swiss and western Austrian Alps. Young shepherds especially, so-called *Hütekinder*, have attracted analysts' attention. For 1838 a total of 33,600 migrant workers is recorded, originating from Vorarlberg, Oberinntal and Unterinntal (15,500 from present-day Austria) and from Pusstortal, Ander Etsch,

Trento and Rovereto (18,100 from present-day Italy). It is improbable, however, that they all went to southern Germany.[63] As a counter-argument we can refer to the trek from the Swiss, Austrian and Italian Alps which took workers to Italy — a route for migrant workers which emerges from the answers to the Questionnaire forwarded by a number of Italian prefects. Küther, who recently devoted a special study to *Vagieren* (drifting) in Bavaria, Franconia and Swabia in the second half of the eighteenth century, maintains, moreover, that this region was comparatively backwards economically and without migratory labour.[64]

(c) The Rhine valley has already been discussed during the account of the North Sea System in the text and in Appendix 2.2 concerning migratory labour in France. The left bank of the Rhine, including the French départements Bas Rhin and Haut Rhin together with the arrondissements Mainz and Speier, appear to have attracted thousands of workers from the north, east and south, but also from across the river.[65] On the right bank of the Rhine we can add the trek of the 'Swabians' from Württemberg to Baden, from the Odenwald to Mannheim and Heidelberg; moreover Westerwald, Vogelsberg and Rhön witnessed the departure of large numbers of workers for the vicinity of Frankfurt.[66] Several well-known 'push areas' have already been cited here above: outside the Alpine region, Schwarzwald, Alb, Bayerische Wald, Odenwald, Westerwald, Vogelsberg and Rhön. Further north the Eichsfeld and the Oder — and Warthebruch certainly should still be mentioned.

Prior to the research of Mannhardt and von der Goltz, all these regions were already known as 'push areas', but it still remains far from clear where the workers who came from these places went to find work, and in what numbers.[67] In the absence of these data we must not preclude the possibility that major migratory-labour systems existed, but — in contrast to the situation in other countries such as Italy and France — we are not in a position to prove their existence.

2.5: *Migratory Labour in Scandinavia, Including Schleswig-Holstein*

It is rather unusual to combine Schleswig-Holstein with Scandinavia, but three facts have persuaded me to do so: during the period in which we are primarily interested Schleswig-Holstein was under Danish rule; it was separated from the rest of Germany by the département of Bouches de l'Elbe; and, not unimportantly, the duchy apparently could also be referred to in source materials as 'Denmark'. Little is known about migratory labour to Finland and Norway in the early nineteenth century, so that we can confine our attention here to Sweden and Denmark.[68]

The history of migratory labour in Sweden has been amply mapped in the extensive studies of Rosander.[69] For the period around 1800 Rosander distinguishes one important migratory-labour system: thousands of workers, male and female, left central Sweden, journeying in particular from Dalarna, but also from Jämtland and Harjedalen, to find work on the Swedish east coast near Stockholm. The number of persons involved c. 1800 is difficult to ascertain; Rosander offers only the statistic of 3,500-4,500 migratory workers in a typical year towards the middle of the nineteenth century.

Until the close of the eighteenth century there was also a migratory-labour system in existence in southern Sweden. By 1800, however, this system had all but disappeared. From Värmland, Västergotland, Småland and Halland, in the late eighteenth century, no fewer than 12,000 herring fishermen went every year to Bohuslän, and its leading city, Göteborg. It appears, however, that during the period with which this book is primarily concerned southern Sweden functioned as a 'push' area providing workers for Denmark. In 1802, 6,000 Swedish farmhands were employed on the Danish island of Sjaelland and whether or not these were seasonal workers or actual immigrants to Denmark remains uncertain.[70] The question now is what we should understand the trek to Denmark as entailing. There are indications that the actual Kingdom of Denmark, and particularly Sjaelland with its capital, Copenhagen, employed numerous Swedes. In 1808 this group constituted perhaps even more than 1 per cent of the population. As far as we now know, however, these were for the most part craftsmen in semi-permanent residence.[71] For this period it has not yet proved possible to demonstrate seasonal migration of Swedish agricultural labourers to Denmark. This trek, to the best of our present knowledge, first began in the 1840s, while Polish labour migration to Denmark commenced still later.[72]

On the other hand, migratory labour to Schleswig-Holstein can be demonstrated earlier than the turn of the nineteenth century. From the French Empire 300 agricultural labourers from Bouches de l'Elbe and from Ems Supérieur, as well as a number of vendors and perhaps several brick-makers from Lippe found work on the right bank of the Elbe.[73]

By 'the right bank of the Elbe', Schleswig-Holstein was in all likelihood meant. The questionnaires of Mannhardt (1865) and Von der Goltz (1872) indeed seem to disclose that a trek took place from Sweden and Denmark proper to these more southern duchies.[74]

Closer scrutiny of the Schleswig-Holstein 'pull area' reveals that the main attraction was the coast along the North Sea, from Dithmarschen in the south via Nordfriesland to the area around Ribe.[75] This 'pull area' was divided from the actual North Sea System by the territory between Weser and Elbe which seems not to have drawn any migrant workers.[76]

To the fertile 'Marsch' along this stretch of the north German and Danish coast, not only did the previously mentioned several hundred agricultural labourers from the south of the French Empire come, but also workers from regions to the east of that area, such as the 'Prostei' near Kiel, and from the western situated Nordfriesland islands even as far as Fanö.[77] I have discovered no numerical sources, but see no reason to suggest that this system compared in magnitude to the North Sea System, and we might well consider it as an offshoot of that system. The first recorded journey of brick-makers from Lippe to Denmark dates from 1847.[78]

2.6: Migratory Labour in Great Britain and Ireland at the Beginning of the Nineteenth Century

From the 1820s on, information is abundant concerning migratory labour in Great Britain and Ireland. The phenomenon after this initial period kept increasing in scale and importance. It is difficult, however, to appraise the situation one or two decades earlier. The data at my disposal pertain almost exclusively to Irish workers, and some Scots and Welshmen, but a fog still hangs over internal labour movements within England. We merely have some indications that migrant workers usually confined their search for work to comparatively short distances. Within these limitations we are able nevertheless to gather an idea, albeit rather crude, of how things developed.[79]

Aside from several smaller 'pull areas' where workers came by the thousand and not by tens of thousands, one 'pull area' stands out sharply. This area can be described as including London and its environs (the 'Home Counties') and the counties due north: Hertfordshire, Cambridgeshire, but especially Suffolk, Norfolk and Lincolnshire (East Anglia and the 'Fens').[80] In London itself construction, public works and street hawking were important occupations for migrant workers, while outside the city, market-gardening to feed the metropolitan population was important.[81] Further north migrant labourers came to perform a range of harvest tasks. By far the majority of them were Irish by origin (from Connacht especially), some 15,000 to 20,000. Several thousand Scots found such employment as well, and Welshman were reported too. For this 'pull area' we can calculate, minimally, some 20,000 migrant workers.[82]

Smaller, secondary 'pull areas' attracted migrants as well: in the west of England and the counties of Cheshire, Shropshire and Herefordshire and, perhaps, the adjacent area round about the city of Cardiff in the south of Wales. This was the destination of workers from Cardiganshire in the west and from the north of Wales.[83]

To southern Scotland, especially Ayr in the west and the 'Lothians' in the east, around Edinburgh, and perhaps connecting up with Northumberland in northern England came workers from both the Scottish Highlands, particularly from Argyll, Perth, Ross and Cromarty, and — in this period in ever increasing numbers — the north of Ireland. To what extent migrant workers from the 'Border Counties' and adjacent Cumberland found work in this nearby 'pull area' as well as in the south of England, I am unable to say.[84]

The Irish counties of Limerick, Clare, Tipperary and the north of Cork accommodated workers primarily from further south, from County Kerry and the south of Cork, but also from Galway situated to the north, while the area around Belfast received migrant workers from Donegal in the northwest.[85]

'Push areas', already mentioned, reappear here summarily in order of their importance:

- Connacht in the west of Ireland, consisting of Galway, Mayo, Roscommon and the south of Sligo, provided the lion's share of Irish migrant workers, approximately 15,000 to 20,000. These journeyed via Dublin and Drogheda to Liverpool, and also to Holyhead, moving on through Lancashire and the West Riding of Yorkshire to reach their chosen destinations in Lincolnshire and

further south, even as far away as London.
- Also in Ireland we can distinguish the 'push areas' of Kerry and southern Cork in the southwest, whence workers went solely to neighbouring counties of Limerick, Clare and Tipperary, and the north of Cork. Migrants from the northwestern counties of Donegal, Tyrone and Londonderry, who in addition to the Belfast area, also went to southern Scotland, and left Ireland from the ports of Belfast and Londonderry bound for Glasgow. Finally, construction workers from western Leinster and from the Belfast area were also cited as holding jobs in England.[86]
- In the Scottish Highlands the counties of Ross and Cromarty, Argyll and Perth witnessed the departure of workers for places in the south of Scotland and in Northumberland. During the Coalition Wars their trek to East Anglia and London ended, although these both remained the destinations of workers from the second Scottish 'push area', the so-called 'Border Counties' along the English border[87] together with neighbouring Northumberland.
- In Wales the northern counties and Cardiganshire in the southwest were 'push areas', perhaps neighbouring Shropshire as well. In addition to the valley of Glamorgan in the south of Wales, migrant workers from these places headed above all for Cheshire, Shropshire and Herefordshire in the east of England. Women from these northern counties and from Shropshire pushed on as far as the London area.
- In England itself the south and centre receive mention as 'push areas' although migrant labourers originating from here did not go far, and no clear-cut single 'pull area' seems to have lured them with jobs.[88] This area lies like a wedge sundering eastern and western 'pull areas'. It appears that in the decades following the Napoleonic era the Irish came in such force to work in the south (Gloucestershire, Wiltshire, Oxfordshire, Buckinghamshire, Berkshire, Surrey, West Sussex and Kent) and in the north (Lancashire, the West Riding of Yorkshire and Nottinghamshire), that the two former 'pull areas' fused together. In central England there remained still a region for which no migratory labour is reported: Derbyshire, Staffordshire, Worcestershire, Warwickshire, Leicestershire and Northamptonshire.[89]

'Pull' and 'push' areas have been designated in Figure A2.3.

Figure A2.3: 'Pull' and 'Push Areas' in Great Britain and Ireland *c.* 1800-10

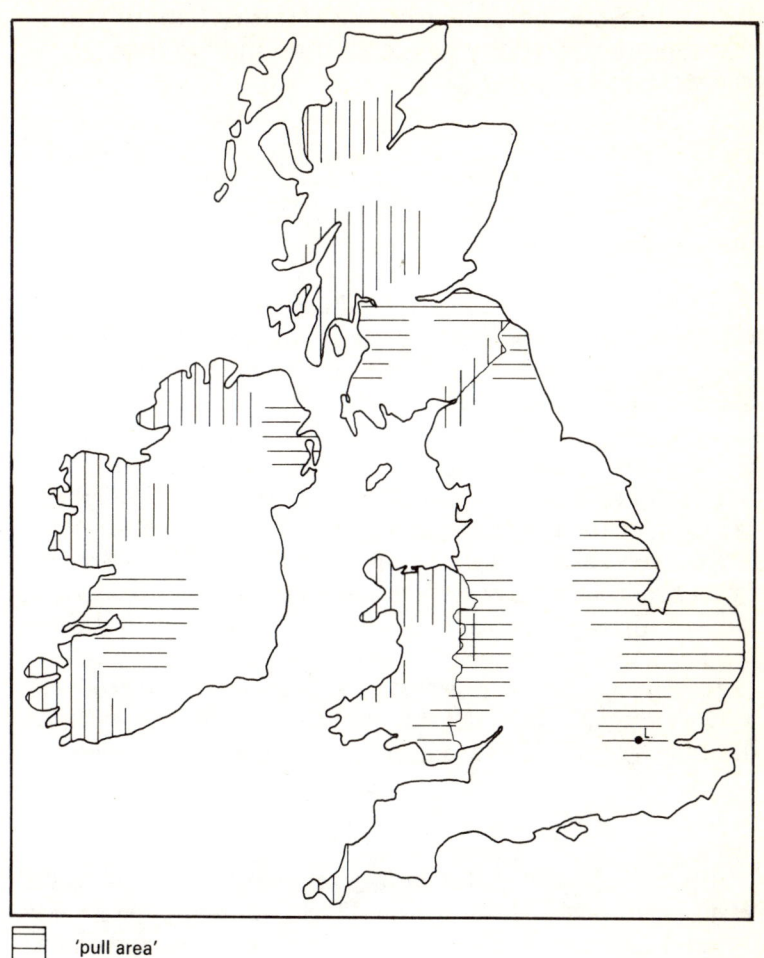

▤ 'pull area'

▥ 'push area'

L.   London

APPENDIX 3
Justification of the Quantitative Comparison Between Different Sources Concerning Migratory Labour from the West of Germany to the Netherlands in the Nineteenth Century

Introduction

The quantitative data in this appendix come from sources which vary widely in character. As a consequence, problems arise in attempting comparisons. First, the geographic units involved frequently differ, especially as the result of political changes which occurred after the collapse of the first French Empire. New divisions were made both of the German portion of the Empire and of various vassal states, such as the Kingdom of Westphalia. Secondly, religious sources account for certain data from 1861. These involve a division of territory according to sees determined by Lutheran church organisation, one which deviates from secular, political division. Thirdly, it is necessary to account for diverse administrative sub-divisions.

All the relevant data of which I am aware have been processed in this appendix in order to facilitate — where possible — deductions about the quantitative development of migratory labour from different German areas. Dubious statistics, and the totals of questionable calculations have been printed in parentheses.

It is to be expected that further research, particularly in the archives of Prussia, Hannover and Lippe, will turn up previously unknown quantitative information. This appendix therefore should be considered as an initial attempt to trace broad developments, one which might encourage efforts in yet greater depth.

The geographical entities used throughout this appendix are the states and their administrative sub-divisions as they existed from 1815 to 1866. This means that statistics from before and after this period have had to be 'translated' to fit the political divisions to which, by choice, the appendix adheres.

We will consider in succession:

Appendix 3 269

(1) The Kingdom of Prussia, in particular the Regierungsbezirke Minden and Münster, 1811-61.
(2) The Kingdom of Hannover, in particular the Landdrosteien Aurich, Osnabrück, Hannover and Stade, 1811-c. 1900.
(3) The Grand Duchy of Oldenburg, 1811-c. 1900.
(4) The Principality of Lippe-Detmold, 1811-1923.
(5) Remaining regions (Braunschweig, Hesse, Mecklenburg) 1865-84.

Figure A3.1 illustrates the location of these areas.

Figure A3.1: The Netherlands and a Number of German 'Push Areas' 1815-66

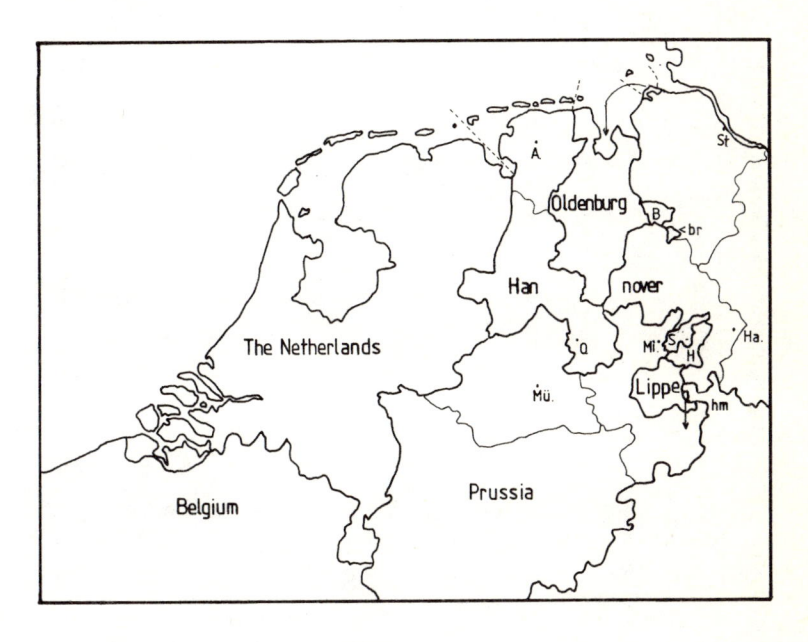

	Cities		Regions
A	Aurich	B	Bremen
St	Stade	S	Schaumburg-Lippe
Ha.	Hannover	H	Schaumburg-Hesse (part of the Electorate of Hesse)
Mi.	Minden	br	Part of Braunschweig
Mü	Münster	hm	Kreis Holzminden (Braunschweig)
O.	Osnabrück		

3.1: Quantitative Data Concerning Migratory Labour from the Kingdom of Prussia, in particular from the Regierungbezirke Minden and Münster, 1811-61

Table A3.1: Migratory Labour from Regierungsbezirk Minden 1811-61[1]

Kreis	Sub-division	1811	1817	1819	1821	1822	1823	1824	1826	1827	1828	1830	1840	1843	1861
Lübbecke	eg Alswede	see Levern													25
	eg Blasheim	see Lübbecke													20
	eg Börninghausen	see Lübbecke													5
	eg Dielingen	see Levern													15
	eg Gehlenbeck	see Lübbecke													4
	eg Holzhausen	see Lübbecke													3
	eg/m Hüllhorst	8													6
	eg/k Levern	22													43
	eg/k Lübbecke	25													20
	eg (Preuss.) Oldendorf	see Lübbecke													30
	eg/kr?/k Rahden	310	182	137	43	37	47	21							183
	eg Schnathorst	see Hüllhorst													20
	eg Ströherr	see Rahden													12
	eg Wehdem	see Levern													21
	Sub-total	365	(182)	(137)	(43)	(37)	(47)	(21)					434	394	407
Minden	eg Friedewalde	44													5
	eg/k Petershagen														15
	eg Ovenstädt														5
	eg/a Hartum									30		11	94	114	10
	eg Lahde	(WF)													40
	eg Windheim	(WF)													25
	eg Buchholz	see Petershagen													10
	eg Heimsen	(WF)													10
	eg/m Bergkirchen	0													20
Herford	eg/kr/m Bünde	0	(63)	(77)	(64)	(83)	(65)	(83)							9
	kr/m Herford	0	(41)	(60)	(10)	(31)	(44)	(22)							—

	eg/k Mennighüffen	12														3
	eg/m Rödinghausen	0														8
	eg Valdorf	(WF)														100
	Sub-total	(12)		104	137	74	114	109	105							120
Halle	eg/m Borgholzhausen	0														10
	eg Brockhagen	(WF)														25
	eg Halle	0														20
	eg Steinhagen	(WF)														10
	Sub-total	(0)		22	91	63	73	72	65							65
Bielefeld	eg Ubbedissen	(WF)								43			58			30
	a/k Versmold	4				48	28	27	35	20	17		53	8	6	—
	Sub-total	(4)				48	28	27	35	20	(17)		53	(53)	(6)	30
Wiedenbrück	eg Gütersloh	(WF)														20
	Sub-total	—		156	240	249	281	258	243							(20)
Paderborn		(WF)		110	162	118	128	110	88							—
Büren		(WF)		226	258	211	222	190	158							—
Warburg		(WF)		14	8	13	16	34	32						7	—
Höxter	kr. Bra(c)kel	(WF)		55	55	50	61	72	72						17	—
	Sub-total	—		(55)	(55)	(50)	(61)	(72)	(72)						(8)	—
Total of data represented here		425	—	940	1,214	947	1,087	1,027	947	—	90	—	122	576	550	782
Total Regierungsbezirk		—	—	940	1,214	947	1,087	1,027	947	1,689	1,794	1,750	—	1,786	1,564	—

Abbreviations: a: Amt; eg: evangelical (Lutheran) Gemeinde in 1861; m: mairie in 1811; k: canton in 1811; kr: kreis; WF: part of the Kingdom of Westphalia in 1811.

Table A3.2: Migratory Labour from Regierungsbezirk Münster 1811-61[2]

Kreis	Subdivision	1811	1828	1861	% Lutherans in 1849
Tecklenburg	eg Brochterbeck			5	35.8
	eg/m Cappeln	10		15	88.4/99.4
	eg Ibbenbüren			10	19.5/32.1
	eg/m Ladbergen	120		130	99.9
	eg/m Ledde	30		3	95.8
	eg/m Lengerich	12		50	89.7/99.6
	eg Mettingen			2	16.5
	eg Recke			21	13.2
	eg/m Tecklenburg	10		3	94.8
	Sub-total	±1000	1398	(239)	
Münster			490		
Ahaus			378		
Steinfurt	eg Steinfurt			3	
	Sub-total		619		
Warendorf			170		
Lüdinghausen			85		
Koesfeld			38		
Borken			12		
Recklinghausen			3		
Beckum			0		
Total			3193		

Abbreviations: eg: evangelical (Lutheran) Gemeinde in 1861; m: mairie in 1811

Yet another comparison between data from 1811 and 1828 is possible: the area of the arrondissement Steinfurt together with that of the mairie Rheine in the canton of Bevergern in 1811 is equivalent to the following in 1828: Kreis Steinfurt, a northern portion of Kreis Koesfeld and Kreis Ahaus, with the exception of the southeast.

This yields the comparison shown in Table A3.3.

Table A3.3: Migratory Labour from the Environment of Steinfurt 1811 and 1828

1811		1828	
Arr. Steinfurt	1,565	Kreis Steinfurt	619
mairie Rheine	± 50	Kreis Koesfeld (northern part)	< 38
		Kreis Ahaus (without the southeast)	< 378
Total	±1,615		<1,035

3.2: Quantitative Data Concerning Migratory Labour from the Kingdom of Hannover, in Particular from the Landdrosteien Aurich, Osnabrück, Hannover and Stade, 1811-c. 1900

Table A3.4: Migratory Labour from Landdrostei Aurich 1811-c. 1900[3]

Kreis	Sub-division	1811	1861	c.1870	c.1900
Wittmund	A. Wittmund		0		
	A. Esens		0		
	Sub-total	*	0		
Norden	A. Berum	*	150/200		
Aurich		*	90/110		
Emden		*	57		
Weener		181	420/475		
Leer	A. Leer		40/ 50		
	A. Stickhausen		20		
	Sub-total	*	60/ 70		
Total		281	777/912	±2,000	300/350

Key: A.: Amt
*: for the department of Ems Oriental a total of 100 (see Appendix 1.3)

Table A3.5: Migratory Labour from Landdrostei Osnabrück 1811-c. 1900

Kreis	Sub-division	1811	1850	1861	1864	1866	1867	1868	1871	c. 1900
Aschendorf		± 250							(0)	100
Sögel		±1,300							(0)	100
Meppen		± 450							(0)	
Bentheim	A. Bentheim	± 400		44						
	A. Neuenhaus	± 100		240						
	Sub-total	± 500		284					(?)	100
Lingen	A. Lingen			7						
	A. Freren			> 441						
	Sub-total	±1,800		> 448		1500			(±1,500)	
Bersenbrück	A. Bersenbrück	±1,885		183	884		1099	999	(±1,000)	
	A. Fürstenau	±1,380		305					(±1,000)	
	— V. Berge		>242							
	A. Vörden	± 75		65						
	Sub-total	3340		553					(±2,000)	
Wittlage		158		7						
Osnabrück		96		0						
Iburg		161		0						
Melle		50		5					(0)	
Total		±8,105		>1,297					≥3,500	200

Key: A.: Amt
V: Vogtei (sub-division of an Amt)

NB: Data for 1861, in comparison with figures for other years, are highly incomplete. Probably the information we have applies solely to Lutherans.

Table A3.6: Migratory Labour from Landdrostei Hannover 1811-c.1900[5]

Kreis	Sub-division	1811	1824	1859	1860	1861	1862	1863	1864	1865 A	1865 B	1866	c.1900
Diepholz		426	±600								100		20/30
Syke	(Amt Freudenberg)	(±50)	± 80								50	877	0
Sulingen	(Amt Ehrenburg-Barenburg)		±300								200		0
Hoya	(Amt Bruchhausen)	±1,002	—	65	1	13	2	2	16	2	200		0
Stolzenau	(Amt Uchte)		—								—	—	0
Nienburg			—								50		0
Total		±1,428	(±980)								(600)	(877)	20/30

Appendix 3

Table A3.7: Migratory Labour from Landdrostei Stade 1811-c.1900[6]

Kreis	1811	1859	1865	c.1900
Achim	⎫	—	—	0
Verden	⎬ ± 725	12	0	0
Rotenburg	⎭	—	—	0
Blumental	⎫			
Zeven	⎬ ± 270			
Osterholz	⎪			
Others	⎭			
Total	±1,000			0

3.3: Quantitative Data Concerning Migratory Labour from the Grand Duchy of Oldenburg, 1811-1900

Table A3.8: Migratory Labour from Oldenburg 1811-1900[7]

Amt	Sub-division	1811	1865	1866	1868	1869	1880	1895	1900
Vechta	eg/m Neuenkirchen	(155)			7				
	Subtotal	1,610	50						
Cloppenburg		742							PM
Friesoythe		174							PM
Wildeshausen	eg/m Wildeshausen	8			4				
	eg/m Huntlosen	0			8				
	eg/m Grossenkneten	0			46				
	eg Dötlingen	*			5				
	Subtotal	(8)			63				
Delmenhorst	eg Ganderkesee	⎫			9				
Oldenburg	eg Wardenburg	⎬ 300			299				PM
	eg/k Hatten	⎪			89				
	Subtotal	⎭			388				
Westerstede									
Total		2,834			(467)				
Grass-mowers and turf-cutters		2,834	300	400	14				
Plasterers		0			453	600	2,000	65	

Abbreviations: eg: evangelical (Lutherans) Gemeinde in 1868
k: canton in 1811
m: mairie in 1811
*: part of arrondissement Oldenburg (probably canton Delmenhorst) in 1811

3.4: Quantitative Data Concerning Migratory Labour from the Principality of Lippe-Detmold, 1811-1923

Because of the dominant position of brick-makers, we can best group data concerning migratory labour from this region according to the kind of work migrants performed. With the passage of time increasing numbers of brick-makers set out for other destinations than places along the North Sea coast. Therefore, the table differentiates brick-makers bound for Groningen and Ostfriesland (the so-called First District) from those who found jobs elsewhere (the Second, Third and Fourth Districts: the rest of Germany, Scandinavia, East and Southwest Europe).

Table A3.9: Migratory Labour from Lippe-Detmold 1811-1923[8]

	Grass-mowers, turf cutters	Brick-makers			Total migrant workers	
	to the Netherlands and Ostfriesland	to the Netherlands and Ostfriesland (1st district)	elsewhere (2nd-4th district)	Total	to the Netherlands and Ostfriesland
1811	250	660	162	822	910
1820		573	487	1,060	
1830		430	686	1,116	
1840		652	1,759	2,411	
1850		794	2,456	3,250	
1860	312	1,267	6,353	7,620	1,579
1865	400	1,254			1,654
1866	500	1,232			1,732
1869		1,151	7,079	8,230	
1882				11,900	
1895				12,400	
1900	0	150	13,850	14,000	150
1912	0			14,227	
1923	0			7,969	

3.5: Quantitative Data Concerning Migratory Labour from Other Areas (Braunschweig, Hesse, Mecklenburg), 1865-84

Duchy of Braunschweig. In 1866 among foreign workers in Friesland 20 grass-mowers were counted who came from Kreis Holzminden in Braunschweig. This kreis bordered on the Prussian Kreis Höxter (see Appendix 3.1) and was extremely close to Lippe-Detmold. In addition another two workers from Braunschweig were reported employed in a brick-works in Veendam (Groningen) in 1873.[9]

278   *Appendix 3*

Electorate of Hesse.

Table A3.10: Migratory Labour from the Electorate of Hesse 1865-84[10]

	1865	1866	1873	1875	1883	1884
Grass-mowers in Friesland	20	30				
Brick-makers in Groningen			13	4	2	>3

Mecklenburg (Grand Duchy of Mecklenburg-Schwerin?). In 1865 there were 50 men from Oldenburg and Mecklenburg digging turf in Dedemsvaart and Lutten. This assertion, wholly unconfirmed, may rest on a mistake.[11]

NOTES

Chapter 1

1. Cf. Tack 1902: 1-8, and Lucassen 1982.
2. Haks 1982: 141-50.
3. See Chapter 4 below.
4. Ibid.
5. See Part II: 120-4.
6. For German *Wanderburschen*: Reininghaus 1981, Roscher 1887, (vol. III, 5th edn): 621-2; for English Travelling Brothers: Leeson 1979; for French *Compagnons*: Coornaert 1966 and Barret and Gurgand 1980. In addition see Le Play 1877/79, V: 1-59; 424-78.
7. Braudel 1976, I: 42; Redlich 1964; Bruijn and Lucassen 1980: 11-29, 134-40. The subject of mercenaries requires not only the study of European armies, but also particularly of colonial ones, such as the French Foreign Legion and the Dutch KNIL (Royal Dutch East Indies Army).
8. Bruijn and Lucassen 1980.
9. Gutton 1981: 101-9; Haks 1982: 19-20; 167-74.
10. See Chapter 4 below.
11. This is true not only for historical writing in the Netherlands, but outside as well. For prominent titles, see the notes to Appendix II. Bade (1980) is an exception; one of his concerns is the relation between migrant labour and migration itself in late-19th century Germany. Bade, too, has an extensive bibliography.
12. E.g. Penninx and Van Velzen 1977: 89-107.
13. Until now the most important publications about this North Sea area are Tack 1902, Van Asselt 1976 and 1977, and Lucassen 1982. Obviously Great Britain also has a coast on the North Sea, indeed a coast, as will be made clear, with a major 'pull area'. Nevertheless, in this study, unless otherwise stated, in talking of The North Sea coast, I will be referring to the continental coastline along the eastern shore of the sea.
14. For the United Provinces in the 17th century, see De Vries 1974; for the origins of labour migration to Holland, see Lucassen 1982 and pp. 133 ff. of this book.
15. For examples of such obstacles, see, for one, Tack 1902.
16. Chatelain 1976: 23-7; cf. also Pijnacker's answer to the questionnaire (ARA, GB 1807-1815: 921); the mayor has listed those persons 'qui se trouvent encore ici à cause qu'ils sont été ici peut être juste dans les annees Lorsque le Conscription était dans leur Pays'; and the remark of the Prefect of Bouches du Weser to the Sub-prefect of Bremen (SAB, F 3a III: 28/5/1811):

> il est nécessaire ... de prévenir une absence qui favoriserait ceux dont l'intention est de se dérober à la conscription et qui nous priverait en outre des ouvriers qui nous sont si nécessaires pour l'exécution des travaux de la nouvelle route.

17. Cf. Appendix I: 6 and Boot, Lourens and Lucassen 1983.
18. For various possibilities about how to interpret the information concerning Westphalia, see Appendix I: 34.

19. See Appendix II.
20. RAL, Nedermaas 2808 (letter Paris 4/3/1811 to the prefect of Meuse Inférieure); Chatelain 1976: 25; Corsini 1969: 143.
21. For the following discussion, see Annex I and its citation of sources, for France, see Chatelain 1976: 23-51.
22. For license taxes, and their relevance to 'foreign workers', see Lucassen 1982: 343.
23. Quoted from the answer sent from Ouder-Amstel (Zuyderzee).
24. For a complete account of the steps which I followed in processing data concerning the North Sea System, see the original Dutch version of this study: Lucassen 1984: Appendix I (250-333). An abbreviated description of this work method appears on pp. 217 ff. below.
25. In Appendix I, see the answers to Question E; for West Flanders, to name one place, it may be supposed that considerable internal migratory labour took place about which we have no clear knowledge; cf. Appendix I: 21.
26. Data from an overwhelming majority of the départements in the North Sea System pertain to the year 1811. Where this was not true (see list below), the number of migrant workers for 1811 has been estimated, in Appendix I according to criteria which are set forth in the appendix. Data for 1809: Frise, Ardennes; 1809-10: Moselle; 1808-10: Ourthe; 1810: Pas de Calais, Dyle, Escaut, Jemappes, Lys, Rhin et Moselle, Sarre; 1812: Bouches de l'Elbe. These départements are thus concentrated in the southern and southeastern part of the study area. For replies from the rest of the Empire, see Appendix III: 2 and III: 3.
27. See below p.148 and, e.g., Appendix I under different départements sub H (Lucassen 1984) and Appendix 2-3, note 60.
28. See below, p. 86.
29. See below, p. 65.

Chapter 2

1. Substantiated by conclusions drawn from data in Appendix I.
2. From Appendix 1.21 it would seem uncertain whether migrant workers avoided the stretch of coast at Lys. For additional doubts, see also Mendels 1978: 336. In any event the entire Flemish North Sea coast was a 'pull area' around 1900, see Blanchard 1905: 512-17.
3. Appendix 1.
4. Appendix 1.
5. See below, Chapter 3. Such a distance meant a maximum of ten days travel should the whole route be covered on foot — something which practically never took place. Cf. Reininghaus 1981: 9.
6. De Vries 1978: maps on pp. 65 and 88; for Belgium and Northern France, see specifically 43-4. For shipping canals in Ostfriesland, see e.g. Wiarda 1880: 33.
7. De Zeeuw 1978: 16-19.
8. Faber et al., 1965; see also Slicher van Bath 1975.
9. De Vries 1974 and Swart 1910: 224-7 (comparison of the Dutch and German coastal area).
10. Van der Woude 1980: 137-9.
11. De Meere 1980A: 358-9 (Table 1, column VIII); De Meere 1982: 71-7; for the difference between Ostfriesland and the interior, see Wiarda 1880: 72-3.
12. Bouman 1946: 15, 58.
13. See below, Chapter 4.

14. For Flanders see also Mendels 1978.
15. Sources: For Flanders: Vandenbroeke 1975: 371 and map XIX; for Regierungsbezirk Münster: Gladen 1970: 58 (looms); Reekers 1956: 6 (population 1818) and Appendix 3.1A (migrant workers); for Lippe: Steinbach 1976: 170 (population 1835) and Meyer 1895: 63 (looms 1836); for Regierungsbezirk Minden: Von Reden 1853: 4: 810-94, and 1597-1600 and Mager 1982: 465-6; for Twente: De ontwikkeling 1963: 9 and Table 2 (looms 1811) and Ramaer 1931: 266 (population 1815). For Westphalia, see also Schlumbohm's outstanding study (1979).
16. Linen weaving was probably only of marginal importance in Wiedenbrück (see Table 2.3). This observation can also be derived from simple mathematics: if we compare the total number of looms in the Gemeinsame Handelskammer Bielefeld/Halle/Wiedenbrück/Vlotho/the west of Lippe (6,038 looms) with separate totals for Lippe (±3,500), Bielefeld (2,500), Herford (1,200) and Halle (210), few looms remain that can possibly be ascribed to Wiedenbrück. (For sources see Table 2.1.)
17. Based on Table 2.1.
18. Gladen 1970: 68-9. Numbers for eastern municipalities in 1811 are reported exactly, but statistics for the western municipalities in some instances involve difficulties since only totals per canton are available — among which certain places are included which fall outside Tecklenburg. The numbers cited: Ladbergen 120; Ibbenbüren, Mettingen and Recke together 520, Bevergern, Riesenbeck (probably including Dreierwalde) and Brochterbeck together with the non-Tecklenburg municipalities Rheine, Salzbergen and Saerbeck 362; and Hopsten and Schale together with the non-Tecklenburg places of Freren, Beesten, Schapen, Thuine, Messingen and Backum together 1,025. My estimate of 1,000 is a conservative one.
19. Households: Gladen 1970: 203; migrant workers, see note 18; looms: Gladen 1970: 57 (cf. also p. 55 for similar production in 1816). In the totals for households per migrant and per loom and the number of all households and of Heuerlinge households in particular, Lienen in the east and Ladbergen in the west have been excluded because of lack of data. Both were included, however, in calculation of the number of migrant workers (30 and 120, respectively).
20. Source: Mager 1982: 465-6 (families in linen manufacture 1838); Von Reden 1853/4: 810-69 (linen manufacture in 1846 and inhabitants in 1849; Appendix 3.1.
21. Mager 1982; Schlumbohm 1979. Not only weaving, but spinning as well could be engaged in so intensively that it precluded migrant labour. See Mager 1981: 154 concerning Spenge where he maintains there was no labour migration, a fact confirmed by the questionnaire in the département Ems Supérieur to which Spenge belonged in 1811 (see Appendix 1.4).
22. Steinbach 1976: 61 and 130. It was above all from the eastern Aemter where there was little textile industry that grass-mowers and peat-cutters came (see Boot, Lourens and Lucassen 1983); cf. also Meyer 1895: 61-6 and 98-103.
23. For the area between the Rhine and the Ruhr, see, for example, Hohorst 1977 (especially good about Kreis Hagen), Denzel 1952 and Huck and Reulecke 1978.
24. For industries in the southern Netherlands, see Hasquin 1979.
25. Von Reden 1853-4: 876; 909-12.
26. Klep 1981.
27. Source: Calculated from *Agriculture 1850*. For the limitation of the small-size farm category to 1 ha, cf. Vandenbroeke 1979: 75-6; see p. 74 of the same work for the size of Flemish farms during the 18th century. For the demographic history of Charleroi, the area with the greatest difference between large and small farms, see André 1970.

28. Delatte 1945: 157, 237-8.
29. Vandenbroeke 1979: 74. We should keep in mind that during the census thousands of Flemish migrant labourers already went every year to France; in 1811, on the other hand, this journey had not yet become an established phenomenon.
30. For the following description, see Klep 1981: 288-308; Vandenbroeke 1979; Vandenbroeke and Vanderpijpen 1981.
31. Cited in Dutch in Klep 1981: 301 from J. Arrivabene: 'Sur la condition des laboureurs et des ouvriers belges et sur quelques mesures pour l'améliorer. Suivie d'une nouvelle édition de l'enquête sur l'état des habitans de la commune Gaesbeeck, augmentée de quelques notes', Bruxelles 1845: 49-62. For Germany, cf. Meurer 1871: 12-21.
32. Von Reden 1853-4: 869-94.
33. Van Aelbroek 1823: 188-9.
34. Von Reden 1853-4: 909-12; farm size there was, for example, comparable to farm size on the Island of Cadzand, see Appendix 1.22.
35. Mager 1982: 442. The author indicates a connection between domestic industry and seasonal job opportunities on large local farms in Ravensberg.
36. For a general introduction to the agriculture of these regions, see Sneller 1943: 302-3 and Roessingh 1979.
37. For cultivation of hemp, see Verrips 1977: 20-30; Landbouwenquête 1953: 166 and 179; idem 1954: 173; Roessingh 1979: 40-1.
38. Possible exceptions: in the west the 'push' compelling dike-workers from Sliedrecht and the vicinity to migrate (see Appendix 1: 12); in the east the 'pull', slight though it quite possibly was, attracting workers for the harvest (see Appendix 1.15).
39. *Oeconomischen toestand der landarbeiders 1909*: 117-24.

Chapter 3

1. Regtdoorzee-Greup Roldanus 1936: 166: travel expenses incurred by Brabanters going to Haarlem were Dfl.5 for the return journey.
2. Cf. Lucassen 1982: 345.
3. Cf. Appendix 1.5, sub G (Lucassen 1984).
4. ADW,CA 369II Report from Ludwig Meyeringh 1865: 'Die Paterborner, Lipper und Kurhessen reisen bekanntlich über Zwolle den Ijssel und Rhein hinunter bis Duisburg'; cf. also Staring 1868: 675-76: 'Except for the masses who descended along the Rhine and the Waal to find employment in the growing of flax, among whom were a very large number of women to do weeding ...'. I did not find any other confirmation such work was performed by German workers of either sex.
5. In this context Van de Graaff made a rather remarkable comment when he wrote: 'Norden is the usual gathering place of the Westphalian day workers who go to Holland to work for a limited time' (1808: 63). Given the eccentric location of Norden in the 'pull area', it is difficult to believe that many workers congregated there.
6. Scheper 1971: 22-3 (without citation of any further source).
7. De Vries 1978: 46 and 65 (map 2.2) where further connections for those going north are indicated. For a vivid description of this border crossing, see Waring 1876: 14-15.
8. Mulder 1973. They crossed the Frisian border near Slijkenburg in Weststellingwerf where they had to pay duty on the tobacco and bacon which they

brought with them. See Wichers Wierdsma 1885: 3.
9. Cited in Ornée 1970: 10.
10. For such music, see Lührmann 1978: 117 and Van Maurik 1901: 66-7. Not only were Wanderburschen known for their songs, but the compagnons as well; Barret and Gurgand 1980: 300-2.
11. For goods imported into Friesland in the eighteenth century, see Wumkes 1930: 6/6/1734 and 12/6/1734; Wichers Wierdsma 1885: 3; and GA Hasselt, OA: 875.
12. Schulte 1970: 38; Lührmann 1978: 117; Leget 1979: 13. Nearby Bippen was also a spot many migrants passed (±1850 2,000 from Oldenburg and Diepholz); Schröder 1976: 85.
13. Wrasmann 1919.
14. According to Van Asselt (1977: 232-33) and Kiel (1941: 108) some 25,000 to 33,000 people crossed this bridge each year during the period under discussion.
15. GA Hasselt OA: 875. (Hardenberg and Dalfsen helmsmen 1733; 11 Hardenberg expediters and 7 Hardenberg helmsmen in 1788); Van der Aa 5, 1844: 130.
16. Unless otherwise indicated, information about the route between Hardenberg and Hasselt derives from a bicycle trip which I made during the summer of 1982. Recognisable landmarks survive in the landscape. Oral tradition, moreover, has preserved various place names which include the term *poepen* (cf. note 20). See also Kleine Staarman 1967: 49-56 (no source cited).
17. Cf. Lucassen 1982: 345-7, unless stated otherwise.
18. GA Hasselt, OA: 875 (Complaint from Hasselt to the States of Overijssel ±19/3/1733, with annexes).
19. See, for example, GA Hasselt, OA 872 and 875.
20. 'Poep' is a term of abuse for German workers in the Netherlands. See Woordenboek der Nederlandse Taal: *poep*. A journey via the Lichtmis, as Lucassen describes (1982: 346), seems rather unlikely prior to 1800. In any event this route would also include the *poepenstouwe* and proceed as described in the above text.
21. Van der Aa 5 1844: 212; Tegenwoordige Staat van Overijssel 1803: 207-8; Frijhoff 1978: 34 (in contradiction to the *Tegenwoordige Staat* which reports that the chapel still stood in 1803.
22. Van der Aa 5, 1844: 210 (Hasselt) and 130 (Hardenberg).
23. Langendijk 1971: 71, verses 635-45 and 647-51. Similar descriptions occur in the early 17th-century farce *Klucht van de Mof* by I. Vos and in various versions of Slennerhincken's exploits. For a crossing with 100 prisoners in 1823, see Sepp, 1823: 492-3; 501-2.
24. De Vries 1978: 83-5; 88.
25. The following description derives from Van Maurik 1901: 15-67. He depicts the situation c. 1860-5.
26. GA Hasselt, OA: 875 (statement of 21/9/1728 by Koert Sitvast, Dirk van Elten and Hendrik Taal in the presence of public notary Gerard Burghout in Amsterdam, no. 336). Many other clashes are known, too.
27. Leget 1979: 17-18 (2/8/1781 robbery of Herman van den Berge from Horstmar in the *slaapstal* (sleeping-stable, i.e. a cheap dormitory arrangement) run by the widow Jan van den Berg on the square in the Wagenmakerslaan outside the Grote Houtpoort in Haarlem by the bleacher's assistant Willem Cloppenburg from Fürstenau, who was on his way home); for two murders under similar circumstances, one in 1822 (see the story which follows) and one in 1847 (concerning two peat-diggers from Bentheim working on the Stadskanaal), see respectively ARA, Staatssecretarie 15/1/1824, 61 and ARA, KdK 520, 17/11/1848, 79. Sibo van Ruller called my attention to these sources.
28. For background information about the madder crop, see below pp. 58 ff;

for the journey, cf. de Vries 1978: 82-4, 87-9; for the place of origin of the two migrants, see Appendices 1.15 and 1.17.

29. E.g. AN, F 20/435 (Dyle); SAO, Rep. 240,751, passim (including Amtmann Bütemeister from Diepholz); RAZ, Archief Monden van de Schelde 18, 15/4/1812; Leget 1979: 14; Lührmann 1978: 117; Doeks 1827; De Bruijne 1939: 167; Schröder 1978: 97-8; Kroniek 1978: 204; Statistieke beschouwing 1853: 290.

30. Gladen 1970: 97.
31. Kiel 1941: 97.
32. GA Zwolle, AA 201-322, folio 742 (by-law 28/11/1773).
33. See, for example, RAO, Statenarchief after 1813, Gemeenteverslag Hasselt 1849. This reports the introduction of a steamboat between Zwolle and Amsterdam which carried migrant workers for Dfl. 0.75, sharp competition for ships from Hasselt; Van Maurik 1901: 20; Beetstra 1979: 119.

34. Leeson 1979; Barret and Gurgand 1980; see also note 121 on page 89 and note 125 on page 90.

Chapter 4

1. See Appendices 1.2, 1.3, 1.7/1.16. For under-estimation of the number of grass-mowers in Friesland, see Appendix 1.8. For Ostfriesland: Swart 1910: 40-1, 47.
2. De Vries 1974.
3. For expert explanation of proper timing for mowing, see Kroniek 1978: 51; cf. Staring 1868: 52.
4. Kroniek 1978: 309 (*re* 1843).
5. Beetstra 1979: 117; Scheper 1971: 22-3.
6. See Kroniek 1978: 69 (*re* 1827) and 309 (*re* 1843); Kleine Staarman 1967: 56; Gewin 1898: 123 and 280. In Groningen workers assembled at the cattle market (Tiesing II 1974: 92); see also note 128 below.
7. Staring 1868: 660. One should realise that in turn grass is considerably heavier than hay.
8. In Streng n.d.: xxviii (after Lucas Rotgans: Poëzy, van verscheidene Mengelstoffen, Leeuwarden 1715, Boek I: 643).
9. A *zwade* is probably illustrated in Griffis 1899: 98 and Waring 1876: 110; for the short scythe, see Figure 4.1 above.
10. Kroniek 1978: passim, Beetstra 1979: 117-19; Hellema (Kroniek 1978: 134) also gave bacon to 'his' mowers; cf. also Spahr van der Hoek 1952: 354-8 and 665-6.
11. Wages: Questionnaire of 1811 (especially responses in Frise, Zuyderzee and Bouches de la Meuse); Kroniek 1978: 51, 143,156; Beetstra 1979: 119; 'Statistieke Beschouwing' 1853: 290; Staring 1868: 678 — on pp. 743-4 he over-estimates the capacity of a mowing machine drawn by a horse to compete with the 'ants'. According to Kroniek 1978: 280 non-Catholic workes also mowed on Sundays; they paused then from 11 until 2 or 3, but it is my impression this was exactly the same work-break that they permitted themselves during the week.
12. See e.g. Appendix 1.5 under Gb and note 15 (Lucassen 1984). To be sure, there are not many references to women hay-makers as migrant workers; for England, see Roberts 1979: 11, 17-18. Cutting in swathes is to mow grass in such a way that it falls in continuous winding-rows.
13. Cf. also Scheper 1971: 22-3.

14. Kroniek 1978: 204.
15. The response from the département of Zuyderzee provides us with more than the usual information concerning the following municipalities: Westzaandam, Enge Wormer (high wages but at individual's own expense), Ouder-Amstel, Breukelen-St. Pieter, Vleuten and the Meern (mowing with scythe), Harmelen c.s. (work from 2.00-21.00!), Zegveld (mowing and hay-making), Barsingerhorn (farmer pays cost of boarding), Harenkarspel (some make hay), Koedijk (German grass-mowers and hay-makers from Gelderland).
16. See Appendix 1.15, note 3 (Lucassen 1984).
17. Kroniek 1978: 280; département Zuyderzee: in Veenhuizen some remain 'who mow the second hay'.
18. See Appendices 1.2, 1.3, 1.11, 1.12, 1.22, 1.28, 1.29.
19. Staring 1868: 53-5 (rye and rape in July; other grains in August; cutting-rye, buckwheat, peas and beans in September).
20. See e.g. Appendix 1.11, sub E, Appendix 1.15, sub D6 (Lucassen 1984); in Bouches de la Meuse, e.g. the places Rozenburg (40-45 women for the weeding, binding of the grain and hay-making) and Zoetermeer (28 girls for weeding, binding and other work in the fields); for weeding, see also Baars 1973: 194. Weeding apparently was woman's work. There are few indications except those cited above that binding in major grain-producing areas was primarily done by women. Cf. also Appendix 1.12, sub F (Lucassen 1984).
21. Radcliff 1819: 124-7, 189-93; cf. also Ab Utrecht Dresselhuis 1819: 107, 111-12.
22. De Hullu n.d.: 114-17.
23. For these tools, see Roberts 1979; Chatelain 1976: 158-60 and 180-3; Weber-Kellermann 1965: 309-28, 456-7, Map 4; for the Netherlands, cf. Appendix 1.11 (in all places where grain was harvested, use of *zichten*, (reaping-hooks) is cited; Baars 1973: 194; on the island of Zuid-Beveland local workers still cut the grain and bound it using sickles, thus work continued to be done in the slower fashion with little differentiation of tasks (Van Hertum 1836: 206); in contrast to Radcliff, Ab Utrecht Dresselhuis (1819: 107) states categorically that reaping with sickles was practised in Sluis district. I suspect that he is mistaken.
24. Over the advantages of the zicht, see Chatelain 1976: 181 and Weber-Kellermann 1965: 312.
25. One could postulate that the spread of the zicht beyond the North Sea coast was connected to the places of origin of migrant workers drawn to 'pull areas'; the zicht spread further still during the nineteenth century, from northwest Germany to regions on the right bank of the Rhine; cf. Weber-Kellermann 1965: Map 4 and 321.
26. See Appendix 1.22, note 5, (Lucassen 1984) and Weber-Kellermann 1965:347.
27. For labour brokerage activities see *Oeconomischen toestand der landarbeiders* 1909:186-8 and sources cited in note 23.
28. Unless stated otherwise, for madder cultivations see Wiskerke 1952 and Van der Kloot Meyburg 1934.
29. See Appendices 1.12 and 1.13.
30. Van Hertum 1981: 186.
31. We know little about the size of itinerant teams. The number ten is one I deduced from a number of diggers detained in Zierikzee in 1811 (See Annex 1.13, note 6 (Lucassen 1984)). It is possible, however, that diggers worked two by two, see p. 50 and Plate 6.
32. Calculated as follows: average farm-size on Schouwen-Duiveland was 45-50 ha (Bouman 1946: 58). With a 7-year crop rotation scheme (Wiskerke 1952: 37), farmers would be planting some 6 ha. with madder. With biennial

madder some 3 ha had to be harvested each year, with triennial madder 2 ha. Assuming that the wage paid for digging 1 ha of biennial madder was some Dfl.30, and of triennial some Dfl.40 (De Kanter 1802: 39; Van Hertum 1981: 186; Landbouwenquête 1954: 49), we can calculate annual digger costs per harvest per farm of Dfl.360 or Dfl. 320, respectively. With a day wage of Dfl.50 per digger, a team of 10 diggers could be paid for about four weeks of work.

33. We know of a team of 70 to 80 men, for example, that worked in the Wilhelminapolder (Bouman 1946: 147).
34. Van Hertum 1981: 186; Wiskerke 1952: 34.
35. Tegenwoordige Staat, Zeeland I, 1751: 354.
36. Bouman 1946: 86 (from a report dating from 1841).
37. Weber-Kellermann 1965: 360.
38. Van der Kloot Meyburg 1934: 73, 115.
39. For flax, unless otherwise indicated: Appendices 1.12 sub D and 1.13 sub C2d (Lucassen 1984); Damsma and Noordegraaf 1982; GA Hendrik-Ido-Ambacht: annexes to Notulen Raad 1867 (with thanks to Leo Noordegraaf); Enquête 1887, Bundel III (testimony of witnesses 28/1/1887, no. 9395-9944); *Verzameling geneeskundig staatstoezicht* 1872: 179-84; in other places within the region under study (especially in Flanders and Westphalia) where flax was raised, the cultivator himself, or local workers, performed the necessary tasks; as things now stand it is difficult to understand Staring's comment (1868: 675-6): 'the masses who come down the Rhine and the Waal to find work in the flax fields of South-Holland and Zeeland, and among whom there are indeed many women to do the weeding'.
40. Van Hertum 1981: 197 (in 1836 Zeeland farmers first planted flax seeds, then leased out their land); Baars 1973: 135-6 (since the 17th century the farmers in the Beijerlanden rented their fields ready to be sown); Lindemans 1952 II: 224 (in the early 1700s Flemish farmers sowed their own flax in Zeeland-Flanders).
41. Everyone left to take part in the weeding: GA Hendrik-Ido-Ambacht, Memorie 31/12/1867 and Enquête 1887: 9404; wife and toddlers stayed home: Enquête 1887: 9756-59 and 9810-15.
42. Heidema and Dijkema 1979: 413 (*re* Hunsingo, Groningen 1871).
43. See Appendix 1.12, sub E and F (Lucassen 1984).
44. For the following, see Appendices 1.7, sub C6; 1.9, sub C2; 1.10, sub D2 and 1.11, sub Fe (all: Lucassen 1984); Van Heerde 1978, Van de Ven 1920: 27, 62, 84, 281-3; 'Statistieke Beschouwing' 1853: 290; Wentzel 1973: 51-4; for Frisian workers who prepared firewood, not treated here, see Kroniek 1978: 203 (a group of 40 workers from beyond Heerenveen employed near Leeuwarden in 1836) and Klaver 1974: 108-17 (*re* stripping oak bark in 1892; in both instances migrant workers, employed by contractors).
45. Van Heerde 1978: 155 (paraphrase of Haasloop Werner in the *Gelderse Volksalmanak* 1840).
46. De Zeeuw 1978: 25.
47. See Appendices 1.11 to 1.14, 1.16, 1.17, 1.21 and 1.22. As harbour workers only those actively involved in ground work are counted here, yet for the Grand Canal du Nord it is impossible to separate out masons, stone-cutters and brick-makers.
48. Text below derives from the following contemporary sources: Vierlingh 1920 (*re* 16th century); Kroniek 1978: 70, 75, 216-19, 230, 232, 287, 324-5, 329, 331, 382, 432 (*re* 1827-53); Van Koetsveld 1868: 124-63; GAA, Nut: 258-60 (*re* 1872-4); Waring 1876: 90-1; Tutein Nolthenius 1890: 493, 534-8; Klaver 1974: 117-19 (*re* 1897-98); Conrad 1902: 204-5; Van Ysselsteyn 1913: 62-74; I have also used the following secondary sources: Baars 1973: 27-65; Bos 1969; De Bruin 1970; Burgler 1979; Doedens 1981; Giele 1979: 224-8; Lucassen and Lucassen 1983B; Pistor and Smeets 1979: 12-17; Roberts and Bos 1982; Sprenger and

Vrooland 1976; Taverne 1978: 363, 370-7; for France: Chatelain 1976: 776-880; for England: Coleman 1968.

49. See especially Bos 1969; the term comes from Van Koetsveld 1868: 141.

50. German workers are actually cited often, but their place of origin is practically never specified; cf. Dobelmann 1963: 23-5 (about a band of dike workers and their boss from the vicinity of Bersenbrück in 1781-1805); for workers from Ostfriesland, see Appendix 1.3.

51. This inclination is strong in Van Koetsveld (1868) so that the prejudice reappears in writers who use him as a source, including Sprenger and Vrooland (1976) and Burgler (1979).

52. Conrad 1902: 205.

53. On this point most authorities disagree, even at times contradicting themselves, e.g. Coleman 1968: 37 ($7,079m^3$/man/yr. according to my calculations), 41 ($14.6m^3$ idem), 55 ($5.04m^3$ idem) and Sprenger and Vrooland 1976: 31-2 (Dfl.0.69 wages/m^3) and 46 (Dfl.1.21/m^3). An estimate of 1 to $1^1/_2m^3$/hr would yield a volume of 10 to $15m^3$/day for each worker. The greater the distance the dug earth had to be carted away, the less a worker could excavate and clear, and the less any given team could accomplish in a day. My figures and estimates derive from De Vries 1978: 128 and 75-7 ($5^1/_2m^3$ by my calculations), Leeghwater 1710: 19, 32 (if one assumes a day's wage of Dfl.1, then $10m^3$ would be a day's work), Lucassen and Lucassen 1983B ($5m^3$), Tutein Nolthenius 1890: 493 ($16m^3$), Vierlingh 1920 XXXVII,105,279 (5 to $6m^3$ by my calculations). Cf., too, note 65 below.

54. Bos 1969; Van Ysselsteyn 1913; Van Koetsveld 1868: 41 ('nine-weekers' from Brabant).

55. GA Gouda, Secretarie Moordrecht 1813-1900: 633 and 649. My data comes from the original forms that were filled in (inv. no. 649): of the 34 household heads, only 7 could sign their names.

56. E.g. Doedens 1981 and MacLean 1979.

57. Cf. Doedens 1981: 60-72 (the first incident he reports happened in 1838).

58. ARA, Waterstaat 1830-1877: 337, Dossier 21 (1843/44).

59. See Appendices 1.3, 1.7/1.9, 1.11, 1.12.

60. De Zeeuw 1978; Van Schaik 1970: 201-20.

61. Van Schaik, for one, is fragmentary (1969 and 1970).

62. Alstorphius Greveling 1840: 175; for the dating of these mining activities in the bogs, see van Schaik 1969: 157-61.

63. Van Schaik 1969: 141-8; Crompvoets 1981: 101-45 (for the various kinds of work teams, an important source for Crompvoets, and one which I too consulted, is Streekarchief Peelland, Deurne, ms.VI/4-13a: J. Hermans: Vergelijkende begrooting en opgave der werkzaamheden ... om eene nieuwe veenderij te ontginnen ..., Deurne-Neerkant 1871); Gerding 1980: 31-6; Aden 1964: 70-2.

64. Crompvoets 1981: 113 (in the *Monden* of the Stadskanaal, a 'communion' of 80-90 men); cf. Van der Hoek 1979: 86-7 (a photo with a team of 79 men).

65. Crompvoets 1981: 121, 122, 127, 128; as together 127 sods (*turven*) make up $1m^3$, this meant 16 $^1/_3m^3$ could be due per person per day; cf. note 53 for ground-work.

66. De Bruijne 1939: 75-7; Crompvoets 1981: 71-82; Van Schaik 1979: 183; 'Uitkomsten van den landbouw' 1890 (Sloten).

67. Crompvoets 1981: 105.

68. For wages and work hours, see literature cited in notes 63, 66 and 70 and in addition the Questionnaire of 1811: note 59.

69. E.g. Tiesing 1974 I: 117. For the mistaken idea that one 'daywork' would be all a man could cut per day, see, among others, Gerding 1980: 36.

70. The cubic measure used in low peat areas was called the *stobbe*: ARA, BZ 1796-1813: 1062 (not in Verhoeff 1982). One stobbe which contained 50 *Leidse*

turftonnen (Leiden peat barrels), required at least 5 to 6 workers to fill it (just as the 'daywork' measure for high peat which could hold 150 Leidse turftonnen). One might infer that three times as many workers were necessary in low bogs as in high to achieve the same result — an assertion De Zeeuw makes based on other evidence (1978: 15). This is to forget, however, both that high peat required far more wheelbarrow transport after removal and that high and low peat commanded far different prices — as De Zeeuw reports — because of their different efficiencies as fuels, the one consumed in domestic hearths, the other destined for industrial ovens. I believe it would be more accurate to say that twice as many workers were needed in low bogs to match production results in high bogs, and not three times as many. This means that exploitation of low peat was of more significance for the local labour market.

71. De Bruijne 1939: 77.
72. Tiesing 1974 I: 116; Aardema 1981.
73. Tiesing 1974 I: 119; Van der Hoek 1979: 85-8 (Van der Hoek calls this functionary a *vervener* (peat owner) but to judge from his measuring stick he must have been an overseer; cf. Crompvoets 1981: 101.)
74. See p. 60 for analogous speeches, see Weber-Kellermann 1965: 93ff.
75. Streekarchief Peelland, Deurne, Gemeentelijke vervening Deurne (not in any particular order): ms. of J. Hermans (1845-1898): 'Gedicht op onze Duitsche werklieden ...' (Poem about our German workers).
76. Tiesing 1974 I: 127 (Lippe workers in the bogs of Drenthe were old hands at beating on their wooden shoes as a signal that on Saturday mornings the week was practically over, or that rain or something else was forcing them to stop working).
77. Cf. van Schaik 1969: 147. Although van Schaik is emphatic that high peat was not for the most part exploited by small companies, none the less, the most important employers in Ems Occidental usually had only some tens of workers in service (ARA, BZ 1796-1813: 1193: Industrial Enquiry 1812 *re* Ems Occidental: idem, 1062).
78. Tiesing 1974 I: 118. Tiesing maintains that the day's wage was decided upon only at the end of the season.
79. In addition to construction workers, brick-makers and bleachers, I came across the following industrial vocations in the Questionnaire of 1811: weavers, primarily from Westphalian departments to Friesland and Groningen, but to the Veluwe as well (Appendices 1.3, 1.4, 1.5, 1.8, 1.10) and also to Belgian 'pull areas' both from North-Brabant and from départements in northern France (Appendices 1.14, 1.15, 1.21, 1.22, 1.24, 1.26, and 1.28); miners from Jemappes to Nord (Appendices 1.23,1.28); factory workers such as lead casters, cotton printers, tobacco processors, brewers (Appendices 1.4, 1.11, 1.12, 1.14, 1.16, 1.17) and craftsmen, frequently designated as *Wanderburschen*, artisans or *compagnons*, among whose numbers could be found tailors, shoemakers, hatmakers, joiners and smiths, primarily towards France (Appendices 1.5, 1.7, 1.10, 1.11, 1.14 to 1.16, 1.19, 1.21, 1.24 to 1.27, and 1.31). Except for itinerant artisans (See Chapter 1, note 6), we know little concerning these other workers. For weavers in Friesland, see Faber 1972: 229-37 and Frijhoff 1977: 228; for sail weavers in the region of the Zaan, see Lootsma 1950: 73-6. Further study of this route for migrant workers is without doubt necessary. For general information cf. De Jonge 1976: 57, 196, 269, 279, 383 and de Graaff 1845: 360-1. For the journey of artisans to the Netherlands, see Penners 1960.
80. Van Tijn 1965: 74; Van Maurik 1901: 30, 62 (bakers).
81. Knotter 1984; cf. also *Staatscommissie over de werkloosheid* 1913A: 13, 26.
82. See Appendices 1.3 to 1.7, 1.9, 1.11 to 1.17, 1.21 to 1.24, 1.28, 1.29, 1.32.

83. See Appendix 1.7, note 8 (Lucassen 1984); GAA, Nut: 258-60 presents the same picture still for 1872-4. From the evidence one might conclude that in Groningen and Ostfriesland — in contrast to Friesland — a lower level of services existed, provided by for example teachers, clergymen, lawyers, etc., cf. Faber 1972: 444-7. Yet eighteenth-century Friesland scored low with 4.48 carpenters per 1,000 inhabitants, whereas Overijssel scored 5.26 and the Noorderkwartier in North-Holland 8.93 (calculations based on Van der Woude 1972: 270).

84. See Knotter 1984 (first citation 1836); GA Gouda, Secretarie 1816-1920: 2023 (security passes); Van Maurik 1901: 30; GAA, Commissie van de arbeidsenquête te Amsterdam 1897-1900. Résumés der verhooren van getuigen voor de bouwbedrijven: 98-107, 121-123.

85. GA Amsterdam, *Commissie van de arbeidsenquête*: 125-31.

86. See Appendix 1.15, note 12 (Lucassen 1984) and Van Iterson 1868: 2, 13-15.

87. *Staatscommissie over de werkloosheid* 1913A: 35-6; Appendix 1.24, note 2 (Lucassen 1984).

88. The best known are the Brabantine workers, who during the winter made wooden clogs, shoes or bundles of firewood; see note 86 and Gewin 1898: 52.

89. ARA, BZ 1796-1813: 1193, Tableau 56, Bouches de la Meuse.

90. See Appendices 1.1 to 1.7, 1.12, 1.13, 1.16, 1.17, 1.22, 1.23, 1.26 and 1.28; in addition cf. the summary of Dutch and Belgian brick ovens in 1816 which appears in Brugmans 1956 and Damsma, de Meere and Noordegraaf 1979 (this last source makes clear that in Gelderland brick manufacture at the time was incidental and of little importance; cf. Hollestelle 1982). All these areas were situated close to navigable waterways.

91. Lucassen and Lucassen 1983B: 46; Appendix 1.13, sub Clb (Lucassen 1984); in Belgium (especially in Hesbaye and 'Pajottenland' roundabout Brussels) the system of temporary ovens persisted on a large scale well into this century; see Peirs 1979: 96-9.

92. Specifically: 822 from Lippe, 50 from Bentheim to the Oude Rijn, 750 from Hainaut and Nord to Rupelmonde, 130 from Nord to French départements; a total of 1,752 workers to which we must add the brick-makers employed on the Grand Canal du Nord — some 50 at least, considering that between Weert and Venlo alone there were 6 brick ovens (Lucassen and Lucassen 1983B: 42-3).

93. In many respects, however, they will have been comparable to brick-makers from Lippe. For brick-makers from Liège in North-Limburg in the first half of the nineteenth century, see SHCL, Doc 7 (concerning Broekhuizenvorst 1833).

94. The account derives primarily from Lourens and Lucassen 1984.

95. ARA, BZ 1796-1813: 1121 (answers in Ems Occidental).

96. For the position and function of the *tichelbode* (brick-messenger), see Lourens and Lucassen 1984; Fleege-Althoff 1928: 110ff; Falkmann 1846: 81-87, 97-101, 168-72, 193-200, 339-43, 369.

97. For discussion of the *Lipper Kommune*, see among others Marijnissen and Raben-Fabels 1978 and the relevent literature cited there; see also Fleege-Althoff 1928.

98. See Appendices 1.4, 1.11, 1.15, 1.16; in the Belgian provinces of Hainaut, East- and West-Flanders there were still far many more bleacheries in the nineteenth century (Brugmans 1956: 282, 329-30). It is striking, however, that in these places, especially where linen was treated, an entirely different organisation seems to have existed from the way bleaching was done in Haarlem: on the average they had only from one to four workers.

99. E.g. Rotterdam (GA Nederweert 1368, domicilie van onderstand); Gouda (idem and another example in GA Nederweert 1061, Strateris, folio 269, house 258; GA Gouda, Secretarie 1816-1920: 2023, security passes); Dordrecht

290 *Notes*

(Regtdoorzee Greup-Roldanus 1936: 23, 151, 287-8; Brugmans 1956: 196-7, 868); in addition to the places of origin summed up in Regtdoorzee Greup-Roldanus, workers also came from Meijel (Peeters, n.d.: marriages Meijel, 14/2/1831, 28/4/1831 and witnesses at christenings no. 99,239, 1094,1127; RAL, Schepenbank Meijel, Schepen boek 8, 5/7/1716) and Beegden (RANH-ORA 685 Heemstede, 16/6/1711).

100. A general picture of the development of jobs in Haarlem bleach-works follows:

	c. 1650			*c.* 1750			*c.* 1811		
	men	women	total	men	women	total	men	women	total
linen-bleacheries	200	800	1,000	120	480	600	30	120	150
thread-bleacheries	140	60	200	140	60	200	70	30	100
clothing-bleacheries	140	210	350	180	270	450	160	240	400
Totals	480	1,070	1,550	440	810	1,250	260	390	650

Sources: in addition to Regtdoorzee Greup-Roldanus 1936, I consulted separately: Brugmans 1956; Van der Woude 1973; RANH, DZZ 458 and arrondissement Amsterdam 645a, answers to the industrial enquiries of 1811 and 1812; *Verslag van de toestand der Provincie Noord-Holland* 1854; GA Velsen, OA 366; 82, 83, 84; GA Bloemendaal, OA 88; 144;Nierhoff 1963: 146-48; Hoekstra 1947: 130-142, 153-55; GA Heemstede, OA 240 and gemeenteverslagen 1853-1882.

101. The following account derives from Regtdoorzee Greup-Roldanus 1936 (unless otherwise specified).

102. Regtdoorzee Greup-Roldanus 1936: 81-2; the men sang while they watered the bleaching field in pairs.

103. Ibid 158; RANH, ORA 618, no. 9 (statement 1749).

104. Regtdoorzee Greup-Roldanus 1936: 156-57.

105. These earnings reflect a standard work week which included Sundays; Regtdoorzee Greup-Roldanus 1936: 237-41, 168-9.

106. Calculated from information concerning nine thread bleach-works appearing in Regtdoorzee Greup-Roldanus (1936: 150); in Bloemendaal in 1742 in 10 thread-bleacheries the average breakdown of personnel, by sex, was 10 men, 4 women (GA Bloemendaal, OA 88).

107. Clothing-bleachers made their appearance especially in Heemstede; see the sources concering Heemstede cited in note 100, and see Groesbeek 1972: 93-5. Calculations in note 100 reveal that the Questionnaire of 1811 did not take clothing-bleachers into account.

108. Once again, cf. sources for Heemstede in note 100.

109. Appendices 1.3, 1.8, 1.14 (see Lucassen 1984: here the largest numbers: 400 for coastal navigation and 300 for river transport and fishing); 1.17; 1.26; for an earlier time, cf. Bruijn and Lucassen 1980.

110. Appendix 1.15; packmen are discussed later (Lucassen 1984); cf. also Funken 1959: 190 and Knippenberg 1974: 38ff.

111. Appendices 1.18 to 1.20, 1.27, 1.30, 1.34.

112. Appendix 1.30: the 6 raftsmen from Ardennes journeyed on the Loire, Maas, Schelde and Mosel; all the rest on the Rhine and its tributaries (Lucassen 1984).

113. For qualitative information, see Leemans 1981: 31-3, 46, 101-7, 109-10; Thon 1833 and Middelhoven 1978: 86-7; for the much smaller French rafts, see Chatelain 1976: 417-19.

114. According to the number of sheds on board, we might think of units of 50 men to a team, but smaller groups, such as the 6 or 7 men who manned each rudder, are also conceivable.

115. The question remains whether or not Leemans's findings are representative (he reports two dates in April, one in June, three in July, six in

August, one in September, four in October and two in November; as for boatmen heading upstream, he mentions four in March and one in November — information which does not prompt any conclusions, Leemans 1981.

116. For 1809 Thon (1833) reports a total of 82 rafts on the Rhine. If the same number were afloat in 1811, this would mean that, on the average, a raft would have offered work for less than 200 men; two voyages per worker per season would then yield more plausible results. For this period, see also Leemans 1981: 107.

117. According to the prefect of Rhin et Moselle.

118. In addition to *marskramers* (pedlars), the predecessors of later travelling salesmen and sales representatives, often on the road because of the nature of their business, were active in the trade sector; cf. note 121. In the Questionnaire of 1811, in the service sector chimney sweeps, musicians, falconers, tinkers and similar figures are also reported.

119. Appendices 1.4, 1.5, 1.15 to 1.17, 1.26, 1.27, 1.29, 1.31 to 1.34.

120. The straw-hat makers from these places do not belong to the industrial but to the trade sector because, together with their fellow villagers (in Glons, for example, in 1816 there were 1,100 workers employed in this industry; see Caulier-Mathy 1962: Tableau I,2), they usually braided the most important parts of the hats at home during the winter. In the summer then, at known distribution points (thus far, for the early 19th century, we are certain of Amsterdam, Rotterdam, Gouda and Brussels), migrant workers, consisting especially of master craftsmen and girls, assembled the hats and sold them (see Appendix 1.16; GA Gouda 1816-1920: 2023; Diederiks 1982: 170; van Tijn 1965: 96; GAA, NSB 267, annexes to the mayor's official report 1347, 1811 and idem, 238, table of factories 1808, folio 18; Damsma, de Meere and Noordegraaf 1979: 356-7.

121. Research into this sector should without fail make use of the passport registers to be found in over-abundance in government archives (see Appendix 1, passim) and of the lists of foreigners spending the night which had to be drafted weekly by local police at the beginning of the 19th century. For the United Kingdom of the Netherlands, at least, such lists have been preserved for the months of February-March 1820 (ARA, Justitie 1813-1876, 467B and 468). Locally these lists also crop up (e.g. GA Gouda 1816-1920: 2023; here, in addition to female bleachers and stucco workers from Oldenburg, straw-hat makers, musicians, seamen and all kinds of merchants and pedlars appear); for Amsterdam *c.* 1860, see Van Maurik 1901.

122. See Part II.

123. For spice vendors from Turócz-Szent Márton, about 50 km north of Kremnitz, formerly Hungary but now Czechoslovakia, see the sources cited in note 121 and Appendix 2.4.

124. For what follows I have made use especially of Knippenberg 1974; Lucassen and Lucassen 1983A; and Gladen 1970: 71-5. See also note 119.

125. This emerges clearly from the sources mentioned in note 121: persons whom the pedlars knew locally and the places where they lodged had to be reported to the authorities. If we trace a particular group of itinerant tradesmen in a particular region through time, we keep coming across the same inns, lodgings and personal relations.

126. For the Netherlands the *Rusluie* (Russia-goers), from Vriezenveen and the pedlars from Muntendam appear to have been exceptions to the rule; for Moselle, in this context, Jewish hawkers from the cantons of Longwy and Longwyon are conspicuous (Appendix 1.32).

127. Especially Van Winkel in Knippenberg 1974: 29-47, based primarily on J. Frederix's MA thesis of 1969 (Leuven University); cf. too literature concerning Breyell in Appendix 1.17 (Lucassen 1984).

128. The 'mob-fairs' in England (see literature cited in note 9 Ch. 1 and

Samuel 1975: 96-7); for France, see Chatelain 1976: 479-81 and 792; for Germany, Swart 1910: 47, Ludwig 1915: 78-104, Hartman 1865, and Baudassin 1865; see also note 6 above.

Chapter 5

1. See summary of Appendix 1.
2. See Appendix 1.4 sub Gg (Lucassen 1984).
3. Here, in addition to a number of cantons in Ems Supérieur, I am also thinking of the 'push area' near Liège (see Appendix 1.26) and certain *Aemter* in the principality of Lippe (see Appendix 1.6) (both Lucassen 1984).
4. SAO, OED 751:

Alle Cantonnisten welche nach Holland gehen haben geringes Grundeigenthum welches nicht so viel einbringt nur die Abgaben zu tragen. Sie müssen also diesen Nebenerwerb wählen, dessen vortheilhaften Seite um so weniger zu verkennen, als kein anderes Erwerbszweig vorhanden, und die Abwesenheit, nicht die mindesten Nachtheile erzeugt. Denn gegen Jacobi sind alle ausgewanderte wieder zürück; und da das Gehen nach Holland erst nach der Saatzeit statt hat; So wird weiter nichts als die Heuernte versäumt, welche durch die zurückgebliebenen weiblichen familien-Mitglieder beschaffet werden kann.

Dadurch das der Hollandsgänger seinen Speckbedarf, von dem geschlachtem Schweine mit nimmt wird die höchste Versilberung des eigenen Erzeugnisses bewirket, und ist das ein Staats Vortheil der sehr in Anschlag gebracht werden muss.

Eben so ist es in Statistischer Hinsicht sehr wichtig, dass fast ein jeder Hollandsgänger einige Stücke Linnen mit nimmt, und selbige ohne zwischen Händler für den höchst möglichsten Preis verkauft.

5. See p. 33.
6. The annual income of a migrant worker from the Osnabrück area c. 1846 can be estimated at 130 Reichsthalers, see Lucassen 1982: 340-1 (in Lucassen's Case b, part of the worker's income from self-sufficient enterprise is apparently not included); cf. also Tiesing 1974 II: 94. Tiesing reports earnings of Dfl.50 in the late 19th for workers from Drenthe who spent six weeks employed away from home; this was the equivalent of 30% of the worker's annual household income.
7. For Diepholz 1811, see note 4; for Work Cycle b,cf. earlier version in Lucassen 1982: 340; see also Meyer 1895: 83-7.
8. See p. 33.
9. Cf. Mager 1982: 459; in 1846 the farms in Osnabrück (specified already in note 6 above) leased, respectively 0.6, 1.3 and 1.8 ha of farm and grazing land. Yield would of course depend on the quality of the land, as well as its extent. For the possibility of yet smaller farms, see Gutmann 1980: 24-5 and the sources he cites.
10. Thorner, Kerblay and Smith 1966: 55-60.
11. Not only with respect to spinning, but to weaving in the summer as well; see Schlumbohm 1979: 282-4.

Part One, Conclusion

1. Tydeman 1819: 16 (our area = the province of Holland).
2. The term 'alternatif' is from Lis 1982: 114.

Chapter 6

1. Based, just as Figures 6.2 and 6.3, on Appendix 2.
2. Meijide Pardo 1960: 562 and 557; Le Play 1877/1879 V: 249-58. To cover the 300 to 400 km on land from Galicia to Castile, 15 to 20 days were needed; see Meijide Pardo: 529. Cf. Poitrineau (1983: 71-2) for the long journey undertaken by some French migrant workers who went as far as Spain.
3. Based on Appendix 2.6 unless indicated otherwise.
4. Morgan 1982: 42; Redford 1976: 71-2; Chambers and Mingay 1966: 92-5.
5. For the following: Ó Gráda 1973; Kerr 1943; Redford 1976: 142-3.
6. Ó Gráda 1973: 62 (two budgets from the 1890s; the respective portions in each of earnings from migrant labour were between 23.7 and 23.9%.)
7. Sources: Redford 1976: 147; Ó Gráda 1973: 74; cf. Kerr 1943: 379, for similar work cycles in the Scottish Highlands, see Lis and Soly 1979: 134-5.
8. De Vries 1976: 162-4.
9. Poitrineau 1983: 5-14.
10. Meijide Pardo 1960: 589.
11. What follows derives from Meijide Pardo 1960.
12. Idem: 476-7.
13. Idem: 492.
14. Idem: 510 and 591.
15. Idem: 467; 528 (golondrina); 529 (cuadrillas).
16. Idem: 135.
17. Idem: 529, 565, 594-6.
18. Idem: 592 and 595.
19. Braudel 1976: 67; see, too, Davico (1968: 159-60) who considers developments in the Pô Valley comparable to those in Catalonia, Basse Provence and Venetia. For migrant labourers journeying to southern France, see Poitrineau 1982 and Claverie/Lamaison 1981: 209.
20. Davico 1968: 150-1 and 158 and AN F 20 435 (Gênes and Marengo).
21. Braudel 1976: 66-7.
22. For what follows, see AN F 20 435 (Rome, Ombrone, Trasimène). For such 'seduction' of workers during the winter, i.e. 19th c. Russia, see Sagarsky 1907: 107,175.
23. AN F 20 434 (Arno).
24. Idem (Golo, Liamone) and AN F 20 435 (Elba).
25. For shepherds, see AN F 20 435 (Trasimène, Ombrone, Méditerranée).
26. AN F 20 435 (Sésia, Stura, Gênes); cf. the percentages in Appendix 2.3y; the vast majority of Galician migrant workers came from the provinces of Orense and Lugo. If we assume some 20,000 to 25,000 workers were involved, this would mean, c. 1800, 4.2 to 5.2% of the total population of both provinces. See Meijide Pardo 1960: 476.
27. Braudel 1976: 46; cf. Chatelain 1976 and Hufton 1974: 72.
28. Sella 1973: 550-1.
29. Sella 1973: 552-3.

30. Chevalier 1950: 217-23, 225-7; Chatelain 1976: 776-893.
31. Chatelain 1976: 548-9 and 604.
32. Idem: 564-6.
33. Chevalier 1950: 217-23.
34. See Appendix 2 for sources: of special interest for specific cities: for Paris, Girard 1979; for Milan, Woolf 1979: 289; for Madrid and Lisbon, Meijide Pardo 1960: 536-8, 551-3, 580 and Bahamonde 1980.
35. AN F 20 435 (Rome).
36. See note 6 of chapter 1.
37. Chevalier 1950: 217-23.

Chapter 7

1. Information which I have come across concerning migratory labour in these areas c. 1800 is scarce indeed; see Appendix 2, introduction and 2.5.
2. There were migrant workers in southern Russia; see note 9. For additional reports on migrant labour in eastern Europe, see, among others, Le Play 1877/9 V: 250 (the Carpathians); Idem II: 179-230, especially 215-22 (central Russia). Kriedte, Medick and Schlumbohm (1978: 49-56) specify 'Ostmitteleuropäischen Gebirgszonen' and the 'Zentrale russische Nichtschwarzerdegebiet' as places where 'second serfdom' was not instituted.
3. Miskimin 1977: 56-64; De Vries 1976: 55-9; Weber-Kellermann 1965: 48-92; Kriedte, Medick and Schlumbohm 1978: 49-56; Millward 1982: 539-43.
4. See note 2 above; there were also serfs who did not deliver labour personally but were obliged to pay a fixed sum yearly, the *obrok* or *abrok*, as it was known; see Thorner, Kerblay and Smith 1966: 13-22. In connection with this financial obligation, migratory labour might also occur; see Le Play 1877/9 II: 86-7, 215-22.
5. See the vivid description of Russian serfdom in Kropotkine 1902 I: 24-5, 44-6, 53-63, 69-84.
6. Freely derived from Knapp (probably from his *Die Bauernbefreiung und der Ursprung der Landarbeiter in den älteren Teilen Preussens*, 1877), cited in Sombart 1919: 51-2.
7. Weber-Kellermann 1965: 49-50, 385; Schissler 1978.
8. Ipsen 1972.
9. Sagorsky 1907, Mendelson 1911, Rosander 1967. Cf. also Trotsky's recollections of his youth in the vicinity of Cherson (1930: 38, 132-9).
10. Even in the lands where slavery had been abolished it is recognised that after the lapse of some years migrant labour emerged. For the transition from slavery to 'indentured labour' to migrant workers in the United States, see Thomas-Lycklama à Nijeholt 1980: 22-5; for the trek from Mexico to the USA, see also Corbett 1979: 226-7; for the change from slavery to migratory labour in West Africa, see Hopkins 1973: 222-31; there are indications of the reverse process in Millward (1982: 541), who reports a seasonal flow of workers from Masovia to Prussia and Silesia in the 16th century. Might this early migratory-labour 'system' have been eroded by the institution of 'second serfdom'?

Chapter 8

1. For an earlier version of the sections of this chapter headed 'Conditions for the Rise of Migrant Labour ...' and 'The Actual Development of Labour Migration ...', see Lucassen 1982: 233 ff.
2. Sources: Van der Woude 1980: 131; Table 7 (division into urban and rural areas in 1680 and south of the IJ in 1750); idem: 135 (Table II); idem 137-8 (urban residents). In the end I have made estimates of separate population figures for the Zaan region and the remaining North-Holland countryside, using an average of the known populations in the Zaan region between 1650 and 1750 and thereby arriving at 92,000 for the total number of inhabitants elsewhere in rural settings. See too, Van der Woude 1962: 35-76 and Faber *et al.* 1965: 50-62.
3. Van der Woude 1980 and 1982.
4. According to Van der Woude (1980: 126, Table 6) in 1833 in North-Holland there were 1,528 km^2 of arable land. Little was added to the total between 1640 and 1833. During the period 1607-40, however, the total rose by 196 km^2 for the large polders alone (see Hartogh Heys van Zouteveen 1870: 56 and Van der Woude 1972: 46-60).
5. Vierlingh 1920: 134, 173; Baars 1973: 38, 45; Kranenburg 1946: 105 (fishermen as farmers' sons, 16th century); Bruijn 1977: 163.
6. Sources: Van der Woude 1972: 46, 126; for the 18th century: Hartogh Heys van Zouteveen 1870: 59 (Boekelermeer).
7. Bruijn and Lucassen 1980: 14; Kranenburg 1946: 28, 39; Van der Woude 1972: 806, 408 (he reports a loss of about 900 jobs in the North-Holland herring fleet in the second half of the 17th century, and about 1,800 jobs in the first half of the 18th).
8. For reactions to the crisis in animal husbandry areas, see De Vries 1980: 35, 40, 42 and Roessingh 1979:23-5. The scaling up of farms is also treated in De Vries 1974: 134. Impoldering also resulted in large farms.
9. For *greppelen*, see Baars 1973: 176, 178, 194. For the longer intervals between maintenance work, see Roessingh 1979: 24.
10. Roessingh 1979: 59; Slicher van Bath 1975: 326; De Vries 1974: 194; for work on harbours, see Sigmond 1977: 90 (figure); for shipping canals, see De Vries 1978.
11. De Vries 1974: 67-73, 132-3; Van der Woude 1972: 413-16.
12. Van der Woude 1972: 427.
13. The building of dikes on the Islands of South-Holland may account for the following estimates of new arable land:

	km^2
surface area in *c.* 1500	1,900
acquisitions 16th century	150
acquisitions 17th century	125
acquisitions 18th century	25
acquisitions 1800-1833	25
surface area in 1833	2,225

See note 4: land gains calculated in keeping with Hartogh Heys van Zouteveen 1870: 31-41.

14. Diepeveen 1950; for the situation in adjoining parts of Utrecht see, among others, Trouw 1948 and Gottschalk 1956.
15. Sources: acquisition of new land on the Islands of South-Holland, see note 13; marsh reclamation calculated from Hartogh Heys van Zouteveen 1870: 59-60;

digging peat in Rijnland calculated from Lucassen 1982: Annex 1 (the average of the first four sample years for each 20-year period is used — e.g. the figure in Table 8.3 for 1600-20 is the average of figures for the years 1600, 1605, 1610 and 1615). For attempts to convert known production figures into statistical estimates of manpower, see note 17 and De Zeeuw 1978: 15-16.

16. Roessingh 1979: 31-2; he also reports the introduction of labour-saving machinery in farming, such as the threshing block on large farms in Groningen and Friesland and the winnowing-mill (28-9).

17. De Vries 1978: 56-64 and 127-32. He maintains that from 1628-1648 there were 266 km (elsewhere he says 243 km) of barge-canals dug, and from 1656 to 1665, 351 km. (elsewhere he says 415). A large portion of these waterways was created in South-Holland. De Vries posits that 100,000 man days were needed per 15 km of canal. For 618 km of canal, therefore, we can calculate that roughly $5^{1}/_{2}$ million days of work would have been required.

18. De Vries 1974: 68; Van Deursen 1978: 30-3; Van Dillen 1970: 186-7; Posthumus 1908-39, especially I: 129-45, 302; II: 418-37; III: 955-64, 1096, 1120-3; rural textile production in the environs of Leiden appears to have already gone into decline before 1650.

19. See, e.g. Van der Woude 1962 and Frijhoff 1977: 177.

20. For peat cutting data per village, see the source cited in Lucassen 1982 (Annex 1); for demographic material: Van der Woude 1962 and De Vries 1974: 93. An inverse relation might be a sign that migrant labourers were being employed.

21. Tack 1902: passim.

22. For Twente, see Slicher van Bath 1957: 55, 59 and Faber *et al.* 1965: 72-89; for Westphalia, see Hömberg 1968: 86-112; for Lippe, see Steinbach 1976: 170. Population statistics for Osnabrück are so vague and contradictory that I have chosen not to use them; see Wrasmann 1919: 119-20, Wrasmann 1921: 1, Stüve 1789, and Hirschfelder 1971: 52-4 and 160.

23. Slicher van Bath 1960: 227-43; Abel 1967: 265ff.

24. See note 22 (Wrasmann 1919 and 1921; Hirschfelder 1971). We may translate *Hauptfeuerstätten* and *Nebenfeuerstätten* roughly as large and small farms. For the same development in Ravensberg, see Mager 1981 and 1982: 458. For the Heuerlinge, see also Mooser 1981.

25. Concerning the relation between population growth and expansion of rural textile production, see Fischer 1973: 158-70; and Kriedte, Medick and Schlumbohm 1978: 171ff.

26. In the second half of the 17th century we can discern a marked increase in the number of laws and regulations passed against the *Hollandsgänger* in practically all 'push areas' (see Tack 1902: passim and Fleege-Althoff 1928: passim). There appears to have been a strong impulse among noblemen and landowners to place workers under obligation to them in order to weather the economic crisis by keeping wages low — or at any rate in order to resist wage increases.

27. Mager 1981: 154 (confirmed by the Questionnaire of 1811 for Ems Supérieur).

28. Faber 1980: 202-3; Gladen 1970: 70.

29. See p. 98 above.

30. Discussed above, p. 45.

31. See p. 67ff.

32. Among others, see Tack 1902: 11 and Fleege-Althoff 1928: 56.

33. See Appendices 1.11 and 1.12.

34. Lucassen 1982.

35. Sources: number of migrant workers from sources cited in Appendices 1.11 and 1.12; population of the department of Bouches de la Meuse taken from

Noordegraaf 1977; for the département of Zuyderzee, the population of the arrondissement Utrecht is from Kemper 1812; the population of remaining arrondissements is from RANH (with thanks to Leo Noordegraaf). The cantons with the highest proportion of migrant workers were Mijdrecht (22.7% — a land reclamation project was in progress), Ouder-Amstel (16.4%), Purmerend (16.3%), Baambrugge (13%) and Edam (12%).

36. See notes 37 and 38; see also pp. 64 and 86 above.

37. Sources: GAA (GA Weesperkarspel: 225; GA Watergraafsmeer: 67-70; GA Buiksloot 66); GA Alkmaar (GA Graft OA 230[1]; GA Schoorl OA 51; GA Heilo OA 45; GA Akersloot OA 8; GA Oudorp OA 3); GA Velsen (OA 83); GA Bloemendaal (OA 114); RAL (Nedermaas 2808).

38. For data extracted from licensing records and for Limburg, see note 37; for information provided by maires from municipalities surrounding Osnabrück (Belm, Rulle, Wallenhorst, Hagen, Glane, Westerkappeln, Lengerich, Lienen, Dissen, Wellingholzhausen, Versmold) and by the former Amtmann of Diepholz, see SAO, OED 751; this decline has also been established for another 'pull area', Groningen — see RAGR, Rechterlijk Archief XXVIIy -$^{1}/_{4}$ (licenses for foreign workers in Fivelingo, respectively 516, 244, 316, 254).

39. See Chapter 3; for calculating the extent of migration of workers from Ireland to England comparable sources were consulted — see Ó Gráda 1973. For Italy, cf. crossings from the mainland to Corsica and Elba (Appendix 2.3).

40. Source: GA Hasselt, OA 929. Note: the total number of regularly scheduled voyages is reconstructed in keeping with the regulation that three ships sail from Hasselt each week. In December 1728, however, a number of such voyages were not registered, and perhaps not undertaken (December 1728 was extraordinarily cold; from 1706 to 1752 the average temperature for any month was lower on only two occasions). The fact that records for January 1729 are missing may also come from a stoppage of traffic as the consequence of freezing temperatures (of all Januaries from 1706 to 1752, only three were colder; the 37 days that the Haarlem ship canal was closed down in 1729 will also have fallen, for the most part, in January). Traffic was probably normal during February 1729, yet registration of these voyages, and of those that took place during the first half of March, are not to be found in the archives. (For data on the climate, see Labrijn 1945: 89-94; De Vries 1977: 198-226, especially 200).

41. For 1812: GA Hasselt, Ensergeld 1812. For 1754: idem: 78, 875.

42. Based on Lucassen 1982: 358 (Annex 6).

43. Slicher van Bath 1957: 220-1; the *Passagegeld* in Hasselt (idem 224), however, is not consistent with this picture; in any event it cannot have been dependent on the shipping movement. The increase in Passagegeld should not be ascribed to a larger transport capacity: from c. 1650 the ships in use were the so-called *wijdschepen* of 24-30 *last* (c. 48-60 tons) burden; these could carry 80 migrants with baggage from Hasselt to Amsterdam, and 100 migrants from Amsterdam to Hasselt. Only once a ship was filled to capacity might it weigh anchor and the next ship take on passengers. (GA Hasselt, OA 78, 875). Perhaps traffic overland explains fluctuations in Passagegeld; for traffic between Amsterdam and the eastern provinces and in Groningen, see De Vries 1978: 260-1, and 272-3 respectively.

44. Yben 1941: 29-35; GA Zwolle, AAZ 01-339, 327, 470. Here too changes in the number of skippers agrees with changes in the amount of Ensergeld — but not with Passagegeld (sharing this discrepancy with Hasselt). See Slicher van Bath 1957: 220,224.

45. Calculated as follows: (1) migrant workers from Bouches du Weser, Ems Supérieur, the département of Lippe, the principality of Lippe, Ems Occidental, Bouches de l'Issel and Issel Supérieur to Zuyderzee, minus 315 from Ems Supérieur and 300 from Bouches du Weser who went by way of Friesland — a

total of 8,158 persons; (2) plus the Germans who went to Bouches de la Meuse, minus 200 workers counted twice and 275 workers from Berg/Westphalia, plus 125 from Ems Occidental and Issel Supérieur — a total of 2,350 persons. The sum of (1) and (2) is 10,508, which I have rounded down to 10,000 (for specific numbers see Appendices 1.11, 1.12).

46. See note 44 (80 workers per ship on the voyage out).
47. Tack 1902: 11, 59, 202; Wrasmann 1919: 115.
48. Tack 1902: 71, 180; Wrasmann 1919: 116.
49. Wrasmann 1919: 118-20 (based on special taxes).
50. Stüve 1789: 20 (alas, he fails to say how he reached his total).
51. The ancient Bishopric of Osnabrück is equivalent to the following administrative units in 1811 (Joulia 1973: 82-9): from arrondissement Lingen: canton Fürstenau; from arrondissement Quackenbrück: canton Ankum, canton Quakenbrück without Essen, canton Vörden; from arrondissement Osnabrück: cantons Bramsche, Osnabrück-Stadt and Osnabrück-Land, Iburg, Osterkappeln, Essen, Melle, canton Dissen without Borgholzhausen, Laer from canton Versmold, Glandorf from canton Ostbevern. Numbers for 1811 in SAO OED 751. The number for 1811 in Wrasmann (1921: 21) is inaccurate.
52. See p. 148.
53. Sources: Tack 1902: 140-3; the first report idem: 79-85. This geographical area is equivalent to part of canton Bassum, arrondissement Nienburg, département Bouches du Weser, for which only the total number of migrants per arrondissement is known. Perhaps several tens of workers would be a safe estimate for 1811.
54. If we compare certain totals from the Brunswick-Lüneburg Aemter Wildeshausen and Diepholz (Tack 1902: 141-2 and 144) dating from the second half of the 18th century with statistics collected in 1811 (Lucassen 1982: annex 3), we can merely demonstrate that migration began to ebb between 1767 and 1811; other numbers are unreliable. Tack's often cited figure for the Netherlands as a whole in 1750 — 27,000 migrant workers — is based on dubious sources and calculations (Tack 1902: 141-2). Fleege-Althoff (1928) presents detailed data for Lippe from 1778 onwards. Here too, however, there are objections; the information is at present being processed by P. Lourens and myself. Gladen (1970: 68-9) has published figures for Tecklenburg for 1750, 1802 and 1811; because these pertain to different geographical entities, however, they can only be compared with difficulty. The statistic he cites for 1811, moreover, derives from Tack's misleading report (Tack 1902: 146).
55. Van der Woude 1962. For an attempted interpretation, see Lucassen 1982: 344-5 and Annex 4.
56. The text which follows is based on Bruijn and Lucassen 1980: 11-29.
57. Source: Bruijn and Lucassen 1980: 24 (Graph 5).
58. Sources: the population of Holland: see Table 8.1 (p. 134); the population of Friesland: Faber 1972: 413-14; calculation of the number of newcomers to the non-agrarian labour market each year on the basis of considerations expounded in Bruijn and Lucassen (1980: 26) — if we imagine that the average age of the economically active population was actually somewhat older, so that annually not $1/20$ but $1/30$ of the total economically active population had to be replaced, this would only serve to increase the difference between successive percentages ((B) as a % of (A)) in the bottom row of the table: e.g. from 1650(A) to 1680 the percentage would rise from 25.3 to 33.8; the annual recruitment of VOC soldiers and sailors in the maritime provinces is calculated by combining percentages from Tables A and B with numbers from Table C in Bruijn and Lucassen (1980: 139-40).
59. The population of South-Holland began to decline only after the 1680s, cf. pp. 133-4.

60. Gerbenzon 1960: xxxviii and 13-4 (citation); for agricultural developments in Friesland in general, see Faber 1972: 149 ff.
61. See Appendix 1.3 and among references cited there (Lucassen 1984) see especially Aden 1964: 27, 40-5, 53.
62. Sources: production figures from Aden 1964: 54, 95, 120, 144; population figures from idem: 200. Around 1770 the production and population lines will have crossed, given that Aden maintains (1964: 55) population growth trailed the increase in turf production prior to 1789.
63. Slicher van Bath 1960: 222-4; although much about the development of the labour market in the Groningen peat-bogs remains unclear, apparently expansion of production in the first half of the 17th century attracted many German seasonal workers, see Van Dijk, Foorthuis and Van der Sman 1984: 25.
64. Lourens and Lucassen 1984.
65. Wiarda 1880: 30-4; Van Eyck van Heslinga 1982.
66. Slicher van Bath 1960: 220-5; cf. pp. 136-41 above.
67. Vierlingh 1920.
68. Van der Kloot Meyburg 1934: 73-4 (the earliest ordinance which fixed 1 October as the day when the harvest could start — in connection with necessary work on the dikes that had to be finished first — dates from 1444); Wiskerke 1952: 86-8 (earliest mention dates from 1441).
69. Verlinden and Craeybeckx 1962: 98-105.
70. Among others, see Van Vooren 1973 and Appendix 1.22.
71. See note 68 above.
72. See Appendix 1.13, note 7 (Lucassen 1984) and Tegenwoordige Staat, Zeeland, 1751: 354-83; Idem 1753: 367-9.
73. For further data about the historical development of migratory labour in this region, see references in Appendices 1.12, 1.13, 1.14, 1.21 and 1.22.
74. The demand for German and Scandinavian seamen for European shipping also increased in Holland during the first half of the 17th century (Bruijn and Lucassen 1980: 11-29); similarly the number of permanent migrants from South Netherlands rose, especially workers coming to hold jobs in the textile industry (Briels 1978 and Van der Woude 1980: 140-1).
75. Chambers and Mingay 1966: 102.
76. Kerr 1943: 365-6; Lis and Soly 1979: 131-6; cf. Cobbett's pronouncement: 'the more purely a corn country, the more miserable the labourer' (cited in Chambers and Mingay 1966: 134); in East England 'enclosures' were of little importance, see Chambers and Mingay 1966: 77-8; Redford gives examples of population increase as the result of enclosure in Lincolnshire (1976: 71-9 and maps a and b), but of depopulation there as well (65, 76), and of depopulation in the Scottish Lothians, another 'pull area' (65). See also Burton 1972, Handley 1970 and Brooke 1983.
77. Hobsbawm and Rudé 1969: 35-6, 44.
78. Redford 1976: 23.
79. Chambers and Mingay 1966: 133.
80. For what follows, see Ó Gráda 1973; Kerr 1943; Redford 1976: 142-3.
81. Jacquart 1974: 140-5, 248-54, 262-3, 267, 283-4, 302-15, 340-54, 383, 446-50, 486, 493, 623-31, 691, 713-43; it is too bad that Chatelain (1976: 71-101) only offers data beginning with the 18th century; for wider application of Jacquart's conclusions, cf. Le Roy Ladurie 1975: 412-14, 429.
82. Jacquart 1974: 741-3; by analogy with the situation in Zeeland-Flanders (see Appendix 1.22 note 5) at least a hundred workers would have been required on these four farms to harvest the grain.
83. Jacquart 1974: 262-3, 486, 493; Appendix 2.2.
84. Le Roy Ladurie 1975: 406, 418-26.
85. Poitrineau 1983: 19ff.

86. Le Roy Ladurie 1975: 428; cf. Appendix 2.2.
87. Meijide Pardo 1960: 496-517 (reports from 1709, 1713, 1720, 1733 and 1740).
88. Idem: 468, 503, 531.
89. Idem: 468 and 503; cf. Hufton 1974: 87 (note 4).
90. Idem: 507, 519, 521, 525; Slicher van Bath 1960: 255-8; Förster 1969: 111. For South Spain, see Le Play 1877-9 V: 249-58.
91. Davico 1968: 143-4.
92. Idem: 153, 158. Cf. AN F 20 435 (Marengo, Stura, Gênes for rice fields and Ombrone and Trasimène for the Campagna) and 434 (Arno also for the Campagna).
93. Davico 1968: 147; Hufton 1974: 117-27; Redford 1976: 137-41; also cf. Küther 1983.
94. Cf., among others, Hufton 1974: 127.
95. Collins 1976: 47-8.
96. Collins 1976; Ó Gráda 1973; Appendix 2.6; Adams 1932 (maps).
97. Davico 1968: 159.
98. Coleman 1968: 25 (As points of origin for the navvies, in addition to Ireland and Scotland he mentions Lancashire and Yorkshire); Redford 1976: 120-1.
99. Slicher van Bath 1960: 216-62; Wallerstein 1980: 3-34; Kriedte 1983; Jansen 1981.

Chapter 9

1. Tack 1902: 122-7.
2. See p. 182 ff.
3. Workers in bogs: de Bruijne 1939: 74-8 (Germans in Vinkeveen 1856-60); van der Aa, 3, 1841: 199 (600 migrant workers in Dedemsvaart, calculated by deducting winter and summer totals from each other) and ADW, CA 369 II (Bericht Meyeringh 1865 and 1867: respectively 300 and 600 German migrant workers in Dedemsvaart in 1865 and 1866); grass-mowers: I know of only two pieces of information — for Twisk in North-Holland where in 1811 59 workers from Münster, Hannover and Overijssel (see Appendix 1.11) came to mow and work on ditches, and in 1871 30 mowers from Overijssel, Gelderland and Germany joined forces with 8 local mowers (GA Amsterdam, Nut, antwoord Twisk 1871); and for Watergraafsmeer where in 1811 13 mowers arrived from Paderborn and Osnabrück (see Table 10.6, p. 148) and where both in 1855 and 1864 11 German grass mowers are reported (GAA, GA Watergraafsmeer 174).
4. Van der Aa, 5, 1845: 210, idem 130 (for Hardenberg there were not yet any complaints about declining flow of traffic); idem 7, 1846: 836-7 (Meppel).
5. RAO, Statenarchief 1813-, municipal reports Hasselt 1842 and 1845.
6. Tack 1902: 150; RAO, Statenarchief 1813-, municipal report Hasselt 1849.
7. Appendix 3.2 (Diepholz and Syke).
8. For the period 1811-1817-9, see also Appendix 1.34.
9. Appendix 3.1 (for Tecklenburg, in particular those places where the situations in 1811 and 1861 can be compared); 3.2 (Lingen and Bersenbrück; in 1811 about 250 hawkers came from this last area, see Appendix 1.4, sub Gc (Lucassen 1984) — these, however, already disappeared before 1861, cf. Rickelmann 1976 and Gladen 1970: 74-5); 3.2C (Diepholz 1865 provided an

improbably small number, in all likelihood because more workers from Diepholz worked outside than in Friesland).

10. Appendices 3.1 to 3.3; Tack (1902: 106-9) asserts that migration from Aemter along the Weser in the neighbourhood of Bremen already decreased in the 1820s, while in Zeven and Verden it continued until the beginning of the 1850s and in Rotenburg lasted as late as the 1860s. The north of Landdrostei Hannover is said to have conformed to this pattern as well.

11. Appendix 3.2 to 3.3 and 3.4. The last reports date from c. 1910 (Ludwig 1915: 17) and c. 1920 (Van der Ven 1920: 225).

12. For developments in Bentheim, see Tack 1902: 120.

13. Source: based on Appendix 3.1: Regierungsbezirk Minden total: 1824-6.

14. Sneller 1943 and De Meere 1982: 5-19; for changes as a result of economic fluctuations, see De Vries 1971.

15. For sugar beet, see Sneller 1943: 417-20; cf. sugar beet in Germany; Olbrich 1982; in France: Chatelain 1976: 677-724.

16. Van Schaik 1969: 148-72; de Zeeuw 1978; Gerding 1983.

17. Grashof 1882.

18. Cf. Teijl 1971: 256-7; from De Zeeuw (1978) we might sooner deduce that turf production increased during the second half of the 19th century, largely because increased production in Drenthe, Overijssel and the Peel more than compensated for diminished production in Holland-Utrecht; Van Tijn and Zappey argue that to the contrary production after 1870 took a steep dive (1977: 225). I am inclined to place the turn around some two decades later.

19. Hartogh Heys van Zouteveen 1870 and Staatscommissie over de werkloosheid 1913 A, 5-8; idem 1914 A: 542.

20. For bleach-works and brick-making, see sources cited in Chapter 4 'Industrial Jobs'.

21. Van der Poel 1967: 159-65, 226-8, 248; in addition, numbers appear in Staring 1868: 739-40 (for 1861) and in Staatscommissie over de werkloosheid 1913B, annex 27 (for 1883, 1893 and 1904); qualitative comments in Uitkomsten van de landouw 1890 (remarks re 1 Laren, 20 Aduard, 22 Bierum, 23 Eenrum, 26 Baarderadeel, 27bis Texel, 33 Grootebroek, 56 Loosduinen and 92 Beek).

22. In 1910 the *Weidestreken* (grassland regions) encompassed practically half a million hectares with an average farm size of 14.6 ha; i.e. almost 35,000 farms with an average of 13 ha in grass (Tenge 1923: 363). If we imagine that the almost 3,000 mowing machines which were in the Netherlands in 1904 (see preceding note) were in use only on these farms — a situation which, given the distribution of these farms throughout the provinces, can be shown to be untrue — even then not yet 10% of the farms in typical hay-producing areas of the Netherlands would have had such a mower. Cf. Van der Poel 1967: 248 (71,366 mowing machines in the Netherlands in 1940).

23. Sneller 1943: 325.

24. Mededelingen Hollandsche Maatschappij van Landbouw 1860: 85-120; 1862: 114-119 (the report of H. Bosker); 1869: 191. Cf. too De Vries 1971: 69 and Van der Poel 1967: 159-65.

25. Indications concerning the use of more Dutch migrant workers in Mededelingen Hollandsche Maatschappij van Landbouw, e.g. 1851: 198; Aardema 1981: 45-6, 60, 83-9; Staatscommissie over de werkloosheid 1914A-580-587 and 590-595; van Maurik 1901: 65; Oeconomischen toestand der landarbeiders 1909: 45ff.; references to more local workers: towards this end the Hollandsche Maatschappij van Landbouw ran a campaign from 1848 to 1851 featuring (hand) mowing competitions; with what measure of success the campaign met is unclear (Mededelingen Hollandsche Maatschappij van Landbouw 1848: 104-5; 1849: 216-18; 1851: 186-7, 194); see, too, van Maurik 1901: 30; Staatscommissie over de werkloosheid 1914A: 575-80.

26. Bijdragen van het Statistisch Instituut 1891: 149-50.
27. Staatscommissie over de werkloosheid 1914A: 529-34; Aardema 1981: 84; Oeconomischen toestand der landarbeiders 1909.
28. Van der Poel 1967: 159-65, 183. For France, cf. Chatelain 1976: 215-16, 710, 718ff.,858.
29. An early plea for mechanisation is found in Sloet tot Oldhuis 1860: 420-1. See also Van Schaik 1969: 176; Crompvoets 1981: 144-5.
30. See, among others, Chatelain 1976: 858.
31. Tack 1902: 96, 106-9; cf. also Pitsch 1974.
32. Markow 1889: 169-70, 174, 183, 190; Mager 1981: 178 (note 34) and 1982: 471.
33. For England, see Thompson 1981: 297-346; for Germany, Schlumbohm 1979; Mager 1981 and 1982: 436-7, 471-2; Steinbach 1976: 55-71. The employment of Silesians in laying the railway between Düsseldorf and Elberfeld in 1839 is startling in this context; see Fremdling 1975: 188; for workers from Ravensberg employed to lay the Köln-Mindener line, see Mager 1982: 469. For the rout of domestic industry in France, see, among others, Claverie and Lamaison 1981: 209-10; for building railways: Chatelain 1976: 818-19, 850-6.
34. Schepens 1973; Chatelain 1976: 669-718.
35. Schepens 1971: 23, 39, 67. *De Oogst* was first published in 1899; *Werkmenschen*, on which Streuvels had been at work since 1896, saw its initial publication in 1926.
36. GAA, Nut: 258-60; the only previous mention known to me concerns *brikkenbakkers* from Stein in South Limburg who were migrating annually to Germany as early as the 1840s. See Marijnissen and Raben-Fabels 1978. An important number of jobs was also available as part of railway construction; see Fremdling 1975: 92-100, 174-83, 186-92.
37. Uitkomsten van den landbouw 1890 (Agricultural results 1890), in particular responses about Laren (G), Bemmel, Bellingwolde, Heythuisen, Beek (L), Schinnen and Voerendaal.
38. Cf. Marijnissen and Raben-Fabels 1978.
39. Klaver 1974: 125-55.
40. See also Aardema 1981: 51-66; Marijnissen and Raben-Fabels 1978: 84ff; *Verstooteling*, H.H. J. Maas's novel from 1907, deals with the same subject matter — cf. Van den Dam and Lucassen 1976: 42.
41. Nichtweiss 1959: 177 (*c*. 1910 60,000 Belgians and Dutchmen); Staatscommissie over de werkloosheid 1914B: 258-81, especially 272 (June 1907: 100,709 Dutch workers employed in Germany); Gargas 1928: 193-201, 211-23, 242-3, 252-5; Olbrich 1982: 68 (in 1907 and 1908, *c*. 100,000 migrant workers from the Netherlands in Prussia); Marijnissen and Raben-Fabels 1978: 252 (practically 150,000 for 1913); far from all migrant workers from the Netherlands, moreover, were registered — for a telling example, see Aardema 1981: 60.
42. Klaver 1974: 129-33, 135, 151-3, 221-3; for Italians, cf. Gargas (1928: 194) who describes the remarkable division of labour between Italian (in German summers) and Dutch (in German winters) ground-workers.
43. Source: Nichtweiss 1959: 177; cf. note 41. In order of magnitude the total arrived at in Table 9.1 agrees with the 1,200,000 foreign workers which the German Ministry of Foreign Affairs accepted as the number employed in Germany in 1912-13.
44. Idem and Table 2/4b.
45. Cf. Nichtweiss 1959: 44-5.
46. Nichtweiss 1959: 20; cf. Wehler 1961 (critical analysis of the number of Poles) and, with regard to the Netherlands, Brassé and Van Schelven 1980.
47. For the complicated processes which accompanied this development, see the excellent summary by Bade (1980).

48. Nichtweiss 1959: 38-40 (the Ansiedlungsgesetz of 1886, aimed against the Poles, played a crucial role in these developments as well); Bade 1980: 312.
49. Aden 1964: 160-2.
50. Cf. Aardema 1981; Klaver 1974; Bijdragen van het Statistisch Instituut 1891.
51. Source: Appendix 3.4.
52. For what follows, see Steinbach 1976: 31-54, 124-55; Fleege-Althoff 1928 and 1930; and Lourens and Lucassen 1984.
53. What is needed especially is research about the lives of individual workers from Lippe; for a start in this direction, see Boot, Lourens and Lucassen 1983.
54. For potato-growing in nearby Ravensberg, see Mager 1982: 445-6.
55. For the following, see Chatelain 1976: 581-1005. For a recent treatment of the trek from the Massif Central, see Girard 1979 and 1982, and Poitrineau 1983.
56. Chatelain 1976: 699-701.
57. Idem: 615, 625-31; Girard 1982: 86, 115, 143.
58. Chevalier 1950; Chatelain 1976; Girard 1979: 129-43; idem 1982.
59. Girard 1979: 132.
60. Girard 1982: 45, 100 (Auvergnians in Paris are indignant that they do not share in the distribution of communal land at home); Girard 1979: 1.
61. Girard 1982: 27,72,107-8; Girard 1979: 134.
62. Girard 1982; passim; Girard 1979: 135ff.
63. Chatelain 1976: 690-1; for Germany, see Bade 1980.
64. Chatelain 1976: 704.
65. Idem: 712.
66. Idem: 214-5, 684.
67. Idem: 721-4.
68. All in all, France provided work to about $1^1/_2$ million migrant workers, an average of 250 days a year; see Prato 1912: 191.
69. Kerr 1943: 371-3; Redford 1976: 146-7; Collins 1976: 48-52; Morgan 1982: 84 (note 9).
70. Ó Gráda 1973: 52-4, 62-3.
71. Redford 1976: 71-2 and Morgan 1982: 34-57.
72. E.g. Collins 1976: 38-40.
73. Ó Gráda 1973: 57.
74. Collins 1976: 40 note 5, 42-3. For 1921 Collins reports 184,000 'part-time seasonal workers in British agriculture' and on the eve of World War II, 100,000. If we are able to accept figures on this order of c. 1900, then English developments will not have differed so considerably from continental ones. For English migrant workers, see also Morgan 1982: 47-54, 76.
75. Cf. Thompson 1981: 469-85; that such bonds might indeed have endured can be induced from the fact that even in the years after the World War II, the remittances of emigrants from Ireland were considered 'too valuable to the Irish economy for emigration to be discouraged', see Hollingsworth 1972: 263.
76. Coleman 1968: 20, 236 (the number for c. 1900 is based on the size of printings of *The Quarterly Letter of the Navvy Mission Society*); also Handley 1970, Burton 1972 and Brooke 1983.
77. Ó Gráda 1973: 58; Collins 1976: 45-8; Redford 1976: 146-7.
78. See also numbers cited in note 74.
79. Förster 1969 and Marchetti 1914.
80. Corsini 1969: 107.
81. Marchetti 1914: 613.
82. Chatelain 1976: 604-5, 631, 978-88. My principal objection to otherwise informative passages is Chatelain's suggestion — launched without supporting evidence — that continuity exists between the departure of Corsican soldiers in the 16th and 17th centuries, and migratory labour in the second half of the 19th

century. It is also not clear to what extent Italian migrant workers stopped to visit the island in this late period, and, for those who did, what measures were taken to make up for their loss. For the trek from Corsica at the dawn of Early Modern History, see Braudel I 1976: 41-2 and 44.
83. Chatelain 1976: 981-2.
84. Marchetti 1914; 611 and 612 (specifications for Foggia and Potenza).
85. Marchetti 1914: 607; Förster 1969.
86. Förster 1969: 28.
87. Marchetti 1914: 607, 616; Förster 1969: 23-42; 122-6.
88. See Appendix 2.4, Hoffmann-Nowotny 1973: 37-66; Cinanni 1969: 151-61; Prato 1912: 197-200, 227-9, 255-6.
80. Research in progress, P. Lourens and J. Lucassen, University of Utrecht, Social-Economic History Dept; Nielsen 1944: 182ff (he reports that seasonal migration from certain Danish islands to the brick factories of Jutland also took place at this time); Willerslev 1952: 114-23, in particular 118; Nellemann 1981: 51 (even Polish brick-makers).
90. Nellemann 1981: 28-31; Swedes and Danes also worked in Germany (idem: 25-6).
91. Idem: 42-54.
92. For Spain as well a vast increase in the volume of migratory labour during the 19th century may be considered as probable, not only in agriculture (Avance Estadística 1891), but also in public works (Bahamonde 1980: 156 ff.) and in mining.
93. Kondratieff 1935; for a review of theories concerning economic fluctuations throughout history, see Jansen 1981.
94. For the period following World War II, see Lucassen 1982: 330-1; for Germany, see Lohrmann 1974: 103-6 and Elsner 1974: 17-40; for France see Granotier 1973: 41-54; for Switzerland, Hoffmann-Nowotny 1973: 37-66.

Appendix 1

1. Lucassen 1984: 250-333.
2. Boot, Lourens and Lucassen 1983. My appreciation to Piet Lourens who provided me with processed data for 1811.
3. The German Reiderland also belonged to this département. For the arrondissement of Assen, see also Lucassen 1985.
4. Here, the relation of this Appendix and Appendix 1.33 is not discussed.
5. Population figures from: Almanach 1812; for the first four départements somewhat different statistics in Schwarting 1936: 13 — the discrepancy, however, is consistently less than 1%; for the principality of Lippe: Steinbach 1976: 170 (concerning 1812). For a different figure for Ems Supérieur, see Joulia 1973: 88. In Appendix 1.34 the only calculation undertaken is for the Regierungsbezirk Minden, (Lucassen 1984) to which migrant workers from Kreis Lübbecke have been added, see Appendix 3.1; population in 1817 according to Kolb 1862: 164.

Appendix 2

1. Certain references to migratory labour in eastern Europe appear in: Roscher III, 1887, 5th edn, 94; Roscher I, 1894, 21st edn, 769; Burke 1978: 95-7; Redford 1976: 5; Le Play 1877-9, vol. II: 86-7, 179-230 and vol. V: 250. It is

remarkable, moreover, how little attention Chayanov devotes to the phenomenon of migratory labour (Thorner, Kerblay and Smith 1966: 107); see too p. 125.

2. For the Balkans data remain too fragmentary; see Appendix 2.4, note 62 and also Redford 1976, XIII (gardeners from Trnovo and, among others, Albanians to Thessaly); Braudel 1976, I: 39, 40,43 and 66 (Albanians to Kosovo Metohija, Thessaly and as mercenaries; Bulgarians to Thrace, the inhabitants of Attica to Thessaly); Mendelson 1911: 551 (Trnovo gardeners).

3. This appendix derived in the first place from Meijide Pardo 1960; in addition, there are interesting facts in: Chatelain 1976: 47-8, 54, 285, 288, 290, 423, 429-30, 442, 445-6, 469-71; Poitrineau 1983: passim; Hufton 1974: 78-9, 85, 87-90; Lis and Soly 1979: 190-1; Falkmann 1846: 66; Meurer 1871: 3; Redford 1976: 4-5; Braudel 1976,I: 40; Le Play 1877-9,IV: 247-90 and V: 240-2, 249-58; Girard 1979: 57-8.

4. For the following, see primarily Chatelain 1976 (cf. note 3).

5. Chatelain (1976: 471) reports two to three thousand workers from Auvergne in 1898 who worked on a regular basis in Spain. Cambon (1890: 31-2) also cites skilled French industrial workers in Catalonia and Basque regions.

6. See Appendix 2.2.

7. Hufton (1974: 87) mentions Père Labat in 1730 as her source, but according to Roscher (I, 1894, 21st edn: 769) Jean Bodin already cited this number in his *Responsio ad paradoxa* of 1568 (p.49); lastly, Le Play (1877-9, V: 241) reports 200,000 Frenchmen in Spain in 1669 basing this claim on 'Mémoires de Gourville: tome LII de la collection des Mémoires relatifs à l'histoire de France'.

8. Kamen 1980: 60-1; Cambon 1890: 31-2 (Madrid bakers from Auvergne); Meijide Pardo 1960: passim; Bahamonde 1980 (migratory labour to Madrid) the previously mentioned tinkers also went to Burgos. It is well worth studying the connection between Galician migration to America and migratory labour within the peninsula, especially since even into this century most migration to America has not been permanent. Between 1901 and 1976, 3.7 million persons, from Galicia above all, migrated to, primarily, Latin America, but during the same period 2.3 million of them — 63% — came back; see Bernitt 1981: 8; cf. also p. 200.

9. Meijide Pardo 1960: 465, 469, 475, 494, 530, 576, 583-4, 590.

10. In addition to literature cited in notes 3 and 8, see also: Bosque Maurel 1978; Bihourd 1890: 66; Roscher I, 1894, 21st edn, 769; and Burke 1978: 97 (for migratory labour of actors, the so-called *farsantes*).

An interesting example of the trek from northern Italy to Andalusia is, moreover, reported by the prefect of Montenotte (AN F 20 435): before the Spanish revolution various inhabitants of coastal cantons in the arrondissement of Savona went to Spain, above all to Cadiz 'where for the most part they carried out their vocations, or engaged in smuggling. The majority thrived there and a certain Montesisto from Savona, 80 years earlier [thus *c.* 1730], amassed a fortune of four million *pièces*'.

11. A trek to the rice fields of Valencia is reported in Garcia Fernandez 1971: 165, whereas migratory labour to Algeria and Central Spain is known to have begun only later in the 19th century.

12. Chatelain 1976 — which wholly replaces Mauco 1932 and, to a large extent, Hufton 1974: 69-106 (who, without making any reference to her source, uses one of Mauco's maps on page 75). Despite Chatelain's monumental achievement, so many inconsistencies remain that only a method such as the one applied in Appendix 1 can produce a more statistically reliable basis for anyalysing the development of migratory labour in France during the period which concerns us. Such an effort, however, exceeds the scale of what is possible here. See too Poitrineau 1983, Barret and Gurgand 1980, and Burke 1978: 92-102 (*re* opérateurs, bateleurs, chanteurs, chansonniers). In connection with Appendix 2.3 I have studied further data concerning, primarily, southern France (AN F 20 434

and 435: reports from Alpes Maritimes, Hautes Alpes, Léman, Isère and from the Italian departments Doire, Pô, Sésia, Stura and the Swiss département Simplon).
13. Chatelain 1976: 48, 615.
14. Idem: 162-9.
15. Idem: 111-2.
16. For Pas de Calais, see Appendix 1.19; nothing is known about Somme; 750 workers went to take part in the harvest in Oise (Chatelain 1976: 163), but far more workers from Oise headed south to find work.
17. Chatelain 1976: 599-604.
18. Idem: 169-78.
19. Idem: 110; for the total: 49.
20. See Appendix 2.1.
21. Chatelain 1976, III. Considering similarities which characterise the apposite 'push areas', I prefer to classify Corsica as part of the Central Italian System; see Appendix 2.3 p/q.
22. Idem: 108 (Loire Inférieure and Maine et Loire are cited as well).
23. Idem: 178; for the total: 49.
24. Idem: 168-9.
25. See Appendices 1.20 and 2.5.
26. Chatelain 1976: 49.
27. Idem: 42. Here, Chatelain estimates that total number of migratory workers in France at the time of the Questionnaire of 1811 at 200,000. Adding the sub-totals of the 'pull areas' discussed in this appendix, I reach a sum of 110,000, whereas together the sub-totals of 'push areas' yield a total of 144,000. For this inconsistency, cf. note 12 above.
28. Idem: 41, 44, 615; Poitrineau 1983.
29. Chatelain 1976: 46.
30. Idem: 48.
31. Idem: Map I-1; Appendices 1.31 and 1.32.
32. Idem: 47; Appendix 2.1.
33. Idem: 48; Appendices 1.28 to 1.30.
34. Corsini 1969: tables on pp. 106 and 110 (concerning the areas 3b-3o treated below), and some answers *in extenso* 143-57. Mauco, moreover, presents results in brief for the départements Gênes, Trasimène and Rome (1932: 69-71) and Woolf, too, appears familiar with the report of the prefect of Rome (1979: 277-8).
35. These data also in AN F 20 434 (Alpes Maritimes) and 435 (Hautes Alpes, Isère and Léman).
36. Corsini (1969: 106, 110) reports 10,300 for reasons unknown to me.
37. Idem: 5,500.
38. Idem arrives at a total of 7,500, above all because — for reasons unknown to me — he includes 6,000 workers in agriculture, compared to my moderate figure of 2,000.
39. Idem combines figures for internal migration with those for migratory workers from Pô, and as a result his total for the département comes to 2,700 (p. 110) or 2,800 (p. 106).
40. Idem only includes the 1,200 construction workers in his calculation of the trek to Marengo.
41. Idem — for reasons unknown to me — includes 500 more agricultural workers in his figures.
42. Idem estimates 300 construction workers and 200 others; thus, a total of 500.
43. Idem, employing sources unknown to me, reports the following trek from Apennins:

agricultural workers	4,500
woodcutters/charcoal burners	1,550
others	2,800
total	8,850

He does cite the prefect who reported in 1807 that as a result of a sizable increase in the number of public works jobs, migratory labour from Apennins declined from 10,000 in 1806 to 2,000 in 1807. This stream of workers headed primarily for Tuscany, the Papal States, Rome and Corsica.

44. Idem, for reasons that remain obscure to me and without specification, cites a total of 3,500 workers.

45. Not in Corsini (1969: 106, 110).

46. Idem.

47. Bovenkerk, Eijken and Bovenkerk-Teerink 1982: 80-6.

48. Almanach 1811; for 3b to 3o slightly different figures in Corsini 1969: 106.

49. The notes below refer primarily to literature which provides information further illuminating data from the questionnaire, and not to questionnaire responses themselves. The trek of Abruzzi shepherds to Apulia (Woolf 1979: 278) is the one example I have found in secondary literature of the pull-force in southern Italy — an area considered by most authors to be a 'push area' (see Romano 1973: 497; cf. also note 59). Strong doubts persist, however, when we consider the great trek within and from southern Italy that was characteristic of the second half of the 19th century (cf. p. 201-2).

50. Mauco 1932: 69; Sella 1973; Meurer 1871: 3; Braudel 1976 I: 66; Davico 1968.

51. Woolf 1979: 150 and 275-83; Sella 1973.

52. For examples, see Roscher I, 1894, 21st edn: 769 and idem III, 1887, 5th edn: 95; Woolf 1979: 289; Bovenkerk, Eijken and Bovenkerk-Teerink 1982: 31-44,159-63; Braudel 1976 I: 40-4,66-7.

53. Chatelain 1976: 792-4.

54. This 'watershed' was not leak-proof: workers from north of the line were reported in Tuscany, the Roman Campagna and on Corsica and Elba. Cf. too Sella 1973: 548-9 (Alps inhabitants bound for the south); Roscher I, 1894, 21st edn: 769 (from Modena to Corsica and from Parma to England).

55. As late as 1848 most migrant workers from Tessin still went to the Pô valley (Roscher 1894, 21st edn: 769).

56. Although masons from Lake Como and Lake Lugano went south, in 1831 workers from Vicenza and Fruili headed for Austria and Hungary (Roscher I,1894, 21st edn: 769); until 1766 workers from Graubünden still journeyed to Venice, but thereafter they probably veered farther north (idem: 771).

57. Mauco 1932: 69-71; Meurer 1871: 3; Staring 1868: 675; Woolf 1979: 277-8; Romano 1973: 498.

58. Mauco 1932: 69-71; Bovenkerk, Eijken and Bovenkerk-Teerink 1982: 80-6.

59. Chatelain (1976: 603-4) reports that even Neapolitan and Calabrian tinkers had already reached Bouches du Rhône; Roscher 1894, 21st edn: 769 (Calabrians to Naples).

60. AN F 20 435, responses from Marengo, Stura, Montenotte, and Trasimène; Corsini 1969; Poussou 1974: 9.

61. Summarised in Map 3, Weber-Kellermann 1965. For these changes, especially the arrival of the Poles, see pp. 189 above.

62. From, respectively, Meurer 1871: 3; Staring 1868: 675 and Roscher I 1894, 21st edn: 769 (only Roscher reports his source and gives a date: 1831); cf.,

too, Roscher III 1887, 5th edn: 94 for Slovakia provinces as 'push areas' and Tack 1902: 7-8 for Bulgarian market-gardeners who also crop up in Timisoara (Romania), Vršac (Yugoslavia), Szeged and Budapest (Hungary) and Vienna. Cf. Braudel 1976 I: 43 (Albanian migration to the Podrina) and Le Play 1877-8 V: 1-59 (Moravia); and 250 (Bohemia and Carpathians).

63. Ludwig 1915: 78-107 (the statistic for 1838 probably also underpins von Reden's report in 1848 of 16,000 to 17,000 men from the German Tirol; see Roscher I, 1894, 21st edn: 769).

64. See Appendix 2.3 (Arno, Doire, Pô, Rome, Simplon, Trasimène, Alpes Maritimes and Hautes Alpes); Küther 1983: 11; see, too, Ludwig 1915: 8 (sauerkraut cutters) and Meurer 1871: 3-4.

65. See Appendix 2.2.

66. Respectively Ludwig 1915: 150ff. (he maintains the trek of the Swabians began in the 18th century); idem:148-50 (the trek from the Odenwald he dates similarly): idem: 7 (the trek from Westerwald and Vogelsberg he traces back to the 17th century); for the Rhön (without dates): Meurer 1871: 3 and Weber-Kellermann 1965: 301. For Rhön, also see Annex 1-4 sub F (Lucassen 1984); in general see Mendelson 1911: 542-4.

67. Weber-Kellermann 1965: 287-308 and her Map 3, based on Mannhardt (1865) and Von der Goltz (1872); Meurer 1871: 3-4; Ludwig 1915: 6-8; Mendelson 1911: 542-4, 550.

68. In the second half of the 19th century brick-makers also went from Lippe to Norway and Sweden. Never very many, however: for the period 1849-69, P. Lourens and I found the highest number of such migratory workers in 1863, when 192 Lippe workers went to seventeen Swedish brick-workers and 16 to three Norwegian brickworks, totals of little significance compared to the thousands who found jobs that year in Danish brick-works (research in progress, University of Utrecht, Dept of Social-Economic History). For Finland, see Hoffman 1982: 41 and Rosander 1967: 54-7; for Norway: Rosander 1967: 57-60.

69. Rosander 1967 and 1976; cf. also Le Play 1877-9 V: 250 and Hekscher 1954: 169-72 and 226.

70. Rosander 1967: 105, 115.

71. In 1808, when Denmark was at war with Sweden, all Swedes in Denmark had to be counted. To the extent that the results of this enumeration have been preserved, it appears that 8,300 Swedes were registered for Amt Copenhagen, Frederiksborg, Sorø, Odense and Hjørring (see Andersen 1982; a study not quoted by Willerslev 1983, who dates the start of the Swedish trek some decades later).

72. Willerslev 1983: 11-12; Nellemann 1981.

73. See Appendix 1.34. This trek, in particular migration from Ems Supérieur, was of extremely recent origin. Later these 'Danes' also set out for Sweden among other destinations; see Wrasmann 1921: 23 and Dobelmann 1963: 25-6.

74. Weber-Kellermann 1965: Map 3.

75. In 1895 the distribution of land ownership was comparable in Jever, Butjadingen, Brade and Elsfleth, in the 'marschen' of Regierungsbezirk Stade and in the Kreise Süderdithmarschen, Norderdithmarschen, Eiderstedt, Husum and Tondern (farms of between 20 and 50 ha were the most common, see Swart 1910: 227). Outside this area after 1750-1800 migrant workers also turn up in Fehmarn (Wiepert 1982: 29).

76. This is not altogether certain for the 'marschen' in Regierungsbezirk Stade; cf. note 75 above.

77. Staring 1868: 675; Baudassin 1865: 233-4 (from Fanö to Ribe); Weber-Kellermann 1965: 198-204.

78. According to the research cited in note 68 above, and also Nielsen 1944: 182ff. (he reports Danish migrant workers in brick-works as well), Willerslev 1952:

114-23 and idem 1983: 13 (Swedish brick-makers in Denmark already in 1855) and 109-18.

79. In what follows the trek of craftsmen, vendors, entertainers and similar figures has largely been left out of consideration; cf. Leeson 1979; Roscher III 1887, 5th edn: 95; Burke 1978: 39-42 and 106-8. 'Navvies' too employed at the time to dig canals (and not yet to lay railways) suffer from all too cursory attention (Coleman 1968: 25-6, 35, 59; Kerr 1943: 374). Burton 1972: 160-1; Handley 1970: 42-64. Agricultural labour and entertainment were at times combined in one and the same group of migrant workers, as illustrated by 'morris dancers'; see Morgan 1975: 51.

80. Thompson 1981: 471; Redford 1976: 133; Ó Gráda 1973: 49-50.

81. Kerr 1943: 371, 373; Ó Gráda 1973: 49.

82. According to Morgan 1982: 84 — on the basis of a PhD dissertation written by Collins in 1970 which I was unable to consult — in 1820 there were 22,000 Irish migrant workers in Great Britain. From this total we must subtract Irish employed in the south of Scotland, but we need to add the Welshmen (Collins 1976: 45-7) and the Scots who journeyed to England (Collins 1976: 47-8; Redford 1976: 135: c. 1790-1800 there were 10,000 Scots arriving annually to work in London), and the English workers who took part in internal migratory labour (e.g. from Cumberland and Leicestershire; see, respectively, Collins 1976: 47 and Redford 1976: 133) Kerr's estimates (1943: 371) are lower than Morgan's; those of Ó Gráda (1973: 50-2) for later years are consistent with Morgan's. (It is rather startling that Ó Gráda's excellent article is cited in none of the works mentioned here whereas it is often pertinent to the matter at hand; what is more, Ó Gráda himself appears to be ignorant of the existence of Collins' dissertation.)

83. Collins 1976: 45-7.

84. idem: 47/8; Redford 1976: 142, 147; Handley 1870: 18.

85. Collins 1976: 48-52; Redford 1976: 141-6; Ó Gráda 1973: 49-51, 58, 60 (an estimate of nearly 40,000 for the number of internal Irish migrant labourers in the 1830s).

86. Collins 1976: 48-52; cf. Kerr 1943: 347 and Thompson 1981: 469-85.

87. Redford 1976: 135 (cites Roxburgshire and Dumfriesshire).

88. Collins 1976: 54-6; Morgan 1982: 47-54, 76 (difficult, however, to date); Redford 1976: 135. Cf., however, Thompson (1981: 246-7) who, speaking about 'the Speenham land Counties of the south', quotes an author from 1836: [the farmer] keep us here [on poor rates] like potatoes in a pit, and only take us out for use when they can no longer do without us.' Cf. also Brooke 1983: 10-37 and 171-92 for navvies in 1851 originating from the south.

89. Redford 1976: 133 and 145-7; Kerr 1943: 372-3; Ó Gráda 1973; Collins 1976.

Appendix 3

1. Sources:
1811: see Appendices 1.4 and 1.34
1817-24: Tack 1902: 146
1826-43: Sahner 1950: 7, 17 (specifications probably only concern Roman Catholics)
1861: ADW, CA 369 I (only concerns Lutherans); Tack (1902: 146) makes incorrect use of these statistics, placing them mistakenly in the 1840s.
2. Sources:
1811: See Appendix 1.4 (Lucassen 1984; with the understanding that Ledde =

Ledde und Leeden and Cappeln = Westerkappeln). For the sub-total, see explanation of Table 1.2 in the text (p. 33).
1828: Tack 1902: 146.
1861: ADW, CA 369 I (only concerns Lutherans). Comparison with 1811 (see right-hand column of the table) has only been attempted for places which were predominantly Lutheran, using the religious census of 1849 (Gladen 1970: 213).
  3. Sources:
1811: See Appendices 1.3 and 1.7.
1861: ADW, CA 369 I.
1870: ADW, CA 369 XI: c. 1870 3,000 German mowers and haymakers to Holland, 2/3rds of whom were Lutherans, mostly from Ostfriesland.
1900: ADW, CA 369 XI: in 1902 320 mowers from Ostfriesland attending the services of Father Voss in Friesland; Tack 1902: 125-6: at these same services in 1900, a congregation of 235 to 245, leading him to conclude that 300 to 350 grass mowers from Ostfriesland, most of them *Reformiert*, (Calvinist Protestant) went to Friesland.
  4. Sources:
1811: See Appendices 1.4 and 1.5 (Tack 1902: 144 presents calculations which in many instances differ from mine, especially for Aschendorf, Sögel, Bentheim and Lingen. Apparently Tack interprets the sub-division borders differently).
1850: Schröder 1976.
1861: ADW, CA 369 I.
1864-71: Meurer 1871: 5-6 (the minimal number of 3,500 for Osnabrück I have taken to be valid for the landdrostei Osnabrück; from a combination of data for the period 1861-8 I have myself undertaken a reconstruction per Kreis and Amt — and print the results in parentheses in the table above.
1900: Tack 1902: 126-7 and 132-4.
  5. Sources:
1811: See Appendices 1.2 and 1.4 (Lucassen 1984; NB1: for Kreis Diepholz I have taken the following marieën: Diepholz, Aschen, Jacobidrebber, Sankthülfen, Lemförde, Varrel, Rehden, Wetschen, Barver, Eidelstedt, Dörpel, Heiligenloh, Dickel, Barnstorf, Kornau and Auburg. This combination differs from that given by the ex-Amtmann of Diepholz in 1811. Basing my calculations on the places he cites, I would reach a total of 376 workers, whereas his own estimate was in the neighbourhood of 1,000. NB2: The estimate for Syke is based on the number for 1808: 69, according to Tack (1902: 144). NB3. The number 1,002 is the result of my calculations for the French arrondissement Nieubourg increased by workers from the marieën Diepenau, Warmsen, Uchte, Kirchdorf, Ströhen, Dörriehloh, Varrel, Gross Lessen, Schmalförden and Heiligenloh, all in Ems Supérieur, approximately equivalent to the Kreise Syke, Sulingen, Hoya, Stolzenau and Nienburg. The inaccuracy arises from the fact that in this way in 1811 migrant workers from the cantons of Rethem and Walsrode were wrongly included in the count whereas those from several villages on the right bank of the Weser in Kreise Stolzenau and Nienburg were wrongly excluded.)
1824-65A: Tack 1902: 144 (NB Tack maintains that in 1824 we should base our calculations on an unofficial total of 1,000 workers from Diepholz, a number close indeed to that reported in 1811 by the ex-Amtmann from Diepholz; see above).
1865B: ADW, CA 369 II (Bericht Meyeringh 1865: estimate of the number of grass-mowers in Friesland).
1866: ADW, CA 369 II (Bericht Lenhartz 1866: enumeration of all German Lutheran workers based on a letter from the Konsistorium of Hannover, 11/5/1866).

1900: Tack 1902: 126, 145.
   6. Sources:
1811: Appendices 1.1 and 1.2 (Lucassen 1984 NB: Kreise Achim, Verden and Rotenburg roughly coincide with the arrondissement of Bremen; the remaining Kreise with the arrondissement Bremerlehe and with the western part of Bouches de l'Elbe, from which no migrant workers came; statistics have therefore been retained which represent the situation in the specified arrondissements.)
1859 and 1865: Tack 1902: 144.
1900: No longer mentioned in the sources cited elsewhere in this appendix for that year.
   7. Sources:
1811: Appendices 1.1 and 1.2 (Lucassen 1984; Amt Vechta = Visbeck; canton Vechta without Eidelstedt, Dörpel, Heiligenloh, Dickel and Barnstorf/Kornau; canton Dinklage; Amt Cloppenburg = canton Cloppenburg, canton Löhningen and mairie Essen; Amt Friesoythe = canton Friesoythe; Amt Wildeshausen = canton Wildeshausen without Visbeck but with Dötlingen/Neerstedt; the remaining Aemter coincide with the 'push' cantons of arrondissement Oldenburg, but without Dötlingen/Neerstedt; Tack 1902: 144 arrives at other figures primarily because he omits the arrondissement of Oldenburg and comes to a lower total for Vechta).
1865: ADW, CA 369 II (Bericht Meyeringh 1865: 200 Roman Catholic grass-mowers in Friesland, 50 turf-diggers from Amt Vechta in Hoogeveen and 50 turf-diggers from Mecklenburg (sic)/Oldenburg in Dedemsvaart and Lutten).
1866: Meyeringh 1867 (400 grass-mowers in Friesland).
1868: Die Hollandsgänger 1869 (only Lutherans).
1869: ADW, CA 369 IV (Bericht A. Wolter 1869).
1880 and 1895: ADW, CA 369 XI and Schauenburg 1886: 42; cf., however, ADW, CA 369 VIII (Bericht Kuhlmann 1889: in his opinion such an estimate seems rather high).
1900: Tack 1902: 113-16, 126.
   8. Sources:
1811: Appendix 1-6.
Brick-makers in other years: Fleege-Althoff 1928: 122, 124, 162, 174-5 and Steinbach 1976: 134-55 (it is possible that the number for 1900 is too high: Fleege-Althoff (1928: 174) reports 100 brick-makers for Groningen in 1902, whereas only 30 are mentioned for 1900 in ADW, CA 369 XI. In 1923 some 925 masons and 702 other migrant workers still also departed).
Grass-mowers/turf-cutters: 1860: ADW, CA 369 I: 1865: ADW, CA 369 II (Bericht Meyeringh 1865: grass-mowers in Friesland); 1866: Meyeringh 1867 (grass-mowers in Friesland).
   9. Sources:
1866: Meyeringh 1867.
1873: Lourens and Lucassen 1984.
   10. Sources:
1865: ADW, CA 369 II (Bericht Meyeringh 1865).
1866: Meyeringh 1867 (the place specified, Kreis Neundorf, does not exist; Nenndorf, situated in the Hessian exclave of Schaumburg, bordering on Lippe-Detmold, appears the only likely solution to the confusion).
1873-84: Lourens and Lucassen 1984.
   11. Source: ADW, CA 369 II (Bericht Meyeringh 1865).

BIBLIOGRAPHY OF PRIMARY AND SECONDARY SOURCES[1]

Primary Sources[2]

The Netherlands

Algemeen Rijksarchief, 's-Gravenhage (ARA)
  Binnenlandse zaken 1796-1813 (BZ 1796-1813)
  JUSTITIE 1813-76
  WATERSTAAT 1830-77
  STAATSSECRETARIE
  Kabinet des Konings (KDK)
  *COLLECTIE GOGEL
  Gewestelijke Besturen 1807-15 (GB 1807-1815)
Rijksarchief in Drenthe, Assen (RAD)
  *Oude Statenarchieven (OSA)
Rijksarchief in Gelderland, Arnhem (RAG)
  *Archieven van de Franse tijd (AFT)
Rijksarchief in Groningen, Groningen (RAGR)
  *Gewestelijke Besturen 1798-1814 (GB 1798-1814)
  RECHTERLIJK ARCHIEF
Rijksarchief in Friesland, Leeuwarden (RAF)
  *Lands- en gewestelijke besturen 1795-1813 (BRF)
Rijksarchief in Limburg, Maastricht (RAL)
  Departement van de NEDERMAAS
  SCHEPENBANK MEIJEL
Rijksarchief in Noord-Brabant, 's-Hertogenbosch (RANB)
  *Departement van de Monden van de Rijn (MR)
Rijksarchief in Noord-Holland, Haarlem (RANH)
  Departement van de Zuiderzee (DZZ)
  Oude Rechterlijke Archieven (ORA)
Rijksarchief in Overijssel, Zwolle (RAO)
  *Departement van de Monden van de IJssel (DEP)
  STATENARCHIEF NA 1813
Rijksarchief in Utrecht, Utrecht (RAU)
  *Archief van de Staten van Utrecht (SA)
Rijksarchief in Zeeland, Middelburg (RAZ)
  ARCHIEVEN van de PREFECTUUR
Streekarchief (SA) EINDHOVEN
  *Gemeentearchief (GA) EINDHOVEN
  *Gemeentearchief (GA) WOENSEL
STREEKARCHIEF PEELLAND, Deurne
  *Gemeentearchief (GA) AARLE-RIXTEL
  *GEMEENTELIJKE VERVENING DEURNE
   MANUSCRIPTEN
Streekarchief (SA) WAALWIJK
  *Gemeentearchief (GA) WAALWIJK
  *Gemeentearchief (GA) BAARDWIJK
Gemeentearchief (GA) ALKMAAR
  Gemeentearchief (GA) AKERSLOOT

Gemeentearchief (GA) GRAFT
Gemeentearchief (GA) HEILO
Gemeentearchief (GA) OUDORP
Gemeentearchief (GA) SCHOORL
Gemeentearchief AMSTERDAM (GAA)
   NIEUW STEDELIJK BESTUUR
   COMMISSIE VAN DE ARBEIDSENQUÊTE TE AMSTERDAM
   1897-1900
   Gemeentearchief (GA) BUIKSLOOT
   Gemeentearchief (GA) WATERGRAAFSMEER
   Gemeentearchief (GA) WEESPERKARSPEL
   Maatschappij tot NUT van het Algemeen (Particuliere archieven 211)
Gemeentearchief (GA) BLOEMENDAAL
   Oud Archief (OA)
Gemeentearchief (GA) GOUDA
   SECRETARIE Gouda 1816-1920
   SECRETARIE MOORDRECHT 1813-1900
Gemeentearchief (GA) 's-GRAVENMOER
Gemeentearchief (GA) HASSELT
   Oud Archief (OA)
Gemeentearchief (GA) HEEMSTEDE
   OUD ARCHIEF
   GEMEENTEVERSLAGEN
Gemeentearchief (GA) HELDEN
Gemeentearchief (GA) HENDRIK-IDO-AMBACHT
*Gemeentearchief (GA) LOON-OP-ZAND
Gementearchief (GA) NEDERWEERT
*Gemeentearchief (GA) RAAMSDONK
Gemeentearchief (GA) SPRANG-CAPELLE
   *Gemeentearchief (GA) 's-GREVELDUIN-CAPELLE
   *Gemeentearchief (GA) SPRANG-CAPELLE
Gemeentearchief (GA) VELSEN
   *Oud Archief (OA)
*Gemeentearchief (GA) WASPIK
Gemeentearchief (GA) WEERT
   *Oud Archief (OA)
Gemeentearchief (GA) ZWOLLE
Sociaal Historisch Centrum voor Limburg, Maastricht (SHCL)
   Documentaire verzamelingen betreffende Noord- en Midden-Limburg
   (DOC 7)

Belgium

Algemeen Rijksarchief, Brussel (ARAB)
   *préfecture de la DYLE
Rijksarchief in Antwerpen, Antwerpen (RAA)
   *PROVinciaal ARCHief
Rijksarchief in Oost-Vlaanderen, Gent (RAGB)
   *Département de l'ESCAUT
   Gemeentearchief (GA) BRUSSEL

France

Archives Nationales, Paris (AN)

Germany

Haupt Staatsarchiv, Düsseldorf (HSAD)
  *Roer-Département
Staatsarchiv Bremen (SAB)
Rheinisch-Westfälisches Staatsarchiv, Detmold (SAD)
Niedersächsisches Staatsarchiv, Osnabrück (SAO)
  Oberemsdepartement (OED)
  *Arrondissement NEUENHAUS
  *Arrondissement LINGEN
Archiv des Diakonischen Werkes der Evangelischen Kirche in Deutschland, Berlin (ADW)
  *Central-Ausschuss für die Innere Mission der Deutschen Evangelischen Kirche (CA)

Notes

1. Abbreviations used in the notes following each chapter are printed in parentheses.
2. Primary sources for this study and mentioned in the Dutch text (Lucassen, 1984, especially Annex 1) but not in this English version, are indicated with an asterisk.

Secondary Sources

Van Der AA, A.J., *Aardrijkskundig woordenboek der Nederlanden*, Gorcum 1836-51
Aardema, M., *Uit het leven van een veenarbeider. Herinneringen van Mindert Aardema, veenarbeider, polderjongen, gastarbeider, AOWer*, Baarn 1981
Abel, W., *Geschichte der deutschen Landwirtschaft vom frühen Mittelalter bis zum 19. Jahrhundert*, Stuttgart 1967
Ab Utrecht Dresselhuis, J., *Het distrikt van Sluis in Vlaanderen*, Middelburg 1819
Adams, W.F., *Ireland and the Irish Emigration to the New World from 1915 to the Famine*, New Haven, London and Oxford 1932
Aden, O., *Entwicklung und Wechsellagen ausgewählter Gewerbe in Ostfriesland von der Mitte des 18. bis zum Ausgang des 19. Jahrhunderts*, Aurich 1964
Van Aelbroek, J.L., *Werkdadige landbouw-konst der Vlamingen*, Gent 1823
Agriculture, 'Recensement Général (15 octobre 1846). Résumés par arrondissement et par province', Bruxelles 1850
Almanach Impérial, Paris 1811 and 1812
Alstorphius Greveling, P.W., *Statistiek van de provincie Drenthe, voornamelijk uit het oogpunt van Nijverheid en Volkswelvaart; met opgave der hoofd-middelen ter opbeuring van dat gewest*, Assen 1840
Andersen, F., 'Svensk af fødsel. Personalhistorisk kildemateriale opstået som følge af udenrigspolitikkens konsekvenser for dansk lokaladministration 1808', in: *Personalhistorisk Tidsskrift 102*, 1982: 55-80
André, R., *La démographie du Hainaut. Tome 1: Charleroi et son agglomération*, Bruxelles 1970
Van Asselt, G.F., 'De Hollandgänger: gastarbeid in de 19de eeuw. De Conferentie

te Oeynhausen op 27 februari 1866; een hoofdstuk uit de geschiedenis van de Reisepredigt', in: *Tijdschrift voor Sociale Geschiedenis 2*, 1976 (no. 4): 4-41
—— De Hollandgängerei, in: *Spiegel Historiael 12*, 1977: 226-35 *Avance Estadistica sobre el cultivo cereal y de leguminosas asociadas en España*, 3 vols, Madrid 1891
Aymard, M., 'La Sicile, terre d'immigration', in: *Les migrations dans les pays méditerranéens au XVIIIeme et au début du XIXeme*. Actes des journées d'études. Bendor 6 et 7 avril 1973, Nice 1974: 134-157
Baars, C., *De geschiedenis van de landbouw in de Beijerlanden*, Wageningen 1973
Bade, K.J., 'Massenwanderung und Arbeitsmarkt im deutschen Nordosten von 1880 bis zum ersten Weltkrieg. Überseeische Auswanderung, interne Abwanderung und kontinentale Zuwanderung', in: *Archiv für Sozialgeschichte 20*, 1980: 265-323
Bahamonde, A., 'El mercado de mano de obra madrileño (1850-74)', in: *Estudios de Historia Social 15*, 1980: 143-75
Barret, P. and Gurgand, J.-N., *Ils voyageaient la France. Vie et traditions des Compagnons du Tour de France au XIXe siècle*, Paris 1980
Baudassin, A., 'Der Mägdemarkt in Ripen', in: *Die Illustrierte Welt 13*, 1865: 233-4
Beetstra, W.T., 'It libben by in greidboer om 1865', in: *It Beaken. Tydskrift fan de Fryske Akademy 41*, 1979: 115-21
Bernitt, M., *Die Rückwanderung spanischer Gastarbeiter. Der Fall Andalusien*, Königstein 1981
Bihourd, M. 'Les Conditions du travail en Portugal', in: M. Cambon, *Les conditions du travail en Espagne*, Paris/Nancy, 1890
Blanchard, R., *La Flandre*, Lille 1905
Boot, M., Lourens, P. and Lucassen, J., 'A linguistic preprocessor for record linkage in socio-economic historical research', in: *Computers and the Humanities 17*, 1983: 45-64
Bos Jzn., W., *Sliedrecht, dorp van wereldvermaardheid*, Zaltbommel 1969
Bouman, P.J., *Geschiedenis van den Zeeuwschen landbouw in de negentiende en twintigste eeuw en van de Zeeuwsche Landbouw-Maatschappij 1843-1943*, Wageningen 1946
Bovenkerk, F., Eijken, A. and Bovenkerk-Teerink, W., *Italiaans ijs. De opmerkelijke historie van de Italiaanse ijsbereiders in Nederland*, Amsterdam 1983
Brasse, P. and Van Schelven, W., *Assimilatie van vooroorlogse immigranten. Drie generaties Polen, Slovenen, Italianen in Heerlen*, 's-Gravenhage 1980
Braudel, F., *La Méditerranée et le monde méditerranéen à l'époque de Philippe II*, Paris 1976, 3rd edn., 2 vols
Briels, J., *De zuidnederlandse immigratie 1572-1630*, Haarlem 1978
Brooke, D., *The Railway Navvy. 'That Despicable Race of Men'*, Newton Abbot, London, North Pomfret (Vt) 1983
Brugmans, I.J., *Statistieken van de Nederlandse nijverheid uit de eerste helft der 19e eeuw*, 's-Gravenhage 1956, 2 vols
De Bruin, M.P., 'Over dijkgraven en polderjongens', in: *Archief van het Koninklijk Zeeuwsch Genootschap der Wetenschappen* 1970: 100-14
Bruijn, J.R., 'Zeevarenden', in: *Maritieme geschiedenis der Nederlanden 3*, Bussum 1977: 146-90
—— and Lucassen, J. (eds), *Op de schepen der Oost-Indische Compagnie. Vijf artikelen van J. de Hullu ingeleid, bewerkt en voorzien van een studie over de werkgelegenheid bij de VOC*, Groningen 1980
De Bruijne, F.H., *De ronde venen. Een sociaal-geografische studie van een gedeelte van het Hollandsch-Utrechtsche weidelandschap*, Rotterdam-Utrecht 1939

Burgler, R., 'Stakingen van polderwerkers in de 19e eeuw', in: *Amsterdams Sociologisch Tijdschrift* 6, 1979: 51-78
Burke, P., *Popular Culture in Early Modern Europe*, London 1978
Burton, A., *The Canal Builders*, London 1972
Bijdragen van het Statistisch Instituut, 7, 1891: 149-50 (letter from J.A. Tours in Beilen)
Cambon, M., *Les Conditions du travail en Espagne*, Paris, Nancy 1890
Caulier-Mathy, N., *Statistiques de la province de Liège sous le régime hollandais*, Louvain-Paris 1962
Chambers, J.D. and Mingay, G.E., *The Agricultural Revolution 1750-1880*, London, Sydney 1966
Chatelain, A., *Les migrants temporaires en France de 1800 à 1914*, Lille 1976, 2 vols
Chevalier, L., *La formation de la population parisienne au XIXe siècle*, Paris 1950
Cinanni, P., *Emigration und Imperialismus. Zur Problematik der Arbeitermigranten*, München 1969
Claverie, E. and Lamaison, P., 'Der Ousta als Produktions- und Wohneinheit im Haut-Gévaudan im 17., 18. und 19. Jahrhundert', in: N. Bulst J. Goy and J. Hoock (eds), *Familie zwischen Tradition und Moderne. Studien zur Geschichte der Familie in Deutschland und Frankreich vom 16. bis zum 20. Jahrhundert*, Göttingen 1981: 202-13
Coleman, T., *The Railway Navvies. A History of the Men Who Made the Railways*, Harmondsworth 1968
Collins, E.J.T., 'Migrant Labour In British Agriculture in the Nineteenth Century', in: *The Economic History Review*, Second Series, 29, 1976: 38-59
Conrad, J.F.W., (Opening address) in: *Tijdschrift voor Sociale Hygiëne en openbare gezondheidsregeling*. Orgaan van het Nederlands Congres van de openbare Gezondheidsregeling 4, 1902: 204-6
Coornaert, E., *Les compagnonnages en France du Moyen Age à nos jours*, Paris 1966
Corbett, J.G., 'Mexico-United States and West European Labor Migration: A Comparative Analysis,' in: R.E. Krane, *International Labor Migration in Europe*, New York 1979: 223-44
Corsini, C.A., 'Le migrazioni: stagionali di lavoratori nei dipartimenti italiani del periodo Napoleonico (1810-1812)', in: *Saggi di Demografia Storica* 2, 1969: 89-157
Crompvoets, H.J.G., *Veenderijterminologie in Nederland en Nederlandstalig België*, Amsterdam 1981
Van Den Dam, J.P.A. and Lucassen, J.M.W.G., *H.H.J. Maas, 1877-1958. Onderwijsman, literator en journalist*, Tilburg 1976
Damsma, D., de Meere, J.M.M. and Noordegraaf, L., *Statistieken van de Nederlandse nijverheid uit de eerste helft der 19e eeuw*. Supplement, 's-Gravenhage 1979
—— and Noordegraaf, L., 'Een vergeten plattelandsnijverheid. Vlasarbeid, bevolkingsgroei en proto-industrialisatie in Zuid-West-Nederland 1700-1900', in: *Economisch en Sociaal-Historisch Jaar-boek* 44, 1982: 145-54
Davico, R., 'Démographie et économie. Ville et Campagne en Piémont à l'époque française', in: *Annales de démographie historique 1968*: 139-64
Delatte, L., *Les classes rurales dans la principauté de Liège au XVIIIe siècle*, Liège 1945
Denzel, E., 'Wirtschafts- und Sozialgeschichte der Stadt Wetter', in: *Beiträge zur Geschichte Dortmunds und der Grafschaft Mark* 49, 1952: 1-270
Van Deursen, A.Th., *Het kopergeld van de Gouden Eeuw. I. Het dagelijks brood*, Assen 1978
Diederiks, H., *Een stad in verval. Amsterdam omstreeks 1800*, Amsterdam 1982

Diepeveen, W.J., *De vervening in Delfland en Schieland tot het einde der zestiende eeuw*, Leiden 1950
Van Dillen, J.G., *Van rijkdom en regenten. Handboek tot de economische en sociale geschiedenis van Nederland tijdens de republiek*, 's-Gravenhage 1970
Dobelmann, W., 'Ein altes Heuerlingsgeschlecht', in: *Heimat gestern und heute. Mitteilungen des Kreisheimatbundes Bersenbrück e.V.* 11, 1963: 23-5
Doedens, A. (ed.), *Autoriteit en strijd. Elf bijdragen tot de geschiedenis van collectief verzet in de Nederlanden, met name in de eerste helft van de negentiende eeuw*, Amsterdam 1981
Doeks, F., *Einige Bemerkungen über die Holländischen Sumpffieber als complicirte und verlarvte Wechselfieber*, Hannover 1827
Van Dijk, J.D.R., Foorthuis, W.R. and van Der Sman, M.-C., *Martinus Schookcius, Tractatus de turfis 1658; Martin Schoock en zÿn beschrÿving van het turfgraven in de hoogvenen*, Groningen 1984
Elsner, L., 'Zum Wesen und zur Kontinuität der Fremdarbeiterpolitik des deutschen Imperialismus', in: *Wesen und Kontinuität der Fremdarbeiterpolitik des deutschen Imperialismus*, Rostock 1974: 2-76
Enquête betreffende werking en uitbreiding der wet van 19 september 1874 (Staatsblad no. 130) en naar den toestand van fabrieken en werkplaatsen, I-V, Sneek 1887
Van Eyck van Heslinga, E.S., 'De vlag dekt de lading. De Nederlandse koopvaardij in de Vierde Engelse oorlog', in: *Tijdschrift voor zeegeschiedenis* 1, 1982: 102-13
Faber, J.A., 'Drie Eeuwen Friesland. Economische en sociale ontwikkelingen van 1500 tot 1800,' in: *A.A.G. Bijdragen 17*, Wageningen 1972
—— 'De Noordelijke Nederlanden van 1480 tot 1780. Structuren in beweging', in: *Algemene Geschiedenis der Nederlanden 5*, Bussum 1980: 196-250
—— et al., 'Population Changes and Economic Developments in the Netherlands: A Historical Survey', in: *A.A.G. Bijdragen* 12, Wageningen 1965; 47-110
Falkmann, 'Historische Bemerkungen über die s.g. Frieslandsgänger, in: *Vaterländische Blätter (Detmold)* 4, 1846: 51-5, 65-71, 81-7, 94-104, 113-18, 129-35, 166-72, 193-200, 339-43, 356-9, 369-75, 385-9, 433-8
Fischer, W., 'Rural Industrialization and Population Change', in: *Comparative Studies in Society and History* 15, 1973: 158-70
Fleege-Althoff, F., *Die lippischen Wanderarbeiter*, Detmold 1928
—— 'Die lippischen Wanderarbeiter', in: H. Volmer and E. Stein (eds.), *Das Land Lippe*, Berlin-Friedenau 1930: 65-71
Förster, R.F., *The Italian Emigration of Our Times*, New York 1969
Fremdling, R., *Eisenbahnen und deutsches Wirtschaftswachstum 1840-1879. Ein Beitrag zur Entwicklungstheorie und zur Theorie der Infrastruktur*, Dortmund 1975
Frijhoff, W., 'De paniek van juni 1734,' in: *Archief voor de geschiedenis van de Katholieke Kerk in Nederland* 19, 1977: 170-233
—— 'De heilige stede van Hasselt (Ov.). Gestalte, waarden en functies van een herleefde bedevaart in een diaspora-parochie,' in: *Archief voor de geschiedenis van de Katholieke kerk in Nederland* 19, 1978: 31-71
Funken, J., Breyeller 'Handelsleute-ohne Kiepe', in: *Breyell, was huckste knäbbig. Ein Heimatbuch bearbeitet von Dr. Hanna Meuter. Schriftenreihe des Landkreises Kempen-Krefeld* 12, 1959: 189-201
Gargas, S., 'Die niederländische Auswanderung,' in: *Economisch-Historisch Jaarboek* 14, 1928: 179-281
García Fernandez, J., 'El cultivo de arroz e su expansion en el siglo xviii en los llanos litorales del golfo de Valencia', in *Estudios Geográficos* 32, 1971: 163-70
Gerbenzon, P. (ed.), 'Het aantekeningenboek van Dirck Jansz,' in: *Estrikken 31*, Groningen 1960

Gerding, M.A.W., 'Turfgraverÿ rondom Hoogeveen 1750-1850', unpublished MA thesis. Dept of Economic and Social History, University of Utrecht 1980
—— 'De economische ontwikkeling van Hoogeveen 1625-1815', in: Keverling Buisman, F., et al. (eds), *Hoogeveen, oorsprong en ontwikkeling 1625-1813*, Hoogeveen 1983: 93-142
Gewin, B., *Arbeidsbeurzen*, Utrecht 1898
Giele, J., *Arbeidersleven in Nederland 1850-1914*, Nijmegen 1979
Girard, R., *Quand les Auvergnats partaient conquérir Paris*, Paris 1979
—— *Journal d'un Auvergnat de Paris (1882-1982), Les Fondations (1882-1907)*, Paris 1982
Gladen, A., *Der Kreis Tecklenburg an der Schwelle des Zeitalters der Industrialisierung*, Münster 1970
Gottschalk, M.K.E., 'De ontginning der Stichtse venen ten oosten van de Vecht', in: *Tijdschrift van het Koninklijk Nederlands Aardrijkskundig Genootschap* 73, 1956
De Graaff, M.H., *Landbouw, fabrijkwezen en koophandel in Nederland*, Leeuwarden 1845
Van de Graaff, S., *Statisties overzigt van Oostvriesland en Jever*, The Hague 1808
Granotier, B., *Les travailleurs immigrés en France*, Paris 1973
Grashof, A., 'Aus dem Leben der Hollandsgänger. Bilder aus dem Natur-, Volks- und Seelsorgerleben', in: *Monatsschrift für innere Mission* 2, 1882: 328-31, 377-80, 414-19, 465-70
Griffis, W.E., *The American in Holland: Sentimental Rambles in the Eleven Provinces of the Netherlands*, Boston New York 1899
Groesbeek, J.W., *Heemstede in de historie. Leven, werken, handel en koehandel in de woonplaats van Emece*, Heemstede 1972
Gutmann, M.P., *War and Rural Life in the Early Modern Low Countries*, Assen 1980
Gutton, J.P., *Domestiques et serviteurs dans la France de l'Ancien Régime*, Paris 1981
Haks, D., *Huwelijk en gezin in Holland in de 17de en 18de eeuw. Processtukken en moralisten over aspecten van het laat-17de- en 18de-eeuwse gezinsleven*, Assen 1982
Handley, J.E., *The Navvy in Scotland*, Cork 1970
Hartmann, A., 'Ein Menschenmarkt', in: *Die Illustrierte Welt* 13, 1865: 7-8
Hartogh Heys van Zouteveen, H., 'De Bodem', in: *Algemeene Statistiek van Nederland, deel* 1, Leiden 1870: 10-62
Hasquin, H., 'Nijverheid in de Zuidelijke Nederlanden 1650-1795', in: *Algemene geschiedenis der Nederlanden* 8, Bussum 1979: 124-59
Van Heerde, H., *Onder de clockenslach van Nunspeet*, Alphen aan den Rijn 1978
Heidema, Sr., P. and Dijkema, E., 'Beschrijving van den landbouw in het district Hunsego, Provincie Groningen', in: G.H. Kocks and J.M.G. van der Poel, *Landbouwkundige beschrijvingen uit de negentiende eeuw*. I Groningen, Wageningen 1979
Hekscher, E.F., *An Economic History of Sweden*, Cambridge Mass. 1954
Van Hertum, J., 'Landbouwkundige beschrijving van een gedeelte der provincie Zeeland, betreffende hoofdzakelijk de eilanden Walcheren, Schouwen, en Zuid- en Noord-Beveland (1836)', in: G.H. Kocks and J.M.G. van der Poel, *Landbouwkundigebeschrijvingen uit de negentiende eeuw*. II *Overige provincies*, Wageningen 1981
Hirschfelder, H., *Herrschaftsordnung und Bauerntum in Hochstift Osnabrück im 16. und 17. Jahrhundert*, Osnabrück 1971
Hobsbawm, E.J. and Rudé, G., *Captain Swing*, 1969
Van der Hoek, S., *Door den vreend'ling met eerbied te naderen, Tijdsbeeld van een veenkolonie*, Groningen 1979

Hoekstra, P., *Bloemendaal. Proeve ener streekgeschiedenis*, Wormerveer 1947
Hoffman, K., 'Sawmills-Finland's Proto-Industry', in: *The Scandinavian Economic History Review* 30, 1982: 35-43
Hoffmann-Nowotny, H.-J., *Soziologie des Fremdarbeiterproblems. Eine theoretische und empirische Analyse am Beispiel der Schweiz*, Stuttgart 1973
Hohorst, G., *Wirtschaftswachstum und Bevölkerungsentwicklung in Preussen 1816 bis 1914*, New York 1977
'Die Hollandsgänger', in: *Kirchliche Beiträge zum Ausbau der evangelisch-Lutherischen Kirche des Herzogtum Oldenburg* 15: 1869
Hollestelle, J., 'De Nederlandse steenbakkerij in de zeventiende en achttiende eeuw', in: *Economisch en Sociaal-Historisch Jaarboek* 44, 1982: 11-21
Hollingsworth, Th.H., 'Emigration from the United Kingdom and the Republic of Ireland', in: M. Livi Bacci (ed.), *The demographic and Social Pattern of Emigration from the Southern European Countries*, Firenze 1972: 261-77
Hömberg, A.K., *Wirtschaftsgeschichte Westfalens*, Münster 1968
Hopkins, A.G., *An Economic History of West Africa*, London 1973
Huck, G. and Reulecke, J. (eds), *... und reges Leben ist überall sichtbar. Reisen im Bergischen Land um 1800*, Neustadt an der Aisch 1978
Hufton, O.H., *The Poor of Eighteenth-century France 1750-1789*, Oxford 1974
De Hullu, J., *Uit het leven van den Cadzandschen landbouwer in vroeger dagen*, (Oostburg)
Ipsen, G., 'Die preussische Bauernbefreiung als Landesausbau', in: W. Köllmann and P. Marschalck (eds), *Bevölkerungsgeschichte*, Cologne 1972: 154, 189
Van Iterson, W.J.D., *Schets van de landhuishouding der Meijerij*, 's-Hertogenbosch 1868
Jacquart, J., *La crise rurale en Ile-de-France 1550-1670*, Paris 1974
Jansen, J.C.G.M., 'Lange golven in de economische geschiedenis van Limburg', in: *Studies over de sociaal-economische geschiedenis van Limburg* 26, 1981: 1-62
De Jonge, J.A., *De industrialisatie in Nederland tussen 1850 en 1914*, Nijmegen 1976
Joulia, A., 'Ein französischer Verwaltungsbezirk in Deutschland: Das Oberems-Departement (1810-1813)', in: *Osnabrücker Mitteilungen* 80, 1973: 60-89
Kamen, H., *Spain in the Later Seventeenth Century 1665-1700*, London-New York 1980
De Kanter, J., *De meekrapteler en bereider*, Dordrecht 1802
Kemper, J.M. (ed.), *Jaarboeken van het Fransche Regt en de Fransche Regtsgeleerdheid voor de Hollandsche Departementen*, Leiden 1812
Kerr, B.M., 'Irish Seasonal Migration to Great Britain, 1800-1838', in: *Irish Historical Studies* 3, 1943: 365-80
Klaver, I., *Herinneringen van een Friese landarbeider. Enkele opgetekende zaken uit het jongste verleden tot 1925*, Nijmegen 1974
Kleine Staarman, J.H., *Historie van Lutten en Slagharen*, Utrecht 1967
Klep, P.M.M., *Bevolking en arbeid in transformatie. Een onderzoek in Brabant 1700-1900*, Nijmegen 1981
Van der Kloot Meyburg, B.W., 'Bijdrage tot de geschiedenis van de meekrapcultuur in Nederland', in: *Economische-Historisch Jaarboek* 18, 1934: 59-153
Knippenberg, W.H.Th. (ed.), *De Teuten. Buitengaanders van de Kempen*, Eindhoven 1974
Knotter, A., 'De Amsterdamse bouwnijverheid in de 19e eeuw tot ca. 1870. Loonstarheid en trekarbeid op een dubbele arbeidsmarkt', in: *Tijdschrift voor Sociale Geschiedenis* 10, 1984: 123-54
Van Koetsveld, C.E., *Ideaal en werkelijkheid. Nieuwste schetsen en novellen*, Schoonhoven 1868

Kolb, G.Fr., *Handbuch der Vergleichenden Statistik der Völkerzustands- und Staatenkunde*, Leipzig 1862
Kondratieff, N.D., 'The Long Waves in Economic Life', in: *The Review of Economic Statistics* 17, 1935: 105-15
Kranenburg, H.A.H., *De zeevisserij van Holland in den tijd der Republiek*, Amsterdam 1946
Kriedte, P., *Peasants, Landlords and Merchant Capitalists. Europe and the World Economy, 1500-1800*, Leamington Spa 1983
— Medick, H. and Schlumbohm, J., *Industrialisierung vor der Industrialisierung. Gewerbliche Warenproduktion auf dem Land in der Formationsperiode des Kapitalismus*, Göttingen 1978
Kroniek van een Friese boer. De aantekeningen (1821-1856) van Doeke Wijgers Hellema te Wirdum, bewerkt door H. Algra, Franeker 1978
Kropotkine, P., *Gedenkschriften van een Revolutionair*, Gorinchem 1902, 2 vols
Küther, C., *Menschen auf der Strasse. Vagierende Unterschichten in Bayern, Franken und Schwaben in der zweiten Hälfte des 18. Jahrhunderts*, Göttingen 1983
Labrijn, A., *Het klimaat van Nederland gedurende de laatste twee en een halve eeuw*, Schiedam 1945
De Landbouwenquête van 1800, reported by J.M.G. van der Poel, in: *Historia Agriculturae* 1, 1953: 48-194; 2, 1954: 45-233; 3, 1956: 105-68
Langendijk, P., *De Zwetser. Kluchtspel, opnieuw uitgegeven en van inleiding en aantekeningen voorzien door W.A. Ornée en M.A. Streng*, Zutphen 1971
Leeghwater, J.A., *Haarlemmermeerboek*, 1710
Leemans, W.F., *De grote Gelderse tollen en de tollenaars in de 18de en het begin der 19de eeuw. Een bijdrage tot de geschiedenis van de Rijnhandel*, Zutphen 1981
Leeson, R.A., *Travelling Brothers. The Six Centuries' Road from Craft Fellowship to Trade Unionism*, London 1979
Leget, J.N., 'Hollandgangers uit Fürstenau', in: D.F. Goudriaan *et al.* (eds.), *Gedenkboek 1948-1978. Afdeling Kennemerland van de Nederlandse Genealogische Vereniging*, Haarlem 1979: 9-19
Lindemans, P., *Geschiedenis van de landbouw in België*, Antwerpen 1952, 2 vols
Lis, C.L.A., 'Problematike relatie pre-moderne industrialisering en maatschappij,' in: *Economisch- en Sociaal-Historisch Jaarboek* 44, 1982: 111-15
— and Soly, H., *Poverty and Capitalism in Pre-Industrial Europe*, Hassocks, Sussex 1979
Lohrmann, R., 'Politische Auswirkungen der Arbeitskräftewanderungen auf die Bundesrepublik Deutschland', in: R. Lohrmann and K. Manfras, *Ausländerbeschäftigung und internationale Politik. Zur Analyse transnationaler Sozialprozesse*, München-Wien 1974: 103-40
Lootsma, S., *Historische Studiën over de Zaanstreek*, Tweede Bundel, Koog aan de Zaan 1950
Lourens, P. and Lucassen J., 'Mechanisering en arbeidsmarkt in de Groningse steenbakkerijen, gedurende de negentiende eeuw', in: *Jaarboek voor de Geschiedenis van Bedrijf en Techniek* 1, 1984: 188-215
Lucassen, J., 'Beschouwingen over seizoengebonden trekarbeid naar het westen van Nederland, ca. 1600-ca. 1800', in: *Tijdschrift voor Sociale Geschiedenis* 8, 1982 (no. 28): 327-58
— *Naar de Kusten van de Noordzee. Trekarbeid in Europees perspektief, 1600-1900* Gouda 1984
— 'Trekarbeid in Drenthe in de negentiende eeuw', in: *Nieuwe Drentse Volksalmanak* 102, 1985: 60-8
— and Lucassen, L.J., 'Marskramers uit Meijel en omgeving: De "Teuten", 1750-1830', in: *Medelo* 2, 1983: 50-9 (A)

—— and Lucassen, L.J., 'De arbeiders aan het Grand Canal du Nord, het traject Weert-Meijel-Venlo in 1809/1810', in: *Medelo* 2, 1983: 41-9 (B)
Ludwig, J., *Die wirtschaftliche und soziale Lage der Wanderarbeiter im Grossherzogthum Baden. Ergebnisse einer Enquête Juli 1911-Mai 1912*, Karlsruhe i.B. 1915
Luhrmann, H., 'Die "Hollandgänger", die "Gastarbeiter" des 18. Jahrhunderts', in: *Heimatjahrbuch für Osnabrück-Stadt und Land 1978*; 116-17
Maclean, J., 'Arbeidsconflicten in de periode 1813-1872', in: *Tijdschrift voor Sociale Geschiedenis* 5, (no. 16) 1979; 292-312
Mager, W., 'Haushalt und Familie in protoindustrieller Gesellschaft: Spenge (Ravensberg) während der ersten Hälfte des 19. Jahrhunderts. Eine Fallstudie', in: N. Bulst, J. Goy and J. Hoock (eds), *Familie zwischen Tradition und Moderne. Studien zur Geschichte der Familie in Deutschland und Frankreich vom 16. bis zum 20. Jahrhundert*, Göttingen 1981: 141-81
—— 'Protoindustrialisierung und agrarisch-heimgewerbliche Verflechtung in Ravensberg während der Frühen Neuzeit. Studien zu einer Gesellschaftsformation im Übergang', in: *Geschichte und Gesellschaft* 8, 1982: 435-74
Marchetti, L., 'Die inneren jahreszeitlichen Wanderungen der Landarbeiter und die wirtschaftlichen Stellenvermittlungsämter in Italien', in: *Zeitschrift für Socialwissenschaft, Neue Folge* 5, *1914*: 605-17 and 683-93
Markow, A., *Das Wachstum der Bevölkerung und die Entwicklung der Aus- und Einwanderungen, Ab- und Zuzüge in Preussen und Preussens einzelnen Provinzen, Bezirken und Kreisgruppen von 1824 bis 1885*, Tübingen 1889
Marijnissen, H. and Raben-Fabels, A., *De weg over de grens*, Nijmegen 1978
Mauco, G., *Les migrations ouvrières en France au début du XIXe siècle d'après les rapports des préfets de l'Empire, de 1808 à 1813*, Paris 1932
Van Maurik, J., *Toen ik nog jong was*, Amsterdam 1901
Mededelingen en berigten van het hoofdbestuur en van de afdelingen der Hollandsche Maatschappij van Landbouw 1, 1848-
De Meere, J.M.M., 'Daglonen in België en Nederland in 1819 — een aanvulling', in: *Tijdschrift voor Sociale Geschiedenis* 6, 1980 (no. 20): 357-84
—— *Economische ontwikkeling en levensstandaard in Nederland gedurende de eerste helft van de negentiende eeuw*, Cahiers Sociale Geschiedenis 1, The Hague 1982
Meijide Pardo, A., 'La emigración Gallega intrapeninsular en el siglo XVIII', in: *Estudios de Historia Social de España* 4, 1960: 461-606
Mendels, F.F., 'Landwirtschaft und bäuerliches Gewerbe in Flandern im 18. Jahrhundert', in: Kriedte, Medick and Schlumbohm 1978: 325-49
Mendelson, F., 'Wanderarbeiter', in: *Handwörterbuch der Staatswissenschaften* 8, 1911: 541-61
Meurer, H., *Das Hollandsgehen mit besonderer Rücksicht auf die Lage der Heuerleute im Osnabrückischen*, Osnabrück 1871
Meyer, E.H.W., *Teilungsverbot, Anerbenrecht und Beschränkung der Brautschätze beim bäuerlichen Grundbesitze Lippes. Eine volkswirtschaftliche Untersuchung*, Berlin 1895
(Meyeringh, F.), 'Hollandsgänger und Reisepredigt', in: *Fliegende Blätter* 24, 1867
Middelhoven, P.J., 'De Amsterdamse veilingen van Noord-Europees naaldhout 1717-1808. Een bijdrage tot de Nederlandse prijsgeschiedenis,' in: *Economisch- en Sociaal-Historisch Jaarboek* 41, 1978: 86-114
Millward, R., 'An Economic Analysis of the Organization of Serfdom in Eastern Europe,' in: *The Journal of Economic History* 62, 1982: 513-48
Miskimin, H.A., *The Economy of Later Renaissance Europe 1460-1600*, Cambridge 1977
Mooser, J., 'Soziale Mobilität und familiale Plazierung bei Bauern und

Unterschichten. Aspekte der Sozialstruktur der ländlichen Gesellschaft im 19. Jahrhundert am Beispiel des Kirchspiels Quernheim im östlichen Westfalen,' in: N. Bulst, J. Goy and J. Hoock (eds), *Familie zwischen Tradition und Moderne. Studien zur Geschichte der Familie in Deutschland und Frankreich vom 16. bis zum 20. Jahrhundert*, Gottingen 1981: 182-201

Morgan, D.H., 'The Place of Harvesters in Nineteenth-Century Village Life', in: R. Samuel (ed.), *Village Life and Labour*, London, Boston 1975

—— *Harvesters and Harvesting 1840-1900. A Study of the Rural Proletariat*, London, Canberra 1982

Mulder, R.D., 'Twee en een halve-eeuw tolheffing en toerisme in Drenthe (1700-1950),' in: *Nieuwe Drentse Volksalmanak* 90, 1973: 24-5

Nellemann, G., *Polske landarbejdere i Danmark og deres efterkommere*, Copenhagen 1981

Nichtweiss, J., *Die ausländischen Saisonarbeiter in der Landwirtschaft der östlichen und mittleren Gebiete des Deutschen Reiches. Ein Beitrag zur Geschichte der preussisch-deutschen Politik von 1890 bis 1914*, Berlin 1959

Nielsen, A., *Industriens historie i Danmark*, Vol. III, 2, Copenhagen 1944

Nierhoff, A.M.G., *Bloemendaal, lanen en wegen hun naam en geschiedenis*, Bloemendaal 1963

Noordegraaf, L., 'Armoede en bedeling. Enkele numerieke aspecten van de armenzorg in het zuidelijk deel van Holland in de Bataafse en Franse tijd,' in: *Holland* 9, 1977: 1-24

Rapporten en voorstellen betreffende den Oeconomischen Toestand der Landarbeiders in Nederland, 's-Gravenhage 1909

Ó Gráda, C., 'Seasonal Migration and Post-Famine Adjustment in the West of Ireland', in : *Studia Hibernica* 13, 1973: 48-76

Olbrich, H. (eds), *Sozialbericht von Johannes Hesekiel, 1866. Über die Wanderarbeiter beim Rübenanbau und in den Zuckerfabriken der Provinz Sachsen, Schriften aus dem Zucker-Museum* 16, Berlin 1982

Ornée, W.A., 'De Mof in de Nederlandse blij- en kluchtspelen uit de 17e en 18e eeuw', in: *Voordrachten gehouden voor de Gelderse leergangen te Arnhem* 27, 1970

Peeters, J.H., *Klapper op doopjes, huwelijken en overlijdens van de Parochie van Sint Nicolaas te Meijel 1608-1860*

Peirs, G., *Uit klei gebouwd. Baksteenarchitectuur van 1200-1940*, Tielt-Amsterdam 1979

Penners, Th., 'Die Abwanderung aus Lingen a.d. Ems nach einer Absentenliste vom Jahre 1729', in: *Osnabrücker Mitteilungen* 69, 1960: 62-101

Penninx, R. and Van Velzen, L., *Internationale arbeidsmigratie. Uitstoting uit 'thuislanden' en maatschappelijke integratie in 'gastlanden' van buitenlandse arbeiders*, Nijmegen 1977

Pistor, R.-G. and Smeets, H., *Die Fossa Eugeniana. Eine unvollendete Kanalverbindung zwischen Rhein und Maas 1626*, Cologne 1979

Pitsch, F.J., *Die wirtschaftliche Beziehungen Bremens zu den Vereinigten Staaten von Amerika bis zur Mitte des 19. Jahrhunderts*, Bremen 1974

Le Play, F., *Les Ouvriers Européens. Etudes sur les travaux, la vie domestique et la condition morale des populations ouvrières de l'Europe. Précédées d'un exposé de la méthode d'observation*, Tours 1877-1879, 6 vols

Van der Poel, J.M.G., *Honderd jaar landbouwmechanisatie in Nederland*, Wageningen 1967

Poitrineau, A., *Remues d'hommes. Les migrations montagnardes en France 17e-18e siècles*, Paris 1983

Posthumus, N.W., *De geschiedenis van de Leidsche lakenindustrie*, I-III, 's-Gravenhage 1908-39

Poussou, J.P., 'Introduction à l'étude des mouvements migratoires en Espagne,

Italie et France méditerranéenne au XVIIIe siècle', in: *Les migrations dans les pays méditerranéens au XVIIIeme et au début du XIXeme. Actes des journées d'études. Bendor 6 et 7 avril 1973*, Nice 1974: 4-24
Prato, G., *Le protectionnisme ouvrier (l'exclusion des travailleurs étrangers)*, Paris 1912
Radcliff, T., *A Report on the Agriculture of Eastern and Western Flanders*, London 1819
Ramaer, J.C., *Geschiedkundige Atlas van Nederland. Het koninkrijk der Nederlanden (1815-1931)*, 's-Gravenhage 1931
Von Reden, F.W., *Erwerbs- und Verkehrsstatistik des Königsstaats Preussen in vergleichender Darstellung*, Darmstadt 1853-4, 2 vols
Redford, A., *Labour Migration in England 1800-1850*, Manchester 1976
Redlich, F., *The German Military Enterpriser and His Work Force. A Study in European Economic and Social History* 1, Wiesbaden 1964
Reekers, S., *Westfalens Bevölkerung 1818-1955. Die Bevölkerungsentwicklung der Gemeinden und Kreise im Zahlenbild*, Münster 1956
Regtdoorzee-Greup Roldanus, S.C., *Geschiedenis der Haarlemmer bleekerijen*, The Hague 1936
Reininghaus, W., 'Die Migration der Handwerksgesellen in der Zeit der Entstehung ihrer Gilden (14./15. Jahrhundert),' in: *Vierteljahrschrift für Sozial-und Wirtschaftsgeschichte* 68, 1981: 1-21
Rickelmann, H., *Die Tüötten in ihrem Handel und Wandel und die Wollen- und Leinenerzeugung im Tecklenburger Land*, Paderborn 1976
Roberts, M., 'Sickles and Scythes: Women's Work and Men's Work at Harvest Time,' in: *History Workshop Journal 1979* (no. 7): 3-28
Roberts, P. and Bos, J., *50 Jaar afsluitdijk. Herinneringen van dijkers, denkers en drammers*, Bussum 1982
Roessingh, H.K., 'Landbouw in de Noordelijke Nederlanden 1650-1815,' in: *Algemene Geschiedenis der Nederlanden* 8, 1979: 16-72
Romano, R., 'Autour de quelques problèmes d'histoire du travail en Italie,' in: *Mélanges en l'honneur de Fernand Braudel. Histoire économique du monde méditerranéen 1450-1650*, Paris 1973: 497-509
Rosander, G., *Herrarbete. Dalfolks säsongvisa arbetsvandringar i jämtförande belysning*, Uppsala 1967
—— *Dalska arbetsvandringar före nya tidens genombrott*, Stockholm 1976
Roscher, W., *System der Volkswirtschaft. Ein Hand- und Lesebuch für Geschäftsmänner und Studierende*, Stuttgart 1875-94, 5 vols
Le Roy Ladurie, E., 'De la crise ultime à la vraie croissance (1690-1789)', in: *Histoire de la France rurale, 11*, 1975: 355-599
Sahner, W., *Katholische und evangelische Seelsorge des Deutschtums in Holland*, Emsdetten (Westf.) 1950
Sagarsky, S., *Die Arbeiterfrage in der Südrussischen Landwirtschaft*, München 1907
Samuel, R. (ed.), *Village Life and Labour*, London/Boston 1975
Van Schaik, P., 'De economische betekenis van de turfwinning in Nederland', in: *Economische-Historisch Jaarboek* 32, 1969: 141-205; 33, 1970: 186-235
Schauenburg, L., 'Die Arbeit unter den Hollandsgängern,' in: *Monatsschrift für innere Mission* 6, Gütersloh 1886: 23-88
Schepens, L., *Kroniek van Stijn Streuvels 1871-1969*, Bruges 1971
—— *Van Vlaskutser tot Franschman. Bijdrage tot de geschiedenis van de Westvlaamse plattelandsbevolking in de negentiende eeuw*, Bruges 1973
Scheper, B., 'Die Niederlande und der Unterweserraum', in: *Nachbarn* 14, 1971
Schissler, H., *Preussische Agrargesellschaft im Wandel*, Göttingen 1978
Schlumbohm, J., 'Der saisonale Rhythmus der Leinenproduktion im Osnabrücker Lande während des späten 18. und der ersten Hälfte des 19. Jahrhunderts: Erscheinungsbild, Zusammenhänge und interregionaler Vergleich', in: *Archiv*

für Sozialgeschichte 19, 1979; 163-298
Schröder, A., 'Heimindustrie und Hollandgängerei um 1850. Aus einem Bericht des Fürstenauer Amtmanns über die wirtschaftliche Situation in den Gemeinden der Kirchspiele Berge und Bippen', in: *Heimat-Jahrbuch Osnabrücker Land 1976*: 82-5
—— 'Hollandgänger werden zu Niederländern-Fürstenauer heiraten nach Amsterdam', in: *Heimat-Jahrbuch Osnabrücker Land 1978*: 97-9
Schulte, H., 'Hollandgängerei vor 200 Jahren. Treffpunkt war der "Breite Stein" zwischen Ankum und Üffeln', in: *Heimat-Jahrbuch des Kreises Bersenbrück 1970*: 38-40
Schwarting, A.C., *Die Verwaltungsorganisation Nordwestdeutschlands während der französischen Besatzungszeit 1811-1813*, Oldenburg 1936
Sella, D., 'Au dossier des migrations montagnardes: l'exemple de la Lombardie au XVIIe siècle,' in: *Mélanges en l'honneur de Fernand Braudel. Histoire économique du monde méditerranéen 1450-1650*, Paris 1973: 547-54
Sepp Jzn., C., 'Tweede reis naar Ommerschans etc.', in: *De Star 1823*: 490-503
Sigmond, J.P., 'Havens', in: *Maritieme Geschiedenis der Nederlanden* 2, Bussum 1977: 78-105
Slicher van Bath, B.H., *Een samenleving onder spanning. Geschiedenis van het platteland in Overijssel*, Assen 1957
—— *De agrarische geschiedenis van West-Europa (500-1800)*, Utrecht 1960
—— 'De demografische ontwikkeling tijdens de Republiek', in: *Vaderlands verleden in veelvoud. 31 Opstellen over de Nederlandse geschiedenis na 1500*, The Hague 1975: 312-36
Sloet Tot Oldhuis, B.W.A.E., Gemengde berigten en mededelingen, in: *Tijdschrift voor Staathuishoudkunde en Statistiek* 19, 1860: 420-1
Sneller, Z.W. (ed.), *Geschiedenis van den Nederlandschen landbouw, 1795-1940*, Groningen-Batavia 1943
Sombart, W., *Die deutsche Volkswirtschaft im neunzehnten Jahrhundert und im Anfang des 20. Jahrhunderts*, Berlin 1919
Spahr van der Hoek, J.J., *Geschiedenis van de Friese landbouw*, Leeuwarden 1952
Sprenger, J. and Vrooland, V., *'Dit zijn mijn beren!'. Een onderzoek naar de arbeidsverhoudingen bij de aanleg van het Noordhollands kanaal*. Amsterdam 1976
Staatscommissie over de Werkloosheid (ingesteld bij K.B. van 30 juli 1909, no. 42), *Verslag van de eerste subcommissie*, 's-Gravenhage 1913 (A)
—— *Verslag van de vierde sub-commissie*, 's-Gravenhage 1913 (B)
—— IX *Eindverslag*, 's-Gravenhage 1914 (A)
—— X *Eindverslag Bijlagen eerste bundel*, 's-Gravenhage 1914 (B)
Staring, W.C.H., *Huisboek voor den landman in Nederland*, Amsterdam 1868
'Statistieke Beschouwing van en toestand der geringe plattelandsbevolking op de Veluwe langs de Zuiderzee [...]', in: *Tijdschrift voor Staathuishoudkunde en Statistiek* 9, 1853: 290
Steinbach, P., *Industrialisierung und Sozialsystem im Fürstentum Lippe. Zum Verhältnis von Gesellschaftsstruktur und Sozialverhalten einer verspätet industrialisierten Region im 19. Jahrhundert*, Berlin 1976
Streng, M.A., *De Zwetser van Pieter Langendijk*, unpublished MA thesis, University of Nijmegen, (no date)
Stüve, J.E., *Beschreibung und Geschichte des Hochstifts und Fürstenthums Osnabrück mit einigen Urkunden*, Osnabrück 1789 (reprint 1978)
Swart, F., *Zur friesischen Agrargeschichte*, Leipzig 1910
Tack, J., *Die Hollandsgänger in Hannover und Oldenburg. Ein Beitrag zur Geschichte der Arbeiter-Wanderung*, Leipzig 1902
Taverne, E., *In 't land van belofte: in de nieuwe stadt; Ideaal en werkelijkheid van de stadsuitleg in de Republiek 1580-1680*, Maarssen 1978

Tegenwoordige Staat, Zeeland, vol. 9, Amsterdam 1751: vol. 10, Amsterdam 1740
Tenge, J., 'De menschelijke arbeidskrachten in den Nederlandschen landbouw', in: *Tijdschrift voor Economische Geographie* 14, 1923: 357-72
Teijl, J., 'Nationaal inkomen van Nederland in de periode 1850-1900-Tasten en testen', in: *Economisch en Sociaal-Historisch Jaarboek* 34, 1971: 232-62
Thomas-Lycklama à Nijeholt, G., *On the Road for Work. Migratory Workers on the East Coast of the United States*, Boston 1980
Thompson, E.P., *The Making of the English Working Class*, Harmondsworth 1981
Thon, F., 'Holländerholz,' in: *Allgemeine Encyklopaedie der Wissenschafte und Kuenste, Zweite Section-Zehnter Teil*, Leipzig 1833: 38-41
Thorner, D., Kerblay, B. and Smith, R.E.F. (eds), *A.V. Chayanov on the Theory of Peasant Economy*, Homewood (Illinois) 1966
Tiesing, H., *Over landbouw en volksleven in Drenthe*, Assen 1974 2nd edn, 2 vols
Trotsky, L., *Ma vie. Essai autobiographique, I, 1879-1905*, Paris 1930
Trouw, J., *De West-Nederlandse veenplassen*, Amsterdam 1948
Tutein Noltheniüs, R.P.J., 'Langs het Merwede-Kanaal', in: *Eigen Haard 1890*: 358-61, 379-81, 490-3, 534-8, 744-7, 825-9
Tydeman, H.W., *Verhandeling ter beantwoording der vrage: Welke zijn de grenzen van het nut en van de schade welke door het gebruik van werktuigen [...] worden aangebragt? [...]*, Haarlem 1819
Van Tijn, T., *Twintig jaren Amsterdam. De maatschappelijke ontwikkeling van de hoofdstad, van de jaren '50 der vorige eeuw tot 1876*, Amsterdam 1965
—— and Zappey, W.M., 'De negentiende eeuw 1813-1914', in: J.H. van Stuijvenberg (ed.), *De economische geschiedenis van Nederland*, Groningen 1977: 201-59
Uitkomsten van het onderzoek naar den toestand van den landbouw in Nederland, ingesteld door de Landbouwcommissie, benoemd bij koninklijk besluit van 18 september 1886, no. 28, 4 vols, 's-Gravenhage 1890
Vandenbroeke, C., *Agriculture et alimentation. L'agriculture et l'alimentation dans les Pays-Bas Autrichiens. Contribution à l'histoire économique et sociale à la fin de l'ancien régime*, Gent Leuven 1975
—— 'Landbouw in de Zuidelijke Nederlanden 1650-1815', in: *Algemene Geschiedenis der Nederlanden* 8, Bussum 1979: 73-101
—— and Vanderpijpen, W., 'Landbouw en platteland in de Zuidelijke Nederlanden 1770-1844', in: *Algemene Geschiedenis der Nederlanden* 10, Bussum 1981: 183-209
Van der Ven, D.J. *Neerlands volksleven*, Zaltbommel 1920
Verhoeff, J.M., *De oude Nederlandse maten en gewichten*, Amsterdam 1982
Verlinden, C. and Craeybeckx, J., *Prijzen- en lonenpolitiek in de Nederlanden in 1561 en 1588-89. Onuitgegeven adviezen, ontwerpen en ordonnanties*, Brussel 1962
Verrips, J., *En boven de polder de hemel. Een antropologische studie van een Nederlands dorp 1850-1971*, Baarn 1977
Verslag van den Toestand der Provincie Noord Holland 1854
Verzameling van stukken betreffende het geneeskundig staatstoezicht in Nederland 1872, 's-Gravenhage 1872
Vierlingh, A., *Tractaat van dyckagie*, J. de Hullu and A.G. Verhoeven (eds), 's-Gravenhage 1920
Van Vooren, G.A.C., 'De armenzorg voor de katholieken in het Middelburgse Missiegebied gedurende de 18e eeuw', in: *Appeltjes van het Meetjesland. Jaarboek van het heemkundig genootschap van het Meetjesland* 24, 1973: 5-72
De Vries, H., *Landbouw en bevolking tijdens de agrarische depressie in Friesland (1878-1895)*, Wageningen 1971
De Vries, J., *The Dutch Rural Economy in the Golden Age 1500-1700*, New Haven, London 1974

―― *The Economy of Europe in an Age of Crisis, 1600-1750*, Cambridge 1976
―― 'Histoire du Climat et économie,' in: *Annales E.S.C.* 32, 1977: 198-226
―― 'Barges and Capitalism. Passenger Transportation in the Dutch economy, 1632-1839', in: *A.A.G. Bijdragen* 21, 1978: 33-398
―― 'Landbouw in de Noordelijke Nederlanden 1490-1650', in: *Algemene Geschiedenis der Nederlanden* 7, Bussum 1980: 12-43
Wallerstein, I., *The Modern World-System II. Mercantilism and the Consolidation of the European World-Economy, 1600-1750*, New York 1980
Waring, G.E., 'A Farmer's Vacation', reprinted (with additions) from *Scribner's Monthly*, Boston 1876
Weber-Kellermann, I., *Erntebrauch in der ländlichen Arbeitswelt des 19. Jahrhunderts auf Grund der Mannhardtbefragung in Deutschland von 1865*, Marburg 1965
Wehler, H.-U., 'Die Polen im Ruhrgebiet bis 1918', in: *Vierteljahrschrift für Sozial-und Wirtschaftsgeschichte* 48, 1961: 203-35
Wentzel, G., *Sprokkelen op de Noord-west-Veluwe*, Berkel en Rodenrijs 1973
Wiarda, D., *Die geschichtliche Entwicklung der wirtschaftlichen Verhältnisse Ostfrieslands*, Jena 1880
Wichers Wierdsma, W.W., *Geschiedenis van het administratief toezicht op de lage verveening in Friesland*, Leiden 1885
Wiepert, P., 'Die Monarchen auf der Insel Fehmarn', in: *Wohnsitz: Nirgendwo. Vom Leben und Überleben auf der Strasse. Herausgegeben vom Künstlerhaus Bethanien*, Berlin 1982: 29-44
Willerslev, R., *Studier i dansk Industriehistorie, 1850-1880*, Copenhagen 1952
―― *Den glemte invandring. Den svenske invandring til Danmark 1850-1914*, Copenhagen 1983
Wiskerke, C., 'De geschiedenis van het meekrapbedrijf in Nederland', in: *Economisch-Historisch Jaarboek* 25, 1952: 1-144
Woolf, S., *A History of Italy 1700-1860 The Social Constraints of Political Change*, London 1979
Van der Woude, A.M., 'De weerbare mannen van 1747 in de dorpen van het zuiderkwartier van Holland als demografisch gegeven,' in: *A.A.G. Bijdragen* 8, 1962: 35-76
―― 'Het Noorderkwartier. Een regionaal historisch onderzoek in de demografische en economische geschiedenis van westelijk Nederland van de late middeleeuwen tot het begin van de negentiende eeuw,' in: *A.A.G. Bijdragen* 16, 1972
―― 'De Goldberg-enquête in het Departement van Texel, 1801', in: *A.A.G. Bijdragen* 18, 1973: 95-250
―― 'Demografische ont wikkeling van de Noordelijke Nederlanden 1500-1800', in: *Algemene Geschiedenis der Nederlanden* 5, Bussum 1980: 102-68
―― 'Population developments in the northern Netherlands (1500-1800) and the Validity of the "Urban Graveyard" effect', in: *Annales de Démographie Historique*, 1982: 55-75
Wrasmann, A., 'Das Heuerlingswesen im Fürstentum Osnabrück,' in: *Mitteilungen des Vereins für Geschichte und Landeskunde von Osnabrück* 42, 1919: 53-171; 44, 1921: 1-154
Wumkes, G.A., *Stads- en dorpskroniek van Friesland, I, 1700-1800*, Leeuwarden 1930
Yben, 'De veerdienst Amsterdam-Zwolle onderhouden door de Zwolsche Carveelschippers en het Amsterdams Grootbinnenlandsvaardersgilde', unpublished thesis, Amsterdam 1941 (copy in GA Zwolle)
Van Ysselsteyn, H.A., 'Verslag omtrent een onderzoek der polderjongens (1910)', in: *Staatscommissie over de werkloosheid (ingesteld bij KB van 30 juli 1909, no. 42)*, II. Verslag der eerste sub-commissie, 's-Gravenhage 1913

De Zeeuw, J.W., *Peat and the Dutch Golden Age. The Historical Meaning of Energy-Attainability*, in: *A.A.G. Bijdragen* 21, 1978: 3-31

Sources of Plates

Algemeen Rijksarchief (ARA)
   Gewestelijke Besturen 1807-1815
Rijksarchief in Gelderland, Arnhem
   Gelderse Rekenkamer
Gemeentearchief (GA) Amsterdam
   Topografische Atlas
Rijksmuseum voor Volkskunde 'Het Nederlands Openluchtmuseum', Arnhem
Atlas van Stolk, Rotterdam
Provinciale Bibliotheek van Zeeland, Middelburg
Nationalmuseet, Copenhagen

INDEX OF PLACE NAMES

Names of French départements are printed in capitals.

Aachen 35, 221
Aalst 31
Aar, Ter 14, 141
Aarlanderveen 141
Abruzzi, The 119, 123, 256, 260, 307
Achim 276, 311
Achterhoek 145
Acqui 244
Aduard 301
Africa 215
Agogna 252
Ahaus 30-2, 42-4, 175, 272-3
AIN 234
AISNE 223, 235
Ajaccio 251
Akersloot 148
Alb 261-2
Alba 244
Albania 305, 308
Alblasserwaard 29, 39
Alessandria 242
Algeria 305
Almelo 14, 44
ALPES MARITIMES 233-4, 236-7, 241-4, 252, 256, 306-8
Alps, The 109-10, 119, 234, 240, 253, 259-62, 307
Alsace 234
Alswede 270
America 305
Amsterdam 14, 44-9, 76-7, 89-90, 122-5, 134, 149-55, 173-4, 180, 221-3, 284, 291, 297, Pl 2, 17
Andalusia 112, 232, 305
Ander Etsch 261
Ankum 45, 298
Anna Paulownapolder 183
Antwerp 36-7, 42, 64, 77, 91, 163, 221
Aosta 120, 240
Apennines, The 119, Pl 15
APENNINS 235, 238, 244-8, 251-5, 258-60, 306-7
Apulia 307
Aquitaine 112, 234-5

Ardennes, The 223
ARDENNES 10-11, 26, 222, 225, 235, 280, 290
Argentina 202
Arezzo 247
Argyll 265-6
ARIÈGE 231, 235
Arnhem 87, 211, 221
Arno (river) Pl 15
ARNO 118, 235-8, 242, 245-52, 255, 258, 293, 300, 308
Arnsberg 35, 38
Arras 222
Aschen 310
Aschendorf 175, 178, 184, 190-1, 274, 310, Pl 19
Asia 156, 215
Assen 179, 304
Assendelft 134
Asturia 110, 115, 231-2
Ath 36
Attica 305
AUBE 235
Auburg 310
Aurich 175, 219, 269, 273
Austria (-Hungary) 107, 189, 202, 230, 260-2, 307
Auvergne 89, 166-7, 196-9, 204, 231, 303-5
AVEYRON 231-3
Avila 116
Avrainville 166
Axel 26
Ayr 265

Baambrugge 297
Baarderadeel 301
Backum 281
Baden 262
Balcans (Balkans) 107, 230, 305
Baltic 125
Barcelona 110, 231
Barkhausen 15
Bar-le-Duc 223
Barnstorf 310-11

328

Index 329

Barsingerhorn 285
Barver 310
Basilicata 202
Basqueland (-territories) 115, 305
BAS RHIN 26, 221, 234, 262
Basin of Paris, The 89, 108-9, 114, 165-7, 170, 186, 194-8, 201, 212-14, 232-5
Basse Provence 293
Bassenge 88
BASSES ALPES 89, 223, 231, 234
BASSES PYRENÉES 235
Bassum 298
Bastia 251
Bavaria 123, 236-40, 249, 259-62
Bayerische Wald 261-2
Beckum 31-2, 35, 175, 272
Beegden 290
Beek 301-2
Beemster 134
Beesten 281
Beijerlanden 286
Beilen 182
Belfast 265-6
Belgium (see also Southern Netherlands) 1, 8-11, 28, 36-7, 57, 71, 77, 81, 89, 189, 198, 209, 235, 280-2, 288-9, 302
Bellingwolde 186-8, 302
Belm 297
Bemmel 302
Bentheim 44-5, 77-9, 175, 178, 220, 274, 283, 289, 301, 310
Benthuizen 141
Berg 8-9, 35, 224, 298
Bergamasque Alps 110
Bergamo 253
Berge 274
Bergen op Zoom 28
Bergkirchen 270
Berkshire 266
Bersenbrück 175, 274, 287, 300
Berum 273
Bessarabia 127
Betuwe 29, 39
Beugen 50
Bevergern 33, 273, 281
Bielefeld 30-5, 40, 86, 185-7, 210, 271, 281
Biella 120, 240, 241
Bierum 301
Biesbos 69
Bingen 87
Bingum 161

Bippen 283
Black Forest see Schwarzwald
Blasheim 270
Bloemendaal 148, 290
Blumental 276
Bobbio 120, 245
Bochum 32
Boekelermeer 295
Bohemia 191, 308
Bohuslän 263
Borculo 186
Bordeaux 195, 233-4
Border Counties 265-6
Borgholzhausen 271, 298
Borgo San Donnino 246
Borinage 35, 186
Borken 31-2, 175, 272
Börninghausen 270
Bosch, Den 28, 50, 77, 221
Both Sicilies 256
BOUCHES DE L'ELBE 10, 25-6, 219-20, 225, 263, 280, 311
BOUCHES DE L'ESCAUT 10, 13, 60, 221, 225
BOUCHES DE L'ISSEL 10, 14, 221, 225, 297
BOUCHES DE LA MEUSE 10, 14; 60, 146-7, 218, 221, 225, 284-5, 289, 296-8, Pl 1
BOUCHES DU RHIN 10, 13-14, 26, 221, 225
BOUCHES DU RHÔNE 233, 307
BOUCHES DU WESER 10, 14, 23-6, 44, 219-20, 225, 279, 297-8
Boxmeer 50
Brabant (Belgian) 35-7, 66, 69, 78-9, 210-11
Brabant (Dutch) 30, 42, 69, 140, 163, 180-2, 223, 282, 287-9, Pl 12
Bra(c)kel 271
Brade 308
Bramsche 298
Braunschweig (Brunswick) 154, 269, 277, 298
Bremen 23, 39, 154, 184-5, 191, 210, 214, 219, 269, 279, 301, 311
Bremerlehe 311
Breukelen-St. Pieter 285
Breyell 88, 291
Briel, Den (Brielle) 50
Brittany 198, 234
Brochterbeck 32-3, 272, 281
Brockhagen 271
Broekhuizenvorst 289

Bruchhausen 275
Brugge 221
Brussels 37, 222, 289, 291
Buchholz 270
Buckinghamshire 266
Budapest 308
Buiksloot 148
Bulgaria 305, 308
Bünde 270
Büren 32, 224, 271
Burgos 305
Butjadingen 6, 23, 28, 42, 56, 210, 308

Cadiz 112, 305
Cadzand (Island of) 56-7, 163, 282
Calabria 202, 256-7, 260, 307
Calais 6, 23, 39, 210
CALVADOS 234
Cambrai 198
Cambridgeshire 265
Canino 250
CANTAL 223, 234
Cape Circeo 260
Cardiff 265
Cardiganshire 265-6
Carpathians 261, 294, 308
Castile 108-10, 115, 167, 170, 212, 231-2, 293
Catalonia 108-10, 116, 212, 230-3, 293, 305
Catania 257
Central Europe 107, 125-7, 190, 213
CHARENTE INFÉRIEURE 233-4
Charleroi 35-6, 281
Cherson 127, 294
Cheshire 265-6
Chiavari 246
China 190
Civitavecchia 250
Clare 169, 265-6
Cloppenburg 276, 311
Coevorden 44
Cologne 35, 221, 302
Connacht 108, 113, 165, 169, 265
Copenhagen 263, 308
Cork 169, 265-6
Corneto 250
Corsica 108-10, 117-18, 201, 204, 212, 233, 237, 246, 260, 297, 303-7
CÔTE D'OR 235
CREUSE 234

Croatia 189
Cromarty 265-6
Crostolo 252-5
Cumberland 265, 309
Cuneo 196, 243
Czechoslovakia 291

Dalarna 263
Dalfsen 45-6, 283
Damme 44
Danish Islands 304
Darmstadt 224
Deolmsvaart 179-80, 278, 300, 311
Delfland 133
Delfzijl 43
Delmenhorst 276
Dendermonde 31
Denmark 9-11, 26, 89, 189-91, 203-4, 220, 262-4, 304, 308-9, Pl 20
Derbyshire 266
Detmold 31, 220
DEUX NÈTHES 10, 26, 221, 225
Deventer 188
Dickel 310-11
Dielingen 270
Diemen 15
Diemerdam 15
Diepenau 310
Diepholz 95-8, 175, 178, 220, 275, 283, 297-301, 310
Dinklage 311
Dissen 297-8
Dithmarschen 264
Ditzum 161
DOIRE 120, 235-43, 252, 257-60, 306-8
Dollart 43
Dolomites 260
Domodossola 260
Don 127
Donau (Danube) 127
Donegal 265-6
Dordrecht 50, 86-8, 218, 289
Dörpel 310-11
Dörriehloh 310
Dortmund 32
Dötlingen (/Neerstedt) 276, 311
Dreierwalde 33, 281
Drenthe 25, 44, 62, 72, 179, 182, 191, 288, 292, 301, Pl 7, 8
Drogheda 265
Dublin 265
Duisburg 282
Dumfriesshire 309

Düsseldorf 35, 188, 302
DYLE 10, 13, 222-5, 280

East Anglia 108, 113-14, 164, 265-6
East(ern) Europe 105-7, 125-7, 190, 213, 230, 277, 294, 304
Ebro 233
Edam 297
Edinburgh 265
Eeklo 31
Eenrum 301
Ehrenburg-Barenburg 275
Eichsfeld 262
Eidelstedt 310-11
Eiderstedt 308
Eifel 26, 89, 210
Eindhoven 86
Ekaterinoslav 127
Elba 110, 117-18, 236-7, 245, 252-60, 293, 297, 307
Elbe 125-7, 191, 255, 264
Elberfeld 302
Elburg 62-3
Elsfleth 308
Emden 44, 161-2, 273
Ems (region) 44-5, 161-2, 173
EMS OCCIDENTAL 10, 14-15, 219-21, 225, 288-9, 297-8
EMS ORIENTAL 10, 13, 23, 219-20, 225, 273
EMS SUPÉRIEUR 10, 14-15, 44, 88, 95, 220, 225, 263, 281, 292, 296-7, 304, 308-10
Enge Wormer 285
England 3, 6, 11, 17, 108, 113, 164-5, 168-70, 185, 195, 198-200, 212-13, 264-6, 279, 284, 287, 291, 297-9, 302-3, 307-9
ESCAUT 10, 13, 23, 26, 221, 225, 280
Esens 273
Essen (Osnabrück) 298, 311
Essen (Ruhrgebiet) 186
EURE ET LOIRE 166, 233
Europe 1, 6, 89, 107-11, 117, 123-5, 128, 133, 136, 156, 164, 171-2, 191-5, 203-5, 209, 212-15, 230-2, 249, 279, 298

Fanö 264, 308
Fehmarn 308
Fens 265
Finland 263, 308
Fivelingo 297

Flanders 26-31, 36-40, 56-7, 66, 69, 79, 162, 183, 186-7, 198, 210, 280-2, 286, 289
Florence 247-9
Foggia 304
Foligno 249-50
FÔRETS 10, 14, 88, 222-5
France 3, 6-7, 11, 26, 57, 77, 89, 106, 109-10, 114-16, 124, 167-9, 184-6, 189, 195-204, 209, 213, 230-43, 260-2, 279-82, 287-93, 301-6
Franconia 262
Frankfurt 234, 262
Frederiksborg 308
French Basqueland 231
French Empire *passim*
French Pyrenees 231
Freren 274, 281
Freudenberg 275
Friedewalde 270
Friesland 13, 25, 28, 44, 48, 53-6, 62, 72, 77-8, 153, 156-9, 162, 173, 179, 182-3, 188-91, 277-8, 282-8, 295-301, 310-11, Pl 4, 14, 17, 19
Friesoythe 276, 311
FRISE 10, 13, 221, 225, 280, 284
Friuli 261, 307
Frosinone 117, 251
Funen Pl 20
Fürstenau 88, 274, 283, 298

Gaasbeek 37, 282
Galicia (Polish) 198
Galicia (Spanish) 110-12, 115-16, 167, 231-2, 293, 305
Galway 169, 265
Ganderkesee 276
Garonne 235
Gascogne 167
Geertruidenberg 28
Gehlenbeck 270
Gelderland 62, 182, 186, 285, 289, 300
Geldern 50
Genemuiden 47
GÊNES 120, 235-8, 244-5, 250-2, 255, 258-60, 293, 300, 306
Genoa 123, 244-5, 249, 260
Gent 31, 64, 221
Germany *passim*
GIRONDE 233-4
Glamorgan 266
Glandorf 298

Glane 292
Glasgow 266
Glons 88, 291
Gloucestershire 266
Goeree (-Overflakkee) 58
Goes 50
GOLO 118, 236-8, 245-6, 251, 254, 258, 293
Göteborg 263
Gouda 86, 289-91
Graft 148
Grand Canal du Nord 24, 42, 64, 79, 286, 289
Graubünden 307
Grave 50
Great Britain 57, 106, 185, 198-200, 204, 230, 264, 267, 279, 309
Groenstraat 88
Groesbeek 62
Groningen 28, 56, 71-2, 77-83, 159-64, 180, 191, 220-1, 277-8, 284-9, 295-9, 302, 311
Grootebroek 301
Groot-Noordhollands Kanaal 70, 180
Gross Lessen 310
Grossenkneten 276
Grosseto 117, 248
Guadalajara 115
Gütersloh 271

Haarlem 83-6, 180, 282-3, 289-90, Pl 10
Haarlemmermeer 133, 140, 180, 183, 297
Hadeln 154
Hagen 281, 297
Hague, The 221
Hainaut 26, 30, 36-7, 42, 58, 77-9, 210, 289
Halland 263
Halle 30-4, 271, 281
Halverde 33
Hamburg 8-9, 26, 141, 184-5, 191, 214, 219, Pl 19
Hamm 35
Hannover 30-2, 82, 175-6, 184, 268-9, 273-5, 300-1, 310
Haps 50
Hardenberg 44-6, 283, 300
Harenkarspel 285
Harjedalen 263
Harmelen 285
Hartum 270
Hasselt 45-9, 149-55, 173-4, 283-4, 294, 297, 300, Pl 17
Hatten 276
Haut Languedoc 167
Haut Pô 252
HAUT RHIN 234, 262
HAUTE GARONNE 231
HAUTE MARNE 235
HAUTE VIENNE 234
HAUTES ALPES 234-7, 241-3, 252-6, 306-8
Heemstede 290
Heerenveen 286
Heidelberg 262
Heiligenloh 310-11
Heilo 148
Heimsen 270
Helden 221
Hendrik-Ido-Ambacht 60, 286
HÉRAULT 233
Herefordshire 265-6
Herford 30-4, 224, 270, 281
Hertfordshire 265
Herve Region 35
Hesbaye 211, 289
Hesse 8, 26, 224, 269, 277-8, 282, 311
Heythuisen 302
Hjørring 308
Hoekse Waard 60
Holland (province) 3, 6-8, 14, 17, 24, 43-7, 51-3, 56, 72, 75-7, 83, 86, 89, 96-7, 101, 133-4, 138-40, 144-59, 162-4, 171, 182-3, 224, 279, 282, 292-3, 298-301, 310, Pl 12
Hollandse IJssel 78
Holyhead 265
Holzhausen 270
Holzminden 269, 277
Home Counties 108, 265
Hoogeveen 73, 179, 311
Hopsten 33, 281
Horstmar 283
Höxter 32, 271, 277
Hoya 275, 310
Hüllhorst 270
Humber 198, 212
Hümmling 88
Hungary 189, 202, 230, 261, 291, 307-8, Pl 14
Hunsingo 286
Hunsrück 26, 210
Huntlosen 276
Hurepoix 165-6
Husum 308

Ibbenbüren 33, 272, 281
Iberian Peninsula 89, 230
Iburg 144, 175, 274, 298
IJ 49, 133-4, 138-41, 145-6, 295
IJssel 28, 282
IJsselmonde 60
Ireland 86, 108, 112-14, 165, 169, 198-200, 230, 264-7, 297, 300, 303, 309
Irish Sea 199
ISÈRE 234, 237-9, 306
ISSEL SUPÉRIEURE 10, 14, 221, 225, 297-8
Issum 50
Italy 6, 11, 17, 106-10, 116-19, 168-9, 189, 195-6, 200-3, 212-13, 230, 233-8, 249, 255, 258-62, 297, 302-7, Pl 15
Italy (Napoleonic Kingdom) 236-58
Ivrea 240

Jacobridrebber 310
Jämtland 263
Jeker 26, 37, 88-9
JEMAPPES 10, 14, 26, 222, 225, 280, 288
Jemgum 161
Jever(land) 23, 308
Joure 53
Jura 234
Jutland 203, 304

Kampen 48, Pl 17
Kassel 8, 9, 26, 141
Kempen 83, 88, 91
Kent 266
Kerry 169, 265-6
Kiel 264
Kirchdorf 310
Kleve 221
Koblenz 87, 221
Koedijk 285
Koesfeld 30-2, 35, 175, 272-3
Kop van Overijssel 28, 72
Kornau 310-11
Kosovo Metohija 305
Kremnitz 291
Krimpenerwaard 29, 39

Ladbergen 33, 180, 272, 281
Laer 298
Lage 298
Lahde 270
Lake Como 123, 253, 307
Lake Maggiore 253, 307
Lancashire 164, 265-6, 300
Land van Goes 50
Land van Heusden and Altena 29, 39
Land van Vianen 39
Langedoc 108, 116, 212, 231, 234
Langstraat 42, 53-5
Langweer 54
Laren 301-2
Latin America 305
Lazio 110, 212, 260
Ledde 272, 310
Leeden 33, 310
Leer 273
Leeuwarden 53, 221, 286
Leicestershire 266, 309
Leiden 296
Leinster 266
Lek 133, 141
LÉMAN 236-9, 306
Lemförde 310
Lengerich 33, 272, 297
Léon 115-16, 231-2
Leonisse 123
Léri 116
Levern 270
LIAMONE 118-19, 236-8, 245-6, 251, 254, 258, 293
Lichtmis 283
Liège 26, 35-7, 42, 77-9, 210, 222, 289, 293
Liemers Pl 5
Lienen 33, 281, 297
Liguria 235, 238, 243
Ligurian Apennines 110, 259
Lille 35, 124, 222
Limburg (Belgian) 36-7, 83, 223, Pl 12
Limburg (Dutch) 72, 77, 83, 88, 180, 188, 223, 289, 297, Pl 12
Limerick 169, 265-6
Limousin 122-3, 166
Lincolnshire 108, 113, 265, 299
Lingen 44-5, 83-5, 88, 175, 220, 274, 298-300, 310
LIPPE 10, 14, 220, 225, 297
Lippe (river) 43
Lippe (-Detmold) 8-10, 26, 30-4, 43, 77-83, 143, 146, 154, 161, 175, 178, 184, 190-4, 203, 217, 220, 224-5, 264, 268-9, 277, 281-2, 288-9, 292, 296-8, 303-4, 308, 311
Lippstadt 32

Lisbon 123-4, 232, 294
Liverpool 265
Livorno 248
Lobith 188
Löhningen 311
Loire 290
LOIRE INFÉRIEURE 306
Lolland-Falster 203
Lommel 91
London 108, 114, 124, 198-200, 212, 264-7, 309
Londonderry 266
Longwy 291
Longwyon 291
Loosduinen 301
Lopikerwaard 29
Lothians 265, 299
Lotte 32-3
LOZÈRE 233
Lübbecke 32-4, 96, 270, 304
Lucca 118, 236-7, 245-8, 251, 254-5, 258, Pl 15
Lüdinghausen 31-2, 35, 175, 272
Lugo 115, 231, 293
Lüneburg 25, 154, 298
Lutten 278, 311
Luxemburg 10, 36, 209, 222, 235
Lyon(nais) 112, 124, 195, 234
LYS 10, 13, 23, 221, 225, 280

Maas 24, 35, 87, 290
Maastricht 11-12, 221
Madrid 110, 115, 123-4, 294, 305
Main 87
Maine 234
MAINE ET LOIRE 306
Mainz 23, 221, 224, 234, 262
Mannheim 262
Marche of Ancona 117, 253
Maremma 117
MARENGO 235-47, 252-8, 293, 300, 306-7
Maribo 203
Mark 35
Marseilles 110, 124, 195, 233, 243
Masovia 294
Massif Central 109-10, 114, 166, 197, 234, 303
Matrice, La 123
Maurice, St. 238-9
MAYENNE 234
Mayo 265
Mecklenburg (-Schwerin) 26, 269, 277-8, 311

Mediterranean Sea (region/coast) 1, 108-10, 116, 120, 202, 231-5, 260
MÉDITERRANÉE 235, 238, 247-50, 254-5, 258, 293
Meern, De 285
Meijel 290
Melle 175, 274, 298
Mennighüffen 271
Meppel 174, 300
Meppen 88, 175, 178, 274
Merwede 66, 69
Merwede Kanaal 68, 180
Messina 257
Messingen 281
Mettingen 33, 223, 272, 281
Metz 223
MEUSE 10-11, 26, 88, 223-5, 235
MEUSE INFÉRIEURE 10-13, 23, 26, 221, 225, 280
Mexico 294
Mézières 222
Middelburg 221
Mijdrecht 297
Milan 110, 123-4, 259, 294
Mill 50
Mincio 252
Minden 25-6, 30-4, 143, 154, 174, 177, 184-5, 220, 224-5, 269-70, 281, 301-4
Modena 307
Modigliana 247
Moldavia 127
Monden 287
Mondovi 243
Mons 36, 222
Mont Blanc 260
Mont Saint Bernhard 260
MONT TONNERRE 10-11, 23, 26, 221, 225
Montalto 250
MONTBLANC 234, 236-41
MONTENOTTE 235-46, 252-3, 256-8, 305-7
Monthey 238
Moordrecht 70
Moravia 308
MORBIHAN 234
Mosel 87, 223, 290
MOSELLE 10-11, 88-9, 223-5, 280, 291
Muiden 28
Mülheim 35
Mulhouse 124
Münster(land) 25-6, 31-2, 35, 38, 44,

Index

146, 154, 174, 178, 184-5, 220, 269-72, 281, 300
Muntendam 291

Namur 36, 78, 222
Nancy 198
Naples 117, 123, 236-7, 242-4, 248-50, 255-8, 307
Nassau 9
Navarra 231
Neckar 87
Netherlands, The *passim*
Neuenhaus 45, 220, 274
Neuenkirchen (Oldenburg) 73, 276
New Castile 115
Nice 196
Nienburg 275, 298, 310
Nieuw-Amsterdam Pl 8
Nieuwe Waterweg 180
Nieuwerkerk aan den IJssel Pl 1
Nieuweschans 43-4
Nieuwkerken *see* Neuenkirchen
Nieuwveen 64
Nijmegen 87
Niklaas, St. 31
Nivelles 36
Noorderkwartier 289
Noordzeekanaal 180
Norcia 247
NORD 10-11, 23, 26, 35, 42, 56, 79, 198, 222, 225, 235, 288-9
Norden 273, 282
Norderditmarschen 308
Nordfriesland 264
Nordhorn 220
Norfolk 265
Normandy 234
Northamptonshire 266
North-Brabant 28, 53, 77, 83, 88
North-Holland 28, 49, 55, 63, 135-41, 158, 171, 183, 213, 289, 295, 300, Pl 2
Northumberland 265-6
Norway 189-91, 263, 308
Nottinghamshire 266
Novi 120, 245
Nunspeet 62

Oberhausen 188
Oberinntal 261
Odense 308
Odenwald 262, 308
Oderbruch 262
Oerlinghausen 31, 34

Oirsbeek 188
OISE 197, 233-5, 306
Old Castile 116
Oldenburg 32, 44, 73, 77, 175, 178, 269, 276-8, 283, 291, 311
Oldendorf 270
Olona 252
OMBRONE 117-19, 236-8, 245-9, 252-60, 293, 300
Ommen 45-6
Oostburg 163
Oostermoer 73
Orense 115, 231, 293
ORNE 166, 234
Osnabrück 25, 30, 143-8, 153-5, 159, 175, 220, 269, 273-4, 292, 296-300, 310
Ostbevern 298
Oste 191
Ostende 64
Osterholz 276
Osterkappeln 298
Ostfriesland 13, 28, 42, 53-4, 71, 77-82, 159-64, 171-5, 184, 190-2, 220, 277, 280, 284, 287-9, 310, Pl 3, 4, 19
Oude Rijn 78-9, 289
Oudenaarde 31
Ouder-Amstel 280, 285, 297
Oudorp 148
Oudshoorn 141
OURTHE 10, 13, 24-6, 88, 222-5, 280
Ovenstädt 270
Overÿijssel 42-7, 62, 182, 209, 300-1, Pl 17
Over-Maas 60
Oxfordshire 266

Paderborn 32, 224, 271, 282, 300
Pajottenland 289
Palermo 257
Pamplona 231
Panaro 253
Papal States 236, 307
Paris 109-10, 114, 122-4, 165-6, 196-9, 204, 233, 294, 303
Paris (French ministry of the Interior) *passim*
Parma 235, 245-6, 260, 307
PAS DE CALAIS 10-11, 23, 42, 198, 222, 225, 233, 280, 306
Peel 75, 180, 301
La Perche 166

Perth 265-6
Perugia 249-50
Petershagen 270
Pfalz 26
St. Philipsland 58
Piacenza 246
Picardy 198, 210
Piedmont 116, 212, 235, 238, 243, 260
Pijnacker 279
Pinerolo 242
Piombino 236-7, 245-8, 254-5, 258-60
Pistoia 118, 247
Po (river, Valley) 108-10, 116, 167, 170, 252, 293
PÒ 235-44, 253-4, 257-9, 306-8
Podhalia 261
Podrina 308
Poland 125-7, 189-91, 194, 198-9, 203-4, 263, 302-4, 307, Pl 20
Pontevedra 112
Pontine Marshes 117, 250
Pontremoli 246
Porto 232
Portoferrajo 255
Portugal 112, 230-2
Potenza 304
Potosi 116
Provence 108-10, 116, 196, 212, 231-4, 243
Prussia 13, 35, 50, 126-7, 161, 174-6, 184, 188-90, 194, 224, 268-70, 277, 294, 302
Purmer 134
Purmerend 297
Pusstortal 261
PUY DE DÔME 223, 231, 234
Pyrenees 110, 233-5
PYRENÉES ORIENTALES 233

Quakenbrück 14, 144, 220, 298

Rahden 270
Ravensberg 143, 154, 282, 296, 302-3
Recke 33, 272, 281
Recklinghausen (-land) 31-2, 35, 175, 272
Rehden 310
Reiderland 78-9, 161-2, 191, 304
Republic of the Seven United Provinces 6, 27, 64, 72, 156, 162, 171, 213, 279
Rethem 310

Rhede 220
Rheine 272-3, 281
RHIN ET MOSELLE 10-13, 221, 225, 280, 291
Rhine (region, Valley) 11, 23-6, 35, 43, 87-8, 112, 190-1, 218, 224, 234-5, 261-2, 281-2, 285-6, Pl 11
Rhön 262, 308
Rhône (Valley) 234, 239
Ribe 264, 308
Ridderkerk 60
Riesenbeck 33, 281
Rijnland 139, 296
Rijswijk 14
Rio de la Plata 202
Roclenge 88
Rödinghausen 271
ROËR 10-11, 14, 23-4, 221, 225
Roermond 148, 186, 189
Romagna 201
Romania 308
Roman Campagna 118-19, 201, 249, 300, 307
Roman States 238
ROME 117, 123, 236-41, 245-60, 293, 306-8
Rome 110, 117-18, 123-4, 250-3, 260, 294, 307
Rooveen 173
Roscommon 265
Ross 265-6
Rotenburg 276, 301, 311
Rotterdam 86, 211, 289-91, Pl 1, 18
Rousillon 235
Rovereto 262
Roxburghshire 309
Rozenburg 285
Ruhr (region, Valley) 40, 184-5, 188-91, 194-5, 204, 210-11, 214, 281
Rulle 297
Rupelmonde 79, 289
Russia 99, 125-7, 189-91, 291-4

Saerbeck 281
Saluzzo 243
Salzbergen 281
SAMBRE ET MEUSE 10, 13, 222, 225
Sankthülfen 310
Saône 234
Sardinia 202, 236, 257-8
SARRE 10-11, 221, 225, 280
Sarzana 246

Sassoferrato 253
Sauerland 89
Savigliano 243-4
Savona 244, 305
Savoye Pl 18
Scandinavia 230, 262, 277, 299
Schale 33, 281
Schapen 281
Schaumburg-Hesse 269, 311
Schaumburg-Lippe 8-9, 269
Schelde 24, 34-5, 79, 87, 290
Schermer (Island) 134
Schinnen 302
Schleswig-Holstein 191, 230, 262-4
Schmalförden 310
Schnathorst 270
Schoorl 148
Schötmar 31
Schouwen (-Duiveland) 58-9, 163, 285
Schwarzwald 223, 262
Scotland 108, 112, 169, 200, 264-6, 299-300, 309
Scottish Highlands 169, 265-6, 293
Segovia 116
SEINE ET MARNE 233
SEINE ET OISE 223, 233
SÉSIA 120, 168, 235-44, 252-3, 257-60, 293, 306
Sevilla 112
Shropshire 265-6
Sicily 107, 112, 202, 236, 256-8
Sienna 248
Silesia 185, 190, 294, 302
SIMPLON 235-41, 252-3, 258, 306-8
Sion 238
Sjaelland 263
Sliedrecht 29, 282
Sligo 265
Slijkenburg 282
Sloten 287
Slovakia 89, 308, Pl 13
Sluis 285
Småland 263
Smilde 15, 73, 179
Sneek 53
Søby Søgård Pl 20
Soest 32, 35, 38
Sögel 175, 178, 274
Soignies 36, 310
SOMME 223, 233, 306
Sorø 308
Southeast Europe 277
South Europe 196, 230

South-Holland 14, 78, 136-42, 155, 158, 183, 286, 296-8, Pl 2, 9
South-Holland (Islands of) 42, 50, 58, 62, 138-40, 295
South-Limburg 88, 188, 302
South(ern) Netherlands 58, 223, 281, 299
Spain 6, 11, 106-7, 110, 116, 169, 230-4, 293, 300, 304-5
Spanish Basqueland 231, 235
Speier 23, 234, 262
Spenge 144, 281
Spessart 223
Spoleto 249-50
Stade 175, 269, 273, 276, 308
Stadskanaal 179, 283, 287
Staffordshire 266
Staphorst 173
Stein 302
Steinfurt 30-2, 42-4, 175, 272-3
Steinhagen 271
Stickhausen 273
Stockholm 263
Stolzenau 275, 310
Ströhen 270, 310
STURA 120, 235-44, 252-3, 256-8, 293, 300, 306-7
Süderdithmarschen 308
Suffolk 164, 265
Sulingen 275, 310
Surrey 266
Swabia 202, 262, 308
Sweden 189-91, 203, 263-4, 304, 308-9
Switzerland 11, 202-3, 230, 235-43, 247, 259-62, 304-6
Syke 154, 275, 300, 310
Szeged 308

TARO 235-8, 242-8, 251-5, 258
Tatra 261
Tauria 127
Tecklenburg 30-3, 51, 88, 97, 144-5, 174, 184, 272, 281, 298-300
Tessin 307
Texel 301
Thessaly 305
Tholen 58, 163
Thrace 305
Thuin 36
Thuine 281
Tiber 123
Tiel 87
Timisoara 308

Tipperary 169, 265-6
Tirol 253, 308
Todi 249-50
Toledo 115
Tondern 308
Toscanella 250
Toulon 243
Toulouse 195
Tournai 36
TRASIMÈNE 117, 236-8, 245-53, 256-60, 293, 300, 306-8
Trento 253, 262
Trier 221
Trnovo 305
Turin 110, 123-4, 241-2, 259
Turnhout 83
Turócz-Szent Márton 291
Tuscany 110, 212, 236-9, 244-5, 249-51, 255, 260, 307
Twente 25, 31, 140-5, 154, 281, 295
Twisk 300
Tyrone 266

Ubbedissen 271
Uchte 275, 310
Ueffeln 45
Uelsen 45
Ukraine 189
Umbria 260
United States 161, 184, 202, 294
Unna 32
Unterinntal 261
Urbino 253
Uruguay 202
Utrecht 28, 72, 75, 87, 139, 146, 295-6, 301, Pl 9

Valdorf 180, 271
Valencia 232, 305
VAR 233
Värmland 263
Varrel 310
Västergotland 263
Vecht (river) 44-6
Vechta 276, 311
Veendam 277
Veenhuizen 285
Velzen 148
Veluwe (zoom) 25, 62-3, 288
Vendée 235
Venebrugge 45
Venetia 123, 293
Venice 249, 259-61, 307
Venlo 289

Vercelli 123, 240-1, 259
Verden 276, 301, 311
Versmold 271, 297-8
Verviers 35
Vicenza 307
Vienna 308
Vigo 112
Vijf Heren Landen 29
Villanueva 112
Vinkeveen 300
Visbeck 311
Viterbo 117, 250
Viù 242
Vleuten 285
Vlissingen 64
Vlotho 281
Voerendaal 302
Vogelsberg 262, 308
Volterra 248
Voorne (-Putten) 50, 58
Voorns Kanaal 180
Vorarlberg 261
Vörden 274, 298
Vreeswijk 87
Vriezenveen 291
Vršac 308

Waal 87, 282, 286
Waldeck 8-9
Wales 108, 200, 264-6, 309
Wallenhorst 297
Walsrode 310
Warburg 32, 271
Wardenburg 276
Warendorf 30-2, 175, 272
Warmsen 310
Warsaw 126
Warthebruch 262
Warwickshire 266
Watergraafsmeer 15, 148, 223-4, 300
Weener 44, 161, 178, 273
Weert 86, 289
Weesperkarspel 148, 223-4
Wehdem 270
Wellingholzhausen 297
Werkendam 29
Wersen 33
Weser 23, 78-9, 82, 264, 301, 310
West Africa 294
West Brabant 66
West England 112
West Europe 1-2, 5-6, 99, 105-7, 122, 125-6, 195, 209, 230
West Flanders 36-7, 280, 289

West Pomerania 190
West Riding of Yorkshire 265-6
West Sussex 266
Westerkappeln 33, 272, 297, 310
Westerstede 276
Westerwald 262, 308
Westfriesland 136
Westphalia 8-11, 31-4, 44, 47, 54, 89, 97-8, 133, 141, 145-6, 155, 185-7, 191-4, 210, 214, 220, 223-4, 268, 279-82, 286-8, 296-8, Pl 16
Weststellingwerf 282
Westzaandam 14, 285
Wesuwe 220
Wetschen 310
Wiedenbrück 26, 30-4, 43, 96, 144, 224, 271, 281
Wieringen 181
Wildeshausen 276, 298, 311
Wilhelminapolder 286
Wiltshire 266
Windheim 270
Winschoten 43
Wirdum 54
Wittlage 175, 274
Wittmund 273
Wonck 88
Worcestershire 266
Wormer 134
Wulpen 163
Württemberg 261-2

YONNE 233-5
Yorkshire 300
Yugoslavia 308

Zaan (region) 87, 133-4, 137-8, 288, 295
Zaltbommel 87
Zeeland (Islands) 17, 26-8, 42, 50, 58-60, 64, 140, 162-3, 183, 189, 286, Pl 6
Zeeland-Flanders 66, 163-4, 171, 286, 299
Zegveld 285
Zegwaard 141
Zeist 28
Zeven 276, 301
Zevenhoven 64
Zierikzee 59, 163, 285
Zoetermeer 14, 285
Zuid-Beveland 50, 285
Zuiderzee 45-7, 51, 62, 146-8, 153, Pl 17
Zuidplas (-polder) 70, 180
Zuid-Willemsvaart 70, 180
ZUYDERZEE 10, 14-15, 146-7, 221, 225, 280, 284-5, 297
Zwartsluis 47
Zwijndrechtse Waard 60
Zwolle 45-51, 149-51, 174, 221, 282-4
Zwolse Diep 47